ETHICAL ISSUES IN CHRONIC PAIN MANAGEMENT

PAIN MANAGEMENT

ETHICAL ISSUES IN CHRONIC PAIN MANAGEMENT

EDITED BY

MICHAEL E. SCHATMAN

Consulting Clinical Psychologist
Redmond, Washington, U.S.A.

CRC Press
Taylor & Francis Group
Boca Raton London New York

CRC Press is an imprint of the
Taylor & Francis Group, an **informa** business

First published 2007 by Informa Healthcare, Inc.

Published 2019 by CRC Press
Taylor & Francis Group
6000 Broken Sound Parkway NW, Suite 300
Boca Raton, FL 33487-2742

© 2007 by Taylor & Francis Group, LLC
CRC Press is an imprint of Taylor & Francis Group, an Informa business

First issued in paperback 2019

No claim to original U.S. Government works

ISBN 13: 978-0-367-45335-0 (pbk)
ISBN 13: 978-0-8493-9268-9 (hbk)

Visit the Taylor & Francis Web site at
http://www.taylorandfrancis.com

and the CRC Press Web site at
http://www.crcpress.com

This book is dedicated to my son, Joshua Harry. May he grow up into a world in which relief of pain and suffering is considered a fundamental human right rather than a commodity.

M.E.S.

Preface

Chronic pain is a phenomenon that impacts the life of the sufferer in profound ways, as it is experienced not only nociceptively, but emotionally, socially, vocationally, financially, legally, and spiritually as well. To the patient, chronic pain represents a challenge unlike that associated with any other type of physical condition. Yet it is not only the patient who is challenged by chronic pain; the wide variety of chronic pain conditions that patients experience certainly represents a unique challenge to the health care professionals who valiantly attempt to treat them. Typically, cure is not a realistic goal for the practitioner or the patient. Accordingly, medical professionals are left with the obligation to reduce suffering, despite a frequent misunderstanding of what suffering entails. Many physicians and other health care professionals want nothing to do with chronic pain patients, simultaneously expressing feelings of frustration relating to their inefficacy in reducing suffering and contempt for the patients who are afflicted. Because of the difficulty involved in effectively treating patients with chronic pain, primary care physicians seek "dumping grounds" for them, hoping that other practitioners will carry the burden. The physician who is brave enough to make chronic pain management a part of his or her practice is faced with a myriad of ethical dilemmas, further complicating the treatment of patients in need of assistance.

While few would question the notion that patients and clinicians experience unique challenges associated with chronic pain, other entities are challenged by this affliction as well. The medical system now includes more than the physician and the patient, between whom a moral covenant ideally exists. This covenant entails a common will, shared by patient and practitioner, to work toward reducing the individual patient's suffering. Parties not directly bound by this covenant have come to be included in the care that the patient ultimately receives, with this seemingly increasing list of parties including the insurance industry, hospital administrations, attorneys, the government (in various forms, including the DEA, the legislature, the executive branch, and the courts), ethics boards of the various professions involved in chronic pain management (whose principles often collide with one another), and research review boards. Sadly, the strength of the covenant between the practitioner and the chronic pain patient is compromised by the involvement of these extraneous parties, some of whom are motivated by the desire to serve the good of society as a whole as opposed to that of the individual patient, with others simply (and, at times, selfishly) motivated by cost-containment and profitability. Both the patient and the physician have lost their autonomy to work together as an effective team, with too many cooks spoiling the broth of patient relief from suffering.

This handbook was written in order to help all the parties involved in the care of the chronic pain patient understand the ethical (and related legal) issues associated with the efforts of professionals to assist patients in their efforts to find relief and reclaim their independence. The opinions of the illustrious group of authors who contributed chapters to the book are not necessarily consistent with each other, and editorial efforts were made to maintain balance in presenting viewpoints that may not be harmonious. All the chapter authors, while renowned in their respective fields of practice and investigation, demonstrated admirable willingness to avoid dogmatic positions in interpreting the literature and offering opinions regarding what constitutes ethical practice.

Ethical Issues in Chronic Pain Management is divided into five sections. The first section, Ethical/Philosophical Issues, includes chapters looking at the pain practitioner's responsibility to practice virtuously (James Giordano), ethical dilemmas experienced by the chronic pain patient (Debra E. Benner), ethical issues associated with treatment of patients at the end of life (Richard Payne), and the ethical failure of society associated with allowing empirically supported multidisciplinary treatment programs to become progressively less accessible to patients (Michael E. Schatman). While seemingly diverse, each of these topics shares the common theme of the integration of classical philosophical thought and the optimal management of chronic pain conditions. The authors of the chapters in this section agree that on both the individual and collective levels, allowing people to suffer needlessly is simply wrong.

The second section of the book, Disparities in Treatment, emphasizes the bioethical principle of justice, which is primarily localized to the domain of distributive justice. The multitiered medical system, which is evident in the American society, results in limited access to high-quality chronic pain management services for many on the basis of socioeconomic factors (1). Chapters in this text include analyses of underservice of specific groups of chronic pain sufferers, including children (Patricia A. McGrath and Danielle A. Ruskin), seniors (Raymond C. Tait), and members of racial and ethnic minority groups (Carmen R. Green). Each of these chapters promotes the mission of the Disparities in Pain Management Special Interest Group of the American Pain Society, which is currently chaired by Dr. Tait.

Part three of the book, Legal and Ethical Issues in the Pharmacological Treatment of Chronic Pain, is extensive, as the included chapters cover the greatest current ethical and legal controversies in the field of chronic pain management. Chronic pain practitioners are in agreement regarding the need to help alleviate suffering in our patients. Considerable disagreement exists, however, regarding the best means of doing so. An emphasis has been placed on chapters relating to the prescription of opioids on a long-term basis, particularly to patients with chronic pain of nonmalignant origin. During the 1990s and the early part of this decade, the pendulum swung from disdain for the practice of chronic opioid therapy to a possible overreliance upon this mode of treatment. The result of this paradigm shift has been not only problematic responses by many patients, but more aggressive monitoring of physicians by the DEA as well. Chapters in this section include an argument for consideration of chronic opioid therapy (B. Eliot Cole), an argument for the need to be cautious in considering long-term treatment with opioid analgesics (Jane C. Ballantyne), and a very important set of recommendations regarding the avoidance of legal and regulatory challenges to physicians who attempt to alleviate patient suffering through the prescription of opioids (Jennifer Bolen). Finally, this section includes a chapter by Ethan B. Russo on the benefits of cannabinoids in the treatment of chronic pain. This chapter was a late addition to the book, as progressively more states are passing legislation supporting the use of cannabinoids for pain treatment. However, in June of

2005, the U.S. Supreme Court curiously ruled that the federal government can ban the possession of the drug, even in states that have eliminated sanctions against its use for the treatment of illness. Dr. Russo's chapter is particularly important given the number of sufferers who have found medicinal marijuana to be an effective pharmacologic agent in their battles with chronic pain.

The fourth section of the book, Medicolegal Issues, consists of chapters on legal issues associated with the treatment of chronic pain. As a considerable proportion of chronic pain patients are injured traumatically or through repetitive motion at work, clinicians are faced with the challenge of providing the best possible care while simultaneously demonstrating sensitivity to the legal aspects of their patients' cases. Additionally, the commodification of medicine in the United States has severely limited the ability of medical professionals to provide optimal care to chronic pain patients. Confusion relating to balancing the interests of multiple clients (i.e., the patient, insurance carriers, case managers, attorneys, the employer, and hospital administrations) often results in an ethical conundrum for the chronic pain practitioner. To provide guidance, this section of the book includes chapters discussing ethical issues associated with disability determination (Jaye E. Hefner), treating chronic patients effectively despite the efforts of managed care to limit treatment (David L. Trueman), and ethical issues associated with providing expert medical testimony in cases involving chronic pain (Barbara L. Kornblau). These chapters have been included in order to help the chronic pain clinician gain perspective on the interaction between the law, ethics, and the provision of medical services.

The final section of the book, Ethical Issues in Standards of Care and Research, covers a wide variety of topics. Chapters in this section examine issues including ethical standards in the psychological evaluation of chronic pain patients (C. David Tollison and Donald W. Hinnant), the need for appropriate physical examination of chronic pain patients and the interaction of legal and ethical issues involved in implementing optimal treatment based upon findings (Nelson Hendler), the importance of clinical practice guidelines (Alexandra Campbell), and ethical issues involved in conducting chronic pain research (Robert J. Gatchel, Perry N. Fuchs, and Colin Allen).

Pain practitioners, as has been suggested by Giordano (2), are obligated to serve as *moral* agents as well as therapeutic agents to their patients. The practice of pain management is under assault by a number of forces (3), although this is thought to be true of medicine in general (4–6). Our hope is that *Ethical Issues in Chronic Pain Management* will provide clinicians with insights that will help them continue to practice the healing art of chronic pain management virtuously, while simultaneously avoiding potential legal pitfalls that may be deleterious not only to health care providers, but to their suffering patients as well. Patients with chronic pain, and society as a whole, cannot afford the demise of the patient–practitioner covenant. Emphasizing ethical and legal treatment will hopefully serve to keep the covenant alive.

Michael E. Schatman

REFERENCES

1. Schatman ME. Racial and ethnic issues in chronic pain management: challenges and perspectives. In: Boswell MV, Cole BE, eds. Weiner's Pain Management: A Practical Guide for Clinicians. 7th ed. Boca Raton, FL: CRC Press, 2006:83–97.

2. Giordano J. Neurophilosophy of maldynic pain: disease, illness and ethical obligation. Paper presented at the 16th Annual Meeting of the American Academy of Pain Management, San Diego, CA. September, 2005.
3. Robbins H, Gatchel RJ, Noe C, et al. A prospective one-year outcome study of interdisciplinary chronic pain management: compromising its efficacy by managed care policies. Anesth Analg 2003; 97:156–162.
4. May WF. Contending images of the healer in an era of turnstile medicine. In: Walter JK, Klein EP, eds. The Story of Bioethics: From Seminal Works to Contemporary Explorations. Washington, DC: Georgetown University Press, 2003:149–162.
5. Pellegrino ED. The commodification of medical and health care: the moral consequences of a paradigm shift from a professional to a market ethic. J Med Philos 1999; 24:243–266.
6. Feldman DS, Novack DH, Gracely E. Effects of managed care on physician-patient relationships, quality of care, and the ethical practice of medicine: a physician survey. Arch Intern Med 1998; 158:1626–1632.

Contents

Contributors

Colin Allen   Department of History and Philosophy of Science, Indiana University, Bloomington, Indiana, U.S.A.

Jane C. Ballantyne   Division of Pain Medicine, Department of Anesthesia and Critical Care, Massachusetts General Hospital, Harvard Medical School, Boston, Massachusetts, U.S.A.

Debra E. Benner   Hershey Medical Center, Hershey, Pennsylvania, U.S.A.

Jennifer Bolen   The Legal Side of Pain, Knoxville, Tennessee, U.S.A.

Alexandra Campbell   Pain Program Accreditation/Outcomes Measurement, American Academy of Pain Management, Sonora, California, U.S.A.

B. Eliot Cole   American Society of Pain Educators, Montclair, New Jersey, U.S.A.

Perry N. Fuchs   Department of Psychology and Biology, The University of Texas at Arlington, Arlington, Texas, U.S.A.

Robert J. Gatchel   Department of Psychology, College of Science, The University of Texas at Arlington, Arlington, Texas, U.S.A.

James Giordano   Center for Clinical Bioethics, Georgetown University Medical Center, Washington, D.C., U.S.A.

Carmen R. Green   Department of Anesthesiology, University of Michigan Health System, Ann Arbor, Michigan, U.S.A.

Jaye E. Hefner   Department of Physical Medicine and Rehabilitation, Spaulding Rehabilitation Hospital, and Department of General Internal Medicine, Massachusetts General Hospital, Harvard Medical School, Boston, Massachusetts, U.S.A.

Nelson Hendler   Mensana Clinic, Stevenson, Johns Hopkins University School of Medicine, and School of Dental Surgery, University of Maryland, Baltimore, Maryland, U.S.A.

Donald W. Hinnant   Carolina Center for Advanced Management of Pain, Asheville, North Carolina, U.S.A.

Barbara L. Kornblau Departments of Occupational Therapy and Public Health, Nova Southeastern University, Fort Lauderdale, Florida, U.S.A.

Patricia A. McGrath Divisional Center for Pain Management and Pain Research, Department of Anaesthesia, The Hospital for Sick Children, The University of Toronto, Toronto, Ontario, Canada

Richard Payne Institute on Care at the End of Life, Duke University Divinity School, Durham, North Carolina, U.S.A.

Danielle A. Ruskin Divisional Center for Pain Management and Pain Research, Department of Anaesthesia, The Hospital for Sick Children, The University of Toronto, Toronto, Ontario, Canada

Ethan B. Russo Department of Pharmaceutical Sciences, University of Montana, Missoula, Montana and Department of Medicine, University of Washington, Seattle, Washington, U.S.A.

Michael E. Schatman Consulting Clinical Psychologist, Redmond, Washington, U.S.A.

Raymond C. Tait Department of Psychiatry, Saint Louis University School of Medicine, St. Louis, Missouri, U.S.A.

C. David Tollison Carolina Center for Advanced Management of Pain, Greenville, South Carolina, U.S.A.

David L. Trueman Columbia University School of Law, New York, New York, U.S.A.

Section I: Ethical/Philosophical Issues

1   Pain, the Patient, and the Practice of Pain Medicine: The Importance of a Core Philosophy and Virtue-Based Ethics

James Giordano

Center for Clinical Bioethics, Georgetown University Medical Center, Washington, D.C., U.S.A.

INTRODUCTION

The classical definition of medicine is the science and art of treating and heal-ing. The applied focus of this science and art is the patient. The word patient is etymologically derived from the Latin *patiens*, the one who suffers. Thus, at its core, medicine is dedicated to the treatment of suffering. However, contemporary medi-cine has embraced a more technocentric, curative model that has utilized advanced diagnostics and therapeutics in the elucidation and treatment of disease. While the efficiency of this orientation upon eradicating disease mortality and improving the public health is incontrovertible, there are certain conditions that are not well served by such a unitary approach. I posit that the illness of chronic pain is one such condition. Although there is a moral obligation to treat pain, the technological advances that have enhanced other aspects of medicine have not led to universal progress in pain therapy and the sole use of the technocentric approach is inad-equate to address and treat the broad dimensionality of chronic pain. Using a phenomenological orientation[a] to examine both the nature of pain and the medi-cine, I argue that the essence of these experiences is such that their clinical intersection requires a virtue-based foundation to allow the physician to best approach the ethical issues inherent to this complex, experiential territory.

A PHENOMENOLOGICAL ORIENTATION TO PAIN[b]

As defined by the International Association for the Study of Pain (5), pain is a noxious stimulus that causes unpleasant sensations and perceptions that can pro-duce cognitive and behavioral responses of avoidance and aversion. Pain that is directly attributable to a noxious stimulus and/or some identifiable organic insult is classified as nociceptive pain, in that it activates a subset of high threshold (i.e., nociceptive) afferent fibers in the "normal" physiologic transduction and trans-mission of information that is "functional" to the organism. Such pain has

---

[a] I do not presume to use the complete phenomenological method. Rather, I utilize the phenom-enological technique of eidetic reduction, or bracketing, to allow for an ataractic identification of the "essence" or eidos of the experience of pain and medicine. A complete description of the phenomenological method from which this approach is derived can be found in Refs. 1 and 2.
[b] A complete phenomenology of pain is beyond the scope of this work; more comprehensive discourse on this topic may be found in Refs. 3 and 4.

recently been called "eudynia," to reflect this physiologic functionality. In contrast, pain can also be generated and perpetuated by nonnociceptive mechanisms through processes of peripheral and central sensitization within the neuraxis from spinal cord to brain (6,7). This is classified as neuropathic pain, and has been termed "maldynia"[c] in light of its pathophysiologic basis. It has become increasingly apparent that such pain exists at the end of the continuum from disease-process to illness manifestation(s), and involves multiple systems affecting the definable "state" or "being" of individual persons. While nociceptive pain may frequently be served by a disease-based, curative medical model, non-nociceptive, maldynic pain most often is not. Maldynic pain can be caused by and induce changes in heterogeneous neurochemical substrates (6,7). While a more thorough definition of these mechanisms may be useful in understanding the "disease-process" that may initiate maldynic pain[d], at present, it is not fully known how the manifestations of this pathology hierarchically advance to affect the subjective experience of the "illness phenomenon" that impacts many, if not all domains of the pain patient[e]. Thus, pain patients cannot be considered as a homogeneous, universal population that can be uniformly fitted into an objectively assessed disease-state. Rather, the illness of maldynic pain is an event that occurs in unique persons, and as such, is defined by the extent and dimensions by which it occupies and distorts the life of each individual.

---

[c] The etymologic origin of the terms eudynia and maldynia may respectively infer notions about the "rightness" and "badness" of these pain states. From a nosologic perspective, this may be relevant to the function of eudynic pain to evoke responses and behaviors that have some benefit to the survival or well being of the organism. Maldynic pain, on the other hand, does not serve any beneficial function, as it persists beyond the point at which chronicity should engage recuperative mechanisms, and thus provokes maladaptive and denigratory effects. This classification speaks of the "purpose" of pain as both biological and perhaps evolutionary function, and can frame maldynia as a modern or postmodern illness (Ref. 8) However, it should be noted that these terms may also lend axiological significance to these conditions, and thus have connotations of blame and stigmatization. In view of these semantic issues, I suggest that these terms be used taxonomically to classify types of pain syndromes according to mechanisms and effects, but not be used as diagnostic categories for patients. Note also that the term "maldynia" and "maldynic illness" are used to address and describe the trajectory of chronic pain to a pervasive experience of the lived body. This trajectory can, and most often does, lead to suffering; however they are not identical terms in this discourse. Suffering can be caused by pain as in the present case, but can also be caused by other life events. In this work, the illness of maldynic pain is presumed to evoke considerable suffering, but the (direct) source of this is pain qua illness. For a discourse on the impact of pain and suffering, see Ref. 9. A detailed discussion of the multidimensionality of suffering and pain can be found in Ref. 10.

[d] According to Ref. 11 "... disease ... is something an organ has; illness is something a man has." I concur with this definition and consider disease as a biologic entity inducing some definable pathologic change in tissue(s) or systems. Illness is herein regarded as a subjective experience that can affect, and be affected by a variety of existential domains of a person's life. There is a considerable dialectic regarding the nature of disease and illness; exploration of this dialectic is beyond the intention of this writing; however, a more complete examination may be found in Ref. 12.

[e] "... However, viable a knowledge of pain mechanisms may be to the scientist or physician, such "secularization" is irrelevant to its first-person experience by the patient. As well, such knowledge does little, if anything to represent the existential experience of a particular patient's pain to the physician" Ref. 13.

In many ways, maldynia defies the technocentric medical model. Contemporary medicine vests considerable heuristic power in images. The ability to "view" sense data has become almost intrinsic to the act of diagnosis (14). While this is an important part of objective evidence-based practice, it may also contribute to what Wittgenstein (15) has termed "picture thinking," which tends to deny the reality of an event or experience unless it can be empirically validated. But, maldynia is less than objectifiable by third person, technologic means (for a broader explanation, see Ref. 9). There are no laboratory tests to specifically confirm the presence or extent of a particular patient's pain. Although advanced neuroimaging [e.g., functional magnetic resonance imaging, positron emission tomography and magneto-electroencephalography (mEEG)] can provide an indication of those brain regions involved in pain processing, even the most sophisticated analyses of neuroimaging data cannot afford an accurate representation of each person's unique experience of pain. The activation of various neuroanatomical pathways may impart significant distinctions in the subjective experience of pain in a particular person. Such variation may hierarchically engage anatomical structures (and/or specific regions within neural fields) to conjoin memories, expectations, beliefs, and the cognitive and emotional variables that create the perceptions and higher consciousness that create the first-person experience of pain (16,17).

Hence, the conscious "self" changes. The patient becomes focused upon a new attunement to numerous (if not all) domains of their existence, which are now experienced as "off-balanced" by pain (18,19)[f]. The lived body is now understood in terms of what cannot be done (disability), difference from the prepainful life (dissonance), emotional suffering (despondence), and vulnerability (dependence). Lieb (22) maintains that a person cannot be wholly in the present, because each is linked to the past and the future. For pain patients, the temporality and perceived horizon of their life worlds are determined by pain: retrospection imparts despair over what was once and is now lost, prospection fosters anxiety about the unknowns in a future seen as increasingly constricted by vulnerabilities and limitations. This may clinically present as comorbid depression and/or anxiety (23,24) that may produce neurochemical changes capable of reciprocally exacerbating the constellation of symptoms to advance the patient further along the illness continuum (6,7,25)[g].

The "self-understood" physical experience of maldynic pain eludes language (9)[h], and the pain patients frequently exaggerate descriptions of the severity of pain and/or its symptoms in an attempt to explain their existential despair (27–29). This can produce enigmatic difficulties in the evaluation of maldynic pain, because many of the research and clinical assessment tools are based upon magnitude estimations (30) that are relative to the patient's prior experience(s). In the absence of technologic means to objectively evaluate and quantify a patient's pain, the physician must rely upon subjective descriptions to gain access into the life world of the patient as affected by pain. However, as can be seen, while explanation may be

---

[f] See also Refs. 20 and 21.
[g] The reciprocity of pain and cognitive and emotional manifestations has led to considerable "chicken-or-the-egg" speculation about the bi-directionality of effect and causation. For a discussion of this issue, refer to Ref. 26.
[h] There is the hypothesis that the capacity for linguistic ability is the basis for higher consciousness. This has led to the proposition that the linguistic issues involved in pain may reflect the fact that pain may represent a unique form of consciousness.

inherently difficult, this narrative is critical to establish the nature, meaning, and impact of pain upon a particular person (vide infra)[i]. This imparts a contextual understanding of the patient as a person, beyond that which can be acquired through solely technical and scientific knowledge. This takes time and cannot be easily accomplished within the confines of a 6 to 16 minute history and physical examination, as has become de rigueur consistent with much of the "turnstile medicine" driven by the technocentric imperative of speed (33). I maintain that the beguiling inadequacies of maldynic pain interventions may reflect an incomplete understanding of this phenomenological construal of pain, based upon the relative refractoriness of these unique patient-centered variables to the diagnostic and therapeutic limitations of a technically oriented model of pain medicine.

A PHENOMENOLOGICAL ORIENTATION TO PAIN MEDICINE[j]

Although pain medicine has developed into a specialty field, its identity remains somewhat noncohesive and its integrity as a practice is subject to the disruptive influence of commoditization and sociopolitical forces that are often economically motivated (35). Yet, it is the nature of pain and the existential dilemma of the pain patient that provides the foundation of what pain medicine should and must be. A phenomenological orientation to medicine may allow a better understanding of the role and ethical obligations of the physician whose focus is treating pain. If we reduce medicine to its essence, we find it to be an intersection of the life world of the clinician as both therapeutic and moral agent, with that of the vulnerable patient who seeks the practice of the clinician to achieve a definable healing end. MacIntyre (36) defines a practice to be a cooperative interaction in pursuit of "goods" (i.e., acts and ends) that are intrinsic to that relationship. Such moral goods are achieved by conforming to standards of excellence within the profession. The literal "profession"[k] of medicine is the act of one person proclaiming to possess the abilities necessary to treat and heal those persons who are made vulnerable by disease and illness (37,38). The moral good of this practice is achieved through virtue, character traits of excellence that predispose the practitioner to act toward the attainment of the moral end, or telos, as professed (39–41). For the pain practitioner, that end is the effective (i.e., biomedically right) and beneficial (i.e., benevolently good) treatment of pain.

To be sure, the act of medicine is a unique experiential event[l]. It is embodied by the clinical encounter that allows for both experiential intersubjectivity (i.e., an intersection of phenomenological life worlds) and the execution of right and good

---

[i] This reflects a component of the hermeneutic circle of that which is "understood" or interpreted in the first-person sense, cannot be "explained," and is the basis of the *ti esti* question, as applied to the phenomena of pain. Further discussion of the hermeneutic approach, with particular emphasis upon the notions of understanding (*Verstehen*), explanation (*Erklaren*) and the nature of self can be found in Refs. 19,31, and 32.

[j] For a more complete phenomenology of medicine, refer to Ref. 34.

[k] Etymologically derived from the Latin, *profiteri*, to declare or publicly announce. Thus, a *profession* is literally a declaration or announcement.

[l] And particularly so of pain medicine given the phenomenological nature of pain, the inherent subjectivity and broad impact of which cannot be evaluated by technologic means, thereby necessitating that the physician return to the intellectual and moral virtues to allow intersection of the life within the patient—physician relationship.

acts (42). The intersection of life worlds is particularly important to pain medicine; it allows the patient to share their lived experience of maldynic illness and thus gives the physician insight to the complexity and uniqueness of a specific patient with this illness. To fully apprehend the impact of each patient's pain, the physician must use a person's narrative and history to establish the concrete reality of the individual life world. Taken together with the objective data, this allows for the establishment of a diagnosis to frame this illness within a generalizable commonality (i.e., the categorical diagnosis). The diagnostic step functions as an act of disclosure, observation, and rationalization for appropriate subsequent intervention (i.e., the relevant diagnosis) (43). However, it is also a moral act of privilege, ritual, labeling, and power. As both a technical and moral act, diagnosis should be based upon both scientific skill and humanitarian art (43,44).

Such disclosure and interpretation position the patient and physician, respectively, at an intersection of their life worlds that allows the patient to ask, "Can you help me?" and the physician to assess, "What is wrong?" and "What can be done?" Recall that in the literal sense, the profession of medicine is a declaration of possessing technical ability as well as a commitment to act in the patients' best interests. Although Veatch (45,46) views this as a social contract, May (47,48) and Pellegrino (49) maintain that it is a moral covenant and the foundation of the reciprocal trust inherent to the medical relationship: the patient must trust that the physician is competent and virtuous; the physician must trust that the patient is truthful and equally committed to the telos of an effective and beneficial treatment/healing (49).

Yet, from this telos also arises the central ethical issue inherent to medicine: for each unique patient, what constitutes a right and good treatment? The complexity of how pain affects the life worlds of unique persons demands that the physician use distinct domains of knowledge (i.e., circumstantial, experiential, abstract, etc.) to apprehend the ontology of maldynic illness (50–52). However, the clinical situation involving a unique pain patient and a particular physician can create numerous therapeutic options that may be based upon technical, social, economic, and personal factors. Thus, according to Pellegrino (49), the critical act of moral agency lies not in the question "what can be done?" but in the question "what should be done for this patient?"

This question is prudential and involves both technical and ethical evaluation. Phronesis, originally defined as the intellectual virtue of "practical wisdom" by Aristotle in Book Six of Nicomachean Ethics and somewhat amended for application to medicine by Pellegrino (49) and Pellegrino and Thomasma (40), affords the ability to weigh multiple, divergent lines of information, and evaluate and resolve ethical issues toward the optimal execution of clinically rational acts in the care of unique patients. This enables the physician to select "the right grounds toward the right people for the right motive and in the right way ... to the best degree" (39,53), thus underscoring the indispensability of phronesis to medicine. Thus, while some explicitly doubt the relevance or possibility of a virtue-based medical ethics in a pluralist society and contemporary medical culture (45,46), I argue for the essentiality of virtue ethics, in general, and the virtue of phronesis, specifically, to guide the physician as a therapeutic and moral agent confronting the ethical dilemmas and medicolegal issues inherent to the practice of pain medicine. As a basis for this argument, I maintain that phronesis provides the capacity to make complex clinical decisions by evaluating the technical options for care, and balancing these accordingly with moral and abstract issues. This allows the physician to appreciate and respect the patient as a unique person in a given circumstance, thereby acknowledging their human dignity, and by extension, their culture, beliefs, and needs. It also enables prudent reliance on, and use of other intellectual and moral virtues necessary to both the clinical encounter with this particular person and the ends of medicine, as a practice. This last point is important in that phronesis enables the physician to appropriately exercise those skills and acts by virtue, rather than by value(s) that have been superimposed upon medicine by societal convention, consensus, or ethical compromise.[m]

PAIN MEDICINE IN THE CURRENT "CULTURE" OF HEALTH CARE

Despite national advocacy statements (55,56), guidelines (57,58), and state-level policies in 45 states (59) endorsing practices to more thoroughly evaluate and control pain, there continues to be considerable ineffectiveness, inequity, and impropriety in the treatment and management of maldynic pain (60). This becomes even more noteworthy in light of Congress having declared the 10-year period of 2000 through 2010 to be "The Decade of Pain Control and Research," the introduction of the Pain Care Policy Act (HR 1863) in 2003, and its reintroduction in 2005 as the National Pain Care Policy Act (HR 1020).

This disparity of intention and execution reflects the realities of the current culture of medicine as created by contemporary society. The pervasive encroachment of postmodern technocentricism into medicine has instilled a climate of moral skepticism and litigiousness. The current medicolegal environment has assumed an increasingly antagonistic stance toward the use of medication. The notoriety of class-action suits related to emergent, initially unrecognized side effects of (analgesic) drugs (e.g., rofecoxib, Vioxx) and several cases in which public figures have been involved in coercive arrangements with physicians for the procurement of opioids have fueled a Zeitgeist of prohibition and retribution. Many physicians have become reluctant or completely opposed to prescribing these medications even when suitable or necessary for the relief of maldynic pain. While recent neuropharmacologic research has led to development of novel, nonopioid analgesics, most of these remain experimental, which precludes their broad use in nonacademic clinical settings (61). Although the serial and combinatory use of currently available nonopioid analgesics for nonterminal pain can be effective, a number of problems frequently occur, leading to asymptotic effects and the recurrence of significant pain: first, many patients rapidly progress through the use of nonopioids for pain control, thus necessitating the addition of an opioid to the regimen; second, the side effects of polypharmacy may warrant discontinuation of a combinatory approach in favor of the use of a single, more potent opioid (62).

Once it has been firmly established that nonopioid pharmacotherapy has become ineffective, there is abundant literature to support that chronic, maldynic pain can be satisfactorily managed or reduced through a stable dose of opioid(s) (63–65). While a standardized paradigm toward achieving analgesia is recommended (64), a simple, dogmatic approach in which "one size fits all" therapeutics are utilized is ineffective (66). It is vital that the physician understand as much as possible about the patient, the pain, and its experience to best select the agent,

---

[m] I use the definition of "value" as stated by Pellegrino 54, p.12: " . . . personal attributions of worth or interest attached to things, ideas, or people . . . but they are not by that fact norms, principles, duties, or obligations."

dose, and regimen that evidence has demonstrated will most likely effect a prudent and beneficial outcome. Pain relief is the end-goal of such therapeutic intervention, and patients have an ethical right to have their pain effectively and beneficially managed (58). The physician and patient must recognize the longitudinal and reciprocal obligations that such treatment entails. To be sure, opioid pharmacotherapy may be both therapeutically and morally sound, but the duration and complex nature of this treatment can create circumstances in which practical and ethical problems arise.

Ethical Issues

The predominant issues of both therapeutic (i.e., scientific/technical and medicolegal dilemmas) and moral (i.e., ethical) relevance to pain medicine involve mismanagement characteristically effected by the inappropriate use of procedures and underprescription or overprescription of drugs (67). Each of these circumstances may reflect a disparity of shared responsibility in clinical decision-making that may have, at its root, a breakdown of beneficence-in-trust. As steward of knowledge, the physician must use scientific knowledge (episteme), skill and art (techne), balanced by phronesis to assess the relative effectiveness, benefit, and burdens of a particular treatment to a unique patient (49,68). Frequently, the overprescription of opioids results from the provision of "too much, too soon," with resultant physiological tolerance necessitating increasing doses of a drug to elicit the desired level of pain control. This may incur opioid-induced hyperalgesia, prompting the cycle of further dose escalation, tolerance, hyperalgesia, etc. (69). The use of an opioid that is inappropriate for a particular patient's type of pain, and/or failure to rotate agents to affect subpopulations of opioid receptors mediating specific and distinct forms of analgesia may also result in pharmacologic inefficacy, dose escalation and therapeutic impropriety (70,71). It is also important to note that patients' expectations of the outcomes of drug treatment may extend beyond pain control to functional domains of their life that may not be changeable and which are not consistent with the telos of pain medicine. Physicians must be sensitive to this and have the obligation to be truthful about the goals and expected attainable ends that a given therapeutic intervention is likely to provide. Describing the limitations of treatment and establishing the parameters for right and good intervention requires courage, integrity, and some degree of effacement of self-interest (72–74). Failure to do this violates a respect for patients' autonomy, deprives them of the knowledge necessary to consent to treatment, and impairs their ability to act with salience and rationality. As a result, patients may become distanced to the therapeutic relationship, increasingly noncompliant and may improperly (self-) medicate in an attempt to control their pain, affect other existential domains or revert the entirety of their life world to the prepain state.

Most commonly, when the right opioid is prescribed and administered at the right dose and schedule, the risk of addiction is rare (70,75,76). However, in cases of inappropriately high-dose opiate use, addiction may, and often does occur, and must be recognized as a clinical entity that requires referral beyond pain medicine to facilitate technically and ethically sound treatment (77). Numerous reasons can contribute to this trajectory: on one hand, it may represent a failure of the physician to utilize technical knowledge and phronesis appropriately to judge what is needed to treat a specific patient's pain, while recognizing their susceptibilities to addiction. However, the medical relationship is built upon a shared intersubjectivity, and patients too have moral obligations that are critical to the integrity of the clinical encounter and the trajectory and success of its outcomes (78,79). Thus, some patients may enter this relationship with the intent to manipulate the physician to accommodate needs that fall outside of the telos of medicine (e.g., procurement of drugs for means beyond pain control). Such intentions and acts fail to respect the autonomy of the physician. Neither physician nor patient can exercise autonomy that is "absolute," and the demands of the patient do not supersede or "trump" respect for the autonomy of the physician (as a person and therapeutic and moral agent). These intentions and acts are a violation of beneficence-in-trust (49) and the physician is not morally obligated to acquiesce to such demands. Yet, irrespective of the cause, the occurrence of addiction is not the basis for labeling or medical disenfranchisement, because such stigmatization and abandonment invariably places the patient in diametric opposition to the healing domains of medicine (80,81). Each patient brings a unique life world to the clinical encounter. The physician must use skill and judgment to apprehend the nature of that patient's pain, and concurrent and past circumstances that may suggest or predispose noncompliance and impropriety of drug use. If these are present, it is the physician's responsibility to insure that these vulnerabilities are addressed so that the patient may receive treatment(s) appropriate to his/her needs.

In contrast to the circumstances and issues inherent to overmedication, the undertreatment of pain may be because of physicians' inadequate knowledge of the extent and nature of a particular patient's pain or due to a lack of familiarity with procedural interventions and pharmacological regimens that would best produce the desired ends of pain control in that unique patient (70,82). However, a more insidious and grave determinant of undertreatment of pain are physicians' manifest anxieties about the potential medicolegal ramifications surrounding the use of opioids and the fear of prosecution or professional sanction in circumstantially and medically complex cases with multiple risks. The progressive ubiquity of postmodern technocentricism has been inculcated in society to adopt a commercialized worldview and led to a pervasive consumerism. The moral and legal difficulties of the patient as a consumer bastardize the patient–physician relationship, and may lead the physician to retreat to a position of reluctance in an attempt to insulate against the resultant demands and burdens of this newly construed interaction. Such defensive posture is incongruous with the core philosophy upon which the practice of pain medicine is based. The profession of pain medicine is a declaration of the promise to help patients in their best interests and is an invitation to trust in the physician's knowledge, skill, and virtue to execute this effective and beneficent care. Pellegrino and Thomasma (40) state that acts of beneficence encompass good on four levels: (i) as an ultimate act toward another human, (ii) as the patient experiences it, (iii) for the patient's choices, and (iv) biomedically. The defensive practice of intentional undertreatment of the pain patient violates each of these domains. Further, by refuting beneficence-in-trust, it disavows respect for the patient as a person, and therefore deprives him or her due equity of care[n].

---

[n] Further vulnerabilities can develop, and these patients may turn to complementary and alternative medicine (CAM) based upon this inequity of care and their disenfranchisement. However, philosophical differences may exist between CAM and mainstream medicine, including distinctions in the moral grounding of practice. CAM providers have an equal obligation to understand the essence of medicine *qua* medicine, its core philosophy, and to uphold the fiduciary responsibilities that are inherent to its profession and practice.

As well, the postmodern skepticism of moral foundation in favor of social contexts has exerted considerable influence upon medicine to adopt a cultural conformity. The plurality of contemporary culture may entail divergent concepts of morality based upon differing value systems and perspectives. These values can contribute to distinct constructs of rationality, and by extension, what constitutes reasonable and expected acts and ends. Together with the aforementioned consumerist manifestations, this has led to a highly litigious climate reflecting divergent societal values rather than a common moral integrity. To confront the often difficult situational complexities that may be superimposed upon medicine, the moral and intellectual virtue of the physician is essential to respond with intention and acts that are both focal to the telos of medicine and which are consistent across time as a matter of character, rather than simple adherence to social convention, or a changing set of values (36,83).

Given this cultural complexity, it can be seen how the sole use of prima facie principles might lead to apparent collision of the principles themselves due to a general lack of moral coherence within a pluralist society and the reliance upon social consensus of how the principles are to be used in differing circumstances. The heterogeneity of social values can produce considerable variation in the interpretation of both a lexical ordering of ethical principles, as well as their inherent meaning. Without a moral grounding, the sole application of principles can be manipulated to meet societal consensus and demands. As matter of fact, the Principlist approach is structured upon more fundamental, normative theories, and at least in concept, acknowledges virtue (84,85), but unless those underlying theories are coapplied and coutilized, the stand-alone use of principles can be somewhat difficult. A virtue-based ethics does not refute the application of prima facie principles. To the contrary, moral and intellectual virtue, in general, and phronesis specifically, allows the physician to intuit the relevance and appropriate use of principles and other ethical concepts (e.g., feminist ethics, casuistry, etc.) to resolve particular dilemmas, and to do so in a way that is consistent with a phenomenological understanding of pain and the telos of medicine qua medicine.

SUMMARY

Maldynic pain is a complex illness that defies technocentric models of evaluation and treatment. To rightly practice pain medicine, the physician must understand the mechanisms of pain, appreciate its phenomenological experience and effects upon the life world and lived body of each pain patient. Intellectual and moral virtue and specifically phronesis, are needed to resolve ethical dilemmas, empower clinical decision-making, and enable rational exercise of skill and art to render a right and good healing to the patient made vulnerable by pain.

ACKNOWLEDGMENT

The author is grateful to Prof. Edmund Pellegrino, M.D. for ongoing intellectual insight and mentorship, and the support of the Center for Clinical Bioethics, Georgetown University, Washington, D.C. This work is based upon a lecture given at the Clinical Meeting of the American Academy of Pain Management, San Diego, CA, September 2005 and on an excerpt of that lecture in Pain Practitioner, which portion is used here with permission. This work was supported, in part by funds from the Hunt-Travis Foundation.

REFERENCES

1. Husserl E. Ideas pertaining to a pure phenomenology and to phenomenological philosophy: Second Book: Studies in the Phenomenology of Constitution. In: Rojcewicz R, Schuwer A (tr.). Dordrecht: Kluwer, 1989.
2. Strauss E. Phenomenological Psychology. In: Eng E (tr.). New York: Basic Books, 1966.
3. Leder D. Toward a phenomenology of pain. Rev Existent Psychol Psychiatr 1984; 9:29–43.
4. Schrag C. Being in pain. In: Kestenbaum V, ed. The Humanity of the Ill: Phenomenological Perspectives. Knoxville, TN: University of Tennessee Press, 1982.
5. International Association for the Study of Pain. IASP pain terminology listing from: classification of chronic pain. In: Merskey H, Bogduk N, eds. 2nd ed. IASP Task Force on Taxonomy Seattle: IASP Press, 1994, accessed online at http://www.iasp-pain.org/terms-p.html.
6. Giordano J. The neurologic basis of pain and analgesia: from molecule to mind. Adv Dir Rehabil 2002; 11(1):25–28.
7. Giordano J. The neurobiology of nociceptive and anti-nociceptive systems. In: Cole EB, Boswell MV, Core BE, eds. Weiner's Pain Management: a Guide for Clinicians. 7th ed. Boca Raton, FL: CRC, 2006.
8. Morris D. The Culture of Pain. Berkeley: University of California Press, 1991.
9. Scarry E. The Body in Pain: The Making and Unmaking of the World. New York: Oxford, 1985.
10. Cassell EJ. The nature of suffering and its relationship to pain. In: Toombs SK, ed. Handbook of Phenomenology and Medicine Dordrecht: Kluwer, 2001:364–383.
11. Cassell EJ. The Healer's Art. New York: Penguin Books, 1979:79.
12. Humber JM, Almeder RF. What is Disease? Totowa, New Jersey: Humana Press, Inc., 1997.
13. Caton D. The secularization of pain. Anesthesiology 1985; 62:493–501.
14. Sulmasy DP. The Healer's Calling: A Spirituality for Physicians and Other Healthcare Professionals. New York: Paulist Press, 1997.
15. Wittgenstein L. Tractatus, Logicus, Philosophicus, 2.1–2.225. CK Ogden (tr.). London: Routledge, 1990:38–43.
16. Chapman RC, Nakamura Y, Flores LY. How we hurt: a constructivist framework for understanding individual differences in pain. In: Kunzendorf RG, Wallace B, eds. Individual Differences in Conscious Experience. Amsterdam: John Benjamin Publications, 2000:17–44.
17. Nelkin N. Reconsidering pain. Philos Psych 1994; 7:325–343.
18. Svenaeus F. Phenomenology of health and illness. In: Toombs SK, ed. Handbook of Phenomenology and Medicine. Amsterdam: Kluwer, 2001:87–108.
19. Gadamer HG. Uber die Verborgenheit der Gesundheit. Frankfurt am Main: Suhrkamp Verlag, 1993.
20. Heidegger M. Being and Time. In: Macquarrie J, Robinson E (tr.). New York: Harper-Row, 1926/1962.
21. Gallagher S. Lived body and environment. Res Phenomenol 1986; 16:139–170.
22. Loeb C. Past, Present, and Future: A Philosophical Essay about Time. Urbana, IL and Chicago: University of Illinois Press, 1991.
23. Ruoff GE. Depression in the patient with chronic pain. J Fam Prac 1996; 43:S25–S33.
24. Smedstad LM, Vaglum P, Kvien TK, Moum T. The relationship between self-reported pain and sociodemographic variables, anxiety and depressive symptoms in rheumatoid arthritis. J Rheumatol 1995; 22:514–520.
25. von Korff M, LeResche L, Dworkin SF. First onset of common pain symptoms: a prospective study of depression as a risk factor. Pain 1993; 55:251–258.
26. Casten RJ, Parmelee PA, Kleban MH, Lawton MP, Katz IR. The relationships among anxiety, depression and pain in a geriatric institutionalized sample. Pain 1995; 61: 271–276.
27. Kleinman A. Illness Narratives: Suffering, Healing and the Human Condition. New York: Basic Books, 1988.

28. Madjar I. Giving Comfort and Inflicting Pain. Edmonton: Qual Institute Pain University of Alberta, 1998.
29. Soderberg S, Norberg A. Metaphysical pain language among fibromyalgia patients. Scand J Caring Sci 1995; 9:55–59.
30. Dionne RA, Bartoshuk L, Mogil J, Witter J. Individual responder analyses for pain: does one pain scale fit all? Trends Pharmacol Sci 2005, 3:125–130.
31. Dilthey W. W. Dilthey: Selected Writings. In: HP Rickman (ed., tr.). Cambridge: Cambridge University Press, 1976.
32. Jaspers K. General Psychopathology. In: Hoenig J, Hamilton M (tr.). Manchester: Manchester University Press, 1963.
33. May WF. Contending images of the healer in an era of turnstile medicine. In: Walter JK, Klein EP, eds. The Story of Bioethics: From Seminal works to Contemporary Explorations. Washington, DC: Georgetown University Press, 2003:149–162.
34. Zaner R. Medicine. In: Embree L, Behnke EA, Carr D, et al., eds. Encyclopedia of Phenomenology. Dordrecht: Kluwer, 1997.
35. Fishman SM, Gallagher RM, Carr DB, Sullivan LW. The case for pain medicine. Pain Med 2004; 5(3):281.
36. MacIntyre A. After Virtue: A Study in Moral Theory. 2nd ed. Notre Dame, IN: University of Notre Dame Press, 1984.
37. McWhinney LR. Focusing on lived experience: evolution of clinical method in western medicine. In: Toombs SK, ed. Handbook of Phenomenology and Medicine. Amsterdam: Kluwer, 2001:325–344.
38. Pellegrino ED. The healing relationship: architectonics of clinical medicine. In: Shelp EE, ed. The Clinical Encounter: The Moral Fabric of the Physician–Patient Relationship. Boston: Reidel, 1983.
39. Aristotle. The Nichomachean Ethics. T. Irwin (tr.). Indianapolis: Hackett Publishing, 1999.
40. Pellegrino ED, Thomasma DC. The Virtues in Medical Practice. New York: Oxford, 1993.
41. Sherman N. The Fabric of Character: Aristotle's Theory of Virtue. Oxford: Clarendon Press, 1989.
42. Pellegrino, E. Philosophy and medicine: problematic and potential. J Med Philos 1976; 1:5–31.
43. Sadler JZ. Diagnosis/anti-diagnosis. In: Radden J, ed. The Philosophy of Psychiatry: A Companion. Oxford: Oxford University Press, :2004; 163–179.
44. Foucalt M. Power and Knowledge. In: C Gordon (tr.). New York: Pantheon, 1980.
45. Veatch RM. Against virtue: a deontological critique of virtue theory in medical ethics. In: Shelp EE, ed. Virtue and Medicine. Dordrecht: Reidel, 1985:329–346.
46. Veatch RM. The impossibility of a morality internal to medicine. J Med Philos 2001; 26(6):621–642.
47. May WF. Code, covenant, contract or philanthropy? Hastings Cent Rep 1975; 5:29–38.
48. May WF. The Physician's Covenant. Revised edition. Philadelphia: Westminster Press, 2000.
49. Pellegrino ED. The anatomy of clinical judgments: some notes on right reason and right action. In: Engelhardt HT, Spicker SF, Towers B, eds. Clinical Judgment: A Critical Appraisal. Dordrecht: Reidel, 1979:169–194.
50. Gorovitz S, MacIntyre A. Toward a theory of medical fallibility. J Med Philos 1976; 1:51–71.
51. Sober E. The art and science of clinical judgment: an information approach. In: Engelhardt HT, Spicker SF, Towers B, eds. Clinical Judgment: A Critical Appraisal. Dordrecht: Reidel, 1979:29–44.
52. Widdershoven-Heerding I. Medicine as a form of practical understanding. Theor Med 1987; 8:179–185.
53. Davis FD. Phronesis, clinical reasoning and Pellegrino's philosophy of medicine. In: Thomasma DC, ed. The Influence of Edmund D. Pellegrino's Philosophy of Medicine. Dordrecht: Kluwer, 1997:173–195.
54. Pellegrino ED, Sulmasy DP. Medical ethics. In: Warrell DA, Cox TM, Firth JD, Benz EJ, eds. Oxford Textbook of Medicine.. Vol. 1 Oxford: Oxford University Press. Oxford: Oxford University Press, 2003:12–16.

55. American Academy of Pain Medicine and American Pain Society. The use of opioids for the treatment of chronic pain: a consensus statement. Glenview, IL, 1997.
56. Federation of State Medical Boards of the United States. Model guidelines for the use of controlled substances for the treatment of pain. Federal State Medical Boards of the United States, Dallas, TX, 1998.
57. Joint Commission on Accreditation of Healthcare Organizations. Comprehensive Accreditation Manual for Hospitals: Official Handbook, 1999.
58. Clark PA. Ethical implications in pain management: can a formalized policy help? Health Prog 2002; 19–28.
59. Pain and Policy Studies Group, University of Wisconsin. Accessed online at: http://www.medsch.wisc.edu/painpolicy, on April 20, 2005.
60. Maher BA, Gallagher R. Dealing with pain. The Scientist: Pain. Accessed online at: http://www.the-scientist.com, on 20 April, 2005.
61. Schmidt WK. An overview of current and investigational drugs for the treatment of acute and chronic pain. In: Bountra C, Munglari R, Scmidt WK, eds. Pain: Current Understanding, Emerging Therapies and Novel Approaches to Drug Discovery. New York: Marcel Dekker, 2003:385–387.
62. Portenoy RK. Opioid therapy for chronic nonmalignant pain: a review of the critical issues. J Pain Symptom Manage 1996; 11:203–217.
63. Brouckoms AJ, Masaud P, Murray GB, Cassem EH, Stern TA, Tesar GE. Chronic nonmalignant pain treatment with long-term analgesics. Ann Clin Psychiatr 1992; 4: 185–192.
64. Fishman SM, Mao J. Opioid therapy in chronic nonmalignant pain. In: Ballantyne JC, ed. The Massachusetts General Hospital Handbook of Pain Management. 2nd ed. Philadelphia: Lippincott Williams-Wilkins, 2002.
65. Zenz M, Strumpf M, Tryba M. Long-term opioid therapy in patients with chronic nonmalignant pain. J Pain Symptom Manage 1992; 7:69–77.
66. Gallagher RM. Pain science and rational polypharmacy. Am J Phys Med Rehabil 2005; 84:S1–S3.
67. Rich BA. Pain management: legal risks and ethical responsibilities. J Pharm Care Symptom Control 1997; 5(1):5–20.
68. Pellegrino ED. From medical ethics to a moral philosophy of the professions. In: Walter JK, Klein EP, eds. The Story of Bioethics: From Seminal Works to Contemporary Explorations. Washington DC: Georgetown University Press, 2003:3–16.
69. Brodner RA, Taub A. Chronic pain exacerbated by long-term narcotic use in patients with nonmalignant disease: clinical syndrome and treatment. Mt Sinai J Med 1978; 45:233–237.
70. Foley KM. Opioids and chronic neuropathic pain. New Engl J Med 2003; 348:1279–1281.
71. Mercadante S. Opioid rotation for cancer pain: rationale and clinical aspects. Cancer 1999; 86:1856–1866.
72. Hauerwas S. Truthfulness and Tragedy. Notre Dame, IN: University of Notre Dame Press, 1977.
73. Pence GE. Ethical Options in Medicine. Oradell, NJ: Medical Economics Press, 1980.
74. Shelp EE. Courage: a neglected virtue in the patient–physician relationship. Soc Sci Med 1984; 18:351–360.
75. Finlayson RE, Maruta T, Morse RM, Martin MA. Substance dependence and chronic pain: experience with treatment and follow up results. Pain 1986; 26:175–180.
76. Porter J, Jick H. Addiction rare in patients treated with narcotics. New Engl J Med 1980; 320(2):123.
77. Frances A, Pincus HA, First MB, et al. Substance-related disorders. Diagnostic and Statistical Manual of Mental Disorders. 4th ed. Washington DC: American Psychiatric Association, 2000:191–295.
78. Dyer AR. Virtue and medicine: a physician's analysis. In: Shelp EE, ed. Virtue and Medicine. Dordrecht: Reidel, 1985:223–236.
79. Lebacqz K. The virtuous patient. In: Shelp EE, ed. Virtue and Medicine. Dordrecht: Reidel, 1985:275–288.

80. Dain N. Reflections on anti-psychiatry and stigma in the history of American psychiatry. Am J Psychiatr 1994; 45(10):1010–1015.
81. Pellegrino ED. Nonabandonment: an old obligation revisited. Ann Int Med 1998; 122(5):377–378.
82. Ballantyne JC, Mao J. Opioid therapy for chronic pain. New Engl Med 2003; 349: 1943–1953.
83. Nagel T. Mortal Questions. Cambridge: Cambridge University Press, 1979.
84. Beauchamp TL, Childress JF. Principles of Biomedical Ethics. 5th ed. New York: Oxford, 2001.
85. Gert B, Cluver C, Clouser KD. Bioethics: A Return to Fundamentals. New York: Oxford University Press, 1997.

2

Ethical Dilemmas of Chronic Pain from a Patient's Perspective

Debra E. Benner

Hershey Medical Center, Hershey, Pennsylvania, U.S.A.

INTRODUCTION

"Pain is a more terrible lord of mankind than even death himself."

Albert Schweitzer

All ethical considerations begin with self. No matter what lens of academic discipline one has acquired along the way, all ethical reflections are ultimately a mirror of self. Individual choices about actions, lifestyle, meaning, and purpose will always spring from this lifelong evolving definition. Any brokenness of self that results from trauma is no respecter of position or credentials. Chronic pain is a trauma that will alter one's view of self, and thus one's ethical outlook in many areas. This is an inevitable consequence of dealing with pain on a daily basis. Every chronic pain patient, therefore, brings a specific set of personal ethics into every encounter with professionals within the health care community. Patients' ethics must be respected and heard. The level of sophistication of thought, knowledge, or language will vary from person to person, but the ethical viewpoint of each person involved in the health care community must be a part of every decision-making process of patient care. The chronic pain patient brings a very unique ethical perspective to the process of health care, and this perspective has been too often overlooked by the medical community. Pain patients should not be regarded as passive observers to whatever the health care community decides. There is much more wisdom in regarding them as teachers in the chronic pain community. In order for any treatment plan to have a chance for success, the patient must be acknowledged as an integral member of the decision-making team.

Because no two people will ever possess the same set of life experiences, there will always be the potential for misunderstanding in any interpersonal encounter within the health care community. This is particularly critical to the chronic pain patient who often feels categorized or judged by his or her presenting pain condition. If the whole patient is not respected, and his or her hopes and fears are not heard by the medical professional, the relationship will end up being just one more frustrating and negative experience for the patient. The health care community should be a place of relative safety and openness for the patient who has usually encountered a substantial lack of understanding and concern from insurance carriers, employers, and even family members and friends. For most chronic pain patients, injustice has taken on a very real and personal meaning in his or her life. Personal integrity and personal ethics have usually been questioned by employers, insurance companies, and even some members of the health care community. Chronic pain patients often encounter either spoken or intimated charges of malingering or overly dramatizing symptoms. Difficulties with insurance companies and their legal representatives have dissolved any sense of security in having protective financial nets for needed medical procedures. These experiences often serve to evoke strong feelings of frustration and bitterness in patients who were formerly hard-working, productive, and trusted members of society.

As a result of coping with a chronic medical condition and working with the health care system, the patient has usually developed some tolerance for the long delays in waiting to see a specialist, some understanding of the busyness and limited time of the specialist's schedule, and some appreciation of the constraints that insurance companies have placed on physician care. But, the hope that reigns eternal in the heart of chronic pain patients is that they will finally meet someone who will have the heart to listen and the mind to hear what every day of suffering is like for the patient. In one study, it was found that doctors interrupt their patients a mean time of 18 seconds after the beginning of the patients' descriptions of their symptoms (1). The patient, who presents with chronic pain, is seeking an understanding ally in the fight against that pain. This will only happen in the ethical milieu of a compassion-filled patient/doctor relationship in which the physician takes the time to listen and to learn. If this does not happen, the patient must once again find the courage and tenacity to continue to search for a medical professional who is able to relate to his or her need for understanding.

As the health care professional moves on to the next patient, the person with chronic pain leaves the relative security of the professional's office to reenter a world that has little practical regard for any perceived weakness or deficiency. Yet, the chronic pain patient is forced to live in such an intolerant world. Any success in coping with this world ultimately rests within the internal ethical worldview of the patient. For the most part, the patient has little control over the inciting cause of the pain condition or the ongoing change in his or her own health status. Any sense of stability and balance must come from within the patient. It is the patient's developing ethical worldview which will determine how well he or she will cope with the devastating life changes that accompany chronic pain. The degree of successful coping will determine the degree of suffering that the patient endures. The ethical issues that influence suffering can be placed in three categories: personal ethics—the choices that determine self-definition and self-value; relational ethics—the choices that define the roles and importance of interpersonal relationships; and, philosophical ethics—the choices that influence the way one views the world and his or her place in it. Practically speaking, for the health care professional, the results of these ethical choices will be reflected in how well the patient responds to various treatment modalities, compliance with physician recommendations, and an observable return to felt purpose and meaning in life.

PERSONAL DILEMMAS

Chronic pain is an isolating condition. Many of the personal ethical dilemmas that confront a chronic pain patient are due to feelings of isolation and alienation from the rest of the world. Some of the stressors contributing to these feelings are either internal or external. The internal stressors begin with the pain sensation itself. The external stressors are the many consequences that accompany a chronic pain condition and add to suffering. Although pain and suffering are often used in conjunction with one another, they are not synonymous. As the term is being used here, pain is mostly the biological/physical sensation of discomfort. It is true that intensification of pain entails the intensification of suffering. However, pain is typically seen as more definite, identifiable, and measurable than suffering (2). Suffering is more inclusive and is the result of both physical pain and the many consequences of that pain. The degree to which the patient suffers depends on the meaning or significance he or she attaches to the pain (3). Attached meaning may be involved in all of these categories, i.e., the physical, emotional, social, relational, financial, and spiritual conditions of the patient. The patient often feels as if he or she has very little control over any of these stressors and, therefore, has little control over the degree of experienced suffering. However, there are important decisions to be made and choices to be followed that will either increase or decrease the amount of the patient's suffering. These often come in the form of personal ethical dilemmas.

Change in Definition of Self (Loss of Roles)

Regardless of whether a chronic pain condition develops quickly as the result of trauma or slowly and insidiously, the patient must deal with a multitude of significant losses. These losses are more readily apparent to those who are close to the patient. Family, friends, and the health care community can observe experiences such as loss of employment, ongoing physical limitations, and changes in the daily routine of the patient. What is not so obvious or observable is the very real feeling of loss of self-identity experienced by the sufferer. This often begins with the loss of one's vocation. If job loss is the direct consequence of declining health due to the chronic condition and an inability to adequately function in a job, the negative effects are far-reaching into the life of the chronic pain patient. It is a leading factor in declining emotional well-being (4). This is a culture that often defines one's worth by the extent to which he or she is able to contribute materially to society. This value is firmly ingrained at a very young age. A person does not need to speak very long to a stranger before the inevitable question of what one does for a living arises. This is a moment of shame and failure felt by the pain patient who is unable to work or is able to work only in a limited role. This shame is especially deep if one suffers from a pain condition that is outwardly invisible. As the explanation is being spoken, the patient is too often met with a look of skepticism or a hurtful reply to the effect that "it must be wonderful to have all that free time."

It has been found that unemployment is extraordinarily stressful and can lead to consequences such as serious health and psychological issues, family violence, other kinds of family conflict, problems with children, and even suicide (4). No matter how internally directed an individual might be, much of one's self-identity is still defined by what he/she does in the work force. There is not only the loss of income, but also the loss of the status and self-esteem derived from being an independent contributing member of society or the main support of the family. Severe grief reactions to job loss are poorly understood by those who have never experienced them. Depending on the degree and nature of the chronic pain condition, the patient may never be able to return to his or her chosen profession. The permanence and finality of such a loss shakes the very essence of the patient. One goes from the role of being a fully functioning member of society to the role of being a disabled person. This is an unwelcome change, to say the least. To varying degrees, it will undermine every aspect of a person's life and being. The patient is forever stigmatized by this change. Unfortunately, adding to the patient's complicated grieving at this time are the frequent battles with workers' compensation and/or insurance companies that challenge the legitimacy of the patient's inability to work. These battles serve to add unneeded fuel to the desperation that the patient is already feeling.

Even if the chronic pain patient is able to continue at the same job, there are usually some accommodations that need to be made by both the patient and his or her employer. Unfortunately, this often results in a lowering of the patient's employment status in some way. Even if the work quality is the same, neither side may feel like it is as good as a *normal* person's work. This may be conveyed to the person with chronic pain in any number of ways, such as lack of promotion or loss of important assignments. In many cases, the patient is never able to return to what he or she was doing prior to the inciting trauma or illness. In this scenario, the person will require some form of assistance to evaluate the limitations and the remaining skills so as to seek alternative employment. This may involve further education or some other kind of skill development. The patient will discover that resources are very limited in finding this kind of assistance. The chronic pain patient may be unable to ever work again in a full-time capacity. If he or she is the significant contributor to the family's income, the results are likely financially devastating. Even if able to continue to perform in the same work environment but with a more limited schedule, the loss of any benefit package the employer may offer is a strong possibility.

In the circumstance in which patients may be able to fulfill the requirements of a part time position, they are often confronted with an ethical dilemma that can rattle their core values. Our country's health care system is in a very severe crisis. For someone with a chronic pain condition who is unable to work at a full time position, it becomes practically impossible to purchase and maintain private health insurance. With the long and involved medical history that a chronic pain patient brings to an insurance application, there is little chance that any insurance carrier will accept the application and offer a policy. If they do, the monthly premium rate is astronomical. In effect, it becomes impossible to obtain health insurance coverage in this circumstance. If the individual strongly desires to be employed (and, contrary to how society too often views someone with a disability, he or she is very likely to be strongly desirous of a return to gainful employment), the prospect of loss of any Social Security benefits that they are receiving, including access to any government health care assistance, exists. Under the current Social Security laws, patients who have been granted full disability and access to Medicare are very limited in the amount of income they can generate before losing all benefits. Therefore, a tremendous internal stress builds up within the patient because the desire to return to work and bring some resemblance of *normalcy* or productivity to one's life meets the financial obstacle of the loss of benefits without the ability to obtain affordable health care. All too often, the chronic pain patient is faced with the dilemma of physically pushing to work a full-time schedule to acquire needed health care benefits and, in doing so, significantly risks exacerbating the medical condition. The other option is to remain unemployed or minimally employed to retain disability status. Neither of these alternatives is conducive to increasing the quality of life of the patient, and both contribute to deepening the feelings of frustration and discontent.

Changes in Self-Esteem (A Journey Through the Early Stages)

A large component of the loss of self-identity is the loss of self-esteem that accompanies the struggle with a chronic illness. Because the very foundation of one's life continues to be shaken by the pain and consequences of the pain, self-esteem falls as a victim to the decline. It is first affected by the diagnosis. Most people can adequately manage the *temporary* role of patient. The very role of being a patient is a regression to a kind of childhood dependency for most adults. However, as long as eventual recovery is likely, one can cope with the indignities—small and large—that accompany this role. The real blow is experienced when the patient is told that there is no further intervention available that will eliminate the pain he or she is feeling. This news promotes more of a loss of self because the realization comes that even one's own body has become an enemy because it is now the agent of the person's daily agony (5). At this point, the primary physician or surgeon often refers the patient to a pain specialist—if one is fortunate enough to have a pain specialist available within a convenient distance. As the patient waits for the day of the first appointment to arrive, subtle changes begin to occur within his or her psyche. First, it feels as if one has been discarded by the physician or surgeon they have come to trust through their medical issues. Second, there is an accompanying sense of failure or shame as if one should have been able to "do better" with his or her recovery. Third, a fear begins to develop at the core of the person that he or she may never again be a fully independent and self-sufficient person. All these feelings are confirmed as patients enter the waiting room of the pain specialist and realize they are now spending what used to be their most productive time of the day with others with whom they never imagined having much common ground. For example, the patient looks around and notices that the other patients do not appear particularly happy or comfortable. There are few smiles or postures of contentment. Instead, there is an almost palpable air of desperation. And then comes the realization that they are spending this experience with many who are decades older than themselves. The "dark cloud" that has followed the patient since the diagnosis grows larger and increasingly more ominous.

Most pain specialists have a true ethical sense of compassion and care for their patients. They have chosen their clinical population with some forethought. They have observed the many struggles and obstacles in the lives of the patients they see every day. Their offices become places of refuge for chronic pain patients. In time, these offices may become the only places where patients feel safe in describing exactly how they are feeling. Nevertheless, that first visit often confirms the patient's worst fears. Chronic pain is presented as something to be managed, not cured. It can no longer be pushed to the edges of life because pain will serve as a constant reminder of limitations and lost dreams. Somewhat paradoxically, the initial affirmation of what the patient has been experiencing is temporarily uplifting. The patient leaves the appointment with the emotional boost of having been heard and understood for the first time since the nightmare began. However, in the days that follow, the sense of isolation again deepens because the patient tries to convey the content of the appointment to family and friends who are neither eager nor willing to accept a diagnosis of chronicity. At best, the patient is met with well-intentioned, but ultimately hurtful, platitudes to the effect that "doctors can be wrong" or "one never knows what cure the future may hold." At worst, the intimation of malingering or somatic hysteria is leveled at the patient.

As the weeks turn into months, it becomes very difficult for the patient to prevent the internalization of such messages. Thinly veiled accusations of malingering can cause even well adjusted patients to want to prove to themselves and others that they are still useful and functional. This kind of compensatory activity, whether in the form of returning to a job in which they are no longer able to physically perform, or doing chores around the house that make them feel *normal*, almost always results in an exacerbation of pain symptoms and the accompanying loss of additional self-esteem. Another factor that adds to this loss is the often-unconscious tendency of others to place the patient in the role of someone who is dependent upon them. This transforms what was formerly a peer relationship into a parent-child relationship. This change is harmful to both parties and can eventually unravel the fabric of a healthy relationship. From personal observations, it seems that in a spousal or other serious romantic relationship, the more quickly a professional therapist is consulted, the better the prognosis for a healthy relationship. In a relationship with another family member or a friend, the therapy option is much more difficult to invoke. However, without awareness and an accompanying *desire* to somehow return to mutuality, the health of any relationship will be in jeopardy. With the loss of each healthy relationship, the patient becomes more isolated and loses more of a sense of self-respect.

In many real ways, the chronic pain patient is not the same person he or she was prior to the onset of the pain condition. There are many challenges in dealing with the physical and emotional toll of daily chronic pain. Each day has to be planned around the *good* times. There can be unpredictable variations in the level of pain from day to day, which makes advance planning difficult. Life becomes a series of trade-offs because the patient must decide how much pain associated with performing a task or accepting a social invitation is acceptable. Many tasks of daily living and maintaining a home become difficult, if not impossible, to manage without assistance. These adjustments are very difficult for someone who formerly lived an independent and vital life. Adding to these difficulties are often the aforementioned financial anxieties. As months turn into years, the patient is stripped of many past enjoyments. These are replaced with practical survival and a growing disdain for the person he or she has become. Because the experience of pain and suffering is a combination of biomedical, psychosocial, and behavioral factors, all these added stressors will diminish the patient's quality of life (6). At this point, chronic pain patients must focus on new ways of defining themselves as worthwhile human beings. Few people can tackle this alone. If the patient is lacking an adequate support system, the task becomes even more monumental. Self-esteem and a new self-identity must be rebuilt brick by brick with the aid of others in their community. New messages must be internalized that promote a healthy recognition of limitations while obtaining a growing respect for what can still be accomplished.

Need for Validation

The chronic pain experience is largely a subjective experience for everyone involved. There are no truly accurate measures for quantifying pain. Physical examinations for chronic pain have inherent subjectivity because it is reported that there is more agreement among various physicians for the same patient regarding the medical history than on the examination findings (6). Much depends on the patient's ability to communicate what he or she is experiencing. Complicating the issue is the great difficulty of adequately describing what is being felt. This is true even for the most articulate patient because pain is an experience that takes one outside the realm of reason and language. It is crucial to find words or phrases that are descriptive enough for the listener to comprehend what the patient is experiencing. This can be a frustrating experience for both the patient and the medical professional. From the patient's perspective, there is the fear of sounding overly dramatic or, conversely, minimizing the report of symptoms. Many factors contribute to how the patient is able to describe his or her chronic pain. These include such diverse factors as prior experiences with other health care professionals, the fluctuating nature of the chronic pain condition, the degree of comfort experienced in the relationship with the medical professional, the ethnic, educational, and cultural backgrounds of the patient, the specific reason for the current visit, and the language skills of the patient and the health care provider. Underlying all these factors is the patient's desperate desire for understanding and validation.

A person does not need to travel the chronic pain journey for very long before meeting with unkind responses, skepticism, and judgmental attitudes from those outside and within the medical community. Such responses only serve to compound the suffering of the patient. It is difficult to understand the ethical mindset of someone who desires to injure another with unkind or judgmental comments. It is this kind of disregard and lack of validation that serves to drive chronic pain patients into deeper isolation. Unfortunately, this lack of empathy is all too prevalent in our world. Especially hurtful to chronic pain patients is encountering these attitudes in groups or institutions in which they found solace prior to the onset of the pain condition. This may even include their religious institutions. Sociologists may excuse the seriousness of this lack of empathy by placing blame on the modern, rapid pace of life. However, it seems that many people do not have the ability or desire to learn to empathize with another's misfortune. Others may fear something similar befalling them, and thus avoid the patient. Still others may consciously or unconsciously reflect an attitude of superiority toward the chronic pain patient. No matter what the cause, the lack of an ethical commitment to assist others who require it reflects a deep flaw within both individuals and institutions. Many chronic pain patients begin to approach every encounter with an air of defensiveness or even anger. Unfortunately, this demeanor serves to increase the likelihood of even further misunderstanding.

Although, the patient ultimately must learn the coping skill of internal validation, doing so is a long and slow process for many with chronic pain conditions. This process is encumbered by a lack of a strong support network. The impact of a chronic pain condition takes its toll on everyone associated with the patient. The patient is no longer able to fulfill many of the same roles he or she had previously. This is true not only in the employment arena, but also in settings with family, friends, and social communities. Generally, people respond to an acute health crisis in a loved one with compassion and a strong desire to help the person. If the acute condition then becomes a chronic condition, relational dynamics begin to change. The patient may experience the gradual withdrawal of compassion and care because those around him or her become frustrated and discouraged by the lack of medical progress. The patient's original support network dwindles or, in some cases, entirely disappears. Martin Luther King Jr. once stated: "In the end, we will remember not the words of our enemies, but the silence of our friends (7)." Because the impact of this huge loss of support begins to be realized by the patient, the health care community often becomes the *substitute* support network. Those who work within the chronic pain community must be aware of this possible scenario and serve the patient well by assisting in efforts to find new alternatives for social support. Although the responsibility for this social reestablishment ultimately rests with the patient, it is initially difficult to move outward to establish new contacts while dealing with the grief and mourning that accompanies such a devastating loss.

Depersonalization in the Health Care System

For anyone who has had experience in the health care community from a patient's perspective, it is not difficult to understand how depersonalizing the system can be. There is not only a lack of dignity and privacy associated with being a patient, but there can also be a loss of *personhood* as well. A patient is often identified by *his or her ailment*. For example, in a hospital setting, one becomes "the back" in room X, or "the neck" in room Y. In a physician's office, it is difficult to maintain any resemblance of self-respect sitting in a paper examination gown while the other people in the room remain fully clothed. It is also difficult not to overhear any discussion about the patient and his or her condition that takes place in the hallway either prior to or after the examination. There are understandably necessary protocols that a patient endures that are less than conducive to retaining a sense of social dignity; however, this situation does not need to be magnified by a health care professional, who seems to forget that he or she is working with a fellow human being. Dr. Oliver Sacks, in his book *A Leg to Stand On*, discussed being thrown into the role of a patient with a chronic injury (8). All his years of medical training did not prepare him for the emotionality associated with suddenly becoming a patient. He noted the arrogant attitudes of certain medical professionals who returned nothing but coldness in the face of his fears. He spoke of being "the leg" during his long stay in the hospital. Through the ordeal of being a patient, he discovered a newfound compassion for dealing with his future patients.

Perhaps the worst scenario in the health care system that a chronic pain patient eventually will face is the independent medical examination (IME). Whether pain is the result of an accident in the workplace, an automobile accident, or some other type of trauma, the patient will frequently be required to undergo a physical examination by a physician hired by an insurance carrier. Sometimes the patient is involved in litigation, which necessitates such an examination by the employer's or the defendant's insurance carrier. Sometimes the patient's own insurance carrier puts them through one or more examinations. This is especially true in those states that have no-fault automobile insurance. Because of these situations, the chronic pain patient and the physician are in an adversarial relationship before the examination even begins. There are those physicians who derive a large percentage of their income from such examinations. It appears obvious that if a physician desires to continue to obtain referrals from insurance carriers, he or she will approach the appointment with a bias against the patient. From the patient's perspective, this examination will almost invariably be a degrading and demeaning experience. IME physicians often question the legitimacy of reported pain and may maintain an air of skepticism throughout the examination. The patient may believe that the report has been written prior to the examination and the physician is simply waiting to add a few details before submitting it. The examination is usually not thorough, and the physician may even intentionally try to invoke painful reactions to observe what response the patient displays. This quickly places the chronic pain patient in a no-win dilemma. If the patient openly exhibits pain, the physician will potentially report that he or she is overly dramatic. If the patient is more stoic in his or her response, the physician may report no indication of pain. Regardless, the IME physician frequently opines that the patient is malingering and/or dishonest in reporting chronic pain. This is an unethical system and one that causes much unneeded stress and anxiety for the patient. Such a system is in opposition to standards of ethical medical practice.

Seeking Adequate Professional Assistance

... medicine professes always to have experience as the touchstone for its workings. So Plato was right in saying that to become a true doctor, the candidate must have passed through all the illnesses that he hopes to cure and all the accidents and circumstances he is to diagnose .... Truly I should trust such a man. For the others guide us like the person who paints seas, reefs and ports while sitting at his table, and sails his model of a ship there in complete safety. Throw him into the real thing, and he does not know how to get at it.

Montaigne (9)

The chronic pain patient and the entire pain community should understand that health care involves more than an amelioration of pain. The relationship between the health care professional and the patient ideally involves a mutual journey of discovery. The patient now interacts with a life altered by the daily struggle with pain and its consequences. Too often, patients feel that they are entitled only to assistance with their medical/biological pain concerns. And, too often, the health care system reinforces this feeling because nociceptive pain, although admittedly subjective, is still somewhat within the comfort range of measurable scientific data. Less quantifiable are the other needs of the person with chronic pain. There are many psychological/emotional needs that arise as a consequence of chronic pain conditions. Until very recently, most chronic pain patients were treated in the psychological community similar to patients who presented with primary depression. However, the depression frequently seen in the chronic pain population is usually due to complicated grief issues resulting from the loss of critical life roles. For the first five years, depression, denial, and especially a sense of entitlement are all a part of the grief cycle and coming to terms with the fact that life will never be the same (7). At the core of the struggle for the patient is the everyday reality of coming to terms with the reduced physical capacity that prevents maintaining routine self-esteem-sustaining roles (4). Although depression and other emotional issues can be a consequence of prolonged pain, chronic pain patients are often reluctant to seek help from the psychological community for fear that they will be told that their pain is "all in their head." This fear is unfortunately reinforced by insurance companies and other legal agencies looking for ways to curtail their responsibilities to pay for patient care. It is essential that the patient seek out professionals who are experienced in dealing sensitively and knowledgeably with chronic pain issues.

Within the psychological domain is the social dimension of chronic pain. Experiencing prolonged pain impacts all the social and relational alliances formerly held by the patient. Helping the patient adjust to these changes and incorporate new ways of social functioning is an important part of health care. This need can be addressed within the psychological community or within some other social or community institution. An important professional in the team of chronic pain consultants, in many cases, is a member of the clergy or some other kind of reputable spiritual director. Shortly following the diagnosis of a chronic pain condition, patients begin to ask the more transcendent questions involving the meaning and purpose of their pain. While some psychologists may be comfortable in this area, others are not. Many patients would clearly benefit by having a spiritual guide as a member of their health care team. The bottom line is that the Cartesian paradigm of an artificial divide of body/mind/soul should be defunct, and ought to be replaced with a multidimensional approach to health care, which seeks to assist the patient in all aspects of his or her being. This should include spiritual aspects.

RELATIONAL/SOCIAL DILEMMAS

Human beings are hardwired for community. Irrespective of one's personality type and temperament, rare is the individual who thrives without the support, companionship, and joy of being part of a welcoming and caring community. In today's culture, this kind of community is becoming increasingly more difficult to find. Some people successfully find it in their extended families, places of employment, social or religious communities, or other groups of common interest. In the shrinking world of the chronic pain patient, finding community is even more difficult. Old avenues of seeking the company of others have been closed or greatly curtailed. Nevertheless, the need for community remains very strong.

Disclosure of Chronic Pain to Others

As chronic pain patients venture out into the community, they are faced with the dilemma of how to respond to inquiries about their health. In our culture, the phrase, "how are you?" is a form of greeting. Few people have the time or interest to hear a full reply. Most people routinely respond with "fine" or "good." What about chronic pain patients? If they encounter friends and acquaintances, there is a decision to be made as to how much to reveal. One must immediately judge whether the person is only making a polite passing inquiry or is really interested in hearing about his or her current health status. If the judgment is incorrect, one can be sure that the person making the inquiry will never ask again. Yet, it does not feel totally honest to provide the standard answer. There will be a few friends who really do want to know the truth. There is a risk of offending these people because not answering honestly will be seen as a form of distancing. With time, the chronic pain sufferers will come to dread the inevitable questions about their health. Few people have the desire to be regarded as perpetual patients. Also to be considered is the added stigma attached to patients who take opioid medications to alleviate pain. Most people do not understand that cognitive impairment or a constant "high" are not experienced with the medical use of opioids for chronic pain.

In social situations, chronic pain sufferers often attempt to assume an air of normalcy. They typically do not want to be reminded about their pain by every acquaintance they meet. This becomes very difficult to convey to others in a way that is diplomatic and respectful of their genuine concerns about the patient. It is perhaps adaptive for the person with chronic pain to construct a reply that expresses gratitude about the inquiry while simultaneously leading the conversation away from the pain issue. Replies such as, "I continue to struggle, but I am dealing with it" or "the pain goes on, but I am managing it" with a "thank you" at the end often allows the patient to then add another remark that refocuses the conversation to a different topic. This kind of reply acknowledges the interest shown by the inquirers while politely reminding the engaged person that chronic pain is so much more than a summary of one's current health status.

Unfortunately, there are also those chronic pain patients who become so focused on their health condition as to limit most, if not every, conversation on that topic. These patients will soon find a paucity of acquaintances with whom to have that type of conversation. Conversations about one's chronic pain, while theoretically cathartic for the patients, produce anxiety and frustration in the listeners. Their early empathy or sympathy quickly turns to despair because they realize there is nothing they can say or do to help the patient. Feelings of "survivor guilt" may also arise. If the listeners genuinely care about the patients, they may find a way of suggesting that they find a member of the professional pain community to whom they can release their emotions and begin to alter their perspectives. This requires tact and a sense of timing because the chronic pain patients are often hypersensitive to suggestions of this type. Conveying the suggestion without triggering abandonment or anger issues within the patients is a difficult task. The recommendation will only be well received when it comes from someone who they trust will continue to care about them and remain in a relationship. This is often a family member, close friend, or another chronic pain patient who has given time and caring to the patient through past episodes of health crises.

Another danger area that most chronic pain patients will encounter is the reality that not everyone is safe to include in the circle of people who know the details about their health condition. There are people who are unsafe because they will use the information to keep the patient in a subordinate role. This may occur in an employment setting or in a social setting. There are people with damaged ego structures that maintain their sense of superiority by finding fault or weakness in others. They will use an individual's chronic pain to identify him or her as weak or unworthy. In this way, they can, and often will, dismiss anything the patient may say that is contradictory to their own narrow view of the world. The patient with chronic pain can be greatly harmed by such a person, especially if this individual has the potential to block or hinder future employment opportunities. If the person is a close friend or family member, ongoing contact may negatively impact the self-esteem of the patient in subtler, but long-lasting ways.

Another potentially toxic group of acquaintances are those who seem to have the need to perpetually care for others in order to feel fulfilled. There is a wide range of responses on this continuum, but all will eventually serve to subvert the independence of the patient. There are very appropriate times during health crises in which strong nurturance and support are needed by the patient. However, if a significant other is entrenched in that type of role, too much focus will be placed on the patient's disabilities rather than on remaining abilities. It is vital for chronic pain sufferers to reclaim as much of their lives as possible within safe medical limits. If the caregiver is thwarting this goal, the patient will either respond with passivity or with anger that can damage the relationship. It is the responsibility of the patient to set healthy limits to care-giving needs.

What to Expect from Others

Making adjustments to reach a level of acceptance with the new way of living that accompanies being a chronic pain patient is a complicated process. One very challenging area that requires much ethical examination by the patient is in knowing what and how much is reasonable to expect from others. When an acute illness or trauma first strikes, there are usually many people around the patient who seem willing and eager to help with physical and emotional needs. As the acute health issue becomes chronic, the patient's social support sphere becomes progressively smaller. With the progression of disability, the chronic pain patient must rely on asking other people for assistance with specific needs. The questions arise—who to ask and what is a proper request. The patient should be encouraged to do as much for him/herself as possible without risking further injury. In some cases, little by way of outside assistance is needed. In other cases, there may be strict medical guidelines as to what tasks the patient can no longer safely perform. These guidelines may necessitate assistance with aspects of daily living. Many of these tasks may involve activities that healthy individuals take for granted. For example, there may be a 5- or 10-pound lifting limitation. If one imagines how many times each week such a limit is exceeded simply to maintain a household, one can begin to realize the dilemma that faces certain chronic pain patients. The patient can make the choice to hire people to assist with tasks. This is the easiest option from an emotional and relational perspective, but is not necessarily economically feasible for chronic pain patients who have drastically curtailed incomes. And, almost invariably, there are no public assistance programs available for chronic pain patients. People in this circumstance are dependent upon family, friends, neighbors, and social organizations for assistance. This places a burden on the very people with whom the patient is trying to reestablish *social* relationships.

It is important for everyone concerned that the patient learns early in the adjustment process to clearly articulate specific needs. Sometimes chronic pain patients are guilty of assuming that others must know what they need. This is seldom true. If needs remain unspoken while waiting for a family member or close friend to fulfill them, the patient often grows embittered and angry. On the other hand, it is also important that those people in the patient's relational sphere offer specific help with specific needs. Too often people tell the patient "to contact them if they need anything." This is not likely to happen because the patient may fear overburdening that individual by asking too often or creating a feeling of obligation. It is also important that the chronic pain patient involves as many people as possible in assisting him or her. In this way, the task does not become overwhelming for a few friends and family members. One vital way in which someone who often assists the patient can maintain a relationship that will be experienced as *symbiotic* is to also ask the patient for assistance. Many chronic pain patients, if they are no longer working on a full time basis, have more time available to help others. Doing so will greatly boost the patient's self-esteem and self-respect.

The Common End Result—Isolation

Chronic pain experience is an isolating one. The losses are many and significant. With each loss, whether it is physical, emotional, social, or financial, there comes a greater sense of isolation. The patient loses many of his or her prior roles. There is the possible loss of employment and the subsequent loss of the workplace *family*, which is often so important in our culture. There is an inevitable shift in family roles because patients may no longer be able to fulfill all the duties and responsibilities within the family for which they had been responsible previously. There is often a loss of financial security and hopes of future career goals. There is a decreasing social sphere as the drain of daily health issues frequently circumvents attendance at social gatherings. For the chronic pain patient, each of these losses narrows one's world and adds to an increasing sense of isolation.

The sense of isolation can become consuming to the point of driving the patient to despair. There are feelings of hopelessness and worthlessness that accompany a poor quality of life. As despair becomes increasingly deep and pervasive, suicidal ideation or the act of suicide becomes an option that creeps into the mind of the patient. These consequences of chronic pain are what cause it to be a potentially fatal condition. It is the social effects of the pain and not the pain itself that may be the determining factors related to suicidal behavior (4).

Isolation begins upon diagnosis and is progressive with the increasing realization that medical science cannot make the pain go away. As previously discussed, language is generally inadequate to fully convey the experience to others. Pain becomes a constant companion and a constant reminder of shattered hopes and dreams. Every chronic pain patient deals with a different set of losses, but loss still remains the underlying theme. With loss comes grieving. With grieving comes the normal reaction to draw inward, further distancing the self from others. The grieving is further complicated if the pain condition is progressive. Any stage of acceptance is difficult to reach if the underlying pain condition is constantly changing. Various emotional and personality factors also play a role in how well a patient tolerates pain as an isolating condition. Those with sound emotional health prior to experiencing chronic pain will tolerate the stresses better than those with preexisting emotional issues. People with varied interests, especially more sedentary interests, will make the transition a little easier. But no matter how emotionally stable an individual is, the isolation that is forced upon him or her by circumstances such as unemployment and poor health will be an extremely stressful life event that will forever change the way the person views the world.

Finding New Ways to Relate and Interact

As with any form of grieving, there exists no hard and fast rule regarding how long it will take one to adjust to a new and unwelcome set of circumstances. The responsibility to adjust rests solely with the chronic pain patient. However, the health care community is a vital component to this adjustment. The patient should be teamed with a physician who is knowledgeable and compassionate about the plight of someone with chronic pain. The patient and physician must work together to create the best combination of modalities to alleviate as much of the patient's pain and suffering as possible. This includes a multidisciplinary approach that addresses the physical, emotional, vocational, and spiritual needs of the patient. Referrals to others within the health care community direct the patient to professionals in the various disciplines that cover these areas. While physicians without expertise in pain management are ethically obligated to make these referrals, it often becomes the patient's responsibility to access these professionals, as well as to cooperate with the treatment plans. Assuming that all these components are in place, the chronic pain patient can begin to make the long journey back to a new normalcy in his or her life.

On the social and relational front, patients must come to realize that the only ones they can change are themselves. It is unrealistic to expect others to change. If others do change in a positive way, it is an added bonus. However, progress should never depend on someone else adjusting or changing to meet the new demands on the social system that chronic pain has imposed. A real phenomenon, which the chronic pain patient experiences that can interfere with relational issues, is the envy of another's health. For example, especially early in the chronic pain experience, it may be difficult to watch a spouse or friends enjoy a beautiful day on a golf course. There will be many such comparable situations that will unconsciously stir up internal resentment in the patient. Over time, without awareness and intervention, this kind of envy can become part of an embittered attitude that will only serve to further isolate the pain sufferer. As a result, instead of participating in social outings such as joining one's friends for dinner after a golf outing, the patient will stay at home and engage in self-pity, dwelling on what has been *missed* rather than maximizing realistic social opportunity. The responsibility for change rests solely with the patient. One may benefit by striving to adjust to his or her own physical limitations while not envying the health of others. This adjustment takes time and the support of others who are able to understand some of what the pain sufferer is feeling. As with most internal changes, cognitive recognition of emotional traps occurs more quickly than changes in feelings. The chronic pain patient must be kind to him/herself in the process of adjustment and expect setbacks along the way.

PHILOSOPHICAL/EXISTENTIAL DILEMMAS

To a certain degree, every chronic pain patient is forced to tackle some of the transcendent dilemmas that define the world and who the individual is within it. Every person coping with a chronic pain condition has been forced to renegotiate his or her way in the world. What served before as answers to the *big* questions in life are no longer adequate. This too-often-neglected aspect of assisting the chronic pain patient must be addressed. Coping strategies should be holistic. To neglect the soul while treating the body and mind is to leave out the most vital part of being human.

Why Me?

The world of the chronic pain patient is entered unwillingly. To those who have never experienced this degree of disruption in life, it may sound overly dramatic to learn of the *pathos* that must be overcome by the patient to again find purpose and meaning to life. An *outsider* may never see any external signs of this abyss into which the chronic pain patient's life has been thrown. Yet, it will be experienced in some way by everyone whose bodily existence is defined by pain. Life's certainties (although always illusionary) are gone. They are replaced by the unknowing that accompanies all plans for the present and the future. Fully independent living is no longer a luxury that the chronic pain patient can enjoy. Instead of planning experiences such as promotions and vacations, the person with chronic pain is planning his or her next set of medical procedures or surgeries. And, sadly, those are the more fortunate patients. The less fortunate have been told that no procedural intervention will diminish their pain. Their only option is a set of medications that may ameliorate their pain—or not. This grim diagnosis is often accompanied by a grim prognosis that predicts a worsening of his or her condition over time. This type of advancing decline in physical health has definite ethical implications for the chronic pain patient. The patient must continue to redefine *self* as each new level of dysfunction is realized. To live with the existential states of progressive dependency and declining productivity is to be constantly in flux about self-definition. To avoid despair, the chronic pain patient must seek new ways of positively experiencing life. Because the patient's social world grows smaller and even close family and friends have turned away during this darkest time, it is easy to well up with bitterness, confusion, and envy (4).

Whether admitted to others or not, it would be the rare individual who would not ask, "why me?" under these circumstances. Paradoxically, the answer to this question-without-an-answer is very prognostically significant in determining how well the person will cope with the chronic pain experience and all of the life changes it entails. If the patient is a spiritual person, his or her faith can be a source of great comfort or a source of great bewilderment. The bewilderment and anger stage will almost invariably be the first stage experienced upon the onset of chronic pain. The patient may doubt the goodness of a higher power or may question the omnipotence of such a being. The sufferer may feel as if he or she is being punished for some transgression from the past. Many beliefs that were once taken for granted are now put to the test. If the patient has a trusted guide through this stage, some degree of spiritual comfort can be found. The degree of comfort varies with the person and over time. It is a comfort characterized by frequent setbacks because each new situational crisis brings even more questions. If the patient is not particularly spiritual, the same questions will be sought within a more strictly existential or rationalistic worldview. No matter what orientation is most prominent, chronic pain patients are groping with the same fear, i.e., that of an unknown future. They are seeking an answer that will give them the needed peace and strength to manage each day. Whatever kind of answer they find will become the ethical lens through which all future personal and medical decisions are made. It will become the starting point toward any possible future happiness or contentment. Without an answer that taps their soul, chronic pain patients are in danger of existential despair.

What Now?

One of the first steps in the process of finding renewed meaning and purpose in life is a change from the question of "why me?" to "what now?" Although seemingly subtle, this change actually reveals a fundamental shift to a forward-looking perspective and an awareness of the need to redefine oneself. This stage is not less emotionally stressful. Answers to the second question can be more difficult to find than to the first. Much of the difficulty of this stage relates to the need to actively seek resources to assist with answering the question. This process cannot take place passively within the patient. It involves time and energy that the patient may feel he or she no longer has. However, it is essential that the patient begin to recover some sense of control in life. This stage must include others in the health care community and in one's social and professional network. It is, essentially, a fact-finding stage in which the chronic pain patient must engage in order to move into a more healthy way of coping with life. The health care community can provide much needed input to the patient with regard to physically limiting factors, constraints in regards to employment, the outline of a medical treatment plan around which the patient must plan other facts of life, and much needed emotional support and encouragement.

As discussed earlier, unless there is another source of financial support, the patient is likely to feel the financial strain of losing or limiting employment. Many chronic pain patients must take a different employment path involving more education or vocational training. In some cases, there is some state or federal assistance, which can aid the person. However, such assistance is minimal and progressively less available, which can make the chronic pain experience even more challenging. Even with retraining, it can be difficult to start over in a new field. It is certainly humbling if a patient was a professional or in management, and is suddenly job seeking at the bottom levels of another profession. Compounding one's frustration is the added complication of explaining a gap in an employment record that occurred if a patient underwent multiple surgeries or any other form of extended treatment for his or her condition. Although it is not legal to discriminate against those with medical disabilities, every person with a disability has met with discrimination. This can be an extremely difficult emotional experience because this discrimination may often come from unexpected sources such as the patient's former employment. Of course, physical limitations will never be the stated the reason for not hiring or rehiring a person with chronic pain. Nevertheless, cases of discrimination are difficult to prove and the patient must gather the strength and courage to move forward.

The patient's personal life must also evolve out of one of isolation and distancing if he or she is to find renewed meaning and purpose. This may involve making amends to those who the patient has alienated during the long process of adapting to a new way of life. The patient ought not expect others to understand or be able to relate to the tremendous amount of energy that is consumed by dealing with chronic pain on a daily basis. Instead, the patient should make every effort to become involved in the lives of other people. Because one's energy is now limited, the chronic pain patient benefits from choosing friends wisely. It is helpful to be surrounded by friends who are genuine positive influences. Careful boundaries should be set around those friends or associates who are often critical and energy consuming. The patient must deal with any guilt that might arise from making these kinds of judgments. This is not an easy task, and depends on the patient's background and personality.

Finding Purpose and Meaning Again

Finding purpose and meaning in life is the defining ethical dilemma of the human condition. For the person with chronic pain, constructing meaning and purpose for a life that is caught in a void of uncertainty, anxiety, and fickleness of bodily control can be exhausting. It may feel as if the only choices are to *give in, give up, or give out*. None of these choices are very conducive to productivity or contentment. Paradoxically, both the good news and the bad news about chronic pain is that it will not kill the patient. Life must be planned with the unwelcome lifelong companion of chronic discomfort. The pain goes wherever the patient goes, and is a part of everything that happens in the person's life. This reality can never be shared or even adequately explained to anyone else because each person's pain is only ever fully known to the self. Within every chronic pain patient striving for a meaningful life is a desire to somehow rise above it. Pain is an unwelcome guest who was never invited into one's life. There is the strong desire to not allow it to enter into any definition of self. Yet, in many ways, it must be part of the new definition of self. Pain's fierce loyalty is unbidden and unwelcome; yet the patient must come to a place of peace with it.

Every life choice either contributes to or detracts from the individual's goal to be who and what he or she has chosen to be. This is no less true for the chronic pain patient. If regarded in this light, the patient may even begin to see the pain as a kind of gift that opens up worlds of compassion for fellow human sufferers. Life lessons can only be learned by experiencing them. Pain is a powerful teacher—emotionally, mentally, physically, and spiritually. Patients with chronic pain have gained unique perspectives on their own suffering and the suffering of others. The very condition that has disrupted life may be the means through which greater self-discovery is achieved. Loss may actually turn into gain. There is enough anecdotal evidence to support the role of self-discovery and spirituality in the healing process (10). Unless a patient chooses the path of embitterment and total isolation, he or she cannot help but see some of the depth of sadness and brokenness that exists in the world. There is a resiliency and tenaciousness in the approach to life that has been forged and tested in the boughs of adversity. Oliver Sacks spoke of experiencing the "purgatorial dark night" that humbled him, took away hope, "but, then, sweetly gently, returned it to me a thousand-fold, transformed (8)." There may be some physical limitations to what can be accomplished, but the person who copes with daily pain has much to offer to others who are suffering—and, no one escapes some form of suffering in life.

Whether this opens the patient's mind to a different set of vocational possibilities is not the critical point. There is so much each person can do to improve life for others within one's sphere of influence. The chronic pain patient is a tremendous resource for others. Instead of assigning a patient role to the person with chronic pain, perhaps there is more wisdom in giving that person the role of sage. Someone who has struggled with physical pain but who refuses to be defined by that pain has made journeys into the soul that few others have made. They have learned many things along the way that can be imparted to others. Extending time to assist with some of the physical needs a chronic pain patient might have is a wise investment if one considers what could be available in return. This way of redefining roles gives a deeper dimension to the relationship. This is a reversal from the role of victim that the world too often places on the person with chronic pain—and, a rejection of a role too often accepted by the person with chronic pain.

There can be much meaning and purpose in life on the other side of a diagnosis of chronic pain. Each person must find what it is that provides motivation to get out of bed in the morning. No one else can do that for the patient. Although no one's life, when examined closely, is *easy*, it cannot be denied that the chronic pain patient has additional hurdles to face each day. It will take time and much encouragement from others to bring the patient to a holistic place where life can once again be lived, rather than just survived. The health care community is not excused from assisting the patient in this achievement. As defined by the World Health Organization: "Health is a state of complete physical, mental, and social well-being and not merely the absence of disease or infirmity (11)." Defined in this way, health care ethics includes the totality of the patient. Therefore, the goal should be as complete a restoration as possible to full functioning as a whole person.

If the chronic pain patient can come to this place of acceptance, new perspectives will be achieved. Joy and happiness will not have to be seen as events of the past. To reach this place will require time, being in a caring community, and much interior soul searching. In the end, however, there will be a new relationship with one's own self-identity and a restoration of self-esteem. Instead of being a chronic pain patient, he or she will become a person who happens to also have chronic pain. With this new mindset firmly locked in place, the person will have regained much of what was once lost—and this will once again enable a life full of possibilities waiting to be explored.

REFERENCES

1. Friedman AM. Treating chronic pain. New York: Plenum Press, 1992.
2. Mayerfeld J. Suffering and moral responsibility. New York: Oxford University, 1999.

3. Chino AF, Davis CD. Validate your pain: exposing the chronic pain cover-up. Sanford, FL: DC Press, 2002.
4. Roy R. Chronic pain, loss, and suffering. Toronto: University of Toronto Press, 2004.
5. Scarry E. The body in pain. New York: Oxford University Press, 1985.
6. Turk DC, Melzack R. Handbook of pain assessment. New York: Guilford Press, 1992.
7. Copen L. Why can't I make people understand? San Diego, CA: Rest Ministries Publishers, 2004.
8. Sacks O. A leg to stand on. New York: Summit Books, 1984.
9. Montaigne M. The complete essays of montaigne (DM Frame, Trans.). Stanford, CA: Stanford University Press, 1957s.
10. Tashner, MC. Ethics of care: pain management and spirituality. In: Weiner RS, ed. Pain management: a practical guide for clinicians. 6th ed. New York: CRC Press, 2002.
11. Ashley BM, O'Rourke KD. Health care ethics. Washington, D.C.: Georgetown University Press, 1997.

3

Life and Death Considerations in Chronic Pain: Secular and Theological Ethical Considerations

Richard Payne

Institute on Care at the End of Life, Duke University Divinity School, Durham, North Carolina, U.S.A.

PERSISTENCE OF POOR PAIN MANAGEMENT AND UNDERTREATED PAIN: IMPACT ON DEATH AND DYING

Numerous reports have documented the undertreatment of acute and chronic pain, even pain related to serious medical illness associated with cancer, HIV/AIDS, and terminally ill patients (1). Pain undertreatment occurs for many complex reasons involving barriers, which span from clinician and patient-related factors to health system factors. These barriers have been well characterized over the past several years (2). What has not been emphasized much are the societal and ethical considerations, which impact clinicians, patients, and the health system in the management of pain.

Unrelieved pain has been cited as a cause of suicide ideation and is implicated in requests for hastened death in patients with cancer, HIV/AIDS, amyotrophic lateral sclerosis (ALS), and a host of other serious medical disorders with terminal prognosis (3). Unrelieved physical pain in these medical conditions may lead to depression, and grief over loss of mental and bodily functions associated with pain, and the disease process may ultimately culminate in existential distress and suffering and requests for assisted suicide or hastened death (4). For example, a recent report on suffering in ALS patients and caregivers found that moderate to severe physical pain occurred in 19% of 100 patients, and was the most significant contributor to suffering (5). Although this report did not find a relationship between current suffering and requests for assisted suicide, the authors did cite the relatively small number of patients studied and that many of the subjects were not making actual decisions about treatment. Another recent study in patients with cancer pain reported that improvements in pain scores were not predictive of a desire for hastened death, but depression was predictive (6). These studies, and anecdotal reports from experienced hospice and palliative care clinicians, point to the complexity of the relationship between pain and suffering in the setting of terminal disease and the difficulty in simply relating unrelieved pain to requests for physician-assisted suicide and euthanasia.

This paper explores secular and theological ethical considerations, particularly because they relate to the persistently poor treatment of chronic pain in serious medical conditions with terminal and nonterminal prognosis. The emphasis will be on ethical considerations in the management of chronic pain in the two cases reported herein, which involved nonterminal diagnosis but nonetheless ended in death of the patients. I will also explore ways in which we might move toward fundamental and systemic change in individual clinicians and caretakers of the health care system to improve the care of patients and the system in which clinicians and patients operate. The following cases put a human face on the problems of poor pain management, which illustrate profound clinical and ethical problems, leading directly or indirectly to death in each case.

CASE 1: COMPLEX REGIONAL PAIN SYNDROME AND UNRELIEVED PAIN LEADING TO SUICIDE

Dr. NP was a 55-year-old gynecologist living in the northeast, referred for evaluation and management of complex regional pain syndrome involving her right arm, neck, and shoulder. She had a complicated medical history involving persistent postoperative pain and cardiac/respiratory arrest following a C5 to C6 laminectomy fusion years earlier. Approximately 10 years later, while dressing to perform a surgical procedure, a swing door struck her from behind; the soft tissue injury led to immediate and persistent moderate to severe lancinating electric shock-like pain involving the left trapezius and paraspinal muscles. Despite multiple pain treatments including physical therapy, oral and intravenous analgesics, and a radio frequency ablation procedure targeted at the facet joints in the cervical spine, she continued to experience episodic severe pain and hypertension (blood pressure recordings during pain episodes could be as high as 210/160).

Reevaluation of her condition by a pain specialist in a distant community confirmed the diagnosis of complex regional pain syndrome (7). Her course over the next two years was quite complicated. She had multiple admissions to a local emergency department with pain exacerbations and severe hypertension requiring admission to intensive care unit. She was managed with oral opioid analgesics (initially methadone and later hydromorphone), gabapentin, and transdermal clonidine; a protocol for acute pain management was negotiated with her local physicians. This protocol involved the use of intravenous opioids in the emergency room when she presented at the onset of pain. She reported that when she received adequate doses of analgesics, her hospital stays were shorter and her hypertensive crises less severe.

Despite this ordeal, there was reluctance on the part of the treating physicians in complying with the protocol regimen, and the pain specialist confirmed significant concerns with the use of intravenous analgesics on the part of the local physicians. Concerns raised by local physicians included fears of regulatory scrutiny of their practices as a result of use of the protocol, and the believability of the patient's pain complaints. The local health care providers maintained this attitude even though there were no allegations of drug diversion and the patient quite adhered to her prescribed medical regimen. The patient also perceived that the nursing and medical staff did not believe her pain, and reported overhearing what she believed to be biased comments about her pain condition. She had been in litigation related to disability claims.

She moved to a distant southwestern city, in part because she had a greater sense of well being in warmer weather, but also to pursue (in her view) better and less biased medical attention and pain management. The treatment protocol based on the use of intravenous opioids during pain and hypertensive episodes was again negotiated with local physicians in her new living area, and again implemented, albeit reluctantly. The patient committed suicide by gunshot wound to the head at home approximately one year after moving to the southwest, and approximately 15 years after the onset of her pain syndrome.

CASE 2: SICKLE CELL ANEMIA-RELATED PAIN, DEATH, AND VICTIM OF DISCRIMINATION

The patient was a 38-year-old African American physician with sickle cell disease. He was referred to a pain specialist during his postgraduate training because of persistent pain related to a nonhealing ischemic ulceration of his leg. Pain occurred daily and was usually quite severe (self reports of daily worst pain ranged typically from 7 to 10/10). The leg ulceration persisted despite use of disease modifying antisickling therapy, including administration of hydroxyurea, frequent blood transfusions, and the use of hyperbaric oxygen therapy.

Pain was successfully managed with a combination of transdermal opioids and oral analgesics (for breakthrough pain). The patient successfully completed his medical training while on opioid therapy, including performing invasive cardiovascular diagnostic and therapeutic procedures, authoring several manuscripts, and testing normally on neuropsychological examinations.

The patient was denied a license to practice medicine after moving to another state after graduation. The basis for this decision rested on his need to use opioids on a daily basis for his pain management. This decision was made despite evidence showing no impairment in his physical or mental abilities to practice medicine, and despite his voluntary submission to a substance abuse treatment program by the medical board (even though there was no evidence of a substance use disorder). Local physicians in his new state were reluctant to prescribe the quantities of oral and transdermal pain medications required for adequate control, necessitating frequent trips of several 100 miles back to a pain treatment center. The patient could not remain abstinent from opioid analgesics as requested by the medical board as a condition of professional licensure, because attempts to do so were invariably associated with severe recurrences of pain and functional impairment. The patient died related to sepsis complicating a sickle cell-related vasoocclusive crisis while in litigation with the medical board.

These cases illustrate the tragic complications associated with poorly treated pain, and point out many ethical implications of the persistent barriers to undertreated pain. These barriers have been highlighted by others (8) and include:

- low prioritization of pain as a clinical problem by clinicians,
- lack of knowledge of clinicians regarding the appropriate assessment and management of pain,
- the impact of fear of regulatory scrutiny on pain management,
- a lack of medical professionalism and a failure of the health care system to insist on accountability for appropriate outcomes of pain treatment,
- resistance to use opioids by patients and clinicians,
- impact of cost constraints on access and quality of pain care.

These cases speak about all these points to some degree, although both patients eventually overcame their reluctance to take opioid administration in the face of severe pain, and cost constraints, although present, were not as severe as in other patient contexts.

Both cases speak about the problem of the low prioritization of pain as a medical and societal problem, and illustrate the fact that poorly treated pain contributes to death by direct and indirect causes. The causal relationship between poorly managed pain and suicide in the first case is unquestioned. The relationship between pain frequency and death in sickle cell anemia has also been demonstrated (9). There are several other similarities and key lessons illustrated by these cases. Both patients were physicians, which could certainly influence, or even complicate, the ways in which clinical decisions were made by their professional caregivers. For example, physicians with access to opioid analgesics and with a substance abuse disorder may be at higher risk of abuse or misuse of these agents (10). It is unclear whether this was a consideration in either case. In case no. 2, the fact that he was a doctor in need of a license to practice his chosen profession became an object of significant contention, and in my view, an opportunity for discrimination based on his need for chronic opioid therapy.

The low prioritization of pain in both cases was reflected in the exaggerated concerns regarding regulatory scrutiny by the treating physicians, and the discounting of the patient's pain complaints in case no. 1. In case no. 2, the arbitrary decision of the medical board to insist on opioid abstinence in the face of clear evidence of a leg ulcer producing ongoing nociception, and the dismissal of evidence showing normal psychological and physical function unequivocally speaks about the low prioritization of pain as a medical problem, and is a model of callous care, in contradistinction to ethical models of compassionate care and "Good Samaritanism" (to be discussed later).

Both patients were members of population groups (women and African Americans) that have been identified as vulnerable to disparities in pain management (11,12). In fact, patient no. 1 specifically voiced that her pain complaints were being discounted because of her gender. Patient no. 2 suspected but never specifically charged racial discrimination complaints, but the literature has consistently demonstrated racial and ethically based differences in pain treatment (13,14).

Finally these cases highlight personal and collective (i.e., societal) failures, which have clinical and ethical implications. Following is a discussion of the secular and theological considerations of these personal and collective clinical and ethical failures that drive the persistence of undertreated pain, and suggestions for improvement.

ETHICAL CONSIDERATIONS IN PAIN AND SUFFERING

As noted above and emphasized by Cassell and others, one must make a distinction between pain and suffering (15). Cassell defines suffering as a "specific state of distress that occurs when the intactness or integrity of the person is threatened or disrupted." The proper assessment of suffering must take into account the person's individual story or narrative, and must include an assessment of the person, and not just an assessment of the body or a list of medical problems.

The ethical and moral requirement of physicians and other health care providers to assess and treat pain is unquestioned, especially in the context of patients with terminal medical conditions (16). For example, the Code of Medical Ethics of the American Medical Association (17) states:

> "Physicians have the responsibility to relieve pain and suffering and to promote the dignity and autonomy of dying patients and the autonomy of dying patients in their care. This includes providing effective palliative treatment even though it may foreseeably hasten death."

The AMA code explicitly embraces the ethical principle of double effect, whose roots can be traced back to the theological philosopher Thomas Aquinas. Palliative care clinicians understand the principle of double effect to have four essential components: (i) the action itself must be either morally good or neutral,

(ii) the bad result must not be directly intended, (iii) the good result must not be proximately caused by the bad result, and (iv) the good result must be proportionate to the bad result (18). Therefore, the use of escalating doses of opioids for the management of pain, dyspnea, and restlessness in dying patients is ethically justified—even if the life of the patient is shortened by a few minutes, hours, or days—if the intent of its use is to relieve otherwise intractable symptoms and there is informed consent to do so by the patient or an appropriate surrogate. This use of opioids is ethically appropriate and lawful and in contradistinction to the injection of an opioid with the deliberate intent to cause death of the patient, which is euthanasia, and an illegal, criminal act. Physician-assisted suicide, currently legal only in the state of Oregon in specifically delimited circumstances, involves the provision of a prescription by a physician for opioids or other substances to a consenting patient, with the understanding that the patient will take such agents to end his or her life. Assisted suicide in Oregon is practiced by a very small number of physicians; many others have expressed ethical reservations (19). It is interesting to note that patient no. 1 chose to take her own life in a violent way, by a self-inflicted gunshot, and not by self-poisoning with her prescription medications, even though she had a large quantity available to her.

SPIRITUAL AND THEOLOGICAL ETHICS, PAIN AND SUFFERING—SOME CONSIDERATIONS

The failure of medicine to attend to the pain and suffering of the individuals represented in our two cases is obvious. Despite this, there is universal acknowledgment of the ethical imperative of physicians to attend to human pain and suffering. However, many theologians, moral philosophers, and ethicists might disagree on how physicians and other agents of medical care should attend to and manage suffering, and what medicine as a profession should promise to individuals and their families.

It is my contention that the tragic outcomes of these cases represent individual failures on the part of clinicians and collective failure of the health care system, and they are related. The great philosopher, Immanuel Kant, wrote about a system of ethics, termed deontological ethics, which speak about the ethics of duty. In Kant's words: "duty is the obligation to act from reverence for moral law ... nothnothing in the whole world ... can possibly be regarded as good without limitation except a good will" (20). Kant further articulated the concept of a "Categorical Imperative" as a way to behave or to "act as if the principle from which you act were to become, through your will, a universal law of nature." The "Categorical Imperative" has been called an unconditional moral command and has been said to be a philosophical restatement of the Golden Rule: "Do unto others as you would have them do unto you." One can but wonder whether the outcome would have been less tragic if the principles of the Categorical Imperative and the Golden Rule had been firmly in the minds of the clinicians and regulators—the embodiment of the "system"—in the narratives of the two case histories reported.

Kant's "Categorical Imperative" and the evocation of the Golden Rule segues into recent theological reflections by the late Pope John Paul II, which are relevant to our consideration. In the Apostolic Letter of John Paul II: On the Christian Meaning of Human Suffering (21) the late Pope states:

> " ... Man suffers in different ways, ways not always considered by medicine, not even in its most advanced specializations. Suffering is something that is still wider than

sickness, more complex, and, at the same time, still more deeply rooted in humanity itself. A certain idea of this problem comes to us from the distinction between physical suffering and moral suffering. This distinction is based upon the double dimension of the human being and indicates the bodily and spiritual element as the immediate or direct subject of suffering...In fact, it is a question of pain of a spiritual nature, and not only of a "psychological" dimension of pain which accompanies both moral and physical suffering..."

The Pope goes on to say in this Apostolic Letter:

"...The parable of the Good Samaritan belongs to the Gospel of suffering. For it indicates what the relationship of each of us must be towards our suffering neighbor...The name "Good Samaritan" fits every individual who is sensitive to the sufferings of others, who is moved by the misfortune of another...In a word, a Good Samaritan is one who brings help in suffering, whatever its nature may be...

...In the course of the centuries, this activity has assumed organized institutional forms and has constituted a field of work in the respective professions...the Good Samaritan of the Gospel has become one of the essential elements of moral culture and, universally, human civilization..."

Kant's philosophical work and Pope John Paul's Letter would point to our individual and collective obligations to relieve suffering. The Pope would agree with Cassell's instruction to focus on the evaluation of the person and not just the body, because suffering is "still wider" than sickness. Most importantly, these observations and reflections would call on us to take a wider view of our clinical responsibilities and professionalism than we currently do, to view ourselves as being accountable as part of the health care and regulatory systems of the profession and society in which we are essential parts. The deontological philosophical perspective of good will expressed through the Kantian "Categorical Imperative," and the parable of the Good Samaritan also leads us to another theological perspective, which I believe is illuminated in the case narratives—this is the concept of social sin.

Social sin is a consequence of collective selfish and immoral acts, and like the doctrine of double effect, originates in the work of Thomas Aquinas (22). Social sin refers to morally culpable acts caused by a community or organization, particularly when individuals in society set up structural processes or so-called "structures of sin," which perpetuate injustice or harm to individuals or groups in a given society. Theologians and moral philosophers point to the pervasive effects of poverty and the growing health care and educational gaps and opportunities between the rich and poor as examples of many individual sins codified in processes or "structures of sin" promoting "social sin" that have harmful or immoral effects. Could the tragic outcomes experienced by the patients in our case examples be related, at least in part, to collective individual failures and "sins" now codified in a health care system that does not insist on the highest degree of professionalism and accountability to improve pain care, and a parallel regulatory system, which does not properly balance the needs of patients with legal or criminal concerns? Is the failure of physicians and other clinicians to abide by the current inadequate system contributing to a collective culture or structure of social sin, in contradistinction to a Good Samaritan culture, and a culture that promotes the greatest good will by putting into operation the "Categorical Imperative?"

These philosophical and theological reflections are mirrored in a recent conceptual model concerning the bioethics of caring, which the author, Stan van Hooft,

PAST ⟺ PRESENT ⟺ FUTURE

THE BIOLOGICAL LEVEL
•Involuntary physical functions (e.g., metabolism, instinctual drives, reflexes, etc.)

•We share this level with all living things

THE PERCEPTUAL-REACTIVE LEVEL
•Involuntary ways of seeing and reacting to things around us—consciousness (e.g., learned responses, emotions, desires, bonds of affection and group memberships, etc.

•We share this level with animals

THE EVALUATIVE-PROACTIVE LEVEL
• Voluntary, purposeful behavior informed by plans and values and the rational pursuit of needs arising from lower levels (e.g., includes most of what we do in our everyday, practical, self-conscious lives)

•This level is distinctively human

THE SPIRITUAL LEVEL
•Thinking which integrates and gives meaning to all the levels of our functioning (e.g., creativity, play, morality, religion, transcendent or ultimate values)

•This level is uniquely human

FIGURE 1 The van Hooft bioethical model of caring. *Source*: Adapted from Ref. 23.

has titled "deep caring" (23). This model is illustrated in Figure 1. As pointed out by van Hooft, caring can be thought of as behavior or motivation. The notion of caring as behavior implies "looking after another person and seeing to their needs"; caring as a motivation implies "feeling sympathy or empathy for someone or being concerned with their well-being or having a professional commitment to seeing to their needs" (23, p. 83). The van Hooft model of "deep caring," with its emphasis on "the formation and maintenance of both the integrity of ourselves and also of our relationships with others and the world around us" (23, p. 84), seeks to understand caring in both senses, and in my view, provides a conceptual lens to merge the philosophical and theological concerns connecting individual actions to community.

The model also incorporates a temporal element in which persons are oriented toward the future, but acting out of experiences in the past, and seems to be able to accommodate the necessity of understanding and respecting the personal narrative of the "whole person" in the assessment and attention to pain and suffering. In the case of physician–patient no. 1 who committed suicide, one might hope that a deeper understanding of her self as an integrated person functioning on the four levels of this model: "biological," "perceptual-reactive," "evaluative-proactive," and "spiritual" might have led to less existential distress and suffering and a different outcome. In the case of physician–patient no. 2 whose death was associated with much distress and suffering related to unrelieved pain, an inability to practice in his chosen vocation, and the psychologically devastating effects of discrimination and arbitrary unsympathetic decision-making on the part of clinicians and medical regulators, this notion of "deep caring" may have also had an impact. Imagine the bureaucrats in the state medical board agencies or the local physicians caring for these patients acting on the principle of the Categorical Imperative, operating with the perspective of creating the greatest goodwill and compassion for another individual. Imagine the regulators and bureaucrats acting with a sense of "deep caring" on the four levels noted by van Hooft in connection with evaluating a fellow human being with a nonhealing ischemic leg ulceration related to a potentially fatal disease, as opposed to seeing him simply as another applicant for medical licensure. Would individuals informed with this perspective insist on opioid abstinence even after evidence that the patient has intractable pain and suffering without these medications?

The van Hooft model also provides insight into how we can move individuals in a system to more compassionate, caring, and ethical action. Many analysts have opined that a major problem for the persistence of pain undertreatment lies in the fact that clinicians do not act even though they have a belief (and even knowledge) that pain should and could be treated more effectively. As described by van Hooft, the deep caring model is "ontological" (i.e., concerned with the nature of how we should act and behave as humans), and should encourage people to act if they come to the understanding that:

> " . . . we realize ourselves by reaching out to the world and to others . . . If the situation is such that I am in a position to help, my belief that another is suffering is a moral reason for me to act and will be immediately motivating. The suffering of another typically calls out to us immediately for a response (We are, of course, free to reject this call, but at a cost to our integrity as self-project and being-for-others)."

CONCLUDING THOUGHTS

What can we take from this dissertation based on the tragic case descriptions of clinical and ethic failures associated with pain management? The important points are that our moral obligation to assess, attend to, and relieve pain and suffering are individual and collective responsibilities. The tragic outcomes of the two patients point to individual and collective (or system) failures that have provided fertile ground for the persistence of pain undertreatment and prolongation of unnecessary suffering. We cannot overlook our moral and ethical obligations to make sure that we are by action or inaction facilitating social sins and structures of sins, which perpetuate needless pain and suffering.

At the root of compassionate care and a better understanding of pain and suffering is attention to the individual narratives of persons, and the promotion of a culture of "Good Samaritanism" to which medicine has traditionally subscribed. Perhaps there should be an emphasis during medical training, which provides a perspective consistent with an ethic of deep caring and attention to the whole person. Training of health care workers—especially physicians and nurses—should provide cognitive interactions and reflective time for clinicians to understand themselves and their roles relative not only to their individual patients, but also to the larger (moral) world. Such training might emphasize how clinicians are formed to contribute to a culture producing the most goodwill and the greatest sense of caring for the whole person, and how the integrity of the clinician is enhanced by the interactions beyond the individual patient. This could provide meaningful systemic behavioral changes in patients and clinicians.

REFERENCES

1. The SUPPORT Principal Investigators. A controlled trial to improve care for seriously ill hospitalized patients. JAMA 1995; 274:1591–1598.
2. Rich BA. An ethical analysis of the barriers to effective pain management. Camb Q Healthc Ethics 2000; 9:54–70.
3. Foley KM. Pain, physician-assisted suicide and euthanasia. Pain Forum 1995; 4:163–178.

4. Field MJ, Cassel CK. Approaching death: improving care at the end of life. Washington, DC: National Academy Press, 1997.
5. Ganzini L, Johnston WS, Hoffman WF. Correlates of suffering in amyotrophic lateral sclerosis. Neurology 1999; 52:1434–1440.
6. O'Mahony S, Goulet J, Kornblith A, et al. Desire for hastened death, cancer pain and depression: report of a longitudinal observational study. J Pain Symptom Manage 2005; 29:446–457.
7. Birklein F. Complex regional pain syndrome. J Neurol 2005; 252:131–138.
8. Rich BA. The ethical dimensions of pain and suffering in Chapter 14.
9. Platt OS, Bambilla DJ, Rosse WF, et al. Mortality in sickle cell disease: life expectancy and risk factors for early death. New Engl J Med 1994; 330:1639–1644.
10. Angres DH, McGovern MP, Shaw MF, Rawal P. Psychiatric comorbidity and physicians with substance use disorders: a comparison between the 1980s and 1990s. J Addic Dis 2003; 22:79–87.
11. Hoffmann DE, Tarzian AJ. The girl who cried pain: a bias against women in the treatment of pain. J Law Med Ethics 2001; 29:13–27.
12. Bonham VL. Race, ethnicity, and pain treatment: striving to understand the causes and solutions to the disparities in pain treatment. J Law Med Ethics 2001; 29:52–68.
13. Todd KH, Samaroo N, Hoffman JR. Ethnicity as a risk factor for inadequate emergency department analgesia. JAMA 2993; 269:1537–1539.
14. Green CR, Anderson KO, Baker TA, et al. The unequal burden of pain: confronting racial and ethnic disparities in pain. Pain Med 2003; 4:277–294.
15. Cassell EJ. Diagnosing suffering: a perspective. Ann Intern Med 1999; 131:531–534.
16. Post LF, Blustein J, Gordon E, Dubler NN. Pain: ethics, culture, and informed consent to relief. J Law Med Ethics 1996; 24:348–359.
17. Council on Ethics and Judicial Affairs of the American Medical Association. Code of Medical Ethics. Chicago: American Medical Association, 1996.
18. Quill TE, Brock DW, Dresser R. The rule of double effect: a critique of its role in end-of-life decision-making. New Engl J Med 1997; 337:1768–1771.
19. Ganzini L, Newlson HD, Lee MA, Kraemer DF, Schmidt TA, Delorit MA. Oregon physicians' attitudes about and experiences with end-of-life care since passage of the Oregon Death with Dignity Act. JAMA 2001; 285:2363–2369.
20. Kant I. The Metaphysics of Morality, translated John Watson, 1901.
21. Pope John Paul II. Apostolic letter of John Paul II: on the Christian meaning of human suffering, 1984.
22. Ragazzi M. The concept of social sin and its Thomistic roots. J Mark Morality 2004; 7:363–408.
23. van Hooft S. Bioethics and caring. J Med Ethics 1996; 22:83–89.

4

The Demise of the Multidisciplinary Chronic Pain Management Clinic: Bioethical Perspectives on Providing Optimal Treatment When Ethical Principles Collide

Michael E. Schatman

Consulting Clinical Psychologist, Redmond, Washington, U.S.A.

INTRODUCTION

In a commentary written 15 years ago in The Journal of Clinical Ethics, Susan Braithwaite described "cruelty" as the "cognizant or willful perpetration, perpetuation, enjoyment of or indifference to cruel effects in another sentient being, without mitigating expectation of proportionate benefit" (1, p. 97). The author went on to state that "cruelty not only occurs but also runs deep, although it remains subordinate to compassion in civilized human society" (2, p. 97). In discussing the concept of beneficence in medicine, Pellegrino and Thomasma refer to the Hippocratic prescription of "at least do no harm" as the most minimal level of this concept, stating that such a level of beneficence is expected in any civilized society (3). With regard to the responsibility of physicians to manage pain, Somerville (4) goes even further, questioning whether failure to manage pain represents infliction of torture. This notion is also addressed by Cousins (5), who suggests that not using available means to provide relief of pain is a form of abandonment, and can actually be considered "torture by omission." The relationship between doing harm to medical patients and incivility is a clear one, and certainly few would argue against the notion that medical professionals are morally obligated to avoid perpetrating both direct and indirect maleficence.

Chronic pain management is not only the domain of the medical community, but is also impacted dramatically by the insurance industry, hospital administrations, the legal system, the pharmaceutical and implantable medical device industries, and a number of other entities. Medical practitioners struggle to balance their obligations and responsibilities to their chronic pain patients with the agendas of the other entities that are involved. Unfortunately, the medical system as a whole is failing in its efforts to meet its obligations and responsibilities to these patients, with perhaps an overabundance of effort being dedicated to balancing the needs and desires of the other parties that claim to have a stake in the care provided to patients with chronic pain. As a result, Braithwaite's (1) description of cruelty unfortunately appears to apply to the pluralistic system responsible for the well-being of chronic pain sufferers, with the insurance industry and hospital administrations primarily responsible for the lack of adequate care so frequently seen. Nevertheless, the indirect role of medical professionals themselves in perpetuating the cruel and uncivilized treatment of chronic pain patients should not be totally dismissed. Numerous authors (3,5–9) have drawn the distinction between "pain" and "suffering," suggesting that pain refers to nociceptive phenomena while suffering is a more complex experience, which involves the psychological response to physical pain. Pain, in isolation, does not necessarily result in suffering. However, because suffering is conceptualized as involving a community's ethical and social structures (7), considerable attention should be paid to the intentionally as well as the inadvertently cruel behaviors of nonpractitioners, which significantly contribute to the suffering of so many chronic pain patients as well as adversely impacting society as a whole.

Perhaps one of the primary causes of the cruelty of the overall system that treats (or, at times, does not treat) chronic pain patients is the conflict between the codes of ethics of the entities involved. Typically, one thinks first of clinicians such as physicians, physical and occupational therapists, nurses, and psychologists as being the primary determinants of the quality of care that a chronic pain sufferer will receive. Each of these disciplines maintains its own code of ethics, to which the chronic pain practitioner within the discipline is expected to adhere. According to the codes of ethics of all health care professions, the well-being of the patient is paramount. Organizations such as the American Academy of Pain Management (10), the American Academy of Pain Medicine (11), and the American Pain Society (12), to which many pain practitioners belong, have their own code of ethics as well, emphasizing patient well-being. In an essay on the moral philosophy of professions, Pellegrino notes that there is a phenomenological and real-world similarity in the human existential realities of persons rendered vulnerable by illness, or by a need for justice, spiritual consolation, or knowledge. These phenomena, by their nature, entail duties, obligations, and virtues of physicians, lawyers, teachers, and ministers (13, p. 9–10). Unfortunately, two of the most influential groups in the treatment of chronic pain, health insurance providers and hospital administrators, would hardly be considered "professionals," as the term is conceptualized by Pellegrino. While Morreim (14) has suggested that health care institutions have a fiduciary obligation to patients similar to that of physicians, she does not present any ethical foundation for such obligation beyond the "business ethic" (15). Accordingly, people who suffer from chronic pain are commonly victimized by the nonprofessionals involved in their care due to the business ethos, the *telos*, or the "ends" of which is profit. Such a *telos* is clearly inconsistent with that of physicians, whose obligation is to help ameliorate suffering.

Not surprisingly, this inconsistency between the ends of business and the ends of medicine is most pronounced with regard to patients who suffer from chronic pain of nonmalignant origin, on the plight of whom this chapter will focus. "Chronic pain" will be used to describe persistent pain of nonmalignant origin throughout the remainder of this analysis. The choice to focus on pain of nonmalignant origin does not suggest that ethical dilemmas are not faced by practitioners and others involved in the treatment of cancer pain. However, terminal cancer patients are more likely to receive the most effective available treatment for their pain—typically oral, transdermal, transmucosal, subcutaneous, or intravenous opioids in combination with adjuvants. More than a decade ago, Portenoy concluded that, "it is generally accepted that the quality of care is adequate for most of these (cancer) patients" (16, p. 77). Unlike the treatment of chronic pain of nonmalignant origin, the ethical duty to relieve cancer pain is infrequently questioned (17). While the Medicare system is grossly inadequate in terms of medication benefits, the system's coverage of hospice care helps reduce the severity of this problem to a certain extent. Although it is outside the scope of this chapter, it should be noted that some problems do exist regarding third party payers' reluctance to cover intrathecal opioid therapy for patients suffering from cancer as well as nonmalignant pain, despite the strong body of literature that empirically supports the use of this delivery system for patients suffering from persistent pain due to malignancy (18–23).

The result of the lack of a teleological ethical foundation among third party payers and hospital administrations is the nontreatment or undertreatment of many chronic pain sufferers, which is of particular concern given that medical science has developed the tools to alleviate pain and suffering for the vast majority of patients who experience chronic pain. Herein lies the cruelty and lack of civility that so many people with chronic pain experience, serving only to exacerbate their suffering. While medical professionals are taught and expected to maintain standards for compassion and respect for human dignity, health insurance companies and all but a small handful of hospitals are primarily concerned with cost-containment and creating profits. Accordingly, chronic pain sufferers often find themselves in the middle of a battle between forces attempting to relieve their suffering and institutions primarily concerned with financial issues. Powerless to impact the overall systems that are in conflict (as well as to impact the severity of their pain and its emotional and behavioral sequelae), chronic pain patients are typically drawn into a downward spiral, which precludes a reasonable quality of life.

In a presentation at the Eighth World Congress of the International Society for the Study of Pain (24), John Bonica was referred to as the "world champion of pain." Certainly, during his illustrious career, Dr. Bonica's efforts to ameliorate pain and suffering among individual patients and chronic pain patients as a group made him a "champion." Given the unfortunate position of chronic pain patients between professionals trying to help them and institutions concerned primarily about financial health, all professionals involved in the treatment of chronic pain must become "champions of pain" if the plight of the population that we treat is to improve. The "economic" model has replaced the "professional" model of accountability to patients. It is well established (25–29) that chronic pain patients utilize a considerable proportion of society's medical resources, which is likely to induce the concern of third-party payers and hospital administrators who are most interested in cost-containment and profitability. Unfortunately, this has led to the insurance and hospital industries turning a blind eye to the misfortune of chronic pain sufferers, which is not surprising given their lack of an ethical obligation to relieve suffering. Because the economic model of accountability to which third-party payers and hospital administrators adhere is not only in conflict with the professional model but also seems to have resulted in bureaucrats displacing practitioners as the determinants of patient care in many situations, professionals who treat chronic pain patients are perhaps ethically obligated to assume the role of "champion of pain." Papadimos (30) has supported this argument through the utilization of stoic thought as an intellectual basis to guide the caregivers of medical outliers, a category into which chronic pain patients seem to fit well. The importance of the "champion of pain" in the treatment of chronic pain patients will be addressed in greater detail later in this chapter.

It has been well noted that managed care raises serious ethical conflicts for physicians (31–37), with a Medline search yielding thousands of articles on the topic. Because practitioners have increasingly become financially dependent upon managed health care organizations, they are forced either to provide their patients with suboptimal care or to exaggerate or even lie regarding patients' symptoms in order to assure that they receive the most appropriate medical care. While a physician is morally obligated to choose the less expensive of two equally effective courses of treatment as well as to avoid providing treatment if unnecessary, his/her primary responsibility certainly remains to the patient (34). Unfortunately, all health insurance, to a considerable degree, can be considered "managed care," because the payer ultimately makes the decision regarding what treatments will be covered. A recent analysis of the health insurance industry in the United States indicates that "traditional insurance plans have also moved toward managed care by adopting features of health maintenance organizations such as utilization controls. As a result, the border between these two types of insurance is now almost nonexistent." (37, p. 4). This is clearly true in cases of chronic pain.

THE IMPACT OF CHRONIC PAIN ON SOCIETY

In looking at the cost of inadequately treated chronic pain, the burden to society, as a whole, is alarming. One must consider not only the monetary cost of medications and other treatments that do not heal the patient (estimated at $125 billion annually in 1999) (38), but also lost wages and disability compensation, lost productivity (estimated at $61.2 billion annually in 2003) (39), lost tax revenue, job absenteeism and disruption in the workplace, and indirect costs such as lost productivity of spouses and other caretakers of chronic pain sufferers. The treatment of patients fortunate enough to enter multidisciplinary chronic pain management programs was estimated in 2002 to result in a total savings in health care expenditures of $45 billion (40). Given that so many patients who could benefit from such treatment are denied access due to third party payer refusals and the diminishing number of available programs, the potential savings in health care expenditures is staggering. For example, Turk (40) noted that only 6% of the patients who are treated by pain specialists are ultimately treated in multidisciplinary chronic pain management programs. This figure does not take into account that the vast majority of chronic pain treatment in this country is provided by primary care physicians, with only 2.5% to 5% of patients who suffer from chronic pain treated by pain specialists (41). It has also been noted that the cost to society of chronic nonmalignant pain is particularly large due to the fact that it generally occurs during mid-life, a time that should be the most productive (42).

BENEFITS OF MULTIDISCIPLINARY CHRONIC PAIN MANAGEMENT

Numerous studies and meta-analyses have indicated that integrated multidisciplinary chronic pain management constitutes the most clinically effective and cost-efficient means of treating most chronic pain conditions. Published supportive meta-analyses and reviews include those by Flor et al. (43), Turk, and Okifuji (44), Okifuji et al. (38), Guzman et al. (45,46), Turk (40), and Schonstein et al. (47). Empirical evidence reported in a recent review (40) indicates that multidisciplinary chronic pain management is superior to treatments such as medications, surgery, and implantable devices such as intrathecal opioid pumps and spinal cord stimulators in terms of pain reduction, improving physical functioning and return-to-work rates. Additionally, multidisciplinary chronic pain management programs are essentially free of treatment-related iatrogenic complications and adverse events, which is certainly not true of the aforementioned unimodal approaches. The literature also indicates that the long-term outcomes of coordinated multidisciplinary care are generally positive, with follow-ups conducted as long as 13 years posttreatment (48). Strengthening the argument for this type of approach is the finding that chronic pain patients who received comprehensive multidisciplinary treatment subsequently utilized medical services in general to a lower extent than did patients not treated in such programs, even in countries that provide their residents with national health insurance (49).

Despite the evidence of cost-efficiency, many insurance carriers are reluctant to pay for the integrated multidisciplinary care of chronic pain. While the reason for this reluctance is likely multicausal, certain speculations can be made. First, insurance carriers tend to be "penny wise and pound foolish" in their efforts to generate profits and control costs. This is actually somewhat confusing, given the aforementioned business *telos* of maximizing profits. Research supporting the cost-efficiency of interdisciplinary chronic pain management is easily and blindly dismissed. Second, as Stieg noted, " . . . there is a tendency of third-party payers to expect pain treatment centers to solve all of their (clients') social problems" (50, p. 302), not recognizing that even the best multidisciplinary programs cannot control all outcomes, just as they cannot control all patient and social variables. Third, pharmaceutical companies have historically marketed medications such as non steroidal anti-inflammatory drugs, opioids, and anticonvulsants to health insurance carriers as inexpensive "quick fixes," despite the lack of empirical evidence supporting monotherapy with medications in the long run as being more cost-effective than multidisciplinary chronic pain management. Because formerly expensive pain medications such as time-released oxycodone, transdermal fentanyl, and gabapentin are now available in much less expensive generic forms, the insurance industry may be even more likely to urge physicians to rely upon medications alone as opposed to multidisciplinary care, which has been empirically supported as superior (40). Additionally, given decreases in reimbursements for actually spending time with patients combined with increases in reimbursements for procedures (51–53), there exists the strong possibility that an interventional pain management specialist will be motivated to maintain control over his or her chronic pain patient as opposed to referring to an interdisciplinary clinic. Chapman notes that, "Concurrent with the decline in intensive programs is the rise of procedural interventions and medication, which receive a great deal of support from medical technology and pharmaceutical companies" (54, p. 1). Also of concern is the proliferation of for-profit, frequently chiropractic-based chronic pain management programs, which refer to themselves as "comprehensive multidisciplinary," when in actuality they are not comprehensive and certainly not multidisciplinary. Third party payers as well as the public and physicians are at risk, not being able to discriminate between these profit-motivated entities and the multidisciplinary programs whose practices are strongly evidence-based and in the practice of tracking outcomes. The lack of cost-efficiency of chiropractic care for chronic pain has been documented (55), although third party payers' ignorance of the literature is likely to perpetuate their universal rejection of multidisciplinary chronic pain management services.

According to Cindy Solochek of the Committee for the Accreditation of Rehabilitation Facilities (CARF) (private communication) (Solochek C. Committee on Accreditation of Rehabilitation Facilities. Oral and email personal communication, October 2005), the number of accredited interdisciplinary chronic pain management programs in the United States has steadily declined from a high of 210 in 1998 to 84 in 2005. While less dramatic, a similar decline between 1997 and 2003 in the number of programs accredited either by CARF, the American

Academy of Pain Management, or the Joint Commission on Accreditation of Healthcare Organizations (JCAHO) has been reported by Marketdata Research (56). As guilty, perhaps, for the demise of multidisciplinary pain management centers as the health insurance industry are hospital administrations. Regardless of whether a chronic pain management program is housed in a for-profit or a not-for-profit facility, programs that do not generate pecuniary gains tend to be discontinued. This issue will be discussed in detail later in this chapter.

The public is unfortunately unaware of the fact that integrated multidisciplinary pain management is becoming progressively less available, with this incomprehension due to disinformation, to a considerable extent. Public awareness campaigns regarding JCAHO's declaration that pain will now be considered a "fifth vital sign" and the proclamation by Congress of this being the "Decade of Pain Control" are meaningless for patients suffering from chronic pain conditions of benign origin. In a curious recent commentary, Haugh states, "Pain management programs have proliferated, focusing on pain experienced during the hospital stay and with chronic conditions" (57, p. 52). Haugh (57) suggests that fear of litigation has driven hospitals and physicians to take steps to avoid under-medication, citing several cases of patients who were undertreated as inpatients or in emergency rooms, which ultimately resulted in successful law suits. While inadequate treatment of pain in hospitals cannot be considered ethical by any means, his commentary suggests that multidisciplinary chronic pain management programs are proliferating, which, according to CARF (Solochek C. Committee on Accreditation of Rehabilitation Facilities. Oral and email personal communication, October 2005) and Marketdata Research (56), is far from the truth.

BIOETHICAL THEORIES AND THEIR APPLICATIONS TO CHRONIC PAIN MANAGEMENT

A number of medical ethicists have provided us with theories of ethics intended to serve as guidelines according to which practitioners can treat patients effectively and ethically. While these theories have merits and are directly applicable to most areas of medicine, they are in conflict with the purely economic model of control of chronic pain treatment by third-party payers and profit-oriented hospital administrations.

Perhaps the most prominent theory in medical ethics is that of principle-based ethics proposed by Beauchamp and Childress (58). Principle-based ethics suggests that clinical appropriateness can be determined by the tenets of autonomy, nonmaleficence, beneficence, and justice. Autonomy refers to the need to respect the independent wishes of the patient to make decisions regarding the treatment that he or she receives. Nonmaleficence refers to the practitioner's duty to avoid causing harm to a patient intentionally or inadvertently. Beneficence is a physician's responsibility to provide intervention that enhances a patient's comfort, health, and overall well-being, currently and in the future. Finally, justice refers to the equitable provision of medical services based upon need (as opposed, for example, to basing the distribution of services upon ability to offer the highest possible remuneration to a health care provider or facility). Each of these tenets should be examined, as doing so sheds light on the current status of chronic pain management service provision.

Integrated multidisciplinary chronic pain management programs emphasize the restoration of autonomy to chronic pain sufferers. While "autonomy" in medical bioethics is typically used to refer to a patient's right to refuse a prescribed treatment, the term can also be used more narrowly to refer to independence. Schatman (59) has suggested that chronicity of pain cannot be determined merely by the period of time one has suffered from pain symptoms; rather, it is the amount of dysfunction experienced across a wide variety of areas due to persistent pain and its negative sequelae that determines chronic status. These areas include the emotional, behavioral, social, recreational, sexual, vocational, financial, and legal spheres as well as the purely physical. Sufferers of persistent pain who have developed "chronicity" have lost their autonomy across most, if not all, of these areas of functioning, with their behavioral patterns moving toward generalized passivity (60–63). Decisions regarding their well-being are often made by family members, physicians and other health care providers, attorneys, and, of course, health insurance carriers. Appropriate cognitive-behavioral intervention in multidisciplinary chronic pain management programs emphasizes helping patients acquire tools that will allow them to regain control of their lives. Unfortunately, if a third-party payer rejects a patient's efforts to enter multidisciplinary rehabilitation, his or her likelihood of receiving the treatment that will help restore autonomy is limited. Ironically, chronic pain sufferers are generally denied the autonomy to choose the very treatment that is most likely to result in the restoration of their autonomy. Despite the numerous meta-analyses and reviews mentioned above (38,40,43–47) that have indicated that multidisciplinary chronic pain management is not only clinically effective but also cost- efficient as well, insurance carriers often look at the price, for example, of a six-week intensive program and experience "sticker shock." What insurance adjustors do not seem to recognize is that chronic pain status is not developed overnight; the maladaptive behavioral patterns that perpetuate the chronicity are reinforced over what is often a prolonged period of time, and helping a patient replace deeply ingrained maladaptive behaviors with more adaptive ones will require more than a week of treatment. Because the impact of persistent pain often results in patients being "broken," healing rather than simply providing obligatory treatment is crucial. May writes of "turnstile medicine," stating that, "Rapid-fire treatment organizes doctors and others as dispensers of technical services rather than teachers of their patients. Teaching is important not only in securing compliance . . . but in helping patients face the great alterations in life . . . . But teaching takes time. It is slow boring through hard wood" (64, p. 157). Health insurance carriers seem to be in a particular rush when the patient is receiving any type of lost-wage indemnity from the same carrier concurrent with treatment (65).

Like all health care professionals, chronic pain practitioners are expected to provide treatment according to the fundamental biomedical ethic of nonmaleficence. Dating back to Hippocrates, the dictum of "first do no harm" has been a cornerstone of medical practice. Irrespective of whether a medical professional increases the suffering of a chronic pain patient through an intentional egregious act, thoughtlessness, or carelessness, doing so is clearly unethical. Ignorance of appropriate methods of treating chronic pain can certainly result in a violation of the principle of nonmaleficence. Outside of maleficence due to ignorance, however, the violation of this principle by practitioners treating chronic pain patients is hopefully uncommon.

According to the business ethic discussed earlier in this chapter, the failure to support multidisciplinary chronic pain management by third party payers and hospital administrators does not necessarily constitute maleficence, because in doing so, they are following the ethos and the laws under which they function.

It is not surprising, however, that those of us who are concerned with ameliorating the suffering of chronic pain patients see this ethos (and perhaps the law) as perverse. Several bioethicists (2,35,66) have suggested that there exists a morality internal to medicine; that is, the *telos* of medicine is always the health and well-being of patients. This assertion appears, on the surface, to be self-evident and irrefutable. Veatch (67), however, has argued that a morality internal to medicine is impossible, because the broader societal norms that impact medical practice make the ends of medicine external to medicine itself. Because the other entities involved in health care have goals that may be inconsistent with those of medical practice, their moralities are not consistent with those of health care providers. Kindly, Pellegrino and Thomasma refer to this discrepancy in values simply as "moral pluralism," (2, p. 25) although they note that physicians need to protect the personal values that shape their practices against usurpation by those forces whose morality is inconsistent with their own convictions.

As mentioned above, multidisciplinary chronic pain management programs have been empirically demonstrated to be cost-efficient as well as effective in terms of relieving the overall suffering of the patients whom they treat (38,40,43–47). The refusal to provide financial coverage for such evidence-based programs to the clinically appropriate insured may not constitute maleficence on the part of third party payers, but certainly constitutes malfeasance. Chronic pain management providers often hear statements such as, "We don't cover chronic pain programs because they don't work" from third party payers. In response, practitioners cite or send the aforementioned meta-analyses supporting multidisciplinary chronic pain management to insurance adjustors, who respond with, "Well, that's just our policy." A policy based upon a refusal to recognize the empirically supported clinical and cost-effectiveness of multidisciplinary chronic pain management clearly constitutes malfeasance. The degree to which such behavior represents intentional malfeasance on the part of third party payers remains in question given the business ethos. Regardless, refusal to fund multidisciplinary chronic pain management services to patients in need represents cruelty and incivility.

Hospital administrators demonstrate malfeasance toward chronic pain sufferers through their decisions to terminate multidisciplinary chronic pain management programs, irrespective of their clinical efficacy. Integrated multidisciplinary chronic pain management programs will never be "cash cows" for hospitals, and are at risk of nonprofitability because of their labor-intensive nature. Because numerous areas of chronic pain patients' lives have been adversely impacted secondary to their pain, it follows that a wide variety of professionals are necessary to treat these patients' suffering effectively. Additionally, the complexity of chronic pain patients' conditions calls for more experienced and specially trained professionals if they are to be treated most effectively, with these professionals commanding higher salaries than generalists (68). According to CARF, the majority of accredited interdisciplinary chronic pain management programs are currently housed in not-for-profit facilities, with many operating within university teaching hospitals (Solochek C. Committee on Accreditation of Rehabilitation Facilities. Oral and email personal communication, October 2005). While a review of the literature does not yield any studies on the specific lack of profitability of multidisciplinary chronic pain management programs, 20 years of personal experience suggests that the losses that such programs incur are likely to be minimal, particularly given the financial resources of most of these institutions. Unfortunately, the maleficent policy of "no profit, no program" comes into play, resulting in the rapidly declining number of facilities for the effective treatment of chronic pain conditions.

The fundamental biomedical ethic of beneficence is likely to be a primary goal of chronic pain management professionals. Despite the consensus that chronic pain patients are a difficult population with whom to work due to the complexity of their cases, practitioners who choose to work with this group are typically seen as dedicated to helping them experience reduced suffering. Once again, however, the business ethos of third party payers and hospital administrators who function under an economic model as opposed to a therapeutic model adversely impacts the quality of care that chronic pain patients in this country receive. Altruism is the domain of the chronic pain practitioner, not of the insurance and hospital industries. States Pellegrino, "The market ethos does not per se foreclose altruism; yet neither does it impose a moral duty to help..." (35, p. 252). Sadly, as mentioned above, the "gold standard" (69) of multidisciplinary chronic pain management will continue to become progressively less accessible to patients in need, unless, of course, someone finds a way to make labor-intensive and patient-centered treatment "magically" less expensive and more profitable.

The final biomedical ethic, justice (primarily localized to the domain of distributive justice) is a challenging one for practitioners of chronic pain management. Results of a 2001 study on ethical dilemmas in pain management (70) were encouraging, as they determined through a survey of pain practitioners that the undertreatment of vulnerable populations was their greatest ethical concern. This finding is particularly important given the positive relationship between poverty and chronic pain (71). Despite indications that most physicians are committed to providing some care to patients on a pro bono or reduced fee basis (72), practitioners are generally interested in being compensated for their time, efforts, and expertise. Few would argue that health care services should be purely charitable. As mentioned earlier in this chapter, the vast majority of the existing comprehensive multidisciplinary chronic pain management programs in this country are housed in not-for-profit hospitals, with most treatment team members salaried by the hospitals in which the clinics are located (Solochek C. Committee on Accreditation of Rehabilitation Facilities. Oral and email personal communication, October 2005). Hospital administrations, accordingly, serve as the "gate keepers" in terms of choosing who will receive treatment. Given the well-documented dual health care system in the United States, patients with chronic pain are eligible for treatment in multidisciplinary programs based upon the quality of their third party coverage. Certain insurance carriers continue to refuse to cover multidisciplinary chronic pain management programs, citing their "lack of efficacy" or "inefficiency" as the reason for refusal, despite the aforementioned plethora of studies supporting their effectiveness and cost-efficiency. Certain Medicare and Medicaid programs offer coverage for such limited multidisciplinary treatment that admitting patients into programs that they will not be permitted to complete would potentially be considered cruel. Unfortunately, a review of the literature fails to yield any studies on the extent to which hospitals are willing to treat chronic pain patients on a pro bono or reduced-fee basis.

While Schatman (73) has concluded that racial and ethnic minority members receive inferior chronic pain management services as compared to nonminority patients, no one has studied the extent to which minority patients are underserved in multidisciplinary chronic pain management based upon minority status per se. However, given the documented relationship between socioeconomic status and minority group membership (74) along with studies that have indicated that racial and ethnic minority group members are less likely to have health insurance coverage than nonminorities (75–77), one can surmise that minority group members, as well as lower socioeconomic status patients, are less likely to receive treatment in multidisciplinary chronic pain management programs than nonminority and higher socioeconomic status patients. If this supposition is accurate, the biomedical ethic of justice is being violated.

The failure of the insurance and hospital industries to respect the biomedical ethical principles of autonomy, nonmaleficence, beneficence, and justice as they pertain to the treatment of chronic pain is clear and unfortunate. However, it has been suggested that relying solely upon these four principles of biomedical ethics can be problematic, because they are often in conflict with each other (78). Accordingly, alternative ethical theories should also be examined because they apply to the cruelty and lack of civility of the involved nonpractitioners in the field of chronic pain management.

Somerville listed seven bases of obligation to relieve pain: trust, human rights, respect for persons, respect for human dignity, relief of suffering, healing, and covenant (3). Few would argue that chronic pain practitioners are not motivated to meet these obligations in their efforts to bring comfort to their patients. Failure to do so by clinicians would represent immoral behavior by any standard. Once again, however, the moralities of medical professionals and those primarily concerned with the economics of health care are in conflict with regard to chronic pain management, because the insurance and hospital industries are not bound by an ethical foundation with the *telos* of reducing suffering.

Practitioners cannot treat chronic pain patients effectively if they do not trust that their patients are motivated to endeavor to mitigate their suffering. Similarly, patients are not likely to ameliorate their distress if they do not maintain trust in the clinicians by whom they are provided treatment. The importance of trust has been described as necessary for the development of the clinician-patient relationship, which is ethically fundamental to all healing relationships (79). While the importance of fiduciary trust between patient and clinician is quite evident, there is a paucity of literature regarding trust between chronic pain patients and third party payers. Nevertheless, clinicians who have worked with chronic pain patients (as well as patients themselves) can attest to the frequently adversarial relationships between third party payers and the insured with chronic pain; "trust" is certainly not the word that is typically used to describe these relationships. Peter and Watt-Watson analyzed the distrust in patients with unrelieved pain. Noting that pain clinicians' work in "elaborate" networks composed of numerous agencies, they state, "Ultimately, the network can act as either a facilitator of or a barrier to care, depending on the trustworthiness of the system" (80, p. 69). Given the commodification of the health care system in the United States, patients have become "fungible" (35). Pellegrino writes, "The special needs of the chronically ill ... are no longer valid claims to special attention. Rather, they are the occasion for higher premiums, more deductibles, or exclusion from enrollment" (35, p. 253). Because they have become viewed as little other than excessive consumers of expensive health care commodities by third party payers, patients who suffer from chronic pain are not likely to elicit trust from the health insurance industry. Conversely, their recognition of being seen simply as costly liabilities does little to enhance chronic pain patients' trust in their insurers. The result is a climate of mutual noncooperation, which can serve only to impede recovery and overall healing. Chronic pain patients' trust in hospital administrations would also likely be diminished if they understood the economic factors discussed earlier in this chapter that have resulted in the ongoing demise of the effective multidisciplinary clinics which have the greatest potential to provide relief and healing.

Allowing an individual to remain in pain and to suffer when the ability to remedy or reduce these experiences has been referred to as a "serious breach of fundamental human rights" (3, p. 51). This notion is undoubtedly recognized by chronic pain practitioners. Unfortunately, the economic model of medicine does not concern itself with human rights, choosing to subordinate them to cost containment and profitability. If third party payers and hospital administrators were concerned with issues of civility, human rights would trump the almighty dollar.

Much of this chapter has focused on the principle-based ethical theory of Beauchamp and Childress (58) because it relates to inadequacies in access to appropriate chronic pain management services. Undoubtedly, principle-based ethical theories have their merits. Sullivan (81) has argued for the superiority of principle-based ethical theories as compared to other theories, including those that are rights-based, in resolving conceptual and bioethical issues. This is questionable with regard to the bioethics of chronic pain management. Can an argument be any stronger than that for the basic human right of relief from pain and suffering when such relief is, in so many cases, available, yet inaccessible? Who has given third party payers and hospital administrators the appanage to deny chronic pain patients high-quality multidisciplinary care? Who has given these agents the sanction to deny chronic pain sufferers the other bases of obligation to relieve suffering which Somerville discusses, respect for persons, and human dignity? (3). Insurance companies and hospital administrators are, at least broadly speaking, a part of the health care system. Accordingly, do they not share in the covenant to provide access to treatment, particularly when treatment such as multidisciplinary chronic pain management has been empirically demonstrated to relieve suffering?

While principle-based and obligation-based ethical approaches help us understand the inadequacies in the health care system that cause so many chronic pain patients to continue to suffer needlessly, they offer little to practitioners in terms of guiding our own behavior in order to impact this quagmire. Virtue ethics, however, perhaps offers us a degree of guidance in dealing with a morally Machiavellian system, which has rendered us incapable of providing the best possible treatment to patients who suffer from chronic pain.

Virtue ethics deemphasizes principles and rules, suggesting that the virtuous individual is disposed to act in accord with the virtue appropriate to the situation (82). In the healing professions such as chronic pain management, this translates to the *telos* of the clinical relationship being the well-being of the patient, which we have the moral duty to pursue. The self-interest of the practitioner needs to be suppressed, with an emphasis on protecting the dignity of the patient (13).

In an essay regarding the "impossibility" of a morality internal to medicine, Veatch (67) suggests that the various parties involved in the health care system have different ends, and accordingly different moralities. It is curious that all of society is not willing to embrace the morality of alleviating suffering as the only legitimate end. Veatch is apologetic for medical practitioners, stating that the climate of cost containment "provides a ready-made basis of condemning physician participation in the economic ends of managed health care: rationing, cost-benefit analysis, and cost-containment" (67, p. 623). By considering the *telos* of medicine to be dependent upon broader societal norms, Veatch's ethical formulation permits pain practitioners to relinquish the position of "champions of pain." Giordano (83) has suggested that practitioners of chronic pain management are ethically obligated to serve as the moral agents as well as the therapeutic agents for our patients. Serving as advocates for our chronic pain patients is perhaps the most obvious and effective manner in which we can serve as their moral agents. If the primary goal of health care insurance carriers and hospital administrators is to contain costs and generate profits, their morality can be considered diametrically opposed to that of the chronic pain practitioner, who is obligated to make all and any effort to relieve suffering. Rationing and cost-containment cannot be considered moral or ethical goals; they are simply financial goals, and ethically need to be subordinated to the practitioner's goal of utilizing the wide range of resources that are available to reduce pain and suffering.

Yet, how far do we go, as "champions of pain," in our advocacy for our patients? In discussing the "virtues" entailed by the medical profession, Pellegrino (84) lists courage along with fidelity, benevolence, intellectual honesty, compassion, and truthfulness. He states, "It also takes courage to be the patient's advocate in a commercialized, industrialized system of care" (84, p. 381). How "courageous" should we be in our advocacy for chronic pain patients? Statements by bioethicists (6,85) have suggested that clinicians should make all efforts and use all strategies to help patients reduce their pain and suffering. As advocates for chronic pain sufferers foundered in a pluralistic and cruel system, is it not our duty to do anything that will help our patients? In an essay on law and ethics, Pellegrino states that, "Physicians have an obligation to advocate the patient's cause whenever it is threatened by a harmful policy or rule" (33, p. 311). As has been discussed throughout this chapter, the rules and policies of the insurance and hospital industries are certainly harmful to chronic pain patients because they are progressively serving to disallow the best possible treatment, thereby perpetuating pain and suffering. Pellegrino goes further, suggesting that, "By denying patients what a good clinician judges to be needed treatment, physicians become accomplices in harming the patient," (33, p. 312) and "It is essential, therefore, to establish some order of priority in the obligations of physicians. In establishing that order, medical ethics puts the vulnerability and genuine needs of the patients at the center. That primacy should not be sacrificed either to law or economics." (33, p. 316). These statements are clearly consistent with virtue ethics. However, in the same essay, the author seemingly contradicts himself, claiming that "gaming" the insurance industry through deception (e.g., exaggeration of a patient's symptoms, manipulating a diagnosis) in order to help gain third party coverage is not morally defensible. In another essay on managed care and ethics, Pellegrino seems to soften his position stating that, "However stringently or loosely one regards the obligation of truth telling, any system of care that makes truth telling an obstacle to beneficence is suspect on the face of it" (24, p. 325).

There exists no definitive to the question of whether manipulating systems in order to help a chronic pain patient represents beneficence and is consistent with virtue ethics. Perhaps doing so is simply as Machiavellian and egregious as is the conduct of the third party payers and hospital administrators who deny the suffering pain patient the best possible treatment due to the business ethos. While personal experience and communication with numerous "champions of pain" suggest that many of us are willing to bend the rules in order to assist disenfranchised and helpless chronic pain sufferers, a number of bioethicists (86,87) argue for adherence to professional standards, the laws of jurisdiction, and the rules of the institutions that provide and fund health care. However, virtue ethics suggest that we will exercise beneficence that goes beyond passive nonmaleficence, even if it puts us at risk of personal loss (2). Nevertheless, as "champions of pain," we can only help a minute percentage of the multitudes suffering from chronic pain because there are so few champions and so many patients. Unfortunately, the progressive demise of the integrated multidisciplinary chronic pain management clinic will serve to decrease the number of champions and accordingly, the number of patients for whom we can advocate aggressively. Something more must be done.

A CALL FOR CHANGE

It is certainly beyond the scope of this chapter to advocate the subversion of the marketplace economy in its entirety, because no evidence condemning the American capitalist system as a whole has been presented in this analysis. However, the private sector does not fare particularly well in the provision of certain fundamental human rights. Access to effective chronic pain management is, undoubtedly, one of these rights. What should be done? What can be done?

Pellegrino (35) suggests that due to the commodification of medicine in our society, the moral answer to inadequate medical care would be a "mixed economy," that is, looking at medical care as a moral obligation, which society owes to its members, and accordingly distinguishing and removing it from the competitive marketplace. He states, "... freedom from acute or chronic pain, disability, or disease, is a condition of human flourishing. Human beings cannot attain their fullest potential without some significant measure of health. A good society is one in which each citizen is enabled to flourish, grow, and develop as a human being." (35, p. 259). While Pellegrino does not actually use the term "socialized medicine," it is clear that this is the system for which he is calling. May's views appear to be consistent with those of Pellegrino. He states, "Because health care is a fundamental good (not an optional commodity such as a Walkman, a tie, or a scarf), it ought to offer universal access and a comprehensive range of services. The covenant cannot exclude...." (64, p. 161).

Socialized medicine has its supporters and detractors in the United States, and the views of the general public on the issue are unclear. However, a recent study (88) suggests that approximately two-thirds of the population favor government guaranteed health insurance, even if implementing it would necessitate raising taxes. Another study (89), however, indicates that legislators are less likely to be in favor of national health insurance than the general population. President Clinton and his wife were vilified by conservatives in the early 1990s for their efforts to make high quality health care a right rather than a privilege. In an interesting analysis, Brock and Daniels (90) outline the ethical foundations of the system which the Clinton administration proposed. The authors note that pain and suffering, disability, and limitation of function restrict the equal opportunity to pursue chosen goals of life, the belief in which our nation was founded.

Although it is beyond the scope of this chapter to call for socialized medicine or even national health insurance, chronic pain that is untreated or undertreated because of the inadequacy of the market system results in such a staggering cost to society as a whole as well as to individual sufferers that sweeping reform is necessary. There exists a moral obligation of a society to relieve the suffering of its citizens, which has been referred to as "beneficent justice" (35). Pellegrino describes beneficent justice as "justice ordered by the obligation to rescue, sustain, and nourish both society and the individual, because each suffers if either is neglected or abused" (35, p. 261). Similar assertions have been made by other theorists (9).

The data on the costs of inadequately treated chronic pain presented earlier in this chapter are relevant with regard to the bioethical theories that emphasize health as a community commodity (1,35,91,92) as well as being important to the individual. Pellegrino has described medicine as "a sensitive societal moral weather vane," stating that, "When its beneficent focus is blurred, it is time for a society to examine its own claim to moral probity" (93, p. 1505). Earlier, Pellegrino (13) had made a strong statement regarding the bioethical trend toward social convention as a means of arriving at moral truths. He states, "Society is not the final arbiter of moral truth per se. There are sadly too many pathological societies past and present to entrust the canons of morality entirely to politics or social convention. Ethics is not a matter of polls or plebiscites." (13, p. 11). Pellegrino is accurate in his identification of society as "pathological," because no society that is healthy would allow so many of its members to suffer with inadequately treated chronic pain when doing so results in such overwhelming societal as well as individual costs. This conceptualization is consistent with the "cruelty" (1) and "incivility" (1,2) of a society that passively condones inadequate treatment of pain among its citizens, which was discussed in the beginning of this chapter.

It is sadly evident that the problem of untreated and undertreated chronic pain will not be ameliorated without strong government intervention. The marketplace economy is not interested in social justice, striving only for profitability. State Emanuel and Emanuel, "We must resist the tremendous tendency within U.S. society to believe that the ideal solution for every complex social problem is the market and economic accountability" (94, p. 238). Accordingly, our government, which strongly endorses and supports the marketplace economy, must take responsibility for and charge of the chronic pain problem. Such action would not be unprecedented, as the government developed the Medicare and Medicaid programs (although it has violated the fundamental bioethical principle of justice in its desire to cut costs). The purpose of these programs was originally to do the right thing, that is, to take care of the medical needs of those who are disempowered and disenfranchised to the extent that they would go without medical care if the government did not provide them with a means of accessing it. The Medicare and Medicaid programs are currently not concerned with assisting society, but only with helping individuals. The development of government funded and managed chronic pain management centers providing quality care to all who require it, on the other hand, would serve both individual patients and society as a whole, ameliorating suffering while simultaneously restoring productivity and the likelihood of not draining and, potentially, contributing to our economy. By removing the *telos* of profit within the chronic pain system, i.e., excluding third party payers and hospital administrations, the needs of individuals and society would simultaneously be served, and the government would meet its moral obligation to help its citizens. Furthermore, disentangling insurance carriers and hospital administrations from the chronic pain management system would potentially create a "win-win" situation, because these entities likely find their involvement to be frustrating due to the dedication of time and the experience of conflict involved, along with their investment of financial resources for generally inefficacious monotherapeutic treatments.

In addition to treating appropriate chronic pain patients, government-managed multidisciplinary chronic pain management centers should provide training opportunities for clinicians who are interested in devoting their professional lives to this critical field. Most of the leading multidisciplinary treatment programs already in existence currently provide fellowship opportunities. If the number of multidisciplinary chronic pain management programs continues to decline, the dedicated fellows might find themselves without the opportunity to utilize the skills that they have acquired. Government-managed centers should also provide opportunities for research; while the science of multidisciplinary chronic pain management has progressed over the years, additional research will enhance its evidence basis and overall effectiveness and cost-efficiency.

One may question the source of funding for such a government-managed undertaking. While start-up costs may be high, the aforementioned literature on the overwhelming cost to society of inadequately treated chronic pain would suggest that the development of these treatment centers would represent an investment in the financial health of our country and meet the government's moral obligation to its citizens in pain. Given the government's willingness to fund costly "programs" that are neither evidence-based nor ethical (e.g., tax cuts for the wealthy, the unprovoked invasion of foreign nations), investing in the rehabilitation of the huge number of chronic pain patients in our society certainly seems reasonable.

The National Pain Care Policy Act (H.R. 1020), introduced in March of 2005, calls for making adequate treatment, education, and research relating to pain management national public health priorities (95). The bill's provision for the creation of six regional pain treatment and research centers represents a start toward solving the crisis of limited access to adequate chronic pain management services in this country. Unfortunately, given the slow pace at which Congress works along with the likelihood that chronic pain management is not at the top of its agenda, it would not be surprising if six or more of the existing comprehensive multidisciplinary clinics are forced to close prior to the development of the six facilities specified by H.R. 1020. More are clearly needed. On a positive note, the bill's provision that the centers are involved in research as well as treatment may yield a strengthening of the evidence-basis of the practice of multidisciplinary chronic management. However, there is no guarantee that the insurance or hospital industries will take note of additional evidence of the clinical effectiveness and cost-efficiency of this type of practice.

In a recent newsletter (96, p. 4), it was noted that H.R. 1020 "faces a long and arduous trek through Congress," with American Pain Society President Dr. Dennis Turk urging grassroots lobbying in order to gain cosponsors for the legislation. More chronic pain practitioners need to become involved at this level. The American Medical Association has noted the responsibility of physicians to seek changes in regulations that are inconsistent with the best interest of patients (97). Geppert has suggested that this stipulation of the AMA code of ethics "enjoins physicians to be invested in political action that will influence policy that undermines good medical practice" (98, p. 158). As mentioned earlier in this chapter, ethical and legal standards limit the extent to which we can realistically "champion" for individual chronic patients without putting ourselves in legal (and perhaps ethical) jeopardy. Accordingly, in order to act virtuously, those clinicians who believe strongly in the primacy of integrated multidisciplinary chronic pain management are obligated to make an effort to help chronic pain sufferers on a macro level as well as individually. Given the early success of the Health Policy and Legislative Awareness Initiative at the Pennsylvania State University College of Medicine, a movement to integrate health policy education into core medical school curricula is being considered (99). Strong calls for obligatory social and political activism in order to help our patients have been made by many of the disciplines involved in comprehensive multidisciplinary chronic pain management, including medicine (100–103), nursing (104–107), psychology (108–111), physical therapy (112), occupational therapy (113), and biofeedback (114). Donohoe (103) wisely suggests that physicians are in a unique position to be politically active in the service of their patients due to their privileged socioeconomic status.

CONCLUSION

Accordingly, the questions to ask regarding the prevention of the demise of high-quality integrated multidisciplinary chronic pain management are not, "What should be done?" and "What can be done?" As champions of pain, our options are currently limited. While we, as chronic pain practitioners, strive to practice ethically, the cruel and uncivil system in which we currently function is progressively prohibiting us from providing the best possible treatment to our patients. Those of us who have worked in centers of excellence have seen the wonderful outcomes that can results from integrated multidisciplinary care. By any ethical standards, allowing our clinics to fade into oblivion due to the competing values and the business ethic of the insurance and hospital industries would be a travesty. The development of government funded and managed multidisciplinary chronic pain management centers for treatment, training, and research is the only feasible answer. As practitioners, we cannot afford, on many levels, to turn a blind eye to the process whereby programs that relieve suffering become extinct. Doing so would represent cruelty and incivility on our part, because we already possess what may be the closest thing to a "cure" for chronic pain. Let us all do the virtuous thing, and sacrifice some of our time and other available resources to advocate for the preservation of effective treatment for those who suffer from chronic pain.

REFERENCES

1. Braithwaite SS. Anticruelty care. J Clin Ethics 1991; 2:97–103.
2. Pellegrino ED, Thomasma DC. The conflict between autonomy and beneficence in medical ethics: proposal for a resolution. J Contemp Health Law Policy 1987; 3:23–46.
3. Somerville MA. Death of pain: pain, suffering, and ethics. In: Gebhart GF, Hammond DL, Jensen TS, eds. Progress in Pain Research and Management. Vol. 2. Seattle, WA: IASP Press, 1994:41–58.
4. Cousins MJ. Pain: the past, present, and future of anesthesiology? Anesthesiology 1999; 91:538–551.
5. Descartes R. Discourse on Method and Meditations on First Philosophy. 4th ed. (Cress DA, tr.). Indianapolis: Hackett Publishing Company, 1999.
6. Cassell EJ. The importance of understanding suffering for clinical ethics. J Clin Ethics 1991; 2:81–82.
7. Loewy EH. The role of suffering and community in clinical ethics. J Clin Ethics 1991; 2:83–89.
8. Rich BA. A legacy of silence: bioethics and the culture of pain. J Med Humanit 1997; 18:233–259.
9. Clark PA. Ethical implications of pain management: can a formalized policy help? Health Prog 2002; 83:19–28.

10. American Academy of Pain Management. Code of Ethics. Sonora, CA, 1988.
11. American Academy of Pain Medicine. Basic Principles of Ethics for the Practice of Pain Medicine. Glenview: IL, 1999.
12. American Pain Society. Ethical Principles of the American Pain Society. Glenview, IL, 1996.
13. Pellegrino ED. From medical ethics to a moral philosophy of the professions. In: Walter JK, Klein EP, eds. The Story of Bioethics: from seminal works to contemporary explorations. Washington, D.C.: Georgetown University Press, 2003:3–15.
14. Morreim EH. To tell the truth: disclosing the incentives and limits of managed care. Am J Manag Care 1997; 3:35–43.
15. Peppin J. Bioethics and Pain. In: Boswell MV, Cole BE, eds. Weiner's Pain Management: A Practical Guide for Clinicians, 7th ed. Boca Raton, FL: CRC Press, 2006: 1377–1392.
16. Portenoy RK. Issues in the economic analysis of therapies for cancer pain. Oncology 1995; 9(suppl 11):71–78.
17. Swenson CJ. Ethical issues in pain management. Semin Oncol Nurs 2002; 18:135–142.
18. Penn RD, Paice JA. Chronic intrathecal morphine for intractable pain. J Neurosurg 1987; 67:182–186.
19. Andersen PE, Cohen JI, Everts EC, Bedder MD, Burchiel KJ. Intrathecal narcotics for relief of pain from head and neck cancer. Arch Otolaryngol Head Neck Surg 1991; 117:1277–1280.
20. Gestin Y, Vainio A, Pegurier AM. Long-term intrathecal infusion of morphine in the home care of patients with advanced cancer. Acta Anesthiol Scand 1997; 41:12–17.
21. Gilmer-Hill HS, Boggan JE, Smith KA, Frey CF, Wagner FC Jr., Hein LJ. Intrathecal morphine delivered via subcutaneous pump for intractable pain in pancreatic cancer. Surg Neurol 1999; 51:6–11.
22. Onofrio BM, Taksh TL. Long-term pain relief produced by intrathecal morphine infusion in 53 patients. J Neurosurg 1990; 72:200–209.
23. Rauck RL, Cherry D, Boyer MF, Kosek P, Dunn J, Alo K. Long-term intrathecal opioid therapy with a patient-activated, implanted delivery system for the treatment of refractory cancer pain. J Pain 2003; 4:441–447.
24. Liebeskind JC, Meldrum ML, John J. Bonica, world champion of pain. In: Jensen TS, Turner JA, Wiesenfeld-Hallin Z, eds. Proceedings of the 8th World Congress in Pain Research and Management. Vol. 8. Seattle, WA: IASP Press, 1997:19–32.
25. Frymoyer JW, Cats-Baril WL. An overview of the incidences and costs of low back pain. Orthop Clin North Am 1991; 22:263–271.
26. Lee P. The economic impact of musculoskeletal disorders. Qual Life Res 1994; 3(suppl 1):S85–S91.
27. de Lissovoy G, Brown RE, Halpern M, Hassenbusch SJ, Ross E. Cost-effectiveness of long-term intrathecal morphine therapy for pain associated with failed back surgery syndrome. Clin Ther 1997; 19:96–112.
28. Hu XH, Markson LE, Lipton RB, Stewart WF, Berger ML. Burden of migraine in the United States: disability and economic costs. Arch Intern Med 1999; 159:813–818.
29. Maniadakis N, Gray A. The economic burden of pain in the UK. Pain 2000; 84:95–103.
30. Papadimos TJ. Stoicism, the physician, and care of medical outliers. BMC Med Ethics 2004; 5:E8. Available at http://www.pubmedcentral.gov/articlerender.fcgi?tool=pmcentrez&artid=539259.
31. Emanuel EJ, Dubler NN. Preserving the physician-patient relationship in the era of managed care. J Am Medic Assoc 1995; 273:323–329.
32. Emanuel EJ. Medical ethics in the era of managed care: the need for institutional structures instead of principles for individual cases. J Clin Ethics 1995; 6:335–338.
33. Pellegrino ED. Allocation of resources at the bedside: the interactions of economics, law, and ethics. Kennedy Inst Ethics J 1994; 4:309–317.
34. Pellegrino ED. Managed care at the bedside: how do we look in the moral mirror? Kennedy Inst Ethics J 1997; 7:321–330.
35. Pellegrino ED. The commodification of medical and health care: the moral consequences of a paradigm shift from a professional to a market ethic. J Med Philos 1999; 24:243–266.

36. Pellegrino ED. Is rationing ever ethically justifiable? The Pharos 2002; 65:18–19.
37. Lagoe R, Aspling DL, Westert GP. Current and future developments in managed care in the United States and implications for Europe. Health Res Policy Syst 2005; 3:4.
38. Okifuji A, Turk DC, Kalauoklani D. Clinical outcome and economic evaluation of multidisciplinary pain centers. In: Block AR, Kramer EF, Fernandez E, eds. Handbook of Pain Syndromes: biopsychosocial perspectives. Mahwah, NJ: Lawrence Erlbaum Associates, 1999:77–97.
39. Stewart WF, Ricci JA, Chee E, Morganstein D, Lipton R. Lost productive time and cost due to common pain conditions in the US workforce. J Am Medic Assoc 2003; 290:2443–2454.
40. Turk DC. Clinical effectiveness and cost-effectiveness of treatments for patients with chronic pain. Clin J Pain 2002; 18:355–365.
41. Market Data Enterprises. Chronic Pain Management Programs: A Market Analysis. Valley Stream, NY: Market Data Enterprises, 1995.
42. Sullivan M, Ferrell B. Ethical challenges in the management of chronic nonmalignant pain: negotiating through the cloud of doubt. J Pain 2005; 6:2–9.
43. Flor H, Fydrich T, Turk DC. Efficacy of multidisciplinary pain treatment centers: a meta-analytic review. Pain 1992; 49:221–230.
44. Turk DC, Okifuji A. Treatment of chronic pain patients: clinical outcomes, cost-effectiveness, and cost-benefits of multidisciplinary pain centers. Crit Rev Phy Rehab Med 1998; 10:181–208.
45. Guzman J, Esmail R, Karjalainen K, Malmivaara A, Irvin E, Bombardier C. Multidisciplinary rehabilitation for chronic low back pain: a systematic review. Br Medic J 2001; 322:1511–1516.
46. Guzman J, Esmail R, Karjalainen K, Malmivaara A, Irvin E, Bombardier C. Multidisciplinary bio-psycho-social rehabilitation for chronic low back pain. Cochrane Database Syst Rev 2002; 1:CD000963.
47. Schonstein E, Kenny DT, Keating J, Kord BW. Work conditioning, work hardening, and functional restoration for workers with back and neck pain. Cochrane Database Syst Rev 2003; 1:CD001822.
48. Patrick LE, Altmaier EM, Found EM. Long-term outcomes in multidisciplinary treatment of chronic low back pain: results of a 13-year follow-up. Spine 2004; 9:850–855.
49. Weir R, Browne GB, Tunks E, Gafni A, Roberts J. A profile of users of specialty pain clinic services: predictors of use and cost estimates. J Clin Epidemiol 1992; 45:1399–1415.
50. Stieg RL. The cost-effectiveness of pain treatment: who cares? Clin J Pain 1990; 6:301–304.
51. Lebovitz A. Ethics and pain: why and for whom? Pain Med 2001; 2:92–96.
52. Reiser WS, Brunicardi BO. Assessing the impact of Medicare payment changes. Healthc Financ Manage 2002; 56:68–71.
53. Weeks WB, Wallace AE. Long-term financial implications of specialty training for physicians. Am J Med 2002; 113:393–399.
54. Chapman SL. Chronic pain rehabilitation: lost in sea of drugs and procedures? APS Bull 2000; 10(suppl 3):8–9.
55. Stano M, Haas M, Goldberg B, Traub PM, Nyiendo J. Chiropractic and medical care costs of low back care: results from a practice-based observational study. Am J Manag Care 2002; 8:802–809.
56. Market data Enterprises. Pain Management Programs: A Market Analysis. 6th ed. Tampa, FL: Market Data Enterprises, 2003.
57. Haugh R. Hospitals and clinicians confront a new imperative: pain management. Hosp Health Netw 2005; 79:51–52, 54–56.
58. Beauchamp TL, Childress JF. Principles of Biomedical Ethics. 5th ed. New York: Oxford University Press, 2001.
59. Schatman ME. Comprehensive outcome measurement: helping patients recognize success. Paper presented at the 14th Annual Meeting of the American Academy of Pain Management, Denver, CO, September, 2003.
60. Alfici S, Sigal M, Landau M. Primary fibromyalgia syndrome—a variant of depressive disorder? Psychother Psychosom 1989; 51:156–161.

61. Sikiv T, Hosterey U. The thematic apperception test as an aid in understanding the psychodynamics of development of chronic idiopathic pain syndrome. Psychother Psychosom 1992; 57:57–60.
62. Vendrig AA, de May HR, Derksen JJL, van Akkerveeken PF. Assessment of chronic back pain patient characteristics using factor analysis of the MMPI-2: which dimensions are actually assessed? Pain 1998; 76:179–188.
63. Hallberg LRM, Carlsson SG. Coping with fibromyalgia. Scand J Caring Sci 2000; 14:29–36.
64. May WF. Contending images of the healer in an era of turnstile medicine. In: Walter JK, Klein EP, eds. The Story of Bioethics: From Seminal Works to Contemporary Explorations. Washington, DC: Georgetown University Press, 2003:149–162.
65. Himmelstein J, Buchanan JL, Dembe AE, Stevens B. Health services research in workers' compensation medical care: policy issues and research opportunities. Health Serv Res 1999; 34:427–437.
66. Brody H, Miller FG. The internal morality of medicine: explication and application to managed care. J Med Philos 1998; 23:384–410.
67. Veatch RM. The impossibility of a morality internal to medicine. J Med Philos 2001; 26:621–642.
68. Moon S. Big demand, bigger paydays: physician compensation survey shows how far primary-care docs lag behind their specialist colleagues in pay range, growth. Mod Healthc 2004; 34:25–29.
69. Large RG, Schug SA. Opioids for chronic pain of non-malignant origin—caring or crippling. Health Care Anal 1995; 3:5–11.
70. Ferrell BR, Novy D, Sullivan MD, et al. Ethical dilemmas in pain management. J Pain 2001; 2:171–180.
71. Aggarwal VR, Macfarlane TV, Macfarlane GJ. Why is pain more common amongst people living in areas of low socio-economic status? A population-based cross-sectional study. Br Dent J 2003; 194:383–387.
72. Council on Ethical and Judicial Affairs, American Medical Association. Caring for the poor. J Am Medic Assoc 1993; 69:2533–2537.
73. Schatman ME. Racial and ethnic issues in chronic pain management: challenges and perspectives. In: Boswell MV, Cole BE, eds. Weiner's Pain Management: A Practical Guide for Clinicians. 7th ed. Boca Raton, FL: CRC Press, 2006:83–97.
74. US Bureau of the Census. Statistical Abstract of the United States: 2000. Washington, D.C.: US Government Printing Office; 2001.
75. Blanchard JC, Haywood YC, Scott C. Racial and ethnic disparities in health: an emergency medicine perspective. Acad Emerg Med 2003; 10:1289–1293.
76. Hargraves JL. Trends in health insurance coverage and access among black, Latino, and white Americans, 2001–2003. Track Rep 2004; 11:1–6.
77. Sudano JJ, Baker DW. Explaining US racial/ethnic disparities in health declines and mortality in late middle age: the role of socioeconomic status, health behaviors, and health insurance. Soc Sci Med 2006; 62:909–922.
78. Gardiner P. A virtue ethics approach to moral dilemmas in medicine. J Med Ethics 2003; 29:297–302.
79. Pellegrino ED. Toward a virtue-based normative ethics for the health professions. Kennedy Inst Ethics J 1995; 5:253–277.
80. Peter E, Watt-Watson J. Unrelieved pain: an ethical and epistemological analysis of distrust in patients. Can J Nurs Res 2002; 34:65–80.
81. Sullivan M. Ethical principles in pain management. Pain Med 2001; 2:106–111.
82. Aristotle. The Nicomachean Ethics (Irwin T, tr.). Indianapolis: Hackett Publishing, 1999.
83. Giordano J. Neurophilosophy of maldynic pain: disease, illness, and ethical obligation. Paper presented at the 16th Annual Meeting of the American Academy of Pain Management, San Diego, CA, September, 2005.
84. Pellegrino ED. Professionalism, profession, and the virtues of the good physician. Mt Sinai J Med 2002; 69:378–384.
85. Borneman T, Ferrell BR. Ethical issues in pain management. Clin Geriatr Med 1996; 12:615–628.

86. Martino AM. In search of a new ethic for treating patients with chronic pain: what can medical boards do? J Law Med Ethics 1998; 26:332–349.
87. Salmon P, Hall GM. Patient empowerment and control: a psychological discourse in the service of medicine. Soc Sci Med 2003; 57:1969–1980.
88. The Pew Research Center for the People and the Press. Religion, a strength and weakness for both parties. The Pew Forum on Religion and Public Life 2005:1–46.
89. Jankel C, Wolfgang AP, Hoff M. Health care priorities: opinions of one state's citizens and legislators: Health Values. J of Health Beh Ed Promot 1994; 18:7–14.
90. Brock DW, Daniels N. Ethical foundations of the Clinton administration's proposed health care system. J Am Medic Assoc 1994; 271:1189–1196.
91. Ethics Committee, Society for Academic Emergency Medicine. An ethical foundation for health care: an emergency medicine perspective. Ann Emerg Med 1992; 21:1381–1387.
92. Jennings B. Healing the self: the moral meaning of relationships in rehabilitation. Am J Phys Med Rehabil 1993; 72:401–404.
93. Pellegrino ED. Medical ethics subordinated by tyranny and war [editorial]. J Am Medic Assoc 2004; 291:1505–1506.
94. Emanuel EJ, Emanuel LL. What is accountability in health care? Ann Int Med 1996; 124:229–239.
95. National Pain Care Policy Act. H.R. 1020. 109th Congress, 2005.
96. American Pain Society. APS president urges member involvement in grassroots lobbying. APS E-News [serial online] 2005; (2):4–5. Available at http://www.ampainsoc.org/enews/september1305/#2 (accessed November 10, 2005).
97. Council on Ethical and Judicial Affairs. Code of Medical Ethics. Chicago: Am Med Assoc, 2002.
98. Geppert CM. To help and not to harm: ethical issues in the treatment of chronic pain patients with substance use disorders. Adv Psychosom Med 2004; 25:151–171.
99. Quraishi SA, Orkin FK, Weitkamp MR, Khalid AN, Sassani JW. The Health Policy and Legislative Awareness Initiative at the Pennsylvania State University College of Medicine: theory meets practice. Acad Med 2005; 80:443–447.
100. Dagi TF. Physicians and obligatory social activism. J Med Humanit Bioeth 1988; 9:50–59.
101. Hill CS Jr. Pain management in a drug-oriented society. Cancer 1989; 63(suppl 11):2383–2386.
102. Weiner S. "I can't afford that!:" dilemmas in the care of the uninsured and under-insured. J Gen Intern Med 2001; 16:412–418.
103. Donohoe M. Causes and health consequences of environmental degradation and social injustice. Soc Sci Med 2003; 56:573–587.
104. Williams A. Community health learning experiences and political activism: a model for baccalaureate curriculum revolution content. J Nurs Educ 1993; s32:352–356.
105. Course-Wozny JL. Caring: a political platform. Revolution 1997; 7:48–52.
106. Brendtro MJ. Breast cancer: agenda setting through activism. Adv Pract Nurs Q 1998; 4:54–63.
107. Boswell C, Cannon S, Miller J. Nurses' political involvement: responsibility versus privilege. J Prof Nurs 2005; 21:5–8.
108. DeLeon PH, O'Keefe AM, VanderBos GR, Kraut AG. How to influence public policy: a blueprint for activism. Am Psychol 1982; 37:476–485.
109. Lewis JA, Cheek JR, Hendricks CB. Advocacy in supervision. In: Bradley LJ, Ladany N, eds. Counselor Supervision: Principles, Process, and Practice. 3rd ed. Philadelphia, PA: Brunner-Routledge, 2001:330–341.
110. Campbell C, Murray M. Community health psychology: promoting analysis and action for social change. J Health Psychol 2004; 9:187–195.
111. Goodman LA, Liang B, Helms JE, Latta RE, Sparks E, Weintraub SR. Training counseling psychologists as social justice agents: feminist and multicultural principles in action. Couns Psychol 2004; 32:793–837.
112. Rothstein JM. Election night lessons (ed. note). Phys Ther 2000; 80:1162–1163.
113. Evert MM. Our journey together. Am J Occup Ther 1995; 49:1065–1067.
114. Andrasik F. Twenty-five years of progress: twenty-five more? Biofeedback Self Regul 1994; 19:311–324.

5 Ethical Challenges in Caring for Children with Chronic Pain

Patricia A. McGrath and Danielle A. Ruskin

Divisional Center for Pain Management and Pain Research, Department of Anaesthesia, The Hospital for Sick Children, The University of Toronto, Toronto, Ontario, Canada

INTRODUCTION

Unprecedented attention has been focused on the unique pain problems of infants, children, and adolescents during the last two decades. Previously, clinical decisions about whether children were experiencing pain and, if so, about the particular pain therapies required, were based primarily on physicians' personal beliefs rather than on scientific evidence. Regrettably, common misbeliefs—that children did not feel pain as intensely as adults and consequently did not require similar analgesics and pervasive fears—that children were at heightened risk for opioid addiction and should receive minimal analgesic doses, caused many children to suffer needlessly (1,2).

Two studies highlight the extent to which children's pain was undertreated. In 1968, Swafford and Allan (3) surveyed analgesic use for all children treated in an intensive care unit during a four-month period. Only 14% of the children (26 of 180) had received any opioids for pain relief. Moreover, only 3% of the children received analgesics after general surgery, presumably because "pediatric patients seldom need relief of pain after general surgery. They tolerate discomfort well" (3). In her doctoral thesis, Eland (4) compared pain medications for 25 children and 18 adults with similar medical conditions. Only 24 analgesic doses were administered to children during their hospitalization, in marked contrast to the 372 opioid doses and 299 nonopioid doses administered to adults. The majority of children did not receive any analgesics, despite undergoing major trauma including amputation of the foot, excision of neck mass, and heminephrectomy.

Subsequent studies dramatically highlighted the adverse impact of untreated postoperative pain in infants (5) and inadequately treated procedural pain for children with cancer (6,7). The ensuing publicity as people learned that minimal anesthesia and analgesia represented "the norm in pediatric postoperative management," rather than the exception, sparked a revolution (2). Amidst increased pressure from health care providers, public advocates, and distressed parents, clinical practice started to change so that children began to receive more appropriate analgesics at adequate doses and regular dosing intervals. Treatment emphasis also shifted gradually from an almost exclusive disease-centered focus—detecting and treating the putative source of tissue damage—to a more child-centered perspective, assessing the child with pain, identifying contributing psychological and contextual factors, and then targeting interventions accordingly.

Increasing attention has been focused on the rights of all children to receive adequate pain control (8). Yet, despite our continuing efforts to make "children's pain control" a higher priority throughout the world, many children still suffer needlessly. In particular, the management of childhood chronic pain is a continuing problem in many centers, creating ethical dilemmas from patient-centered, health care, and societal perspectives. In this chapter, we describe the key ethical dilemmas in caring for children with chronic pain and present child-centered guidelines for integrating ethical considerations into our routine clinical practice.

CHILDREN DO EXPERIENCE CHRONIC PAIN

In contrast to past assumptions, children, like adults, do experience many types of chronic pain caused by disease, injury, and psychological factors or by factors currently unknown and yet to be identified (2,9,10). However, the topic of children's chronic pain has been neglected in comparison to that of adults so that critical questions remain unanswered about the magnitude of the problem, its economic impact, and the personal burden to children and families. Many studies demonstrate that a substantial proportion of children experience chronic pain, but few population-based epidemiologic studies have been conducted on chronic pain in children (11–13). Thus, we either do not know the specific prevalence rates for most pain conditions [i.e., cancer pain, complex regional pain syndrome (CRPS), phantom limb pain, and pain disorder] or our estimate is based on only a single study (i.e., fibromyalgia, knee pain, or somatization disorder) (11). Overall, we know that prevalence of chronic pain increases with age and that the prevalence of certain pain conditions varies with sex or age. For example, data from Pain Clinics indicates that CRPS differentially affects females with a female:male ratio of 6:1 and an age of onset from 9 to 15 years, usually from 10 to 12 years of age (14–16).

It is exceedingly important to obtain accurate prevalence data for chronic pain in children, especially according to age, sex, and ethnicity. Longitudinal studies are required to document the natural history of the varied pain conditions, determine prognostic factors, and identify any high-risk groups that should receive special intervention to reduce the likelihood that their disabling pain will continue into adult life. Many acute pains were undertreated in children because these pain problems were underreported. After the magnitude of acute pain in infants and children was documented, major changes occurred in the clinical management of acute pain. "Similarly, unrecognized chronic pain is untreated chronic pain" (11). At present, we do not know the extent to which children may suffer from inadequately managed chronic pain. Epidemiological data is essential to ensure that we can better identify children at risk for developing chronic pain and provide the health care resources necessary to treat them.

Critical questions remain unanswered about the pathophysiology of almost all complex non–disease-related chronic pain conditions in children. Our understanding of the pathophysiologic processes is often presumed, rather than documented, and based primarily on extrapolation from adult studies. For example, the clinical criteria for diagnosis of CRPS require at least two neuropathic pain descriptors (i.e., burning, dysesthesia, paresthesia, mechanical allodynia, and hyperalgesia to cold) and two physical signs of autonomic dysfunction (i.e., cyanosis, mottling, hyperhydrosis, extremity cooler than contralateral by 3 C, and edema). Yet, the specific pain features and sensory deficits have not been well detailed for most childhood chronic pain conditions, including CRPS, so that we lack sensitive and child-based (i.e., developmentally appropriate) diagnostic classifications. Instead, clinical criteria are based on disease characteristics that were described for adults, even though clinical and community studies indicate that the presentation of pain is often different in children. Thus, descriptive clinical studies are needed to establish developmentally appropriate pain classifications and diagnostic criteria. Otherwise, children with non-disease-related chronic pain may not be diagnosed in a timely manner and treated appropriately.

Children also experience significant cognitive, behavioral, and emotional effects as pain persists, in addition to the altered sensory processing that occurs with chronic pain (17). Although extensive research has been conducted on the impact of adult chronic pain on the quality of life, including the economic costs in terms of lost productivity (i.e., work) and the broader costs to the health care system, comparable meticulous research has not yet been conducted with children. Recent surveys of children's general pain experiences (i.e., acute, recurrent, and chronic) suggest that a significant proportion of children experience impaired quality of life due to pain (18–20). Yet, definitive data on the true impact of chronic pain for children, families, and society is notably absent. Such data should be obtained through longitudinal studies in which children have been diagnosed according to established criteria, so that we can better understand the impact of the different types of chronic pain.

Also, in marked contrast to the regulatory-required data obtained in randomized clinical trials (RCTs) to document treatment efficacy for adults with chronic pain, most regulatory agencies have neglected the need for obtaining comparable efficacy data for children until relatively recently. As a result, the efficacy of almost all therapies used to control children's chronic pain is based on extrapolation from adult data. Yet, increasing responsibility for evidence-based practice dictates that health care providers adopt clear guidelines for determining when treatments are effective and for identifying those children for whom they are most effective. Ethical dilemmas arise from our lack of data from well-designed cohort studies and RCTs to support the efficacy of most interventions (both drug and nondrug therapies) used for children with chronic pain. As an example, most of the pharmacological management of neuropathic pain in children and adolescents is based on extrapolation from adult studies. While tricyclic antidepressants and gabapentin are well-established analgesics for neuropathic pain in adults, evidence for efficacy in children is confined to case reports or very small series (21,22). Similarly, although cognitive-behavioral interventions are critical components of pain management programs for chronic pain, most of the data supporting their efficacy is derived only from studies of childhood headache (23). As Eccleston et al. (24) concluded, we urgently need well-designed studies of nonheadache chronic pain in children and adolescents.

Thus, the lack of definitive information on many aspects of children's chronic pain—age- and sex-related prevalence rates, developmentally appropriate diagnostic criteria, personal and economic impact of pain, and evidence-based treatment guidelines—complicates our clinical management of many types of childhood chronic pain.

CHILDREN ARE NOT "LITTLE ADULTS" WITH RESPECT TO CHRONIC PAIN

Although chronic pain is traditionally defined as pain that persists for a prolonged period (typically > 3 months), it is not simply a prolongation of the same physical mechanisms responsible for acute pain (i.e., injury-induced activation of peripheral nociceptors). Instead, chronic pain often has neuropathic components, wherein injured nerves respond abnormally to normal sensory stimuli. Pain may persist or intensify despite an absence of evidence of continuing injury.

Children are not "little adults" with respect to chronic pain from biologic and psychological perspectives (1). Children's chronic pain is not simply and directly related to the extent of tissue damage. Their developing nociceptive system responds differently to injury (i.e., increased excitability and sensitization) when compared to the mature adult system (25,26). Also, children's pain seems more plastic or modifiable in comparison to adults, so that environmental and situational factors exert a more powerful influence on children's pain perceptions (27).

Even more than in adults, pain can be different, depending on children's expectations, perceived control, or the significance that they attach to the pain (28). Children actively interpret the strength and quality of any pain sensations, determine the relevance of any hurting, and learn how to interpret the significance of their pain by observing how other people respond to them. Children's perceptions of pain are defined by their age and cognitive level; their previous pain experiences, against which they evaluate each new pain; the relevance of the pain or disease causing pain; their expectations for obtaining eventual recovery and pain relief; and their ability to control the pain themselves.

While age, sex, temperament, and cultural background shape how children generally interpret and experience painful sensations, other factors exert a more dynamic impact. The cognitive, behavioral, and emotional factors listed in Figure 1 vary dramatically and profoundly influence children's chronic pain. These situational factors complicate our already challenging efforts to understand and treat chronic pain in children. They add a unique, dynamic dimension that interacts with the more stable characteristics of the child and the situation in which the pain is experienced (11,27,29).

Children's understanding, perceived control, expectations, and the meaning of the pain influence their ultimate perceptions. Moreover, their beliefs (shaped by their parents) guide what they do to relieve pain and shape their emotional

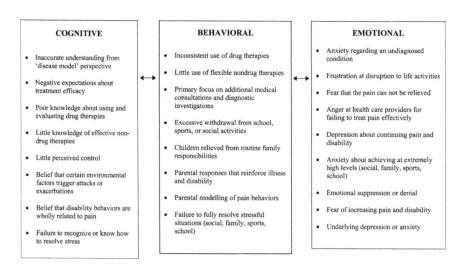

FIGURE 1 Cognitive, behavioral, and emotional contributor to children's chronic pain.

responses to a pain problem—thus, influencing children's pain intensity, pain-related disability, and subsequent emotional distress.

While they may be unable to change the more stable child characteristics, health care providers can dramatically improve children's pain by modifying situational factors. Cognitive factors include parents' and children's understanding of their chronic pain, knowledge of effective therapies, and expectations for continuing pain or pain relief. Behavioral factors refer to the specific behaviors of children, parents, and staff during pain episodes and also to parents' and children's broader actions in response to a chronic pain problem. Emotional factors include parents' and children's feelings about the pain itself or responsible health condition and its adverse impact on the family, as well as any associated emotional disorders (such as anxiety or depression). Parents' understanding of the cause of pain, possible treatments, and long-term prognosis guides their behaviors toward children and shapes children's emotional responses to the pain problem (30).

Situational factors may affect children even more than adults. Adults typically have experienced a wide variety of pains differing in etiology, intensity and quality; their diverse experiences create a broad base of knowledge, realistic expectations, and versatile coping behaviors. In contrast, children, especially very young children, have considerably limited pain experience. They rely mainly on information conveyed within the immediate situation to interpret the pain they experience and to respond appropriately. Thus, children are particularly sensitive to environmental cues and to the behaviors of the adults who are present. Children's chronic pain is not predetermined by the extent of their injuries or disease progression. When health care providers ignore the powerful mediating impact of situational factors on chronic pain, they can easily, albeit inadvertently, increase a child's pain, disability, or emotional distress.

Children with chronic pain depend greatly on their parents (and adult health care providers) to understand, cope, and interpret their pain and its impact on their lives (31). Consequently, they are more susceptible than adults to the influence of situational factors and more at risk of increased pain and suffering. Moreover, parents usually decide (for children) or influence (for adolescents) treatment choices and control access to treatment. While children with chronic pain are not "little adults" from a biological pain perspective, situational factors and parental influence must be recognized as other key factors affecting their pain experience and response to treatment. Ultimately, the ethics of caring for children with chronic pain requires all health care providers to recognize the myriad factors that affect their pain and disability.

CARING FOR CHILDREN WITH CHRONIC PAIN

Irrespective of etiology, chronic pain has profound and prolonged physical, behavioral, and psychological consequences (31). Concurrently, what children (and parents) know, do, and feel all exert a profound impact on their subsequent pain and disability. Thus, to adequately treat chronic pain, health care providers must evaluate the primary pain sources and ascertain which situational factors are relevant for which children and families. Treatment emphasis should shift accordingly from an exclusive disease-centered framework to a more child-centered focus. Health care providers should select specific therapies to target the responsible central and peripheral mechanisms and to mitigate the pain-exacerbating impact of situational factors, recognizing that the multiple causes and contributing factors will vary over time.

Drug therapies—analgesics, analgesic-adjuvants, and anesthetics—are essential for pain control, but nondrug therapies—cognitive, physical, and behavioral—are also essential. As we monitor a child's improvement in response to the therapies initiated, we refine our pain diagnosis and treatment plan accordingly. Pain control is achieved practically by adjusting both drug and nondrug therapies in a rational child-centered manner based on the assessment process. Controlling chronic pain requires an integrated approach because many factors are responsible, no matter how seemingly clear-cut the etiology. Adequate analgesic prescriptions, administered at regular dosing intervals, must be complemented by a practical cognitive-behavioral approach to ensure optimal pain relief.

Certain cognitive, behavioral, and emotional factors may intensify pain, increase distress, and exacerbate a child's disability (Fig. 1). Pain adversely affects all aspects of children's lives. Parents are distressed by the pain itself, its implications for their children's future, its life-threatening potential (if any), and the prospect of continuing pain and progressive disability. Parents and adolescents tend to emphasize and fear the future consequences of children's physical condition, whereas young children are more preoccupied by the immediate situation and disruptions to their daily activities. The dynamics within the family (for children, siblings, and extended family members) inevitably change because chronic pain prevents children from pursuing their normal activities and disrupts family schedules.

Health care providers must realize not only that the situational factors that affect children with chronic pain are very different from those associated with acute pain, but also that almost all families will try to understand childhood chronic pain based on their understanding of acute pain. The vast majority of pains that children experience are acute pains caused by injuries. Such nociceptive pain usually has a rapid onset—obviously linked to injury, and has a protective significance—warning children to avoid further physical harm. The pain lessens progressively as injuries heal. A wide array of over-the-counter analgesics provides effective pain relief. Children usually do not experience any prolonged emotional distress because they understand acute pains and know they can be controlled easily. Thus, the cognitive factors associated with acute pains are generally positive—an accurate understanding of the cause, positive expectations for relief, and a personal sense of control. The aversive significance is shaped mainly by the pain intensity and the temporary disruptions to children's normal activities.

In contrast, chronic pain, often comprising multiple nociceptive and neuropathic components, is not consistently associated with obvious tissue injury and may lack a protective biological significance. Even when triggered by injury, the pain may not lessen progressively as the injury heals. Treatments that relieve acute pain may be wholly ineffective, so that children do not know whether they will ever be pain-free again. The continuing pain adversely affects all interpersonal relationships and all aspects of a child's life—family, social, sports, and school. Children with chronic pain can experience prolonged psychological distress, impaired physical functioning, decreased independence, and may face an uncertain prognosis. Unlike the single treatment approach effective for acute pain, chronic pain usually requires a multimodal treatment approach combining drug therapy, physical therapy, and psychological counseling.

The ethical care of children with chronic pain necessitates that health care providers recognize that complex and dynamic interactions occur among the cognitive, behavioral, and emotional factors listed in Figure 1 children's pain, disability, and distress. What parents understand about the cause of their child's pain, possible treatments, and long-term prognosis guides their (and their child's) behaviors and shapes the family's emotional responses to the chronic pain problem. Parents usually try to understand their child's condition from an acute disease perspective, where pain is due to a single cause and can be relieved by a single treatment. They do not understand that chronic pain, unlike most pains that they have already experienced, may have several interrelated causes.

Particular problems arise for families of children with idiopathic pain or pain with a psychological etiology. Parents often continue medical investigations because they search for some clear-cut physical etiology that will lead them to find the one definitive treatment that will immediately stop their children's pain. Parents may reject potentially effective treatments after only one attempt, even though the treatment would address some of the causes and might reduce children's pain severity over time. Children often "learn" that they will remain very disabled until the "one right treatment" is found. They believe that they have no control and cannot prevent the future course of continuing pain and disability.

ETHICAL PRINCIPLES: "STOP, LOOK, LISTEN, AND COMMUNICATE WITH CHILDREN"

Health care providers should recognize that children with chronic pain have the right to receive optimal, ethically sound care. In essence, children and their parents enter into a unique contract with health care providers. They entrust their care to us because of our knowledge, training, and moral imperative to do good while we, in turn, are responsible to promote their welfare to the greatest extent possible. The integrity of such contracts is upheld by conducting a thorough pain assessment, establishing an accurate diagnosis, formulating an appropriate treatment plan, and effectively communicating the diagnosis and treatment rationale to children and parents. Our ethical guiding principles are to deliver "state of the art" care while adhering to the values of patient autonomy and beneficence, and guarding against harm (Fig. 2).

Every health care provider uses a particular cognitive-behavioral approach when treating patients. Pain modulation begins at the first consultation, when health care providers first shape what children and parents understand about chronic pain, what they will do, and how they will feel. To mitigate the factors that can intensify chronic pain, health care providers should *"stop, look, listen, & communicate"*: *stop* an exclusive disease focus, *look* at the big picture—assess the child with pain, and *listen* to the child's pain history (and listening to the family's perspective), appreciating the potential impact of situational factors, and clearly *communicate* relevant diagnostic and treatment information to the children and parents.

Typically, children have undergone multiple medical examinations and diagnostic tests to determine whether their pain is caused by disease, an underlying health condition, neural dysfunction, or psychological disorder. The diagnostic phase may last several weeks or months, as different specialists rule out various diagnoses. Children and their families become increasingly anxious throughout this period. By the time the etiology (or probable etiology) is known, most children have become extremely focused on any physical signs and symptoms because they searched for cues as to what was wrong in their bodies. If their pain is uncontrolled during this period, they probably did not attend school, enjoy their usual activities,

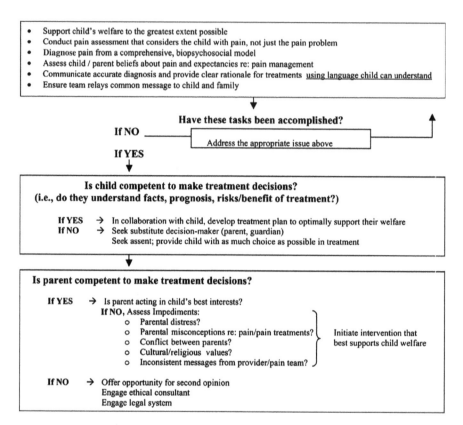

- Support child's welfare to the greatest extent possible
- Conduct pain assessment that considers the child with pain, not just the pain problem
- Diagnose pain from a comprehensive, biopsychosocial model
- Assess child / parent beliefs about pain and expectancies re: pain management
- Communicate accurate diagnosis and provide clear rationale for treatments using language child can understand
- Ensure team relays common message to child and family

Have these tasks been accomplished?

If NO ──────── Address the appropriate issue above

If YES

Is child competent to make treatment decisions?
(i.e., do they understand facts, prognosis, risks/benefit of treatment?)

If YES → In collaboration with child, develop treatment plan to optimally support their welfare
If NO → Seek substitute decision-maker (parent, guardian)
          Seek assent; provide child with as much choice as possible in treatment

Is parent competent to make treatment decisions?

If YES → Is parent acting in child's best interests?
           If NO, Assess Impediments:
             o Parental distress?
             o Parental misconceptions re: pain/pain treatments?   Initiate intervention that
             o Conflict between parents?   best supports child welfare
             o Cultural/religious values?
             o Inconsistent messages from provider/pain team?

If NO → Offer opportunity for second opinion
          Engage ethical consultant
          Engage legal system

FIGURE 2 Ethical considerations in promoting welfare of children with chronic pain.

or socialize with friends. Concurrently, their fears, frustration, and anxiety about the future escalate.

In essence, the situational factors shown in Figure 1 may become secondary causes or contributing factors for children's pain and disability, especially for children whose pain has a complex etiology or has primary psychological components. When diagnostic consultations focus exclusively on the pain features—location, frequency, quality, severity, duration, and accompanying physical symptoms, rather than on the child with pain and potentially relevant situational factors, health care providers inadvertently reinforce the acute disease model of pain. As such, they strengthen parents' beliefs that chronic pain is caused only by a particular physical abnormality and that children's disability will persist until health care providers find the right treatment.

Specialists may emphasize negative test findings—"a failure to find something," rather than a positive confirmation of an understandable and, therefore, treatable pain condition. Lacking a confirmatory and concise diagnosis, parents continue to be anxious and worried about why their children have pain, fearing that the pain signifies an as yet undiagnosed disease or medical condition. Primary care providers should be able to guide families through the diagnostic phase of a child's chronic pain problem, helping them to understand the test results and reports from different specialists, alleviating their unfounded fears, and explaining why assessment should focus on the child with pain and not just the pain symptom.

Communicating a diagnosis is a critical component of pain management. Even when some aspects of the pain condition are puzzling, health care providers should honestly describe what they know and explain what they need to explore further in a straightforward and reassuring manner. Accurate information about the pain source(s) can mitigate the increased distress caused by parents' misinterpretations and anxieties. Moreover, because expectancies can profoundly affect treatment effectiveness (32), health care providers should build on this knowledge and directly address parents' and children's expectancies within the diagnostic appointment.

An accurate diagnosis is the foundation of pain management for children with chronic pain, communicating information about both the primary causes and the secondary contributing factors so that treatments can be targeted at each relevant factor. Because these factors may vary over time, pain assessment remains a critical component of any treatment regimen. The focus of continuing assessment is the child with pain—not only the pain features but also the situational factors that modulate pain. Even when pain is due to actively progressing disease such as for patients with advanced cancer, many other factors can affect their pain and suffering. Health care providers should assess these factors and target treatments accordingly.

For example, we have received consults for children receiving palliative care, whose pain had been well controlled with large (and presumably appropriate) opioid doses, but who were now experiencing increasingly frequent episodes of breakthrough pain. For some children, the increased pain signified advancing disease requiring increased medication. But for other children, the increased pain signified increasing emotional distress related to their fears about death. These children needed counseling to relieve their distress and, concomitantly, their pain (33,34).

Caring for children with chronic pain usually requires a multimodal approach comprising physical, pharmacological, and psychological therapies. Psychological interventions are an essential component of most treatment programs because of the many cognitive, behavioral, and emotional factors that can affect pain and disability. Individualized programs are potentially the optimal and most practical interventions because they match treatments to the particular needs of each child and family. Specific therapies are based on the assessment results to target the responsible central and peripheral mechanisms, and to mitigate the pain-exacerbating impact of situational factors. Thus, the emphasis of the treatment rationale is on the multifactorial etiology of pain and recommendations for a multimodal treatment approach. This is in direct contrast to the "single cause and single treatment" approach normally adequate for relieving acute pain.

SPECIAL ETHICAL CHALLENGES

Health care providers face multiple challenges in caring for children with chronic pain. Not only must they be sensitive to the fact that children experience pain differently than adults, but they must also contend with ethical dilemmas that are inevitably raised when treating child patients. Health care providers routinely tackle questions about determining children's capacity to understand their pain condition and decide among treatment options, resolving disagreements among children, parents, and the health care providers as to the "best" treatment regimen, and judging benefits, risks, and burdens from the child's and the family's perspectives. To do so, they are guided by three ethical standards: beneficence, i.e., making decisions to support the child's best interests; informed consent; and the double principle, an action that promotes well-being that may have a foreseen negative effect, but in which the good effect outweighs the bad.

BENEFICENCE AND MALEFICENCE

All children with chronic pain should receive care that promotes their welfare (beneficence) and guards them from harm (maleficence). Regrettably, several clinical circumstances can compromise our ability to fulfill this ethical principle. Children depend on their parents initially to acknowledge the importance of their pain problem and arrange medical evaluation, and then to select the best treatment options for them. Thus, children are at risk of continued or increased pain if parents fail to appreciate the seriousness of their pain complaints, fail to arrange appropriate medical evaluation, or fail to follow appropriate treatment recommendations. Similarly, children are at risk of continued or increased pain if health care providers fail to diagnose their pain from a comprehensive biopsychosocial perspective or fail to recommend the most appropriate treatments. Health care providers may also fail children when they do not clearly communicate a diagnosis and provide an understandable rationale for the recommended treatments.

Children with chronic pain, and their parents constitute an especially vulnerable population. Typically, all children have been assessed and treated by several physicians and health care providers, but their pain persists and anxieties increase. But, circumstances may be horrendous for children whose pain is not clearly related to an underlying disease. They have usually seen a multitude of medical specialists, have often received different diagnoses and conflicting treatment recommendations, and some children become increasingly disabled because they and their families wait for the "right diagnosis and right treatment." By the time children are referred to a pain specialist or chronic pain clinic, frustrated families are both hopeful and uncertain as to whether their children can ever be helped. Health care providers must be sensitive to a family's vulnerability and should adopt a "Stop, Look, Listen, & Communicate" approach to ensure that they respect children's rights, evaluate all factors contributing to children's pain and disability, communicate a diagnosis clearly, and present a treatment plan with therapies targeted at the primary and secondary causes for pain.

Yet, even with this approach, conflicts may still arise. In our experience, the most common conflicts arise when parents do not agree with the pain team's diagnosis or treatment regimen (i.e., use of particular medication, accepting physiotherapy, or receiving psychological and psychiatric assistance).

CASE EXAMPLES—PARENTS DO NOT ACCEPT DIAGNOSIS

Jen, a 10-year-old girl, was diagnosed with CRPS-Type 1 in her right ankle after twisting her ankle in dance class and had experienced pain for 18 months. At the time of referral to our clinic, we also diagnosed her with an increasing disability problem. In essence, she had progressively developed major behavioral tantrums when her pain increased (or, in the team psychologist's opinion, when Jen did not want to go to school, did not want her mother to leave, and wanted special private time with her parents away from her three siblings). Jen regained full use of her ankle and reported less pain after physiotherapy and with regular medication, but the unpredictable behavioral tantrums continued. Although Jen and her parents accepted a recommendation for cognitive-behavioral therapy and acknowledged that Jen was often a manipulative child, they were unable to set limits with her because they viewed her tantrums as pain based and not behaviorally based. In essence, they did not fully accept our diagnosis and thus could not accept all our treatment recommendations.

Maddie, a four-year-old girl, suffered from epidermolysis bullosa. She was referred for pain management during her regular dressing changes. Maddie's dressing changes had become horrific experiences for her and her mother. Maddie's open leg wounds were so extensive that when her mother and visiting nurse unwrapped her bandages before placing her in the warm bath, she became very distressed and screamed when she was placed in the tub. Although her mother had initially requested some psychological intervention to help Maddie cope during the painful dressing changes, members of the chronic pain team explained that Maddie first required drug therapy to provide her with predictable, pain-free periods to lessen her anxiety and distress. Then, the psychologist could teach her and her mother some psychological therapies to complement her drug therapy. At her first follow-up appointment, Maddie said that the prescribed opioid medicine had helped her but her mother said she did not want Maddie to become addicted and was reluctant to continue to administer it. Despite her young age, Maddie clearly expressed that her medication had helped but her mother preferred to stop using it, despite team members' reassurance and explanations about the difference between tolerance and addiction.

These cases highlight one of the most difficult ethical issues that challenge health care providers—how we should respond when a child chooses one therapy while parents choose another. While each clinical situation is unique, which common principles should govern our deliberations and responses? Based on our clinical experience and consistent with recommendations for managing children's chronic pain, our suggested guiding principles are listed in Figure 2.

Parents may make decisions for children that contradict our beliefs and recommendations as health care providers. Yet, they are acting in accordance with their beliefs, and the vast majority of parents are genuinely making decisions based on what should be best for their children. Health care providers should respectfully ascertain parents' underlying beliefs, fears, and rationale. Then, they are responsible for providing concrete information to refute any erroneous beliefs and alleviate unfounded fears—usually additional information about how chronic pain differs from acute pain, especially its multidimensional aspects and the need for multimodal therapy, and explicit information about the efficacy of recommended drug and nondrug therapies.

Recently, parents have asked us about the use of drugs not labeled for use in children, the use of drugs classified as anticonvulsants or antidepressants, and the rationale for psychological therapy for "real physical pain." Health care providers should assist parents to make decisions on the basis of accurate and understandable information about chronic pain. They should address any misconceptions and acknowledge parents' dissenting views in a sensitive manner, while maintaining that the primary focus is the best interests of the child. Health care providers should also assess the extent to which religious/cultural beliefs may conflict with treatment recommendations and assist families to reach an acceptable solution that is in keeping with their beliefs/values and their child's welfare.

Yet, parents may still not accept treatment recommendations so that their children are at risk for continued pain, pain-related disability, and emotional distress. In most cases, health care providers must accept parents' decisions. However, when parents' actions mean children will likely suffer harm as a result (35), health care providers could seek assistance from an institutional ethical committee or ethical consultant. As a final measure, when decisions represent harm to the child or neglect, legal protection services should be involved and decision-making responsibilities may be shifted to a guardian (35,36).

In our experience, certain circumstances increase the possibility of such situations arising.

- **Complicated pain history**—child received several conflicting diagnoses and treatment recommendations.
- **Presence of contributing psychosocial factors, irrespective of etiology**—cognitive, behavioral, or emotional factors are contributing to child's pain or disability.
- **Rigid belief in acute pain model**—parents or children interpret pain as sign of underlying, as yet unidentified, tissue damage.
- **Heightened parental distress**—at least one parent is exceptionally distressed and family life is significantly disrupted by the child's pain.
- **Major change in parental behaviors since pain onset**—parents often exhibit more crisis-oriented behaviors in response to the child exhibiting inconsistent responses to pain complaints.
- **Mixed messages**—team members present discrepant information or opinions at different times, or fail to communicate a clear diagnosis.

CHILDREN'S CONSENT TO TREATMENT

Children should be involved in their health care decisions to the greatest extent possible (35,37). However, health care providers may have overly protective attitudes or underestimate children's decision-making capacity so that they overlook the right of children to express their views (38). Children usually need a more individualized approach, with concrete age-appropriate examples, to enable them to understand their pain condition and appreciate the benefits and risks of recommended treatments. Due to busy clinic schedules, some pain teams may focus primarily on communicating with parents rather than children. Yet, according to the American Academy of Pediatrics, the dictates of informed consent require that (i) health care providers use language that is appropriate for a child's developmental age to explain their condition, the proposed treatment and associated risks/benefits, and the risks/benefits of alternative treatments (including the choice of no treatment); (ii) children (or parents as surrogate decision makers) have appropriate decision making capacity, including the ability to understand and communicate information, comprehend the consequences of the proposed treatment, nontreatment, and treatment alternatives; and (iii) children have autonomy, so to the greatest extent possible, they are free to choose treatment without being coerced or manipulated (37).

Irrespective of their disease or chronological age, children are deemed capable of decision-making if they possess the cognitive and emotional processes necessary relative to the health care decision at hand (39). Therefore, the greater the risk of possible harm (e.g., discontinuing a life-saving treatment), the greater the competency required. Informed consent should be obtained at the start of treatment and leads to improved treatment adherence and more trusting and collaborative relationships between providers and their patients (40).

Parents are the surrogates for infants, young children, and children with cognitive impairment, who lack the capacity to make complex health care decisions. Yet, when feasible, children should be included in decision making as much as possible and when possible, children should assent to treatment (36). In our experience, even very young children are interested in why they are hurting and how treatments may help. All children have had injuries and learn that parents and different types of health care (e.g., bandages, sutures, casts, and medicine) can relieve their pain. Health care providers should have a versatile repertoire of practical examples to explain chronic pain and why multimodal therapies are required.

CHILDREN'S REFUSAL OF TREATMENT

If children refuse treatment, health care providers are responsible for assessing their decision-making capacity. After using age-appropriate language to explain the pain condition and the potential benefits and risks of available treatments, health providers should ascertain: (i) were children able to understand this information? (ii) were children free to make decision without being coerced or manipulated? and (iii) does the gravity of the situation require that children have greater competency, i.e., high-risk decisions such as discontinuing a life saving treatment.

By 15 years of age, children are able to make informed treatment decisions as competently as adults (39). Yet, health care providers should not assume that younger children are necessarily incompetent. Younger children may be equally competent, especially those who have serious health problems and have grown up with regular interactions with health care providers. All children should be encouraged to be involved in discussions and treatment decisions as much as they would like.

When children adamantly refuse treatment, health care providers should seriously attempt to understand their reasons (e.g., ungrounded fears and misconceptions), clarify any misconceptions, encourage them to reconsider, and force treatment only as a last option. If children reluctantly accept treatment, then health care providers should carefully note any concrete gains because children may have difficulty understanding more subtle signs of improvement. Children should be partners in formulating treatment goals and as necessary, treatment goals should include key individuals in the child's environment (e.g., parents, teachers, and coaches) to maximize children's resumption of regular activities to the extent possible.

FUTURE CHALLENGES

Whether viewed from patient-centered, health care, or societal perspectives, ethical considerations are intrinsic components of caring for all individuals with chronic pain, but especially so for children. As a result of extensive research, we have gained better insights about caring for children with chronic pain. Treatment emphasis has shifted gradually from an almost exclusive disease-centered focus—detecting and treating the putative source of tissue damage—to a more child-centered perspective, assessing the child with pain, identifying contributing psychological and contextual factors, and then targeting interventions accordingly. However, serious challenges remain.

We need to apply the existing knowledge more consistently within our clinical practice. Regrettably, many hospitals still do not require consistent documentation of children's pain, preventing us from ensuring that children's pain is adequately controlled. Hospital administrators or accreditation organizations should establish children's pain control as a priority, as recently mandated by the Joint Commission on Accreditation of Healthcare Organizations for the United States (41). In spite of established analgesic dosing guidelines for infants and children, the undertreatment of postoperative and chronic pain is a continuing problem in many centers.

Evidence-based practice dictates that health care providers adopt clear guidelines for determining when treatments are effective and for identifying children for whom they are most effective. Yet, we lack data from well-designed cohort studies and RCTs to support the efficacy of many interventions (both drug and nondrug therapies) used extensively in clinical practice for children with chronic pain. Although cognitive-behavioral interventions are critical components of pain management programs for chronic pain, most of the data supporting their efficacy is derived from studies of childhood headache. We critically need data on child-centered treatment efficacy—that is, when interventions are selected for the individual child with pain, based on an assessment of the specific cognitive, behavioral, and emotional factors contributing to his or her pain and disability. We do not yet know the specific prevalence of most types of chronic pain in children, but recent research is focusing on the epidemiology of childhood persistent pain to obtain age- and sex-related prevalence estimates, identifying vulnerability and prognostic factors, and determining the long-term impact for children and their families. We need longitudinal studies to identify key risk factors that influence a child's vulnerability to chronic pain, in particular, the increased apparent vulnerability in females. Our ultimate and continuing challenges are to better understand the experience of children's pain and to improve clinical practice so that health care providers use the existing "state-of-the-art" pain scales, interpret children's pain scores to guide therapeutic decisions, and document treatment effectiveness.

REFERENCES

1. McGrath PA. Children—'not simply little adults.' In: Merskey H, Loeser JD, Dubner R, eds. The Paths of Pain: 1975–2005. Seattle: IASP Press, 2005:433–446.
2. Schechter NL, Berde C, Yaster M. Pain in infants, children, and adolescents: an overview. In: Schechter NL, Berde C, Yaster M, eds. Pain in Infants, Children, and Adolescents. 2nd ed. Lippincott: Williams & Wilkins, 2003:3–18.
3. Swafford LI, Allan D. Pain relief in the pediatric patient. Med Clin North Am 1968; 52:131–136.
4. Eland JM. Children's Communication of Pain. University of Iowa, 1974.
5. Anand KJS. Pain, anaesthesia, and babies. Lancet 1987; 330:543–544.
6. Schechter N. Untreated pain in children. In: Schmidt RF, Willis WD, eds. Encyclopedic Reference of Pain. New York: Springer-Verlag. 2006.
7. Hilgard JR, LeBaron S. Relief of anxiety and pain in children and adolescents with cancer: quantitative measures and clinical observations. Int J Clin Exp Hyp 1982; 30:417–442.
8. Eccleston C, Malleston P. Managing chronic pain in children and adolescents. BMJ 2003; 326:1408–1409.

9. McGrath PA. Pain in Children: Nature, Assessment and Treatment. New York: Guilford Press; 1990.
10. McGrath PJ, Finley GA. Chronic and recurrent pain in children and adolescents. In: McGrath PJ, Finley GA, eds. Chronic and Recurrent Pain in Children and Adolescents: Progress in Pain Research and Management. Vol. 13. Seattle: IASP Press, 1999:1–4.
11. McGrath PA. Chronic pain in children. In: Crombie IK, ed. Epidemiology of Pain. Seattle: IASP Press, 1999:81–100.
12. Goodman JE, McGrath PJ. The epidemiology of pain in children and adolescents: a review. Pain 1991; 46:247–264.
13. Van DenDerkhof E. Prevalence of chronic pain disorders in children. In: Schmidt RF, Willis WD, eds. Encyclopedic Reference of Pain. New York: Springer-Verlag. 2006.
14. Wilder RT, Berde CB, Wolohan M, Vieyra MA, Masek BJ, Micheli LJ. Reflex sympathetic dystrophy in children. Clinical characteristics and follow-up of seventy patients. J Bone Joint Surg Am 1992; 74:910–919.
15. Olsson GL, Arner S, Hirsch G. Reflex sympathetic dystrophy in children. In: Tyler DC, Krane EJ, eds. Advances in Pain Research and Therapy. Vol. 15. New York: Raven Press, 1990:323–331.
16. Berde CB, Solodiuk J. Multidisciplinary programs for management of acute and chronic pain in children. In: Schechter NL, Berde C, Yaster M, eds. Pain in Infants, Children, and Adolescents. 2nd ed. Lippincott: Williams & Wilkins, 2003:471–486.
17. Brown SC, McGrath PA, Krmpotic K. Pain in children. In: Pappagallo M, ed. Neurologic Basis of Pain. New York: McGraw-Hill, 2005:225–242.
18. Perquin CW, Hazebroek-Kampschreur AA, Hunfeld JA, et al. Pain in children and adolescents: a common experience. Pain 2000; 87:51–58.
19. Hunfeld JA, Perquin CW, Bertina W, et al. Stability of pain parameters and pain-related quality of life in adolescents with persistent pain: a three-year follow-up. Clin J Pain 2002; 18:99–106.
20. Merlijn VP, Hunfeld JA, van der Wouden JC, Hazebroek-Kampschreur AA, Koes BW, Passchier J. Psychosocial factors associated with chronic pain in adolescents. Pain 2003; 101:33–43.
21. McGraw, Kosek. Erythromelalgia pain managed with gabapentin. Anesthesiology 1997; 86:988–990.
22. Rusy LM, Troshynski TJ, Weisman SJ. Gabapentin in phantom limb pain management in children and young adults—report of seven cases. J Pain Symptom Manage 2001; 21:78–82.
23. McGrath PA, Holahan AL. Psychological interventions with children and adolescents: evidence for their effectiveness in treating chronic pain. Sem Pain Med 2003; 1:99–109.
24. Eccleston C, Morley S, Williams A, Yorke L, Mastroyannopoulou K. Systematic review of randomised controlled trials of psychological therapy for chronic pain in children and adolescents, with a subset meta-analysis of pain relief. Pain 2002; 99:157–165.
25. Fitzgerald M, Howard R. The neurobiological basis of pediatric pain. In: Schechter N, Berde C, Yaster M, eds. Pain in Infants, Children, and Adolescents. 2nd ed. Lippincott: Williams & Wilkins, 2003:19–42.
26. Andrews KA. The human developmental neurophysiology of pain. In: Schechter NL, Berde C, Yaster M, eds. Pain in Infants, Children, and Adolescents. 2nd ed. Lippincott: Williams & Wilkins, 2003:43–57.
27. McGrath PA, Hillier LM. Modifying the psychologic factors that intensify children's pain and prolong disability. In: Schechter NL, Berde C, Yaster M, eds. Pain in Infants, Children, and Adolescents. 2nd ed. Lippincott: Williams & Wilkin, 2003:85–104.
28. McGrath PA, Dade LA. Strategies to decrease pain and minimize disability. In: Price DD, Bushnell MC, eds. Psychological Methods of Pain Control: Basic Science and Clinical Perspectives, Progress in Pain Research and Management. Vol. 29. Seattle: IASP Press, 2004:73–96.
29. Ross DM, Ross SA. Childhood pain: current issues, research, and management. Baltimore: Urban & Schwarzenberg, 1988.
30. McGrath PA, Hillier LM. The Child with Headache: Diagnosis and Treatment. Vol. 19. Seattle: IASP Press, 2001.

31. Craig KD, Lilley CM, Gilbert CA. Social barriers to optimal pain management in infants, children, and adolescents. Clin J Pain 1996; 12:232–242.
32. Meyer B, Pilkonis PA, Krupnick JL, Egan MK, Simmens SJ, Sotsky SM. Treatment expectancies, patient alliance, and outcome: further analyses from the national institute of mental health treatment of depression collaborative research program. J Consult Clin Psychol 2002; 70:1051–1055.
33. Brown SC. Cancer pain and palliative care in children. In: Schmidt RF, Willis WD, eds. Encyclopedic Reference of Pain. New York: Springer-Verlag. 2006.
34. Collins J, Weisman SJ. Management of pain in childhood cancer. In: Schechter NL, Berde C, Yaster M, eds. Pain in Infants, Children, and Adolescents. 2nd ed. Lippincott: Williams & Wilkins, 2003:517–538.
35. Bioethics Committee, Canadian Pediatric Society. Treatment decisions regarding infants, children and adolescents. Pediatr Child Health 2004; 9:99–103.
36. Nolan K. Ethical issues in pediatric pain management. In: Schechter NL, Berde CB, Yaster M, eds. Pain in Infants, Children, and Adolescents. Baltimore: Williams & Wilkins, 1993:123–132.
37. Committee on Bioethics, American Academy of Pediatrics. Informed consent, parental permission, and assent in pediatric practice. Pediatr 1995; 95:314–317.
38. Rylance G. Editorial: making decisions with children. Br Med J 1996; 312:794–796.
39. Fundudis T. Consent issues in medico-legal procedures: how competent are children to make their own decisions? Child Adolesc Ment Health 2003; 8:18–22.
40. Beahrs JO, Gutheil TG. Informed consent in psychotherapy. Am J Psychiatry 2001; 158:4–10.
41. Pain Assessment and Management Standards—Hospitals. Joint Commission on Accreditation of HealthCare Organizations webpage. Available at: http://www.jcrinc.com/subscribers/printview.asp. Accessed February 7, 2006.

6 Ethical Considerations in the Management of Chronic Pain in Older Adults

Raymond C. Tait

Department of Psychiatry, Saint Louis University School of Medicine, St. Louis, Missouri, U.S.A.

INTRODUCTION

The American Medical Association has enumerated principles relevant to the practice of medicine, the first of which states (1) "A physician shall be dedicated to providing competent medical care, with compassion and respect for human dignity and rights." Relative to this principle, the effective management of pain in an older adult, undertaken in order to reduce suffering and to improve quality of life, clearly qualifies as an ethical enterprise. In fact, this chapter is predicated on the assumption that ethical pain care is largely synonymous with effective pain management. Nonetheless, as the following pages will describe, there are a number of obstacles to the effective management of pain in older adults, such that ethical pain care for the geriatric patient continues to represent a clinical challenge to the health care provider.

A recent article devoted to the application of ethics to the practice of pain medicine recognizes the complex ethical dilemmas that have emerged in this field (1). The article was written to provide "a roadmap that allows us to keep practicing in the face of an increasingly complex—and often confusing and contradictory—environment without losing our way...." (2). The American Academy of Pain Medicine (AAPM) statement describes conflicting ethical requirements associated with the array of audiences with which the pain specialist is required to interact, including patients, peers, and a variety of societal agents (e.g., the courts and insurance carriers).

Of the possible audiences, this chapter will focus on patients and, of those, only older adults. Further, its primary concern involves those with persistent, rather than acute pain conditions. There are two reasons for the focus on persistent pain: (i) it is common in older adults, secondary to its association with many diseases of aging (3), and (ii) its management often involves attention to a complex array of factors, some of which require ethical consideration. Although the goals of this chapter are narrower in scope than those described by AAPM, nonetheless, the chapter demonstrates that the roadmap to ethical, effective pain management in older adults has its own share of confusing and sometimes contradictory elements.

While the roadmap to effective pain management may be difficult to discern, its end point (effective pain management, improved quality of life) is arguably more important for this age group than for any other. Surveys have shown that a high proportion of older adults experience persistent pain relative to other age groups, secondary to the many diseases (e.g., cancer, diabetes, and arthritis) associated with aging (3,4). In long-term care (LTC) settings, persistent pain is even more prevalent, affecting up to four of every five residents (5,6). Further, persistent pain often is associated with a number of comorbid conditions in older adults, including depression (7,8), disability (9), and social isolation (10). Therefore, inadequately treated pain can snowball into a complex of problems that can increase morbidity (11) and, in some cases, mortality (12).

The chapter is organized around the seminal work on health care ethics from Georgetown University, the "Georgetown Mantra" (13). That work enunciated four principles to guide health care decisions: beneficence, nonmaleficence, autonomy, and justice. These principles subsequently were subsumed into three (the principles of beneficence and nonmaleficence were combined as two sides of one coin) that were incorporated into the Belmont Report (14): (i) autonomy, (ii) beneficence/nonmaleficence, and (iii) justice. While the latter three principles have been used primarily as guides for clinical research, they apply equally well to practice, making them a good structure for organizing the content of the chapter.

The following section outlines general pain management issues regarding older adults relative to each of the three principles. Subsequent sections speak to the issues in more detail. Those sections address issues relevant not only to clinical practice, but also to clinical research that is needed if we are to elevate clinical practice to levels that meet the highest ethical standards. Finally, the chapter ends with a general consideration of the role of ethics as a guide to clinical research and practice in the older adult population.

THE BELMONT REPORT

The National Commission for the Protection of Human Subjects of Biomedical and Behavioral Research, formed as part of the National Research Act in 1974, developed guidelines regarding the ethical conduct of research that are derived from the three core principles referenced above. The first of the principles, involving respect for autonomy, subsumes two ethical imperatives: (i) that any person should be viewed and treated as an autonomous agent, capable of informed deliberation and choice, and (ii) that persons who are incapable of autonomous decision making for any of a variety of reasons (e.g., illness, disability, circumstance) deserve protections to ensure that decisions are made with respect for their well-being. Clearly, each of these imperatives is consistent with medical practice. Few would argue with the proposition that patients should be treated with respect for their capacity to make independent decisions in regard to their health care. Indeed, current medical practice treats the patient as a partner in treatment, and the patient's input is a crucial element of that practice (15). Further, in regard to vulnerable patients whose capacity for independent decision making is compromised (e.g., a young child, a person who sustained a serious head injury, a patient with dementia), few would dispute that family members and/or other legally authorized representatives should be involved whenever possible in making decisions, especially when the benefits of a decision must be weighed against significant risks.

Although few would argue with either of the above standards, they are of particular importance when treating older adults in pain. The bedrock of effective pain management involves the patient-provider partnership (16), and the evaluation of treatment effectiveness is largely based on patient reports (and provider observations). Consistent with such a partnership, the first imperative speaks to the importance of eliciting and respecting patient reports (e.g., regarding levels of pain and function) in the medical encounter. The second imperative speaks to issues more specific to pain management in older adults whose decisional (and reporting) capacity has been compromised by ill health and/or cognitive impairment. For these patients, who lack a vital channel for pain evaluation (valid self-report), the principle raises questions as to how a provider should make rational treatment decisions, especially because family members or guardians will have access to little (if any) additional information regarding the internal state of the patient that is not also available to the provider.

The second principle, beneficence, speaks to a provider's duty to balance possible benefits against risks in treatment. As with the first principle, few would dispute that this duty is integral to the practice of medicine. The practice becomes more complicated, however, when applied to the management of pain in older adults, secondary to issues related to the ancillary principle, nonmaleficence. Such issues include the greater number of health-related complications found in older adults experiencing pain (3), as well as the greater risk for drug–drug interactions and/or serious drug side effects secondary to different pharmacodynamics and pharmacokinetics in older adults (17). Balancing benefit against risk is even more challenging when treating older adults with cognitive compromise; lacking clear information on changes in pain intensity associated with treatment, it is extremely difficult to determine how a provider should evaluate treatment benefits against the risks of a given treatment. Finally, challenges to the principle of beneficence occur when an older adult is facing the end of life. In particular, it can be difficult to decide when the benefits of treatment directed at the cause(s) of illness are outweighed by the benefits of comfort-oriented care, of which adequate pain control is a prime consideration.

The principle of justice, primarily considered in the context of a fair distribution of benefits and risks, is the third and final organizing principle. The application of this principle to general medical practice is exemplified by the ongoing campaign to reduce treatment disparities related to sociodemographic factors such as race, ethnicity, socioeconomic status, etc. A detailed analysis of this issue may be found in Dr. Carmen Green's chapter in this text. The principle takes on more salience in the context of treating older adults in pain. Not only do disparities related to sociodemographic factors apply to older adults (18), but also there is evidence that pain is generally undertreated in older adults (19–22), possibly secondary to attitudes reflecting "ageism (23)." "...a deep and profound prejudice against the elderly, which...allows the younger generations to see older people as different from themselves." This section of the chapter addresses shortfalls in pain care relative to the ethical principle that equitable treatment should be provided to all patients. Disparities in treatment secondary to sociodemographic factors clearly violate this principle.

RESPECT FOR AUTONOMY

General Considerations
Under the best of circumstances, assessing pain, especially pain of an extended duration, is a challenging enterprise. While objective diagnostic information is important to its assessment, especially in acute pain conditions, it has less value in the assessment of chronic pain (24,25). This is particularly so in older adults where degenerative changes associated with aging can make it difficult to determine whether findings are "normal" relative to aging processes or, instead,

reflect pathology (26). Further, it is well recognized that patients can report pain levels of high intensity in the absence of clear diagnostic findings (27), as well as little or no pain in the presence of obvious lesions (28).

The uncertain association between diagnostic test results and reported pain intensity underscores the importance of provider judgments in the assessment of clinical pain of a chronic nature (29). Those judgments primarily derive from a *medical encounter* and may be influenced by provider attributes (e.g., experience and training), elements of the patient's presentation, and aspects of the environment in which the medical encounter occurs. Any and all of these factors can influence judgments of pain. While some would argue that the latter analysis does not adequately value the contribution of diagnostic test results to pain assessment (as is certainly true in the evaluation of acute pain), few would argue against the importance of the medical encounter in assessing chronic pain effectively. Because of the importance of the medical encounter, the principle of respect for autonomy (and its implied validation of the autonomous agent's experience) is central if assessment is to accurately reflect the experience of the person in pain and treatment is to reduce consequent suffering.

That said, a number of factors have been identified that may lead health care providers to invalidate or discount pain that is reported to them by patients of any age. Such factors include the availability of medical evidence supporting the pain complaint (30), questions as to who bears responsibility for the circumstances of pain onset (31), the degree to which a provider is positively or negatively valenced toward the patient (32), and patient characteristics such as race/ethnicity and socioeconomic status (33,34). In addition, providers seem to discount pain that is reported at high levels relative to that reported at lower levels (31,35).

Clearly, because the medical encounter is central to effective pain assessment and management, the social psychological factors described above cannot be avoided. Moreover, to the degree that judgments of pain intensity influence decisions about treatment, those factors represent threats to effective pain management. Hence, it is crucial that pain management providers be aware of these influences and take steps to reduce their potential impact on their clinical judgments. Most importantly, providers should allocate sufficient time to conduct a thorough assessment. A thorough assessment is less vulnerable to social psychological biases, while those biases are magnified when time urgency limits the information upon which judgments are based (36).

Challenges Specific to Older Adults
While the challenges described above also apply to pain management in older adults, geriatric pain management is further complicated by two additional factors. One involves questions regarding whether geriatric patients underreport levels of pain intensity and, if so, under what conditions (37). The second involves the complications involved in the assessment and treatment of pain in patients with neurocognitive compromise (38,39). Each of these is addressed in more detail below.

The perception that older adults underreport pain is well documented. For example, there are reports of "silent" heart attacks in this age group, as well as evidence of underreporting pain secondary to intra-abdominal infections (40,41). These and other data suggest that older adults may be less sensitive to visceral pain than other age groups (26,37). For the vast majority of painful conditions (e.g., musculoskeletal and postoperative), however, research shows no differences in pain sensitivity between older and younger adults (26,37). Hence, the experimental data do not support the general premise that older adults experience pain less intensely than younger adults.

Despite the experimental literature, the clinical literature continues to describe differences in reported pain severity for older adults in clinical settings (42). Explanations for the apparent tendency of older adults to underreport pain are largely conjectural, and many center on dynamics of the patient-provider relationship. For example, it is possible that older adults simply assume that the health care provider knows that pain is present, so that further description of pain is unnecessary. Alternatively, they may fear the prospect of diagnostic testing or possible hospitalization if significant levels of pain are reported (42). Further, especially if they are in a dependent relationship with the provider (43), they may want to be "good patients" and downplay anything they perceive as a complaint (e.g., about poorly controlled symptoms such as pain).

Alternative explanations of the apparent tendency of older adults to underreport pain invoke cognitive processes, one of which centers on the use of social comparisons (44). Social comparisons are used when people attempt to evaluate the significance of an experience: experiences that are viewed as consistent with those of others elicit less attention than do experiences that are inconsistent with others (45). Thus, the older adults who believe that pain is a natural consequence of aging may attach less significance to it and may minimize their reports of it. Another cognitive explanation involves semantics: older adults may define "pain" differently than younger adults. For example, I recently was asked to evaluate pain in an 80-year-old Caucasian female who had been hospitalized following a fall. When asked to rate her pain on a modified (0–100 point) VAS scale, she reported a pain level of "0." When questioned further about this rating (in the context of rather obvious pain behaviors), she noted that, had I asked her to rate "stiffness," she would have reported it to be "100."

If patient-provider communication about pain is compromised by factors such as those described above, communication problems are even more pronounced in patients with neurocognitive deficits. The problems are especially prominent in patients whose deficits are of such severity that they compromise their ability to describe an internal state such as pain. Although the problem of effectively assessing and treating pain in this patient group is well recognized, they remain particularly vulnerable to undertreatment (22,39,46). Some strides have been made in assessing pain among those with mild-to-moderate cognitive impairment; it is clear not only that their self-reported levels of pain intensity are largely valid (6,47), but also that these levels can be reliably assessed with self-report instruments (38,48).

Pain assessment guidelines have been proposed based on reporting differences among geriatric patients with little or no impairment versus those with moderate impairment. For older adults in the former group, the best estimate of *actual* pain derived from retrospective report involves averaging estimates of *usual* and *least* pain (an estimating process consistent with that recommended with younger adults) (49). For older adults with moderate levels of impairment, the best estimate of actual pain derives from retrospective ratings of *usual* and *worst* pain. The latter formulas, while still somewhat preliminary, may provide the practitioners with a proxy for daily pain assessments upon which they can base reasonable pain treatment decisions.

Although pain can be assessed by self-report in older adults with mild-to-moderate cognitive impairment, the reliability of those self-reports diminishes as impairment progresses (48). Among older adults with severe cognitive impairment, of course, self-report is of little or no value. Alternative approaches to assessment and treatment, however, have proved problematic. Most alternative approaches posit a relationship between pain severity and behaviors reflecting agitation (50–52), assuming that an increase in the former will occasion an increase in the latter in a manner consistent with that observed in young children (53). Unfortunately, older adults with advanced dementia respond variably to pain: although some respond with agitation, others respond passively and become more withdrawn (54).

Because of the variable responses to pain described above, unidimensional rating instruments (e.g., those that equate agitation with pain) are only selectively relevant. Several recent studies, each involving behavioral observations incorporated into analgesic trials, illustrate this point. These trials used well-accepted instruments for rating agitation in the nursing home, the Cohen-Mansfield Agitation Inventory (CMAI) (55) and the Discomfort Scale for Diseases of the Alzheimer's Type (56). Nonetheless, the results failed to show significant differences in behavior among patients during the analgesic phase of the trial compared to behavior during the placebo phase (50,52).

A similarly designed trial that looked both at behavioral measures of agitation and a broader range of behaviors yielded somewhat different results (57). In regard to agitation, measured with the CMAI, the results were comparable to those of the studies described above: there was no analgesic effect. In regard to a broader range of behaviors (assessed with Dementia Care Mapping) (58), the results showed that patients in the analgesic phase of the trial were more active than they were in the placebo phase. The activity increase, however, involved both prosocial behavior (e.g., direct social involvement) and behavior reflecting agitation (e.g., talking to oneself).

While the latter three studies differed in other ways that preclude a direct comparison of findings, the results suggest that observational strategies that are linked to analgesic interventions have potential to improve assessment and treatment in severely demented patients with pain. At the level of clinical practice, any change in behavior subsequent to the initiation of an analgesic is noteworthy and may signal the need to introduce routine analgesic administration. From the research perspective, observational methodologies linked to an analgesic trial should examine a broader swath of behavior than agitation.

BENEFICENCE

Pharmacotherapy Considerations

As noted earlier, the application of the principle of beneficence to older adults in pain appears straightforward: effective management of pain clearly should provide benefit to the patient whose pain is of a severity such that it interferes with general levels of activity and diminishes quality of life. To a degree that is not found in other patient populations, however, the general principle of beneficence is offset in older adults by its corollary, nonmaleficence. Nonmaleficence, the injunction to do no harm, requires that the health care provider balance pain-related treatment considerations against side effects, drug–drug interactions, and the impact of treatment on comorbidities, all issues that are more common in older adults (59,60).

This dilemma is exemplified by recent events associated with the use of a class of nonsteroidal drugs [cyclooxygenase (COX-2) inhibitors] in patients with chronic pain secondary to arthritis. These compounds were developed in order to provide the analgesic benefits associated with standard nonsteroidal anti-inflammatory drugs, while reducing the level of gastrointestinal (GI) and other systemic effects secondary to their more targeted inhibitory actions on inflammation-related prostaglandin synthesis (61,62). The putatively lower side effect profile of COX-2 inhibitors led to strong uptake among health care providers, especially those working with older adults (63).

Of course, the controversy surrounding this class of drugs ultimately had little to do with GI side effects. Instead, it involved the increased risk that patients incurred for thrombotic cardiovascular events, initially linked to the use of rofecoxib. Such risks were suggested in an early study that compared rofecoxib to naproxen (64); they were confirmed by subsequent analyzes by the Food and Drug Administration (FDA) that suggested that rofecoxib caused between 88,000 and 139,000 myocardial infarctions over the five years that it was on the market (65).

Two elements of this drama hold particular relevance to issues of beneficence in older adults. First, this age group is most vulnerable to the cardiac events that led to the class of drugs being withdrawn (violating the principle of nonmaleficence). Second, despite the increased risk of cardiovascular events for patients taking COX-2 inhibitors, many patients complained when they had to discontinue the medications. These patients were willing to trade the cardiac risks for the pain relief and increased quality of life provided to them by these medications. While their argument became academic when the FDA pulled the COX-2 inhibitors from the market, their dilemma exemplifies the risk/reward issues that can characterize treatment in this age group.

While not so publicized, the beneficence/nonmaleficence principle also applies to the use of opioids in older adults, especially in LTC settings. As noted previously, pain is prevalent in LTC, affecting as many as 80% of residents (6,66). Moreover, it often is poorly controlled, both among those capable of self-report (67) and those whose capacity to report pain is compromised (39). In combination with other health problems common to LTC residents, medical decisions regarding the use of analgesics can be complicated, especially for residents who demonstrate levels of pain intensity beyond the mild-to-moderate range (i.e., those for whom routine acetaminophen is inadequate).

Numerous treatment heuristics, both pharmacologic and nonpharmacologic, have been proposed for patients in the latter group (54,68). Of the pharmacologic approaches, many involve the use of psychotropics with analgesic properties (e.g., amitryptiline) and/or anticonvulsants (e.g., carbamazapine). While potentially appropriate, each of the latter medications demonstrates significant side effects and drug–drug interactions that complicate their use. In light of these considerations, arguments have been advanced in favor of long-term opioids (59), largely because they can be managed to maximize their analgesic benefits, while minimizing complications associated with their well-known side effects (e.g., constipation and confusion). Despite the putative advantages of this class of medications, opioids remain relatively underused in older adults secondary to concerns shared by providers, patients, and families.

A recent case exemplifies some of these issues. An 82-year-old white female was admitted to a geriatric psychiatry inpatient service following a suicide attempt in which she shot herself in the abdomen with a 0.22 caliber pistol. The circumstances that led to the suicide attempt relate to the recent retirement of her primary care physician of many years, who transferred her care to a younger colleague. The patient had long-standing abdominal pain of indeterminate origin that had been successfully managed with propoxyphene, one tablet q.i.d. prn. While this treatment had provided adequate pain control with no escalating dosage for years, the patient's new physician was uncomfortable with the patient's propoxyphene use, particularly because it is not indicated for long-term use (58). Consequently, the new physician discontinued the opioid and instituted a course of antidepressant therapy. The patient shot herself when she derived no benefit from the antidepressant regimen and was told that her previous propoxyphene regimen would not be reinstated. After being stabilized medically, a psychiatric transfer was made, and numerous psychotropic combinations were tried without appreciable benefit. Ultimately, the treating psychiatrist recognized that, while propoxyphene was far from an ideal analgesic, its benefits could not be denied. After it was reinitiated, the patient was discharged home to independent living and returned to her former levels of activity.

Neurocognitive Deficits

As with the principle of autonomy, the principle of beneficence is tested when treating pain in older adults with severe cognitive impairment. As noted in the previous section, pain can elicit such divergent responses as agitation and withdrawal. In the former case, the cause of agitation often can be difficult to identify. Consequently, agitation has been managed with frontline psychotropics to treat the putative neuropsychiatric cause, despite evidence that unattended pain commonly occasions agitation (68). Clearly, when undertreated pain underlies a behavioral disturbance, the application of a chemical straitjacket that suppresses agitation without treating the cause fails to meet the standard of beneficence. Fortunately, nursing home practice has become more sensitive to the need to rule out undertreated pain before initiating psychotropics (51,68).

If pain is increasingly recognized as a possible cause of agitation, its role in mediating passivity and/or withdrawal is less well recognized. Indeed, inactive or withdrawn patients are frequently managed observationally in nursing homes; they are brought out of their rooms to facilitate their observation from a nursing station. When inactivity is secondary to pain, more effective pain control can promote increased activity, interaction, and self-care (57). While increased levels of activity sometimes can be disruptive and require additional behavioral management, the principle of beneficence suggests that, on balance, the benefits of more effective pain control outweigh the risks.

A recent case from the latter study (57) illustrates these points. A 95-year-old white female was enrolled into a double blind, crossover trial in which the behavioral effects of an analgesic were compared to those of placebo in severely demented, nursing home patients with significant joint pathology. When in the placebo phase of the study, she exhibited her customary behavior, sitting on a couch beside the nursing station. Her only notable activity involved less-than-subtle flirting with an 83-year-old male (who did not reciprocate her affections) whenever he passed within reach. In the analgesic phase of the trial, however, her active range increased to such a degree that she was capable of demonstrating her affection at various locations on the nursing unit. While she clearly required more staff attention when her mobility increased, it was apparent that her quality of life had improved. When the trial ended, however, her physician did not maintain her on the analgesic, and she returned to her customary location in front of the nursing station.

Palliative Care

The issue of palliative care at the end of life is addressed comprehensively elsewhere in this book. Nonetheless, the issue is particularly relevant to this age group and merits some consideration in this chapter, although the comments are limited only to matters relevant to the issue of beneficence. A substantial subgroup of older adults will depend upon the delivery of palliative care if they are to experience reasonable comfort in their final days (69). Despite the availability of technology that can deliver such care in the vast majority of cases, there is evidence that pain control is adequate in only about 50% of patients in their final days of life (70). This statistic is a stark indicator that palliative care falls short of reasonable ethical standards in an unacceptable number of patients.

Of course, there are many barriers to effective palliative care at the end of life, involving system, patient, and provider factors, many of which have been discussed in several recent volumes (71,72). Of the many barriers, perhaps the one most relevant to beneficence involves the issue of curative versus comfort treatment, particularly the point at which one should give way to the other. Palliative care specialists aver that this distinction is specious: they advocate attention to both, arguing that the pursuit of one does not preclude the other. Nonetheless, in medical practice the decision to focus on comfort measures often occurs only after curative measures have failed (72). Even then, the decision often comes late in the process despite recent legislation (i.e., intractable pain statutes) aimed at promoting earlier, more effective symptom control (73).

Provider reluctance to acknowledge the need for comfort care is illustrated by a fellow investigator's recent experience with an intervention designed to address spiritual, emotional, and practical issues often associated with the end of life. The study projected an enrollment of approximately 350 subjects, and considerable effort was spent educating cardiologists, oncologists, geriatricians, and other physicians in order to facilitate appropriate enrollment. When the study closed three years later, enrollment totaled 72 patients, despite repeated efforts by the investigator to address the enrollment problem. He was informed that many of the physicians did not want to address end-of-life issues with patients, fearing that this would reduce their optimism for life-prolonging treatment and undermine its effectiveness.

JUSTICE

The principle of justice, involving the fair distribution of benefits and risks, applies to two broad issues relevant to older adults in pain. One issue involves attitudes toward older adults that may negatively impact clinical decisions. The second involves attitudes toward subgroups of the older adult population that may eventuate in disparities in pain treatment.

Ageism

Prejudicial attitudes toward older adults ("ageism") contribute to treatment decisions that negatively impact health care across a variety of medical disorders (74), including those associated with chronic pain. Ageism is reflected in a tendency for health care providers to discount symptoms associated with medical disorders, often translating into less aggressive treatment for older adults than for younger adults who present with similar symptoms. Among other factors, such tendencies are likely to underlie the relative infrequency with which older adults are referred to specialty pain clinics for the treatment of chronic pain (75), despite evidence indicating that they are likely to benefit as much as younger adults from the multidisciplinary treatment often provided by such clinics (75,76).

The study to understand prognoses and preferences for outcomes and risks of treatment (SUPPORT) provides direct evidence of undertreatment of pain in older adults (19). Among other findings, that study documented low levels of satisfaction with pain treatment among critically ill older adults. To improve the quality of pain care, a variety of interventions were implemented and studied (e.g., staff education and the display of pain intensity ratings at the bedside). Following the interventions, satisfaction with pain treatment again was assessed, but found to be no better than before. Of course, since the time of the SUPPORT study, the Joint Commission for Accreditation of Healthcare Organizations has identified pain as a "fifth vital sign," and practice standards have been established that facilitate improved pain management in hospital settings. While the latter developments have addressed the most obvious shortcomings in pain care for this vulnerable patient group, it is noteworthy that administrative fiat, rather than provider education, was required to improve that care.

Treatment Disparities

Because ethical issues related to racial/ethnic disparities are addressed elsewhere in this volume, they are only noted here. Nonetheless, it is important to acknowledge that disparities in the provision of health care, including pain management, have been documented for a variety of sociodemographic variables, including race/ethnicity (33,36), socioeconomic status (36), and, as noted above, older age (75). Although age has not been a primary focus in disparities research, there is evidence that treatment disparities related to race/ethnicity exist within the older age group (18,77). Addressing racial/ethnic inequities in pain management constitutes a significant ethical challenge for pain practitioners, albeit one that has gone largely unrecognized until recently (78).

Of course, correcting disparities in pain care requires a clear understanding of factors that mediate and maintain them. Unfortunately, we are only in the early stages of that understanding. At the patient-provider level, it is likely that several factors contribute to disparate care, including negative patient expectations of treatment (79), negative provider stereotyping of patients (36,80), and nonparticipative patient-provider interactions (15). Lacking a clear prescription for ways to eliminate disparities in pain care, the most effective strategy has been noted previously: to allocate sufficient time to conduct a thorough assessment. Not only are more-detailed assessments less vulnerable to psychological biases, but also they directly address dysfunctional interaction patterns that have been implicated in the disparities literature. Further, in light of the communication problems sometimes associated with older age, allocating adequate time for assessment may be particularly important when treating these patients.

Obviously, disparities in pain treatment are related to more than just the medical encounter. Other elements that contribute to racial/ethnic disparities in pain care include differences in access to health care (81), differences in the availability of opioid analgesics (82,83), and biopsychosocial stresses endemic to societal prejudice (84). Hence, the provider, who is invested in the just delivery of health care services will face challenges at multiple levels. Until attention is provided at each level, steps to address inequities at the patient-provider level will meet with only limited success.

FUTURE DIRECTIONS: AN ETHICAL COMPASS

Much as the principles of autonomy, beneficence, and justice have served as a useful framework against which to view current pain management practices in older adults, they serve to frame directions for future improvements in clinical care and for clinical research. From an autonomy perspective (i.e., respecting the patient's role as a partner in treatment), there is a general need for more clearly defined practice standards, especially as they relate to the assessment of geriatric pain, both in outpatient and LTC settings. There is little doubt that the effectiveness of pain care improves when a thorough evaluation is made of the three core dimensions of the pain experience: pain intensity, pain-related disability, and psychological distress. Establishing evidence-based standards to guide assessment, including the identification/development of instruments for patients with mild-to-moderate cognitive deficits, would be particularly helpful for outpatient settings.

The most pressing need, however, involves the development of easily administered protocols for assessing pain in older adults with severe neurocognitive deficits. Without effective pain assessment for this group, it is not only difficult to identify patients in need of treatment, but it is also difficult to assess the effectiveness of any intervention that is implemented. Toward this end, there is a great need for research-driven protocols. Because of the many complications associated with research conducted in LTC settings (85) and the inconsistencies reported in the research to date, progress in this area has been limited. Substantive progress, especially in the development of reliable protocols that can be administered with relative ease (recognizing the practical limitations associated with staffing shortages common in LTC settings), is likely to be limited by funding restrictions. Notwithstanding this obstacle, we clearly need to make progress if we are to meet our ethical imperative to manage pain and improve the quality of life of the 2.2 million citizens of the United States (and countless others outside the United States) who reside in LTC settings.

In terms of beneficence/nonmaleficence, there is a need for more rational management of the analgesics currently available, including opioid analgesics. To accomplish this goal, legislative balance is needed such that undertreatment of pain is accorded the same level of concern that overtreatment has received, a process that is complicated by current administrative and political trends. Changes in patient and provider attitudes toward the rational delivery of palliative care also are needed, especially attitudes that interfere with integration/merging of life-prolonging and palliative treatments. Suggestions as to how to accomplish these changes already have been articulated (72); concrete steps toward implementation now are needed.

Finally, the principle of justice demands attention to ageist attitudes and to inequities in care associated with sociodemographic boundaries, prevalent across all levels of society. Such attitudes militate against ethically responsible, effective pain management through inattention to clinically significant levels of pain and pain-related dysfunction. Current clinical practice can be improved by emphasizing thorough assessment, making greater use of adjunct health care providers (e.g., RNs, MSWs, and PhDs) who are trained and can take the time required for comprehensive assessment. Clinical pain research also can contribute to remedying treatment disparities, although it must focus more closely on the social psychology of the medical encounter if it is to do so. Hopefully, clinical and research progress will inform decisions made and programs administered at the public policy level.

In the meantime, despite our best intentions and ongoing advances in the field of pain management, we continue to fall short. Indeed, in some areas (e.g., assessing and treating pain among those with severe cognitive impairment) we have barely started. Of course, we cannot abrogate our ethical responsibility to older adults in pain until further progress is made. Indeed, this chapter is predicated upon the assumption that we provide ethical care whenever we deliver responsible and effective pain management to each older adult to the best of our current abilities, recognizing that we will do better as the field moves forward. Hopefully, roadmaps, such as that proposed in this chapter, will help to guide further progress toward the ideal of ethically sensitive, effective pain care for the older adult population.

REFERENCES

1. AAPM Council on Ethics. Ethics charter from American academy of pain medicine. Pain Med 2005; 6:203–212.
2. DuBois MY. The birth of an ethics charter for pain medicine. Pain Med 2005; 6: 201–202.
3. Ferrell BA. Overview of aging and pain. In: Ferrell BR, Ferrell BA, eds. Pain in the Elderly. Seattle: IASP Press, 1996:1–10.
4. Mobily P, Herr K, Clark K, Wallace R. An epidemiologic analysis of pain in the elderly: the Iowa 65+ rural health study. J Aging Health 1994; 6:129–154.
5. Ferrell BA, Ferrell BR, Osterweil D. Pain in the nursing home. J Amer Geriatr Soc 1990; 38:409–414.
6. Parmelee PA, Smith BD, Katz IR. Pain complaints and cognitive status among elderly institution residents. J Amer Geriatr Soc 1993; 41:517–522.
7. Parmelee PA, Katz IR, Lawton MP. The relation of pain to depression among institutionalized aged. J Gerontol Psychol Sci 1991; 46:P15–P21.
8. Williamson GM, Schulz R. Activity restriction mediates the association between pain and depressed affect: a study of younger and older adult cancer patients. Psychol Aging 1995; 10:369–378.
9. Scudds RJ, Robertson JM. Empirical evidence of the association between the presence of musculoskeletal pain and physical disability in community dwelling senior citizens. Pain 1998; 75:229–235.
10. Newsom JT, Schulz R. Social support as a mediator in the relation between functional status and quality of life in older adults. Psychol Aging 1996; 11:34–44.
11. Moss MS, Lawton P, Glicksman A. The role of pain in the last year of life of older persons. J Gerontol Psychol Sci 1991; 46:P51–P57.
12. Lissner L, Bengtsson C, Bjorkelund C, Wedel H. Physical activity levels and changes in relation to longevity. Am J Epidemiol 1996; 143:54–62.
13. Beauchamp T, Childress J. Principles of Biomedical Ethics. 4th ed. Oxford, England: Oxford University Press, 1994.
14. National Commission for the Protection of Human Subjects of Biomedical and Behavioral Research. The Belmont Report: Ethical Principles and Guidelines for the Protection

of Human Subjects of Research. Washington, D.C.: DHEW Publication No. (OS) 78–0012, 1978.

15. Cooper-Patrick L, Gallo JJ, Gonzales JJ, et al. Race, gender, and partnership in the patient-physician relationship. JAMA 1999; 282:583–589.
16. Sternbach RA. Pain Patients: Traits and Treatments. New York: Academic Press, 1974.
17. Young RC, Meyers BS. Psychopharmacology. In: Sadavoy J, Lazarus LW, Jarvik LF, Grossberg GT, eds. Comprehensive Review of Geriatric Psychiatry—II. Washington, D.C.: American Psychiatric Press, 1996:755–817.
18. Bernabei R, Gambassi G, Lapane K, et al. Management of pain in elderly patients with cancer. SAGE Study Group. JAMA 1998; 279:1877–1882.
19. Desbiens NA, Wu AW, Broste SK, et al. Pain and satisfaction with pain control in seriously ill hospitalized adults: findings from the SUPPORT research investigations. Crit Care Med 1996; 24:1953–1961.
20. Feldt KS, Ryden MB, Iles S. Treatment of pain in cognitively impaired compared with cognitively intact older patients with hip fracture. J Am Geriatr Soc 1998; 46: 1079–1085.
21. McCaffery M, Ferrell BR. Patient age: does it affect your pain-control decisions? Nursing 1991; 21:44–48.
22. Tait RC, Chibnall JT. Pain in older subacute care patients: associations with clinical status and treatment. Pain Med 2002; 3:231–239.
23. Butler RN. Age-ism: another form of bigotry. Gerontologist 1969; 9:243–246.
24. Jacobson L, Mariano AJ. General considerations of chronic pain. In: Loeser JD, Butler SH, Chapman CR, Turk DC, eds. Bonica's Management of Pain. 3rd ed. New York: Lippincott Williams Wilkins, 2001:241–254.
25. Rudy TE, Turk DC, Brena SF. Differential utility of medical procedures in the assessment of chronic pain patients. Pain 1988; 34:53–60.
26. Harkins SW. Aging and pain. In: Loeser JD, Butler SH, Chapman CR, Turk DC, eds. Bonica's Management of Pain. 3rd ed. New York: Lippincott, Williams & Wilkins, 2001:813–823.
27. Hadler NM. Occupational Musculoskeletal Disorders. 3rd ed. New York: Lippincott, Williams & Wilkins, 2005.
28. Stadnik TW, Lee RR, Coen HL, et al. Annular tears and disk herniation: prevalence and contrast enhancement on MR images in the absence of low back pain or sciatica. Radiology 1998; 206:49–55.
29. Tait RC, Chibnall JT. Symptom judgments in patients with intractable pain. Adv Med Psychother Psychodiag 1997; 9:91–105.
30. Chibnall JT, Tait RC, Ross L. Effects of medical evidence and reported level of pain on medical symptom judgments. J Behav Med 1997; 20:257–271.
31. Tait RC, Chibnall JT. Observer perceptions of chronic low back pain. J Appl Soc Psychol 1994; 24:415–431.
32. Chibnall JT, Tait RC. Observer perceptions of low back pain: effects of pain report and other contextual factors. J Appl Soc Psychol 1995; 25:418–439.
33. Green CR, Anderson KO, Baker TA, et al. The unequal burden of pain: confronting racial and ethnic disparities in pain. Pain Med 2003; 4:277–294.
34. Tait RC, Chibnall JT, Andresen EM, Hadler NT. Management of occupational back injuries: differences among African Americans and Caucasians. Pain 2004; 112:389–396.
35. Grossman SA, Sheidler VR, Swedeen K, Mucenski J, Piantadosi S. Correlation of patient and caregiver ratings of cancer pain. J Pain Symp Manage 1991; 6:53–57.
36. Smedley BD, Stith AY, Nelson AR, eds. Unequal treatment: confronting racial and ethnic disparities in health care. In: Committee on Understanding and Eliminating Racial and Ethnic Disparities in Health Care. Institute of Medicine of the National Academies. Washington, D.C.: The National Academies Press, 2002.
37. Harkins SW. What is unique about the older adult's pain experience? In: Weiner DK, Herr K, Rudy TE, eds. Persistent Pain in Older Adults: An Interdisciplinary Guide for Treatment. New York: Springer Publishing Co., 2002:4–17.
38. Scherder E, Oosterman J, Swaab D, et al. Recent developments in pain in dementia. BMJ 2005; 330:461–464.

39. Sengstaken EA, King SA. The problems of pain and its detection among geriatric nursing home residents. J Am Geriatr Soc 1993; 41:541–544.

40. Barsky AJ, Hochstrasser B, Coles NA, Zisfein J, O'Donnell C, Eagle KA. Silent myocardial ischemia: is the person or the event silent? JAMA 1990; 264:1132–1135.

41. Norman DC, Yoshikawa TT. Intraabdominal infections in the elderly. J Am Geriatr Soc 1983; 31:677–684.

42. Herr K, Garand L. Assessment and measurement of pain in older adults. Clinics Geriatr Med 2001; 17:457–478.

43. Cassell E. The nature of suffering and the goals of medicine. N Engl J Med 1982; 306:639–645.

44. Festinger L. A theory of social comparison processes. Hum Relat 1954; 7:117–140.

45. Hill MG, Weary G, Hildebrand-Saints L, Elbin SD. Social comparison of causal understandings. In: Harvey JH, Weary G, eds. Attribution: Basic Issues and Applications. New York: Academic Press, 1985:143–165.

46. Ferrell BA. Pain management in elderly people. J Am Geriat Soc 1991; 39:64–73.

47. Parmelee PA. Pain in cognitively impaired older persons. Clin Geriat Med 1996; 12: 473–487.

48. Chibnall JT, Tait RC. Pain assessment in cognitively impaired and unimpaired older adults: a comparison of four scales. Pain 2001; 92:173–186.

49. Jensen MP, McFarland CA. Increasing the reliability and validity of pain intensity measurement in chronic pain patients. Pain 1993; 55:195–203.

50. Buffum MD, Sands L, Miaskowski C, Brod M, Washburn A. A clinical trial of the effectiveness of regularly scheduled versus as-needed administration of acetaminophen in the management of discomfort in older adults with dementia. J Am Geriatr Soc 2004; 52:1093–1097.

51. Douzjian M, Wilson C, Schultz M, et al. A program to use pain control medication to reduce psychotropic drug use in residents with difficult behavior. Ann Long-Term Care 1998; 6:174–179.

52. Manfredi PL, Breuer B, Wallenstein S, Stegmann M, Bottomley G, Libow L. Opioid treatment for agitation in patients with advanced dementia. Int J Geriat Psychiat 2003; 18:700–705.

53. Hamers JPH, Abu-Saad HH, van den Hout MA, Halfens RJG, Kester ADM. The influence of children's vocal expressions, age, medical diagnosis and information obtained from parents on nurses' pain assessments and decisions regarding interventions. Pain 1996; 65:53–61.

54. Stein WM, Ferrell BA. Pain in the nursing home. Clin Geriatr Med 1996; 12:601–613.

55. Cohen-Mansfield J, Marx MS, Rosenthal AS. Dementia and agitation in nursing home residents: how are they related? Psychol Aging 1990; 5:3–8.

56. Hurley AC, Volicer BJ, Hanrahan PA, et al. Assessment of discomfort in advanced Alzheimer patients. Res Nurs Health 1992; 15:369–377.

57. Chibnall JT, Tait RC, Harmon B, Luebbert RA. Effect of acetaminophen on behavior, well-being, and psychotropic medication use in nursing home residents with moderate-to-severe dementia. J Am Geriatr Soc 2005; 53:1921–1929.

58. Kitwood T, Bredin K. A new approach to the evaluation of dementia care. J Adv Health Nurs Care 1992; 1:41–60.

59. Guay DRP, Lackner TE, Hanlon JT. Pharmacologic management: noninvasive modalities. In: Weiner DK, Herr K, Rudy TE, eds. Persistent Pain in Older Adults: An Interdisciplinary Guide for Treatment. New York: Springer Publishing Co., 2002:160–187.

60. Virani A, Mailis A, Shapiro LE, et al. Drug interactions in human neuropathic pain pharmacotherapy. Pain 1997; 73:3–13.

61. Miyoshi HR. Systemic nonopioid analgesics. In: Loeser JD, Butler SH, Chapman CR, Turk DC, eds. Bonica's Management of Pain. 3rd ed. New York: Lippincott, Williams & Wilkins, 2001:1667–1681.

62. Vane JR, Botting RM. New insights into the mode of action of anti-inflammatory drugs. Inflamm Res 1995; 44:1–10.

63. Brater DC. Effects of nonsteroidal anti-inflammatory drugs on renal function: focus on cyclooxygenase-2-selective inhibition. Am J Med 1999; 107(suppl 6A):65S–71S.

64. Bombardier C, Laine L, Reicin A, et al. Comparison of upper gastrointestinal toxicity of rofecoxib and naproxen in patients with rheumatoid arthritis. N Engl J Med 2000; 343: 1520–1528.

65. Grassley CE. Grassley questions Merck about communication with the FDA on Vioxx. http://finance.senate.gov/press/Gpress/2004/prg101504.pdf.

66. Fox PL, Raina P, Jadad AR. Prevalence and treatment of pain in older adults in nursing homes and other long-term care institutions: a systematic review. Can Med Assoc J 1999; 160:329–333.

67. Teno JM, Weitzen S, Wetle T, Mor V. Persistent pain in nursing home residents. JAMA 2001; 285:2081.

68. Kovach CR, Weissman DE, Griffie J, Matson S, Muchka S. Assessment and treatment of discomfort for people with late-stage dementia. J Pain Symptom Manage 1999; 18:412–419.

69. King L, Arnold R. Pain and suffering in older adults approaching the end of life. In: Weiner DK, Herr K, Rudy T, eds. Persistent Pain in Older Adults. New York: Springer Publishing Co., 2002:295–315.

70. SUPPORT principal investigators. A controlled trial to improve care for seriously ill hospitalized patients: the study to understand prognoses and preferences for outcomes and risks of treatment (SUPPORT). JAMA 1995; 274:1591–1598.

71. Field M, Cassel C, eds. Approaching death, improving care at the end of life. Committee on Care at the End of Life. Institute of Medicine. Washington, D.C.: National Academy Press, 1997.

72. Foley KM, Gelband H, eds. Improving palliative care for cancer: summary and recommendations. Institute of Medicine and Commission on Life Sciences National Research Council. Washington, D.C.: National Academy Press, 2001.

73. Joranson DE, Gilson AM, Dahl JL, Haddox JD. Pain management, controlled substances, and state medical board policy: a decade of change. J Pain Symp Manage 2002; 23:138–147.

74. Madan AK, Aliabadi-Wahle S, Beech DJ. Age bias: a cause of underutilization of breast conservation treatment. J Canc Ed 2001; 16:29–32.

75. Gibson SJ, Farrell MJ, Katz B, Helme RD. Multidisciplinary management of chronic non-malignant pain in older adults. In: Ferrell BR, Ferrell BA, eds. Pain in the Elderly. Seattle, WA: IASP Press, 1996:91–99.

76. Middaugh SJ, Levin RB, Kee WG, Barchiesi FD, Roberts JM. Chronic pain: its treatment in geriatric and younger patients. Arch Phys Med Rehabil 1988; 29:1021–1026.

77. Cleeland CS, Gonin R, Hatfield AK, et al. Pain and its treatment in outpatients with metastatic cancer. New Engl J Med 1994; 330:592–596.

78. Lebovits A. The ethical implications of racial disparities in pain: are some of us more equal? Pain Med 2005; 6:3–4.

79. Ibrahim SA, Siominoff LA, Burant CJ, Kwoh CK. Differences in expectations of outcome mediate African American/white patient differences in "willingness" to consider joint replacement. Arthrit Rheum 2002; 46:2429–2435.

80. Tait RC, Chibnall JT. Racial and ethnic disparities in the evaluation and treatment of pain: psychological perspectives. Prof Psychol Res Prac 2005; 36:595–601.

81. Mayberry RM, Mili F, Ofili E. Racial and ethnic differences in access to medical care. Med Care Res Rev 2000; 57(suppl 1):108–145.

82. Green CR, Ndao-Brumblay SK, West B, Washington T. Differences in prescription opioid analgesic availability: comparing minority and white pharmacies across Michigan. J Pain 2005; 6:689–699.

83. Morrison RS, Wallenstein S, Natale DK, Senzel RS, Huang LL. "We don't carry that:" failure of pharmacies in predominantly nonwhite neighborhoods to stock opioid analgesics. N Engl J Med 2000; 342:1023–1026.

84. Clark R, Anderson NB, Clark VR, Williams DR. Racism as a stressor for African Americans. A biopsychosocial model. Am Psychol 1999; 54:805–816.

85. Ouslander JG, Schnelle JF. Research in nursing homes: practical aspects. J Am Geriatr Soc 1993; 41:182–187.

Racial, Ethnic, and Sociodemographic Disparities

Carmen R. Green

Department of Anesthesiology, University of Michigan Health System, Ann Arbor, Michigan, U.S.A.

INTRODUCTION

Unprecedented scientific advances have led to a better understanding of pain mechanisms and the ability to alleviate pain and suffering. Yet the literature continues to document the widespread and significant undertreatment of pain (especially for racial and ethnic minorities). Numerous studies describe stark differences in health and health care based upon race, ethnicity, gender, socioeconomic status, and age (1–3).

Overwhelmingly, the literature provides evidence for inferior care of minorities. There is also considerable evidence that acute, chronic, and cancer pain have unique health implications in minority patients, low-income individuals, elderly persons, and women that are often unrecognized or overlooked (4–11). Furthermore, the pain complaints of racial and ethnic minorities receive less attention than those of Caucasians (regardless of the type of pain), putting them at significant risk for inferior quality pain care (12–15). Thus, several ethical challenges essential for health care planning in an increasingly aging and diversifying society exist (16,17).

Like many chronic illnesses, chronic pain (i.e., nonmalignant or benign pain greater than equal to six months) significantly impairs overall health and well-being (18–20). However, most of the literature on disparities fail to address this chronic condition and when it is addressed, the focus is on acute and cancer pain (21–23). In addition, age, ethnicity, and sociodemographic factors may make certain populations more vulnerable to chronic pain (24). There is limited literature to guide us regarding the presenting symptoms, pain duration, and disability due to chronic pain, but it suggests that the health problems commonly seen in chronic pain patients [e.g., depression, posttraumatic stress disorder (PTSD)] are more problematic in minority and underserved populations (25,26). Because there is often a close association between race or ethnicity and income, living in poverty is an additional risk factor for poor health due to pain as well as inferior quality pain care (27). Overall, guidelines designed to improve and reduce barriers to chronic pain care have not adequately addressed disparities in pain care for potentially underserved and vulnerable populations or the ethical implications for disparate pain care (28–31). This chapter primarily focuses on disparities in chronic pain while providing an overview of disparities from an ethical perspective. More specifically, this chapter will address:

- The consequences of pain on overall health and well-being in an ethnically diverse population.
- The consequences of disparities in the context of pain.

- The epidemiology of pain in an ethnically diverse population.
- Pain assessment and treatment in an ethnically diverse population.
- Barriers to accessing quality pain care in an ethnically diverse population.
- The role of provider variability on pain care disparities.
- Pain, disparities, and policy.

DEFINING HEALTH AND DISPARITY

The World Health Organization (WHO) defines health as "a state of complete physical, mental, and social well-being and not merely the absence of disease or infirmities" (32,33). It also proclaims that health is a basic human right (34,35). It follows that chronic pain is a unique disease that impacts multiple health domains: physical (e.g., sleep), psychological, and social functioning, while causing undue suffering (25,26). When compared with the general population, chronic pain patients have significantly more depression (independently increasing morbidity). In addition, increased anxiety and PTSD symptoms as well as social isolation are often associated with chronic pain (25,26). In the presence of chronic pain, minorities are more likely to have PTSD and depression than Caucasians. In addition, they are also less likely to seek counseling to treat these symptoms.

An operational definition of a disparity refers to "differences in the disease burden, illness, injury, disability, or mortality experienced by one population group in relation to another or clinical decisions or outcomes associated with disadvantage for one group as compared to another" (36,37). The disparities literature primarily focuses on Black Americans, Hispanics, and Native Americans in comparison to Caucasians. However, significant disparities in health and those, which are based upon socioeconomic status and geographic location, are well described. Nonetheless, mortality rates are significantly higher for minority persons at all ages as well as for economically disadvantaged people (38–40). There is also evidence for racial and ethnic differences in the prevalence, morbidity, and mortality associated with cardiac disease, diabetes, and other chronic illnesses as well as in the medical care received for these conditions, thereby presenting significant ethical concerns (16,41,42).

Health insurance is considered the great equalizer by ensuring access to medical care and thereby improving health (27). Yet, more than 45 million Americans are currently uninsured, with racial and ethnic minorities disproportionately making up over 50% of the uninsured (43). Currently, nearly one-third of Americans self-identify as a member of a minority population (i.e., African-American, Native American, or Hispanic) and this percentage will increase to 50% by the year 2050 (44–46). Minorities and uninsured persons are more likely to use the emergency department for health care (including acute exacerbation of chronic pain) and to be hospitalized for preventable conditions due to diminished access to quality resources (47). The unfortunate truth is that untold millions of Americans are also underinsured, limiting their access to care and treatment. This problem reduces access for the chronic pain patients who have limited or no coverage for physical therapy or counseling services that have demonstrated efficacy. Another clear example is the injured worker who must pay for health care first and then seek reimbursement from the insurer (e.g., workman's compensation). Thus, the inability to access quality health care as well as to receive treatment to relieve pain and suffering is fundamentally an ethical and policy issue.

Ultimately, the goal for using health services is to maintain and improve health. Many erroneously believe that health care disparities would no longer exist when socioeconomic status and health insurance coverage are similar. However, racial and ethnic disparities in health and health care exist for patients with comparable insurance and the same illness (48,49). Studies also suggest that racial and ethnic minorities, who are Medicare beneficiaries are more likely to rate their health as poor when compared to similar Caucasians (49). The issue of disparities in health due to pain and the undertreatment of pain fits into a troubling overall health picture for minorities, who generally receive lower quality health care (and pain care) than Caucasians, even when their income, insurance, and medical conditions are similar.

HISTORY

Although race and ethnicity are often used interchangeably, race is essentially a social construct that describes people based upon a set of shared physical characteristics that is often associated with real or perceived economic power (50). The literature has the tendency to lump all minorities into one group, although there is growing evidence for intrarace differences in health care experience (24). One challenge to eliminating disparities is confronting this country's problematic and politically sensitive racial relations, when skin color could determine an individual's quality of life, health, occupation, and residence (51–53). More specifically, race has determined the quality of medical care. The federal government (e.g., courts and congress) addressed educational, employment, and housing inequities via the 1964 Civil Rights Acts. Indeed, implementing Medicaid and Medicare in the mid-1960s made enormous differences in reducing this gap (36,37). Although other factors (e.g., genetics, behaviors, and socioeconomic factors) also determine a population's health, persistent health inequities prompted the U.S. Department of Health and Human Services to establish a national goal to eliminate health disparities by the end of this decade (consistent with the decade of pain research and control). Congress again provided leadership by legislatively mandating the Institute of Medicine (IOM) report entitled, "Unequal treatment: Confronting racial and ethic disparities in care" and the National Center on Minority Health and Health Disparities at the NIH (36,37), compelling evidence for disparities in health and the system were detailed in the IOM report. The document speaks to the ethical dilemma presented by disparate care, stating that "racial and ethnic disparities in health care occur in the context of broader historic and contemporary social and economic inequality and because they are associated with worse outcomes in many cases, are unacceptable" (36,37). Among the many overarching goals proposed for the nation's research agenda in Healthy People 2010 was improving health and eliminating disparities in health care (54,55). Unfortunately, scholarly documents discussing unequal treatment and disparities in health care have not provided information about the chronic pain experience. Yet, the impact of chronic pain on the estimated one in six Americans (especially women, minorities, and the elderly) was largely overlooked in Healthy People 2010 and in the IOM report. Furthermore, most research studies examining health status failed to examine the impact of chronic pain and did not include an ethnically diverse population.

EPIDEMIOLOGY OF PAIN

Globally, chronic pain is the third largest health problem. In fact, the WHO proclaimed pain relief as a human right (56,57). With more than 75 million

Americans suffering from chronic pain, poor pain management crosses socioeconomic, geographic, gender, and racial lines. As Americans live longer, they are more likely to suffer from painful chronic conditions (58,59). Conditions such as arthritis and diabetes are also more prevalent among minorities. Pain leads to over 700 million lost workdays and greater than $100 billion in health care expenditures annually (60,61). More specifically, chronic pain is the second leading cause for all physician visits and the most frequent cause of disability in the United States (62,63). Without necessary improvements in the quality of chronic pain management, the increasing prevalence of chronic pain (especially in an aging and diversifying society) will have devastating socioeconomic and health consequences (20,60). From both a public health and ethical perspective, there are tremendous benefits to understanding the effects of chronic pain on both the individual and society that can be translated into improved health and medical care for all.

Women, minorities, and economically disadvantaged persons suffer substantially more impairment due to chronic pain (e.g., sleep perturbations, depression, and physical disability) (60,64). Although women enjoy a longer life expectancy, they have increased disability and diminished quality of life as well as an increased prevalence of chronically painful conditions (e.g., interstitial cystitis, fibromyalgia, and lupus) compared with men (65,66). These stark gender-related disparities are more pronounced in racial and ethnic minority women, providing evidence that both gender and race are important factors in preserving health and wellness (2,67). Thus, it is essential when assessing pain that racial, ethnic, and gender identifiers be included such that outcomes are monitored and interventions can be designed to reduce and eliminate disparities. The failure to do so does not respect the value of each individual.

BARRIERS TO QUALITY PAIN CARE

Although we have the ability to assess and treat pain, clinicians frequently confront complex ethical and moral dimensions that impact patients. Pain assessments by professionals are often lower than the patient's self-report (especially for minority patients), while mild mood disorders are more likely to be attributed to major psychological disturbances in minority people (68–71). The way that women and minorities communicate their pain complaints may reduce the likelihood that they receive adequate attention.

PAIN ASSESSMENT AND TREATMENT

The cornerstone for quality pain care is pain assessment, and the gold standard for pain assessment remains patient self-report (72,73). Chronic pain patients with similar disease activity often may report differences in pain intensity and its impact on their lives (74,75). Differences in sex hormones, central nervous system functioning, pain learning, culturally imposed factors, pain care beliefs, past experiences, socioeconomic status, and social roles may predispose women and minorities toward responses and actions that increase the threat of pain (76–78). Altogether, these are important considerations, because minorities and women often report increased pain intensity, depression, and anxiety in response to chronic pain (25,26,79). Yet, these factors are not consistently taken into account when assessing pain. The failure to do so when assessing pain creates paternalism that prevents the patient from being a full partner in their health care, implying that the clinician makes decisions without taking into account the patient's experience.

Being a full health care partner incorporates the basic ethical principles: justice, respect for autonomy, nonmaleficence, and beneficence (80,81). Justice refers to giving patients what they deserve whereas autonomy asserts that an informed patient has a right to a self-chosen plan. Nonmaleficence is essentially the obligation to avoiding harm whereas beneficence is the active obligation to do good. When factors that influence the pain experience are not considered in assessing the impact of pain on an individual, it does not promote ethical or just practice. Furthermore, it prevents the patient from being fully informed about their condition preventing them from being a full partner in their health care, and thereby leading to potential harm (in terms of diminished health) as well as devaluing their basic rights (42,82).

There is still little known regarding the inciting event, presenting symptoms, pain duration, and disability due to chronic pain in an ethnically diverse population, but there is evidence that the disease course varies based upon gender and race (83). Because chronic pain impacts physical, social, and emotional health, it is important to assess all health domains. Overall, minority persons report significantly more comorbidities, higher pain scores, increased pain severity, more suffering, and less control of pain than Caucasians across the age continuum (25,26). Minorities (regardless of age and gender) also report increased physical disability and more problems with sleep as well as significantly more depression (25,26). They also report more symptoms consistent with PTSD and anxiety than Caucasians (84–86). What remains unclear is whether these findings reflect undertreatment, over-reporting, differences in pain sensitivity, or some combination of these factors (87). Despite emerging research suggesting the multidimensional impact of chronic pain, there is a dearth of longitudinal research specifically addressing the impact of pain on racial and ethnic minorities and women.

Physician patient congruence (e.g., gender and race) may improve the quality of medical care (88). It is interesting that clinicians routinely describe the patient's phenotype (i.e., race) when presenting the patient's chief complaint, but we rarely do this for the health care team delivering their care (89). Yet, the risk for cultural misinterpretations is increased for minority patients (who are often cared for by nonminority clinicians) (90–93). Even when there is racial and gender congruence, there is often noncongruence between the patient and team based upon socioeconomic status; again, this lack of congruence contributes to problematic communication and the potential for cultural misinterpretations (94–96). Because it is often not feasible for every patient to have a clinician that looks like them, the need for culturally sensitive care is critically important. From an ethical perspective, each clinician has the duty to try to understand how a patient's culture may influence the meaning of pain as well as how to deliver culturally competent care (42). Yet, in an increasing multicultural society, most clinicians struggle, and continuing medical education directed at cultural competence is in its infancy.

Assessing and treating chronic pain is often complicated by disability, depression, and pain intensity issues (97). Personal biases in assessing and treating patients (especially patients complaining of severe pain) complicate chronic pain care for all patients but especially for minority patients (98–100). Differences in the way racial and ethnic minorities as well as women communicate their pain concerns may increase the likelihood of their complaints being discounted, especially if the patient's gender, race, or ethnicity is not congruous with the clinician's. Patients with pain due to sickle cell anemia continue to provide stories documenting poor pain assessment and inadequate pain care during an acute pain crisis and for their chronic pain complaints (101–103). In addition, perceptions and stereotypes about addiction in this vulnerable population persist when the provider–patient interaction is fraught with the potential for racial stereotyping, mistrust, and problematic physician–patient communication (both from language and cultural perspectives) (104). Previous ethical lapses (e.g., Tuskegee syphilis trials) as well as negative experiences and interactions with the team contribute to this reluctance and serve as a reminder that trust (the basic tenet for being a partner in health care) is not transferable (42,105–109).

HEALTH CARE PROVIDER VARIABILITY IN PAIN MANAGEMENT DECISION MAKING

Despite therapeutic advances currently available to treat chronic pain, research designed to specifically examine the response to chronic pain in underserved and vulnerable populations is extremely limited. Clinicians are ill-equipped to treat chronic pain and the ethical implications of its undertreatment due to insufficient pain knowledge and ineffective pain management education in the health professional schools (110,111). Overall, education about pain, health care disparities, and ethics in an increasingly complex health care delivery system are neglected topics in most health professional schools. In fact, the physician has a basic duty to the patient to address and treat pain (112). The fact that both women and minorities often do not receive adequate pain treatment indicates the need for chronic pain guidelines as well as the need to more successfully translate research and education into clinical practice. Yet most scholarly documents addressing the ethical practice of pain medicine have not addressed disparate pain care based upon race, ethnicity, age, or gender (17,113).

Unfortunately, universal guidelines for chronic pain management are lacking and pain relief is often not a priority at the clinician or health system level (28,29,114). Physician confidence in their ability to manage pain is often misplaced and is clouded with myths and insufficient knowledge (13,36,37,99,100). They also have lower goals for chronic pain relief, less satisfaction with their chronic pain management, and provide lower quality pain care for chronic pain than for acute and cancer pain (100). The U.S. Agency for Policy and Research sponsored guidelines for acute postoperative and cancer pain treatment, yet 70% of cancer patients die with uncontrolled pain and nearly 40% of postoperative patients experience significant pain (114–116). Furthermore, variability in pain management decision making and unequal treatment based upon race, ethnicity, gender, and age complicates pain management (with minorities, women, and the elderly receiving lower quality care) (14,23,25,50,117). Racial and gender stereotyping may play a significant role (118–122). For instance, the Worker's Compensation literature provides evidence for disparate pain care (6,9,123). These studies reveal that racial and ethnic minorities were twice as likely to be disabled six months following occupational back injuries and those without legal representation received less treatment and lower disability ratings than Caucasians. When untreated chronic pain prohibits a patient from returning to work, the system has failed.

The International Association for the Study of Pain (IASP), WHO, and European Federation of IASP chapters have urged that pain is a pressing problem and that pain relief is a human right (124a). More specifically they released a joint statement: "the control of pain has been a relatively neglected area of governmental concern in the past, despite the fact that cost-effective methods of pain control are available. The time is right to raise the profile of pain, to promote the recognition that chronic pain is a disease in its own right and an important health concern, but above all, to raise global awareness to a fundamental truth— the relief of pain should be a human right." However, in their objectives presented in the global day against pain initiative (124b), disparities in pain care based upon race and ethnicity were not discussed. When one population (e.g., racial minorities) is disproportionately and negatively impacted more than another, it represents a fundamental human rights issue.

The perception of regulatory scrutiny often makes physicians nervous about aggressively treating pain and prescribing opioid analgesics (125,126). Recent prosecutions of pain physicians have increased these concerns and have negatively impacted the quality of pain care for patients with legitimate chronic pain complaints (126–131). It is critically important that government enforcement efforts do not prevent effective pain treatment. Hospitals, insurance providers (including the government), and physicians must examine their guidelines, policies and procedures, and licensure process to make sure that all patients, regardless of sex or race, receive proper pain treatment (132–134). Whenever this does not occur, it represents a failure of medical training, continuing medical education, and medical practice.

ACCESS TO QUALITY PAIN CARE

Most diseases commonly associated with disparities (e.g., cancer, diabetes, cardiovascular disease, and osteoarthritis) are also associated with pain. Despite the impact that chronic pain has on our society as well as an extensive literature documenting the benefits of optimizing pain management, there are limited guidelines for chronic pain management. Adequate assessment and appropriate chronic pain management is a neglected part of medicine. In the United States, chronic pain remains a national problem with significant health and socioeconomic implications, but there is considerable variability in clinician knowledge, perceptions, and goals regarding pain management. Physicians report decreased satisfaction and lower goals for chronic pain therapy than for acute, postoperative, or cancer pain. The lack of a curative model when combined with lower physician goals for chronic pain relief may lead to variability, poor assessment, and suboptimal pain management (13,98–100). Thus, to achieve quality chronic pain care, clinicians may have to move away from a strictly curative model.

Even when patients find a physician who will assess their pain complaints, they may be denied necessary treatments (e.g., opioid analgesics, counseling, and physical therapy) that can improve their quality of life due to insurance issues (135,136). In addition, minority and economically disadvantaged patients continue to report difficulty in obtaining their opioid analgesic prescriptions at their neighborhood pharmacies (137,138). Several studies provide support that pharmacies located in minority neighborhoods were significantly less likely to carry adequate opioid analgesic supplies. Although poor Caucasians had increased difficulty accessing their medications as well, minorities faced similar difficulties in obtaining their opioid analgesics in their neighborhoods regardless of high or low income, suggesting that higher socioeconomic status was not protective. In addition, limited knowledge and misperceptions about addiction, tolerance, and dependence may contribute to variability in prescribing by physicians as well as stocking by pharmacists. Thus, racial stereotyping and perceptions, socioeconomic status, poor pain assessment, and decreased ability to obtain pain medications at neighborhood pharmacies complicate access to appropriate pain management for racial and ethnic minority persons, while impairing their overall quality of life.

BARRIERS

Several patient-related barriers to quality pain care that can be especially problematic for racial and ethnic minority patients exist (117). A common fear among patients is that they will become addicted to "narcotics." Racial and ethnic minority persons with chronic pain tend to have less trust in the health care system and believe to a greater extent than Caucasians that race and ethnicity affects health care and pain care. Minority patients also tend to believe that good patients avoid talking about pain and that pain medications cannot really control pain. In addition, minorities report increased difficulty paying for health care despite having insurance and access to a tertiary care pain center (98,139). They also report that chronic pain was a major financial problem more so than do Caucasians. Minority patients with chronic pain also believe that they should have been referred to a pain center sooner more so than Caucasians (140). These disparate attitudes have significant implications in a potentially vulnerable population at risk for poor pain assessment and management. However, the question remains whether these perceptions or attitudes are based in reality or whether their health care experiences contributed to these beliefs. Thus, failure to optimize pain care is fundamentally an ethical lapse with long-term quality of life implications.

PAIN, DISPARITIES, AND HEALTH CARE POLICY

Medical science has many effective tools to battle pain, but they only work when they are applied uniformly to people who need them. There is little awareness regarding pain as a public health crisis or of racial and ethnic disparities in the pain care experience. The increasing racial and ethnic diversity in the United States and the growing importance of disparities to consumers (e.g., health plans, patients, employers, and providers) prompted the government to lead efforts to reduce and eliminate disparities in health and health care (141–144). Inequities in the health care system result in decreased productivity, increased health care utilization, and increased health care costs. People at risk for disparate care often access the health care system with increased disease burden at higher cost centers (e.g., emergency department). Considering the increasing prevalence of pain and its disproportionate impact on underserved and vulnerable populations, it is critically important that pain is not left out of the health care policy and disparities agenda. Consistent with WHO policy, undertreated pain (when adequate treatment is available) must be considered a human rights issue. It is the signature of a great society.

The IOM report "To Err is Human," provided evidence for preventable medical errors leading to death (44,000 Americans annually). Although the report suggested gaps in quality, it did not address inadequate pain assessment and treatment that leads to the unnecessary suffering of millions due to unrelieved pain. Not until quality health and pain care are available for the most vulnerable in our society, will we be able to improve health and pain care for all.

There is continuing controversy regarding using opioid analgesics for chronic and persistent pain (especially in minority and low-income populations).

For minorities, the use of opioid analgesics for chronic pain is fraught with the potential of racial stereotypes, mistrust, and problematic physician–patient communication. Yet, there is no evidence to support minorities as being more likely than nonminorities to abuse opioid analgesics or divert them for illicit purposes. Nonetheless, stereotyping may complicate pain care for underserved and vulnerable populations.

WHAT WOULD QUALITY, ETHICAL PAIN CARE LOOK LIKE?

1. All patients having access to quality pain care by a knowledgeable health care team that views pain relief as a priority.
2. All patients receiving a comprehensive chronic pain assessment that focuses on their physical, social, and psychological functioning. Pain assessment is performed routinely during primary care and specialty clinics visits using tools that are culturally sensitive and age appropriate, while also taking into account social roles (e.g., parenting).
3. The patient receives culturally and linguistically sensitive education regarding pain and is treated as a full partner in his/her health care. Pain education also includes awareness for family members, health care providers, health care policy makers, and the public.
4. Enhanced educational efforts directed at pain, disparities, and ethics for an increasingly diverse population become commonplace. Toward this end, increased awareness for patients, health care providers, health care policy makers, and the public is achieved.
5. All chronic pain patients having access to multidisciplinary pain management centers and modalities (e.g., physical therapy, counseling, opioid analgesics, and nerve blocks) known to improve functioning, decrease pain, and enhance quality of life.
6. For injured people, pain management is integrated into the patient's rehabilitation regimen.
7. Guidelines are developed to promote quality pain care. Research that is informed by the patient's experience is successfully translated into clinical practice. In addition, racial and ethnic identifiers are used to monitor outcomes until disparities in pain care are eliminated.

CONCLUSIONS

Chronic pain is a significant public health problem that disables more people than cancer or heart disease, while costing the American people more than both combined. In an increasingly aging and diversifying America, there is compelling evidence that minorities often receive less than optimal treatment for fractures, chest pain, and cancer, as well as many chronically painful conditions such as arthritis. Minorities are often prescribed lower quality pain treatment than Caucasians—even when they have similar insurance. When disabled, minorities often receive lower monetary settlements from the Worker's Compensation System. Even when minorities are able to overcome the significant barriers to appropriate pain assessment and receive treatment for their pain complaints, they often receive less pain medication than their Caucasian counterparts and are less likely to obtain opioid analgesic prescriptions at their neighborhood pharmacies.

No one should suffer from pain when effective treatment is available. There is a fundamental need for clinical medicine to address and recognize bioethical issues related to disparities in health and pain care. A great society has a moral imperative to help people, who are particularly vulnerable to the devastating effects of pain. Yet, health profession schools (e.g., medical, pharmacy, and nursing) devote little time to these important issues. From the time of Hippocrates, physicians have vowed to eliminate pain and suffering. In the middle of the decade for pain research and control, it is our moral imperative to optimize pain care and to eliminate disparities in care, wherever they exist. Pain management is a human right's issue and the under treatment of pain (for whatever reason) is fundamentally a medical error with long-term ethical implications.

REFERENCES

1. Institute of Medicine of the National Academies. Smedley BD, Stith AY, Nelson AR, eds. Unequal treatment: confronting racial and ethnic disparities in health care. Washington, DC: National Academic Press, 2002.
2. LeResche L. Gender considerations in the epidemiology of chronic pain. In: Crombie IK, Croft PR, Linton SJ, LeResche L, VonKorff M, eds. Epidemiology of Pain. Seattle: IASP Press, 1999:43–51.
3. Weissman JS, Betancourt J, Campbell EG, et al. Resident physicians' preparedness to provide cross-cultural care. JAMA 2005; 294:1,058–1,067.
4. Aggarwal VR, Macfarlane TV, Macfarlane GJ. Why is pain more common amongst people living in areas of low socioeconomic status? A population-based cross-sectional study. Br Dent J 2003; 194:383–387; discussion 380.
5. Cepeda MS, Carr DB. Women experience more pain and require more morphine than men to achieve a similar degree of analgesia. Anesth Analg 2003; 97:1,464–1,468.
6. Chibnall JT, Tait RC. Disparities in occupational low back injuries: predicting pain-related disability from satisfaction with case management in African, Americans, and Caucasians. Pain Med 2005; 6:39–48.
7. Parrott RL, Silk KJ, Dillow MR, Krieger JL, Harris TM, Condit CM. Development and validation of tools to assess genetic discrimination and genetically based racism. J Natl Med Assoc 2005; 97:980–990.
8. Subramanian SV, Chen JT, Rehkopf DH, Waterman PD, Krieger N. Racial disparities in context: a multilevel analysis of neighborhood variations in poverty and excess mortality among black populations in Massachusetts. Am J Public Health 2005; 95:260–265.
9. Tait RC, Chibnall JT, Andresen EM, Hadler NM. Management of occupational back injuries: differences among African Americans and Caucasians. Pain 2004; 112:389–396.
10. Tamayo-Sarver JH, Dawson NV, Hinze SW, et al. The effect of race/ethnicity and desirable social characteristics on physicians' decisions to prescribe opioid analgesics. Acad Emerg Med 2003; 10:1239–1248.
11. Waisel DB, Truog RD. An introduction to ethics. Anesthesiology 1997; 87:411–417.
12. Einbinder LC, Schulman KA. The effect of race on the referral process for invasive cardiac procedures. Med Care Res Rev 2000; 57:162–180.
13. Green CR, Wheeler JR, LaPorte F. Clinical decision making in pain management: contributions of physician and patient characteristics to variations in practice. J Pain 2003; 4:29–39.
14. Services U.S.D.o.H.a.H. Developing objectives for healthy people 2010, 1997.
15. Todd KH, Deaton C, D'Adamo AP, Goe L. Ethnicity and analgesic practice. Ann Emerg Med 2000; 35:11–16.
16. Bonham VL. Race, ethnicity, and pain treatment: striving to understand the causes and solutions to the disparities in pain treatment. J Law Med Ethics 2001; 29:52–68.
17. Schulman KA, Berlin JA, Harless W, et al. The effect of race and sex on physicians' recommendations for cardiac catheterization. New Engl J Med 1999; 340:618–626.
18. Crombie IK, Croft PR, Linton SJ, LeResche L, VonKorff M. Epidemiology of Pain. Seattle: IASP Press, 1999.

19. Rich BA. An ethical analysis of the barriers to effective pain management. Camb Q Health Care Ethics 2000; 9:54–70.
20. Sondik EJ, Lucas JW, Madans JH, Smith SS. Race/ethnicity and the 2000 census: implications for public health. Am J Public Health 2000; 90:1709–1713.
21. Boulware LE, Cooper LA, Ratner LE, LaVeist TA, Powe NR. Race and trust in the health care system. Public Health Rep 2003; 118:358–365.
22. Brandon DT, Isaac LA, LaVeist TA. The legacy of Tuskegee and trust in medical care: is Tuskegee responsible for race differences in mistrust of medical care? J Natl Med Assoc 2005; 97:951–956.
23. Green CR, Baker TA, Ndao-Brumblay SK. Patient attitudes regarding health care utilization and referral: a descriptive comparison in African and Caucasian Americans with chronic pain. J Natl Med Assoc 2004; 96:31–42.
24. Baker TA, Green CR. Intrarace differences among black and white americans presenting for chronic pain management: the influence of age, physical health, and psychosocial factors. Pain Med 2005; 6:28–38.
25. Green CR, Baker TA, Smith EM, Sato Y. The effect of race in older adults presenting for chronic pain management: a comparative study of African and Caucasian Americans. J Pain 2003; 4:82–90.
26. Green CR, Flowe-Valencia H, Rosenblum L, Tait AR. The role of childhood and adulthood abuse among women presenting for chronic pain management. Clin J Pain 2001; 17:359–364.
27. Lurie N, Jung M, Lavizzo-Mourey R. Disparities and quality improvement: Federal policy levers. Health Aff 2005; 24:354–364.
28. AGS Clinical Practice Guidelines. The management of chronic pain in older persons. Geriatrics 1998; 53(suppl 3):S6–S7.
29. Practice Guidelines for Chronic Pain Management. A report by the American Society of anesthesiologists task force on pain management, chronic pain section. Anesthesiology 1997; 86:995–1004.
30. Parker R, Ratzan S, Lurie N. Health literacy: a policy challenge for advancing high-quality health care. Health Aff 2003; 22:147–153.
31. Ruiz P, Venegas-Samuels K, Alarcon RD. The economics of pain: mental health care costs among minorities. Psychiatric Clin North Am 1995; 18:659–670.
32. Kohn LT, Corrigan JM, Donaldson MS, America, C.o.Q.o.H.C.i., Medicine., I.o., eds. To Err is Human: Building a Safer Health System, ed. In: (U.S.), I.o.M. and America., C.o.Q.o.H.C.i. Washington, DC: National Academy Press, 1999.
33. Tamsen A, Hartvig P, Dahlstrom B, Lindstrom B, Holmdahl MH. Patient controlled analgesic therapy in the early postoperative period. Acta Anaesthesiolog Scand 1979; 23:462–470.
34. Breslow L. A quantitative approach to the World Health Organization definition of health: physical, mental and social well-being. Int J Epidemiol 1972; 1:347–355.
35. Klock PA, Roizen MF. More or better educating the patient about the anesthesiologist's role as perioperative physician. Anesth Analg 1996; 83:671–672.
36. Institute of Medicine. The institute of medicine's goal to eliminate health care disparities: guidance for the national healthcare disparities report. National Academies Press, 2002.
37. Jacox A, Carr DB, Payne R. New clinical-practice guidelines for the management of pain in patients with cancer. New Engl J Med 1994; 330:651–655.
38. Helme RD, Gibson SJ. The epidemiology of pain in elderly people. Clin Geriatrist Med 2001; 17:417–431, v.
39. Ndao-Brumblay SK, Green CR. Racial differences in the physical and psychosocial health among black and white women with chronic pain. J Natl Med Assoc 2005; 97:1369–1377.
40. Turk DC, Brody MC, Okifuji EA. Physicians' attitudes and practices regarding the long-term prescribing of opioids for noncancer pain. Pain 1994; 59:201–208.
41. Council on Ethical and Judicial Affairs A.M.A. Gender disparities in clinical decision making. JAMA 1991; 266:559–562.
42. Francis CK. The medical ethos and social responsibility in clinical medicine. J Natl Med Assoc 2001; 93:157–169.

43. Brown ER, Ojeda VD, Wyn R, Levan R. Racial and ethnic disparities in access to health insurance and health care.

44. Anderson GF, Hussey PS. Population aging: a comparison among industrialized countries. Health Aff (Millwood) 2000; 19:191–203.

45. Crystal S, Johnson RW, Harman J, Sambamoorthi U, Kumar R. Out-of-pocket health care costs among older Americans. J Gerontol Soc Sci 2000; 55B:S51–S62.

46. Stewart WF, Ricci JA, Chee E, Morganstein D, Lipton R. Lost productive time and cost due to common pain conditions in the U.S. workforce. JAMA 2003; 290:2443–2454.

47. Ashton CM, Haidet P, Paterniti DA, et al. Racial and ethnic disparities in the use of health services: bias, preferences, or poor communication? J Gen Intern Med 2003; 18:146–152.

48. Collins FC. What we do and don't know about 'race', 'ethnicity', genetics and genetics and health at the dawn of the genome era. Nat Genet 2004; 36:513–520.

49. Collins K, Hall A, Neuhaus C. U.S. Minority Health: A Chartbook. New York: The Commonwealth Fund, 1999.

50. Green CR, Anderson KO, Baker TA, et al. The unequal burden of pain: confronting racial and ethnic disparities in pain. Pain Med 2003; 4:277–294.

51. Curtin PD. The slavery hypothesis for hypertension among African-Americans: the historical evidence. Am J Pub Health 1992; 82:1681–1686.

52. Ghosh S, Sallam S. Patient satisfaction and postoperative demands on hospital and community services after day surgery [see comments]. Br J Surg 1994; 81:1635–1638.

53. Weisberg JN, Keefe FJ. Personality, individual differences, and psychopathology in chronic pain. In: Gatchel RJ, Turk DC, eds. Psychosocial Factors in Pain; Critical Perspectives. New York: The Guilford Press, 1999.

54. Morris DB. Ethnicity and pain (IASP Newsletter). Clin Updat 2001; 9:556.

55. Shaiova L, Wallenstein D. Outpatient management of sickle cell pain with chronic opioid pharmacotherapy. J Natl Med Assoc 2004; 96:984–986.

56. Haas J. The cost of being a woman. New Engl J Med 1998; 338:1694–1695.

57. Joranson DE, Gilson AM. Pharmacists' knowledge of and attitudes toward opioid pain medications in relation to federal and state policies. J Am Pharm Assoc 2001; 41: 213–220.

58. Fries BE, Simon SE, Morris JN, Flodstrom C, Bookstein FL. Pain in U.S. nursing homes: validating a pain scale for the minimum data set. Gerontologist 2001; 41:173–179.

59. Hilts PJ. In tests on people, who watches the watchers? N Y Times (Print) 1999; F1, F4.

60. Grembowski DE, Martin D, Diehr P, et al. Managed care, access to specialists, and outcomes among primary care patients with pain. Health Serv Res 2003; 38:1–19.

61. Weir R, Browne GB, Tunks E, Gafni A, Roberts J. A profile of users of speciality pain clinic services: predictors of use and cost estimates. J Clin Epidemiol 1992; 45(12): 1399–1415.

62. Saha S, Arbelaez JJ, Cooper LA. Patient–physician relationships and racial disparities in the quality of health care. Am J Public Health 2003; 93:1713–1719.

63. Tait RC, Chibnall JT. Work injury management of refractory low back pain: relations with ethnicity, legal representation and diagnosis. Pain 2001; 91:47–56.

64. Robinson ME, Wise EA, Gagnon C, Fillingim RB, Price DD. Influences of gender role and anxiety on sex differences in temporal summation of pain. J Pain 2004; 5:77–82.

65. Berkley KJ. Vive la difference. Trends Neurosci 1992; 15:331–332.

66. Lillie-Blanton M, Hoffman C. The role of health insurance coverage in reducing racial/ethnic disparities in health care. Health Aff 2005; 24:398–408.

67. LeResche L, Mancl L, Sherman JJ, Gandara B, Dworkin SF. Changes in temporomandibular pain and other symptoms across the menstrual cycle. Pain 2003; 106:253–261.

68. Anderson KO, Richman SP, Hurley J, et al. Cancer pain management among underserved minority outpatients: perceived needs and barriers to optimal control. Cancer 2002; 94:2295–2304.

69. Gunn CC. Chronic pain: time for epidemiology. J R Soc Med 1996; 89:479–480.

70. Katz NP, Sherburne S, Beach M, et al. Behavioral monitoring and urine toxicology testing in patients receiving long-term opioid therapy. Anesth Analg 2003; 97:1097–1102.

71. Whitfield KE, Baker-Thomas T. Individual differences in aging minorities. Int J Aging Hum Dev 1999; 48:73–79.
72. Elliott AM, Smith BH, Penny KI, Smith WC, Chambers WA. The epidemiology of chronic pain in the community. Lancet 1999; 354:1248–1252.
73. Ferrell BR, Borneman T, Juarez G. Integration of pain education in home care. J Palliat Care 1998; 14:62–68.
74. Weisse CS, Sorum PC, Sanders KN, Syat BL. Do gender and race affect decisions about pain management? J Gen Intern Med 2001; 16:211–217.
75. Williams DR. Racial/ethnic variations in women's health: the social embeddedness of health. Am J Public Health 2002; 92:588–597.
76. Gallagher RM. Primary care and pain medicine: a community solution to the public health problem of chronic pain. Med Clin North Am 1999; 83:555–583, v.
77. Green C, Flowe-Valencia H, Rosenblum L, Tait A. Do physical and sexual abuse differentially affect chronic pain states in women? J Pain Symptom Manage 1999; 18: 420–426.
78. Green CR, Ndao-Brumblay SK, Nagrant AM, Baker TA, Rothman E. Race, age, and gender influences among clusters of African American and white patients with chronic pain. J Pain 2004; 5:171–182.
79. Ngo-Metzger Q, Massagli MP, Clarridge BR, et al. Linguistic and cultural barriers to care. J Gen Intern Med 2003; 18:44–52.
80. Dubois MY. The birth of an ethics charter for pain medicine. Pain Med 2005; 6: 201–202.
81. Riley JL III, Wade JB, Myers CD, Sheffield D, Papas RK, Price DD. Racial/ethnic differences in the experience of chronic pain. Pain 2002; 100:291–298.
82. Wallman KK, Evinger S, Schechter S. Measuring our nation's diversity: developing a common language for data on race/ethnicity. Am J Public Health 2000; 90:1704–1708.
83. Pappagallo M, Heinberg LJ. Ethical issues in the management of chronic nonmalignant pain. Semin Neurol 1997; 17:203–211.
84. Gibson SJ, Katz B, Corran TM, Farrell MJ, Helme RD. Pain in older persons. Disabil Rehabil 1994; 16:127–139.
85. Gureje O, Von Korff M, Simon GE, Gater R. Persistent pain and well-being: a World Health Organization study in primary care. JAMA 1998; 280:147–151.
86. LeResche L. Gender differences in pain: epidemiologic perspectives. Pain Forum 1995; 4:228–230.
87. Le May S, Hardy JF, Taillefer MC, Dupuis G. Measurement of patient satisfaction. Anesth Analg 1999; 89:255.
88. Kulich RJ. Screening for chronic opioid therapy. Pain Manage Rounds 2004; 1:1–6.
89. Hoffmann DE, Tarzian AJ. The girl who cried pain: a bias against women in the treatment of pain. J Law Med Ethics 2001; 29:13–27.
90. LaVeist TA, Bowie JV, Cooley-Quille M. Minority health status in adulthood: the middle years of life. Health Care Financ Rev 2000; 21:9–21.
91. Northington-Gamble VN. Under the shadow of Tuskegee: African Americans and health care. Am J Public Health 1997; 87:1773–1778.
92. Schatman ME. Racial and ethnic issues in chronic pain management: challenges and perspectives. Pain Management 83–97.
93. Whaley AL. The culturally sensitive diagnostic interview research project. In: Taylor RJ, ed. A Study on the Psychiatric Misdiagnosis of African American Patients, 2003:57–66.
94. Poobalan AS, Bruce J, King PM, Chambers WA, Krukowski ZH, Smith WC. Chronic pain and quality of life following open inguinal hernia repair. Br J Surg 2001; 88:1122–1126.
95. Rose VL. Guidelines from the American geriatric society target management of chronic pain in older persons. Am Fam Physician 1998; 58:1213–1214, 1217.
96. Zuvekas SH, Taliaferro GS. Pathways to access: health insurance, the health care delivery system, and racial/ethnic disparities, 1996–1999. Health Aff (Millwood) 2003; 22:139–153.
97. Green CR, Wheeler J, Marchant B, LaPorte F, Guerrero E. Analysis of the physician variable in pain management. Pain Med 2001; 2:317–327.

98. Green CR, Wheeler JC, LaPorte F, Marchant B, Guerrero E. How well is chronic pain managed? Who does it well? Pain Med 2002; 3:56–65.

99. Green CR, Wheeler JR. Physician variability in the management of acute postoperative and cancer pain: a quantitative analysis of the michigan experience. Pain Med 2003; 4:8–20.

100. Greenberg PE, Leong SA, Birnbaum HG, Robinson RL. The economic burden of depression with painful symptoms. J Clin Psychiatry 2003; 64(suppl 7):17–23.

101. Benjamin LJ, Sinson GI, Nagel RL. Sickle cell anemia day hospital: an approach for the management of uncomplicated painful crises. Blood 2000; 95:1130–1137.

102. Shavers VL, Lynch CF, Burmeister LF. Knowledge of the Tuskegee study and its impact on the willingness to participate in medical research studies. J Natl Med Assoc 2000; 92:563–572.

103. Tobin JR, Butterworth J. Sickle cell disease: dogma, science, and clinical care. Anesth Analg 2004; 2004:283–284.

104. Joranson DE. Availability of opioids for cancer pain: recent trends, assessment of system barriers, new World Health Organization guidelines, and the risk of diversion. J Pain Symptom Manage 1993; 8:353–360.

105. Bierman AS, Clancy CM. Health disparities among older women: identifying opportunities to improve quality of care and functional health outcomes. J Am Med Womens Assoc 2001; 56:155–159, 188.

106. Blanchard JC, Haywood YC, Scott C. Racial and ethnic disparities in health: an emergency medicine perspective. Acad Emerg Med 2003; 10:1289–1293.

107. Fouad MN, Partridge E, Green BL, et al. Minority recruitment in clinical trials: a conference at Tuskegee, researchers and the community. Ann Epidemiol 2000; 10:S35–S40.

108. OMara AM, Arenella C. Minority representation, prevalence of symptoms, and utilization of services in a large metropolitan hospice. J Pain Symptom Manage 2001; 21:290–297.

109. Shaya FT, Blume S. Prescriptions for cyclooxygenase-2 inhibitors and other nonsteroidal anti-inflammatory agents in a medicaid managed care population: African Americans versus Caucasians. Pain Med 2005; 6:11–17.

110. Jordan MS, Lumley MA, Leisen JC. The relationships of cognitive coping and pain control beliefs to pain and adjustment among African-American and Caucasian women with rheumatoid arthritis. Arthritis Care Res 1998; 11:80–88.

111. Turk DC, Okifuji A. Does sex make a difference in the prescription of treatments and the adaptation to chronic pain by cancer and noncancer patients? Pain 1999; 82:139–148.

112. Dubois M, Banja J, Brushwood D, et al. Ethics charter from American academy of pain medicine.

113. Ethics Charter from American Academy of Pain Medicine. Pain Med 2005; 6:203–212.

114. American Pain Society. Quality improvement guidelines for the treatment of acute pain and cancer pain. JAMA 1995; 274:1874–1880.

115. Carr DB, Miaskowski C, Dedrick SC, Williams GR. Management of perioperative pain in hospitalized patients: a national survey. J Clin Anesth 1998; 10:77–85.

116. Jamison RN, Raymond SA, Slawsby EA, Nedeljkovic SS, Katz NP. Opioid therapy for chronic noncancer back pain. A randomized prospective study. Spine 1998; 23:2591–2600.

117. Green CR, Baker TA, Sato Y, Washington TL, Smith EM. Race and chronic pain: a comparative study of young black and white Americans presenting for management. J Pain 2003; 4:176–183.

118. Auman C. Effect of health-related stereotypes on physiological responses of hypertensive middle-aged and older men. J Gerontol 2005; 60B:P3–P10.

119. Balsa AI, McGuire TG. Prejudice, clinical uncertainty and stereotyping as sources of health disparities. J Health Econ 2003; 22:89–116.

120. Fennema K, Meyer DL, Owen N. Sex of physician: patients' preferences and stereotypes. J Fam Pract 1990; 30:441–446.

121. Phillips DM. JCAHO pain management standards are unveiled. Joint commission on accreditation of health care organizations. JAMA 2000; 284:428–429.

122. Rooks RN, Simonsick EM, Miles T, et al. The association of race and socioeconomic status with cardiovascular disease indicators among older adults in the health, aging, and body composition study. J Gerontol B Psychol Sci Soc Sci 2002; 57:S247–S256.

123. Haythornthwaite JA, Menefee LA, Quatrano-Piacentini AL, Pappagallo M. Outcome of chronic opioid therapy for noncancer pain. J Pain Symptom Manage 1998; 15:185–194.
124a. Morrison RS, Wallenstein S, Natale DK, Senzel RS, Huang LL. "We Don't Carry That"—failure of pharmacies in predominantly nonwhite neighborhoods to stock opioid analgesics. New Engl J Med 2000; 342:1023–1026.
124b. www.iasp.org.
125. Gilson AM, Joranson DE. Controlled substances and pain management: changes in knowledge and attitudes of state medical regulators. J Pain Symptom Manage 2001; 21: 227–237.
126. Lasch KE. Culture, pain, and culturally sensitive pain care. Pain Manag Nurs 2000; 1: 16–22.
127. Fishman SM, Bandman TB, Edwards A, Borsook D. The opioid contract in the management of chronic pain. J Pain Symptom Manage 1999; 18:27–37.
128. Fishman SM, Wilsey B, Yang J, Reisfield GM, Bandman TB, Borsook D. Adherence monitoring and drug surveillance in chronic opioid therapy. J Pain Symptom Manage 2000; 20:293–307.
129. Haywood LJ. Early efforts of blacks in the fight against heart disease and stroke. J Natl Med Assoc 1999; 91:669–675.
130. Johansson EE, Hamberg K, Westman G, Lindgren G. The meanings of pain: an exploration of women's descriptions of symptoms. Soc Sci Med 1999; 48:1791–1802.
131. Kelly MP. The World Health Organization's definition of health promotion: three problems. Health Bull (Edinb) 1990; 48:176–180.
132. Berry PH, Dahl JL. The new JCAHO pain standards: implications for pain management nurses. Pain Manage Nurs 2000; 1:3–12.
133. Gallagher RM. Physician variability in pain management: are the JCAHO standards enough? Pain Med 2003; 4:1–3.
134. Plotnikoff GA, Numrich C, Chu Wu C, Yang D, Phua Xiong P. Hmong Shamanism: animist spiritual healing in Minnesota. Minn Med 2002; 85:24–29.
135. Grossman SA, Sheidler VR, Swedeen K, Mucenski J, Piantadosi S. Correlation of patient and caregiver ratings of cancer pain. J Pain Symptom Manage 1991; 6:53–57.
136. Smith BH, Elliott AM, Chambers WA, Smith WC, Hannaford PC, Penny K. The impact of chronic pain in the community. Fam Pract 2001; 18:292–299.
137. Green C, Ndao-Brumblay SK, West B, Washington T. Differences in prescription opioid analgesic availability: comparing minority and white pharmacies across Michigan. J Pain 2005; 6:689–699.
138. Navarro V. Race or class or race and class: growing mortality differentials in the United States. Int J Health Serv 1991; 21:229–235.
139. Green CR. Pain: racial disparities in access to pain treatment. Clin Updat 2004; 12(6):1–4.
140. The origins of racial/ethnic disparities. Health Aff 2005; 24:316.
141. The public-sector response to disparities. Health Aff 2005; 24:353.
142. Insurer's response to health disparities. Health Aff 2005; 24:397.
143. Maiese DR. Healthy people 2010—leading health indicators for women. Womens Health Issues 2002; 12:155–164.
144. Komaromy M, Grumbach K, Drake M, et al. The role of black and hispanic physicians in providing health care for underserved populations. New Engl J Med 1996; 334:1305–1310.

**Chronic Opioid Therapy: The Argument
for Opioid Therapy to Treat Persistent
Noncancer Pain**

B. Eliot Cole

American Society of Pain Educators, Montclair, New Jersey, U.S.A.

INTRODUCTION

*" . . . For the easing of neurotraumatic pain . . . morphia salts are invaluable. When continu-
ously used . . . hypnotic manifestations lessen, whereas its power to abolish pain continues,
so that the patient . . . may become free of pain . . . ."*

Silas Weir Mitchell (1)

There is no longer any real question that opioid analgesics have the capacity to
relieve pain, regardless of the cause for the pain. Opium has been used for thousands of years to relieve pain and suffering (2). There is currently no evidence
that opioids are any less effective for neuropathic pain than for nonneuropathic pain,
any less effective than other classes of medication, or that any opioid is more specific
for neuropathic pain than another (3). Doses used and potency issues may differ for
various conditions and situations causing pain, but opioids are regarded as the cornerstone of pain management (4). Chronic opioid therapy is the main therapeutic
approach for moderate to severe cancer-related pain (5). Eighty-seven percent of
physician members of the American Pain Society maintain patients with noncancer
pain on opioids and support the long-term use of opioids for patients with chronic
noncancer pain (6). Chronic opioid therapy may allow the return of normal function
without significant adverse side effects in those who have failed other treatments (7).

Those in pain, who have previously failed other classes of medication and
interventional therapies, are now considered for long-term opioid therapy as part
of their overall pain management by reputable practitioners. What was unthink-
able in the past, long-term opioid therapy, is now accepted by many as the
standard of care for chronic and intractable pain unresponsive to other modalities.
With the potential for suffering and the inevitable downward spiral in quality of
life (QOL) due to pain so great, should we not consider it unethical to withhold
long-term opioid therapy, which has no end-organ damage when nothing else is
appropriate for the control of pain?

THE DEBATE STILL GOES ON AND ON AND ON

Cohen et al. stated in their discussion about the management of pain for those
being rehabilitated from significant traumatic events " . . . in light of their long
and unparalleled record of providing pain relief throughout the centuries, opioids
are the gold standard for treatment of severe pain. For many patients with intense,

unremitting pain, opioids are the only group of drugs capable of providing relief from suffering..." (8).

Opioids are the first-line therapy for moderate to severe pain in nociceptive, neuropathic, and mixed pain syndromes associated with terminal illness (9). At the March 2003 American Pain Society's annual scientific meeting, attendees learned that opioids were an effective therapy for chronic, noncancer pain. Proponents stated that it was time for prescribers to move past the stigma associated with opioid use and the worries about addiction, to recognize the value of these agents of patients with intractable pain. Steven D. Passik, Ph.D. bluntly stated, "...it's...outrageous that we're still discussing (the appropriateness of opioid therapy for nonmalignant pain)..." while agreeing in principle that well-controlled long-term studies were still lacking regarding opioid therapy (10).

Opioids relieve pain by working directly on specific receptors in the nervous system to modulate ascending pain transmission, and thereby modulate the experience of pain. Widely accepted as effective analgesics, the greatest reluctance for the use of opioids for pain management prescribers is the fear of reprisals from state licensing boards and the Drug Enforcement Administration (DEA) (11). The practice of medicine is so second-guessed by regulatory overseers that sadly, the safest decision for too many modern practitioners is not to treat pain and leave patients suffering when effective options are readily available. The criminalization of medicine with regard to opioid prescribing has led to the abandonment of the patients, who justifiably seek our assistance managing their pain.

With pain as the most common complaint of patients with rheumatologic diseases, reduction of pain must be an essential feature for meaningful improvement (12). Modification of the disease process without adequate treatment of pain will not improve the quality of any patient's life. Pain surveys with patients having rheumatoid arthritis establish that pain control is generally inadequate, not even formally assessed or treated for many people with this terrible disease (12). This undertreatment of pain is potentially more physiologically and psychologically adverse than any theoretical risk from opioid therapy, yet practitioners routinely limit opioids for their patients, while literally creating toxicity from biological agents, disease-modifying drugs, corticosteroids, and nonsteroidal medications for most of them.

WHAT IS THE EVIDENCE FOR AGGRESSIVE OPIOID THERAPY?

A double-blinded, placebo-controlled study of 104 patients experiencing moderate to severe osteoarthritis pain using controlled-release (CR) oxycodone demonstrated significant reduction in reported pain, improvement in coping, reduction in helplessness, and passive coping. This three-month study found that opioid therapy was most effective when incorporated into a multidisciplinary approach to pain management (13).

A study lasting up to 90 days, with osteoarthritic patients suffering from moderate to severe pain secondary to osteoarthritis uncontrolled by nonsteroidal anti-inflammatory agents, acetaminophen and/or short-acting opioids, was conducted. Its results indicated that CR oxycodone was significantly superior to placebo therapy in decreasing average pain intensity and pain-induced interference with general activities such as daily functioning, walking ability, normal work, mood, sleep, relationships, and enjoyment in life. CR oxycodone provided additional benefits beyond the improvements seen with nonsteroidals and acetaminophen alone, while daily doses of oxycodone averaged 57 mg and remained low despite allowable increases of more than three times stabilized doses, suggesting that patients were not becoming tolerant to their opioid therapy (14).

Beliefs that sufferers of back or muscle pain could not benefit from opioid therapy are no longer valid, with the demonstration that many patients now experiencing chronic spinal pain benefit from long-term opioid therapy without creating adverse physical or behavioral risk. In a study of back pain patients, 152 of 230 subjects found that opioid therapy decreased the intensity of their pain by greater than 50%, caused only mild side effects, and did not result in significant increases in the amount of medication taken. The efficacy of long-term opioid therapy was sustained from three months to three years (15). While it is unknown how long this efficacy can be sustained, chronic back pain remains a vexing condition and a multibillion dollar financial drain annually on the U.S. economy in lost productivity and increased healthcare utilization. Adequate pain management, including opioid therapy when other measures are not effective, not only can decrease suffering, but also decrease the cost burden to society.

A meta-analytic report of randomized, placebo-controlled trials of World Health Organization (WHO) step 3 opioids for efficacy and safety in chronic noncancer pain performed by searching the Oxford Pain Relief Database (1950 to 1994) and Medline, EMBASE, and the Cochrane Library until September 2003, using inclusion criteria of randomized comparisons of WHO step 3 opioids versus placebo in chronic noncancer pain, and double-blind studies reporting on pain intensity outcomes using validated pain scales identified fifteen trials for evaluation. Four of these included trials involved 120 patients receiving intravenous opioid therapy for their pain. Eleven included studies (1025 patients) compared oral opioids with placebo for four days to eight weeks. Six of the 15 included studies had an open label follow-up of 6 to 24 months. The mean decrease in pain intensity in most studies was at least 30% with opioids and was comparable in neuropathic and musculoskeletal pain. The short-term efficacy of opioids was good in both neuropathic and musculoskeletal pain conditions (16).

Another meta-analytic review of articles in any language regarding the use of opioids to treat central or peripheral neuropathic pain of any etiology indexed on Medline (1966 to December 2004) and the Cochrane Central Register of Controlled Trials (fourth quarter, 2004) resulted in 22 that could be classified as short-term (14 that involved opioid therapy < 24 hours) versus intermediate-term (eight with a median length of therapy being 28 days, and a range of 8–56 days). There were no truly long-term studies identified despite the needs for such information. The short-term trials produced contradictory results, while the eight intermediate-term trials demonstrated opioid efficacy for neuropathic pain (17).

In a randomized, double-blind, active placebo-controlled, four-period crossover trial, 57 patients with neuropathic pain (35 with diabetic and 22 with postherpetic neuralgia) received daily doses of an active placebo (lorazepam), CR morphine, gabapentin, and a combination of gabapentin and morphine. Forty-one patients completed the entire study. Each of the four treatment periods involved five weeks, and the main outcome measure was mean daily pain intensity with secondary outcomes including pain, adverse effects, maximal tolerated doses, mood, and QOL. The mean daily pain (from 0–10 with 10 being the most severe) determined for the maximum tolerated dose of each studied medication arm was 5.72 at baseline, 4.49 with placebo (lorazepam), 4.15 for gabapentin, 3.70 for morphine and 3.06 for the combination of gabapentin, and morphine. Using the Short-form McGill Pain Questionnaire, the total scores (on a 0–45 scale with 45 being the most severe pain) at a maximum tolerated dose were 14.4 for placebo (lorazepam), 10.7 for gabapentin, 10.7 for morphine, and 7.5 for the combination of gabapentin and morphine ($p < 0.05$) (18). Together, these findings demonstrate the importance of opioid therapy, and the ability of opioids to work with other agents (e.g., gabapentin) to produce better outcomes than either type of medication administered alone.

In a study involving 36 patients with moderate or greater diabetic neuropathic pain for at least three months, they were evaluated for efficacy, safety, and health-related QOL while receiving CR oxycodone or active placebo (benztropine). Patients were washed out from all opioids two to seven days before randomization to 10 mg CR oxycodone or benztropine 0.25 mg every 12 hours. The doses were increased as necessary to a maximum of 40 mg CR oxycodone or 1 mg benztropine every 12 hours, with crossover to the alternate treatment after a maximum of four weeks. Acetaminophen, 325–650 mg every four to six hours as needed was also provided for breakthrough pain. Treatment with CR oxycodone resulted in significantly lower ($p = 0.0001$) mean daily pain (21.8 ± 20.7 vs. 48.6 ± 26.6 mm visual analogue scale (VAS)), steady pain (23.5 ± 23.0 vs. 47.6 ± 30.7 mm VAS), brief pain (21.8 ± 23.5 vs. 46.7 ± 30.8 mm VAS), skin pain (14.3 ± 20.4 vs. 43.2 ± 31.3 mm VAS), and total pain and disability (16.8 ± 15.6 vs. 25.2 ± 16.7; $p = 0.004$). The number needed to treat, having one patient with at least 50% pain relief, was 2.6 and clinical effectiveness scores favored treatment with CR oxycodone over benztropine ($p = 0.0001$) (19).

In a multicenter, randomized, double-blind, placebo-controlled, parallel-group six-week study with 159 patients having moderate to severe diabetic neuropathic pain, treatment was initiated with either one 10-mg tablet of CR oxycodone ($n = 82$) or identical placebo ($n = 77$) every 12 hours. Doses were increased every three days to a maximum of six tablets (60 mg CR oxycodone) every 12 hours. At an average (SD) dose of 37 (21) mg/day (range 10–99 mg/day), CR oxycodone provided more analgesia than placebo ($p = 0.002$) in the intent-to-treat cohort. From days 28 to 42, overall average daily pain intensity (least squares mean ± SE), rated in subject diaries on a numeric scale of 0 (no pain) to 10 (pain as bad as you can imagine), was 4.1 ± 0.3 in subjects given CR oxycodone and 5.3 ± 0.3 in placebo-treated subjects (20).

In another study, 81 adult patients with refractory neuropathic pain refractory were randomly assigned to receive high-strength (0.75 mg) or low-strength (0.15 mg) levorphanol capsules for eight weeks under double-blind conditions. Levorphanol was patient-titrated to a maximum of 21 capsules of either strength day. Outcome measures studied included the intensity of pain (diary), the degree of pain relief, QOL, psychological and cognitive function, the number of capsules taken daily, and blood levorphanol levels. High-strength levorphanol capsules reduced pain by 36%, compared with a 21% reduction for the low-strength group ($p = 0.02$). Patients in the high-strength group averaged 11.9 capsules/day (8.9 mg/day), while patients in the low-strength group required 18.3 capsules/day (2.7 mg/day). Affective distress and interference with functioning were reduced, and sleep was improved in both groups. The reduction in the intensity of neuropathic pain was significantly greater during treatment with higher doses of opioids than with lower doses (21).

IMPLICATIONS FOR PRESCRIBERS AND THEIR PATIENTS

Regardless of the underlying pathophysiology of the pain, opioids are effective. What is still lacking after decades of modern clinical use is the long-term risk to benefit ratio for maintained opioid therapy. No one has ever conducted a 1-, 5-, or

10-year study of the efficacy of opioid therapy. Physicians, who still claim that opioid therapy is only marginally useful in the treatment of chronic pain, and only has a minimal effect on functioning, are in the minority today. Major medical, nursing and pharmacy organizations strongly support the use of opioids for the treatment of chronic pain in a number of consensus and policy statements (2).

Today, most physicians fear the regulatory bodies more than the patient advocacy rules. While one physician from Oregon was censured for the undertreatment of pain and two physicians from California were civilly sued for elder abuse resulting from their alleged undertreatment of pain, hundreds of physicians are forced to go through prescribing related investigations every year in the United States. To be investigated for excessive opioid prescribing is difficult to defend, time consuming and costly, and often presupposes that one is poorly prescribing based upon the absolute numbers of pills/prescription or the number of prescriptions written in some arbitrary unit of time. Due to this level of scrutiny, it may be easier and safer today for practitioners to avoid treating patients with chronic persistent pain and to limit their prescribing of opioids for extended periods to those with established cancer diagnoses, or other serious types of end organ disease.

However, we are all prospective patients, who may potentially need opioid therapy in the future. How we treat our patients today will have great influence on how we will be treated in the future when it is our turn to be cared for as patients. Opioids have been, are and always will be an essential tool in the management of patients with acute, chronic, and cancer pain (22).

MITIGATION

What are the options for the prescribing practitioner faced with a patient who has persistent, chronic noncancer pain and for whom the use of opioid therapy might be beneficial? These patients need a thorough psychological assessment for the presence or absence of Axis I or II disorders, overt substance abuse/use, and other psychological confounders to the use of known medications of potential abuse. While many prescribers may feel ill prepared to undertake such screening, working with other mental health professionals (substance abuse counselors, social workers, psychologists, and psychiatrists) will increase the likelihood that latent pathology will be recognized early and any aberrant behavior will be detected once opioid therapy is initiated.

I have described 10 Tips for Prescribing Opioids (23). Gourlay, Heit, and Almahrezi have described 10 Steps of Universal Precautions in Pain Medicine regarding opioid prescribing (24). Taken together the key aspects of long-term opioid management include:

- Obtaining a thorough history and performing a thorough physical examination for every patient to accurately determine the etiology of the pain.
- Establishing a clear diagnosis and differential regarding the pain condition.
- Obtaining a second opinion from a pain management specialist, a specialist in the involved organ system or a specialist in the overall disease process before committing to long-term opioid therapy when seeing a patient as a primary care practitioner and not as a pain specialist.
- Identifying those at risk for substance abuse or referring to someone capable of making this determination before initiating long-term opioid therapy.
- Documenting everything contemporaneously seen, felt, heard, and considered about the patient from the first encounter onward.

- Obtaining informed consent from the patient before opioid therapy is initiated, so there is no doubt regarding the treatment proposed or the outcome expected.
- Using a written opioid treatment agreement defining the expectations and obligations for the patient and the practitioner.
- Obtaining patient agreement to use only one provider for opioid prescriptions and one pharmacy to obtain opioid medications.
- Administering pre- and postintervention assessments of pain intensity and function (performance of activities of daily living).
- Seeing the patient receiving opioid analgesics on a regular basis and evaluating the level of analgesia and activity, and emergence of adverse effects or aberrant behavior.
- Prescribing long-acting opioid analgesics on a time-contingent basis so that stable levels are achieved and reinforcement of pill taking is minimized.
- Considering "rational polypharmacy" using adjuvants with opioids and seeing opioid prescribing as part of some larger plan rather than the only plan.
- Determining the minimum dose necessary to maintain function and useful activities of daily living by potentially trying to decrease the dosage (25–35%).
- Ordering urine drug screens for your patients of concern to document that you are able to recover their prescribed medications (to rule out significant diversion) and that you are thinking about their potential use of illicit substances (things you do not prescribe).
- Periodically reviewing the diagnosis and comorbid conditions that contribute to the overall pain experience, including the development of addiction.
- Staying current with opioid prescribing rules, obtaining relevant education from recognized organizations, and keeping politically aware of developments.

One should be creative and flexible regarding opioid administration. While direct access to prescribed oral opioid medications may prove too tempting for some to not abuse, by putting the same medication directly into the nervous system (epidural, subdural, or ventricular) by means of a medication delivery system, the risk of abuse from prescribed opioids is minimized. The same would also be true for those with limited intellectual capacity, who are not able to safely administer their own medications.

ADVICE FROM THE DEA ABOUT OPIOID THERAPY

Much is made about the need for more scrutiny and tighter controls to prevent medication diversion from licit sources. For many years, the DEA has maintained a special website for the purpose of preventing "drug diversion" and to inform prescribers about their responsibilities when prescribing controlled substances (25). The DEA declares that all prescribers share responsibility with society at large for solving the prescription drug abuse and diversion problem, and that they have a:

- Legal and ethical responsibility to uphold the law and to help protect society from drug abuse;
- Professional responsibility to prescribe controlled substances appropriately, guarding against abuse, while ensuring that patients have medication available when they need it;
- Personal responsibility to protect their practices from becoming easy targets for drug diversion.

Accordingly, the prescriber must become aware of potential situations in which drug diversion can occur and enact safeguards to prevent diversion. To accomplish this, the DEA expects prescribers to be able to identify "so-called" common features of drug abusers:

- Unusual behavior in the waiting room;
- Assertive personality, often demanding immediate action;
- Unusual appearance—extremes of either slovenliness or being overdressed;
- Unusual knowledge of controlled substances and/or giving medical history with textbook symptoms, or giving evasive or vague answers to questions regarding medical history;
- Being reluctant or unwilling to provide reference information. Usually has no regular doctor and often no health insurance;
- Requests for a specific controlled drug and reluctance to try a different drug;
- Failure to keep appointments for further diagnostic tests or refusal to see another practitioner for consultation;
- Exaggerating medical problems and/or simulating symptoms;
- Exhibiting mood disturbances, suicidal thoughts, lack of impulse control, thought disorders, and/or sexual dysfunction;
- Displaying cutaneous signs of drug abuse—skin tracks and related scars on the neck, axilla, forearm, wrist, foot, and ankle. Such marks are usually multiple, hyperpigmented, and linear. New lesions may be inflamed. Displaying signs of "pop" scars from subcutaneous injections.

The DEA expects prescribers to understand the motivations and "modus operandi" used by drug-seeking patients. They describe these characteristics as indicative of suspicious behavior:

- Must be seen right away;
- Wanting an appointment toward end of office hours;
- Calling or coming in after regular hours;
- Stating he/she's traveling through town, visiting friends or relatives (not a permanent resident);
- Feigning physical problems, such as abdominal or back pain, kidney stone, or migraine headache in an effort to obtain narcotic drugs;
- Feigning psychological problems, such as anxiety, insomnia, fatigue, or depression in an effort to obtain stimulants or depressants;
- Stating that specific nonnarcotic analgesics do not work or that he/she is allergic to them;
- Contending to be a patient of a practitioner, who is currently unavailable or will not give the name of a primary or reference physician;
- Stating that a prescription has been lost or stolen and needs to be replaced;
- Deceiving the practitioner, such as by requesting refills more often than originally prescribed;
- Pressuring the practitioner by eliciting sympathy or guilt or by direct threats;
- Utilizing a child or an elderly person when seeking methylphenidate or pain medication.

Finally, the DEA has developed lists of behaviors for prescribers to demonstrate. When confronted by suspected drug abusers prescribers must:

- Perform thorough examinations appropriate to the conditions.
- Document examination results and questions asked by the patients.

■ Request picture identification, or other forms of identification and Social Security numbers. These documents should be photocopied and included in the patients' records.
■ Call previous practitioners, pharmacists, or hospitals to confirm patients' stories.
■ Confirm telephone numbers, if provided by patients.
■ Confirm current addresses at every visit.
■ Write prescriptions for limited quantities of medications.

What the DEA ultimately believes is that prescribers must do more than

■ Taking their patients' words at face value when they are suspicious.
■ Dispensing drugs just to get rid of drug-seeking patients.
■ Prescribing, dispensing, or administering controlled substances outside the scope of professional practice or in the absence of formal practitioner-patient relationships.

The DEA holds dispensing pharmacists to a high standard as well, and entrusts them to be another safeguard against bad faith prescribing. In the DEA's "Pharmacist's Guide to Prescription Fraud," pharmacists are instructed that they, too, have a legal responsibility to be acquainted with the state and federal requirements for dispensing controlled substances (26). Pharmacists, too, have a legal and ethical responsibility to uphold these laws and to help protect society from drug abuse.

As pharmacists have a personal responsibility to protect their practices from becoming easy targets for drug diversion, they must become aware of potential situations in which drug diversion can occur and enact safeguards to prevent diversion. To meet this challenge, dispensing pharmacists must maintain constant vigilance against forged or altered prescriptions. The Controlled Substances Act holds pharmacists responsible for knowingly dispensing prescriptions that are not issued in the usual course of professional treatment.

Ultimately, pharmacists must know the prescribers in their communities, and their signatures. They need to know DEA registration numbers of these prescribers, know their patients, and carefully check the dates on all prescription orders. Pharmacists are tasked to know if prescriptions have been presented within a reasonable length of time since written (that prescriptions have not "timed out").

When there are questions concerning any aspect of prescription orders, pharmacists are instructed to call prescribers for verification or clarification. Should discrepancies be noted, patients must have plausible reasons before prescription medications are dispensed. Whenever pharmacists are in doubt, the DEA expects them to minimally request proper identification from patients. Finally, the DEA expects pharmacists to not dispense forged, altered, or counterfeited prescriptions and to call local police authorities. In fact, the DEA expects pharmacists to contact their State Board of Pharmacy and/or the local DEA office whenever a pattern of prescription abuse is discovered.

SUMMARY

"Doing the right thing" for patients is a fascinating ethical discussion. Most would easily agree that it is not ethical or in the best interest of a patient in agonizing pain for a physician to "do nothing at all." With the medications, procedures, and techniques available today, we have the capacity to individualize the care provided and to use opioid analgesics in a safe and responsible fashion. While opioid alkaloids are one of the oldest remedies for the treatment of pain, they are often relegated to second tier status and their use routinely avoided primarily due to regulatory concerns (27).

While the first rule of medicine is to do no harm, with our eyes open to the risks and benefits of opioid therapy, we may do the right thing (relieve pain using opioids) without necessarily creating a significant potential for adverse events or unintended consequences. Philosophers and scholars may continue to debate the merits of opioid therapy, and elected officials will certainly pontificate about the rules of opioid therapy for the management of pain. In the meantime, why must patients live their lives in pain without the benefit of appropriate treatment? The withholding of justifiable, appropriately supervised, opioid therapy is morally wrong and indefensible.

There will likely never be long-term double blinded, placebo controlled, multiyear opioid study to determine all of the risks of opioid medications and resolve all of the questions about it. To do so would require withholding necessary medical care, and would force those who do not receive opioids to live with intractable pain, while putting them at risk for depression, substance abuse, and even suicide. There are many opioid studies that span weeks to months, and more than two decades of practical experience caring for the terminally ill, which have established that opioids improve QOL. We do not need more studies of longer duration to tell us what we know is in the best interest of our patients in pain. Assuming that we follow the rational steps of opioid prescribing outlined above, and we enter into treatment agreements with "all eyes open," we can use opioids to manage all types of pain including chronic, persistent noncancer pain.

Patients, not practitioners, should make the final decision about taking or not taking opioids for their pain. When there is doubt regarding opioid appropriateness, and in the absence of some clear contraindication to opioid therapy, opioids should be provided for the relief of chronic pain. These opioids should be prescribed as part of a time-limited clinical trial with defined end points (decrease in pain intensity or increase in function), coupled to a mutually agreed upon stopping point if no clinical benefit is seen. While not intended to completely eliminate all pain, opioids will improve the QOL for most patients, and take the edge off the misery that prevents them from enjoying their lives.

Physician–patient partnerships allow for the necessary precautions to be taken when prescribing opioids. Use of mutually agreed upon plans of care with defined points of evaluation prospectively developed do remove much of the emotion associated with long-term opioid prescribing for chronic pain. In the end, if a system of credentialing is established for prescribers to demonstrate mastery of knowledge regarding responsible prescribing practices, we can have the win-win outcome we seek and realize the promise that patients who need opioid medications will have access to them and that those who should not have access to them will not.

REFERENCES

1. Mitchell SW. Injuries of the Nerves and Their Consequences. Philadelphia: JB Lippincott, 1872.
2. Ballantyne JC, Mao J. Opioid therapy for chronic pain. N Engl J Med 2003; 349:1943–1953.
3. Katz N, Benoit C. Opioids for neuropathic pain. Curr Pain Headache Rep 2005; 9:153–160.

4. Cepeda MS, Farrar JT, Baumgarten M, Boston R, Carr DB, Strom BL. Side effects of opioids during short-term administration: effect of age, gender and race. Clin Pharmacol Ther 2003; 74:102–111.
5. Indelicato RA, Portenoy RK. Opioid rotation in the management of refractory cancer pain. J Clin Oncol 2003; 21(9):87s–91s.
6. Turk D, Brody MC. What position do APS's physician members take on chronic opioid therapy? Am Pain Soc Bull 1992; 2:1–7.
7. Howard FM. Chronic pelvic pain. Obstet Gynecol 2003; 101:594–611.
8. Cohen SP, Christo PJ, Moroz L. Pain management in trauma patients. Am J Phys Med Rehabil 2004; 83(2):142–161.
9. Thomas JR, von Gunten CF. Pain in terminally ill patients: guidelines for pharmacological management. CNS Drugs 2003; 17:621–631.
10. Mitka M. Experts debate widening use of opioid drugs for chronic nonmalignant pain. JAMA 2003; 289:2347–2348.
11. Grabois M. Management of chronic low back pain. Am J Phys Med Rehabil 2005; 84(suppl):S29–S41.
12. Borenstein D. Opioids: to use or not to use? That is the question. Arthritis Rheum 2005; 52:6–10.
13. Zautra AJ, Smith BW. Impact of controlled-release oxycodone on efficacy beliefs and coping efforts among osteoarthritis patients with moderate to severe pain. Clin J Pain 2005; 21(6):471–477.
14. Markenson JA, Croft J, Zhang PG, Richards P. Treatment of persistent pain associated with osteoarthritis with controlled-release oxycodone tablets in a randomized controlled clinical trial. Clin J Pain 2005; 21(6):524–535.
15. Mahowald ML, Singh JA, Majeski P. Opioid use by patients in an orthopedics spine clinic. Arthritis Rheum 2005; 52:312–321.
16. Kalso E, Edwards JE, Moore RA, McQuay HJ. Opioids in chronic noncancer pain: systematic review of efficacy and safety. Pain 2004; 112:372–380.
17. Eisenberg E, McNicol ED, Carr DB. Efficacy and safety of opioid agonists in the treatment of neuropathic pain of nonmalignant origin. JAMA 2005; 293:3043–3052.
18. Gilron I, Bailey JM, Tu D, Holden RR, Weaver DF, Houlden RL. Morphine, gabapentin, or their combination for neuropathic pain. N Engl J Med 2005; 352:1324–1334.
19. Watson CPN, Moulin D, Watt-Watson J, Gordon A, Eisenhoffer J. Controlled-release oxycodone relieves neuropathic pain: a randomized controlled trial in painful diabetic neuropathy. Pain 2003; 105:71–78.
20. Gimbel, JS, Richards P, Portenoy RK. Controlled-release oxycodone for pain in diabetic neuropathy: a randomized controlled trial. Neurology 2003; 60:927–934.
21. Rowbotham MC, Twilling L, Davies PS, Reisner L, Taylor K, Mohr D. Oral opioid therapy for chronic peripheral and central neuropathic pain. N Engl J Med 2003; 348:1223–1232.
22. Long SP. Opioids have been, are and always will be an essential tool in the management of patients with acute, chronic and cancer pain: there is no debate. ASA Newsletter 2005; 69(9). Available at http://www.asahq.org/Newsletters/2005/09-05/long09_05.html. Accessed on 12/7/2005.
23. Cole BE. Prescribing opioids, relieving patient suffering and staying out of personal trouble with regulators. The pain practitioner, 2002; 12:5–8. Available at http://www.aapainmanage.org/literature/PainPrac/V12N3_Cole_PrescribingOpioids.pdf. Accessed on 12/8/05.
24. Gourlay DL, Heit HA, Almahrezi A. Universal precautions in pain medicine: a rational approach to the treatment of chronic pain. Pain Med 2005; 6:107–112.
25. Drug Enforcement Administration. Don't be scammed by a drug abuser 1999; 1(1). Available at http://www.deadiversion.usdoj.gov/pubs/brochures/drugabuser.htm#resp. Accessed on 12/26/2005.
26. Drug Enforcement Administration. A pharmacist's guide to prescription fraud 2000; 1(1). Available at http://www.deadiversion.usdoj.gov/pubs/brochures/pharmguide.htm. Accessed on 12/26/2005.
27. Zochodne DW, Max MB. An old acquaintance: opioids for neuropathic pain. Neurology 2003; 60:894–895.

Chronic Opioid Therapy: The Argument for Caution

Jane C. Ballantyne

Division of Pain Medicine, Department of Anesthesia and Critical Care, Massachusetts General Hospital, Harvard Medical School, Boston, Massachusetts, U.S.A.

INTRODUCTION

Opioids can effectively treat pain and suffering, can imbue users with a sense of well-being, can increase artistic creativity, and can cause addiction. It is no surprise, then, that throughout their history, opioids have been used for both therapeutic and recreational purposes, and have been associated with varying degrees of disapproval related to their addictive properties. Unfettered opioid use and addiction have tended to be openly tolerated by societies during times of limited supplies, but when increases in supplies have brought addiction into prominence as a pervasive societal problem, politicians have generally felt compelled to introduce controls. In the United States, controls were introduced at the beginning of the 20th century, at a time when the street use of heroin was becoming an obvious source of crime and depravity. Other industrialized nations had similar problems and followed the lead of the United States in introducing controls on opioid use. There was an important difference, however, between the United States and other nations; the therapeutic use of opioids for the maintenance of addiction was not tolerated in the United States, whereas elsewhere it was, at least initially. For example, the British politicians expressed an abhorrence of restricting opioid use: "Heroin addiction in Great Britain is practically unknown and it is difficult to see why administrative action should be allowed to hinder the relief of suffering" (1). The more conservative U.S. politicians felt that: "Drug addiction is an evil" [that should be] "rooted out and destroyed" (2). A 55 years impasse (after Webb vs. the United States under the provisions of the 1914 Harrison Narcotic Drug Act made it illegal for physicians to prescribe opioids for the treatment of opioid addiction) (3) was broken only when the pioneering work of Nyswander, Dole, and Kreek, who demonstrated over years that addicts maintained on opioids can function normally and are less likely to relapse back into crime (4), culminated in the 1974 Narcotics Addict Treatment Act. Now opioids could be prescribed in the United States by certified physicians for the treatment of opioid addiction, but under tight constraints.

In England, Dame Cecily Saunders became a pioneer of present day palliative care. She was a deeply religious woman, and based her ideas for hospice on the ancient monasteries that provided spiritual comfort and refuge to the dying. She recognized, however, that spiritual tranquility was hard to achieve without relief from physical pain, and felt that modern medical science should be combined with the ancient spiritual approach to optimize peace for the dying. In 1967, she founded the first hospice in England, St Christopher's Hospice in South London. Her earliest pain remedy—known as the Brompton cocktail—consisted of heroin, cocaine, and sherry. Later, she and a close colleague, Robert Twycross, came to realize that the only ingredient needed for pain relief was the opioid, and the other ingredients were abandoned. They subsequently worked with pharmacologists to optimize opioid preparations for use in cancer pain—resulting in the development of slow-release opioid formulations. The fact that they realized, only after experimentation, that opioids have unique analgesic properties illustrates an important aspect of opioid history: it was not until the 20th century that pain relief, independent of other central effects, was attributed uniquely to opioids. This special property of opioids was further elucidated when endogenous opioids and opioid receptors were identified in the late 1970s (5,6).

In the United States, aggressive regulation, especially restrictions making it illegal for physicians to prescribe for addicts, had effectively halted opioid prescribing, even for the treatment of pain. Physicians were cowed into not prescribing lest they lose their medical licenses, and the criminalization and subsequent stigmatization of addiction affected physicians and patients alike. It took a different sort of activist to help reestablish opioid use for of the treatment of pain in the United States, and this role was taken up by Kathleen Foley, later joined by Russell Portenoy. They were greatly influenced by the work of Saunders and Twycross and of Nyswander, Dole, and Kreek, and were convinced that opioids could and should be prescribed for the relief of cancer pain, and that during such treatment (and indeed, during the treatment of acute pain), problematic addiction does not arise.

The 20th century saw the emergence of inseparable and unprecedented legal and ethical struggles regarding opioid treatment of pain, especially opioid treatment of chronic pain. While opioids became established as the only systemic treatment capable of relieving severe pain, the introduction and subsequent tightening of regulations markedly changed the way physicians, patients, and others view addiction. The availability of illicit drugs (opioids and others) increased several fold, despite laws attempting to control their production, import, and dissemination. Worse still, prescription drug abuse emerged as a significant societal problem in the United States (7,8) probably related to the liberalization of opioid treatment for pain, especially the secondary liberalization of opioid treatment for chronic pain. Is it reasonable to withhold a uniquely effective pain treatment because of concerns over addiction? Herein lies the core ethical dilemma for physicians prescribing opioids for chronic pain. This chapter will review the state of our knowledge about the addiction risk for patients receiving long-term opioid pain therapy, as well as our knowledge about long-term opioid efficacy, side effects, and complications. The chapter will conclude by assimilating this acquired knowledge about benefits and risks, with the ethical questions that inevitably arise during the long-term treatment of pain with opioids.

ADDICTION RISK

Present-day U.S. physicians experienced a surge of support for the use of opioids for chronic pain during the last two decades of the 20th century. Pain advocacy had promulgated the use of opioids for pain during terminal[a] cancer and for acute

---

[a] Increased cancer survival has resulted in the emergence of a new syndrome—chronic cancer pain. The word "terminal" is inserted advisedly to distinguish terminal from chronic cancer pain. Terminal cancer pain more closely matches the traditional concept of cancer pain being a short-term, terminal condition. The principles of opioid treatment of chronic cancer pain should be similar to those for all chronic pain: careful patient selection, controlled dosing, maximization of nonopioid treatments, careful monitoring of function and quality of life, and willingness to wean if treatment goals are not met.

pain, resulting in vast improvements in pain management for patients suffering severe pain in the hospital setting and during terminal illness. In these settings, addiction was virtually never problematic, and there seemed good reason to extend the principles developed for cancer and acute pain to the treatment of chronic pain. The assumption was that the medical use of opioids for severe pain would be associated with only low rates of addiction, either because addiction was less likely to arise in the presence of severe pain (9), or because the psychosocial situation of medical treatment was not conducive to the development of addiction. However, with increasing experience of chronic opioid treatment, the medical community has revised its estimates of the extent of the addiction problem, and realized that the factors contributing to the development of problematic addiction during opioid treatment of pain (iatrogenic opioid addiction) are complex and poorly understood.

The difficulty of quantifying iatrogenic opioid addiction begins with the difficulty of defining and recognizing the phenomenon. Perhaps this lack of a satisfactory definition for iatrogenic opioid addiction is not surprising because the currently accepted definitions for drug addiction in illicit users were established only after decades of debate. Drug addiction is also known as substance dependence, and defined as such in the Diagnostic and Statistical Manual of Mental Disorders-IV (DSM-IV) of the American Psychiatric Association. In the DSM-IV manual, seven criteria for substance dependence are listed and these are tolerance, physical dependence, and five further criteria that are behaviors chiefly associated with illicit use (Table 1) (10). At least three criteria must be present to diagnose substance dependence. Substance abuse is considered a lesser form of substance dependence, implies spasmodic rather than continuous use, and comprises the same behavioral criteria but not tolerance and physical dependence. The DSM-IV definitions, the most widely used definitions in the United States, are similar in essence, if not in terminology, to internationally accepted definitions of drug addiction.

Anybody treating chronic pain with opioids and experiencing the problematic behaviors of their patients will recognize that the behaviors seen in clinic bear little relationship to those listed in the DSM-IV criteria that are associated

TABLE 1 Diagnostic and Statistical Manual of Mental Disorders-IV Substance Dependence Criteria

Tolerance

Withdrawal, as manifested by either the characteristic withdrawal syndrome or the same or closely related substance is taken to relieve or avoid withdrawal symptoms

The substance is often taken in larger amounts or over a longer period than intended

There is a persistent desire or unsuccessful efforts to cut down or control substance use

A great deal of time is spent in activities necessary to obtain the substance, use the substance, or recover from its effects

Important social, occupational, or recreational activities are given up or reduced because of substance use

The substance use is continued despite knowledge of having a persistent physical or psychological problem that is likely to have been caused or exacerbated by the substance

Note: Addiction (termed substance dependence by the American Psychiatric Association) is defined as a maladaptive pattern of substance use, leading to clinically significant impairment or distress, as manifested by three (or more) of the following, occurring at any time in the same 12-month period.
Source: From Ref. 10.

TABLE 2 Problematic Behaviors That Could Indicate Drug Abuse or Addiction in Patients Treated with Opioids for Chronic Pain

Self-escalation of dosage
Repeated prescription loss with "classical" excuses
  "The pills fell into the toilet bowl"
  "I left the prescription in the changing room"
  "The airline lost my luggage"
  "The dog ate it"
Multiple prescribers
Frequent telephone calls to the office
Focusing mainly on opioid issues during visits
Visiting office without an appointment

more specifically with illicit use and procurement. The behaviors seen in the pain clinic are different; they are nuisance behaviors that annoy the prescribing physician and clinic staff and are often assumed to be indicative of addiction, but have never formally been accepted as signs of addiction (Table 2). These behaviors could as easily be manifestations of a chaotic lifestyle, uncontrolled pain, or fear of withdrawal, as of addiction. In fact, such is the nonspecificity of these behaviors, and the high degree of subjectivity in judging whether an opioid-treated pain patient is addicted, that to a large extent iatrogenic opioid addiction remains nothing more specific than what the reporting person says it is.

Pain and addiction societies, recognizing these difficulties of definition when applied to pain patients, developed definitions that they felt were more appropriate for use in opioid-treated pain patients (Table 3) (11,12). The panel of experts that developed the new definitions attempted to address two issues (i) the poor applicability of the DSM-IV behavioral criteria to patients receiving opioids for pain and (ii) the possible stigma that could be attached to tolerance and physical dependence (both inevitable consequences of chronic opioid use even in the absence of behavioral problems), if these are included in addiction definitions. To address the first, they redefined addiction and identified impaired control over drugs use, compulsive use, continued use despite harm, and craving as signs of addiction. To address the second, they separated out tolerance and physical dependence from their definition of addiction. But the definitions remain unsatisfactory

TABLE 3 Definitions Related to the Use of Opioids for the Treatment of Pain

Addiction
Addiction is a primary, chronic, neurobiologic disease, with genetic, psychosocial, and environmental factors influencing its development and manifestations; it is characterized by behaviors that include one or more of the following: impaired control over drug use, compulsive use, continued use despite harm, and craving

Physical dependence
Physical dependence is a state of adaptation that is manifested by a drug class specific withdrawal syndrome that can be produced by abrupt cessation, rapid dose reduction, decreasing blood level of the drug, and/or administration of an antagonist

Tolerance
Tolerance is a state of adaptation in which exposure to a drug induces changes that result in a diminution of one or more of the drug's effects over time

Source: From consensus document from Ref. 11.

because the signs of addiction listed are difficult to identify other than as the non-specific behaviors listed in Table 2. To complete the circular argument, tolerance and physical dependence might drive such behaviors, so it does not seem logical to remove them from definitions of drug addiction.

In view of these difficulties of definition, it is not surprising that estimated risks of iatrogenic opioid addiction have varied enormously between assessors and throughout the evolution of chronic opioid treatment of pain. During the early years, addiction rates were reportedly very low. A classic report (a letter) by Porter and Jick (13) was taken out of context and often used to support low addiction rates; the report was of 0.03% addiction rates in hospitalized patients (13). More realistically, Portenoy and Foley, in a seminal paper describing opioid therapy for noncancer pain (13), reported rates of addiction of 5% (14). Rates of this order were widely accepted, despite the weak level of evidence (mostly anecdotal studies), probably overlooking the fact that the experts reporting such successes were likely providing exceptionally careful and personalized care. As these authors themselves say: "It must be recognized, therefore, that the efficacy of this therapy and its successful management may relate as much to the quality of the personal relationship between physician and patient as to the characteristics of the patient, drug, or dosing regime" (14). After a decade or more of acceptance that therapeutic opioid use was unlikely to result in addiction, the medical community began to question the supposed low rates of addiction due to a perceived increase in the number of problematic behaviors, as well as the documented increase in prescription drug abuse (15). A systemic review published in 1992 reporting addiction rates of up to 18.9% (16) failed to penetrate the vast number of educational materials that were used during the 1990s to persuade the medical community that addiction was extremely rare during the treatment of pain. Yet today, when we are justifiably more concerned, this higher rate has become widely accepted. Whatever figure we believe or accept, the true incidence of addiction in opioid-treated chronic pain patients is unknown.

Despite the dismal progress made in quantifying addiction risk during opioid treatment of chronic pain, much progress has been made in understanding the underlying mechanisms of addiction. It is now understood that the final common pathway of addiction, whether to drugs or other factors, resides in the mesocorticolimbic system and depends on dopamine activation in the so-called "reward center" of this system (Fig. 1) (17). Also, that each addictive drug has its own characteristic withdrawal syndrome, and a unique molecular basis for physical dependence. In the case of opioids, withdrawal is thought to occur because chronic opioid administration depresses noradrenaline activity in the locus ceruleus (Fig. 1), which, when opioids are withdrawn, results in a rebound outpouring of noradrenaline from this center and the characteristic clinical picture of catecholamine overactivity (central neurologic arousal and sleeplessness, irritability, psychomotor agitation, diarrhea, rhinorrhea, and piloerection) (12,18). These insights, together with the persuasive clinical research and lobbying of Nyswander, Dole and Kreek, and others, finally persuaded politicians that addiction is a disease worthy of treatment rather than a crime. Genetic differences between individuals have been shown to account for differences in opioid metabolism, disposition, sensitivity, and the balance between desirable and untoward effects, and future genetic studies are likely to be bountiful if terms of improving the risk: benefit of opioid therapy. Understanding that addiction risk must depend on the complex interplay between the drug itself and the genetic and psychosocial factors

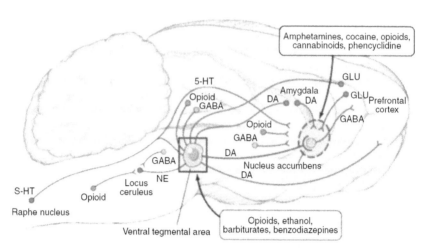

FIGURE 1   Neural reward circuits important in the reinforcing effects of drugs of abuse. As shown in the rat brain, mesocorticolimbic DA systems originating in the ventral tegmental area include projections from cell bodies of the ventral tegmental area to the nucleus accumbens, amygdala, and prefrontal cortex; GLU projections from the prefrontal cortex to the nucleus accumbens and the ventral tegmental area; and projections from the GABA neurons of the nucleus accumbens to the prefrontal cortex. Opioid interneurons modulate the GABA-inhibitory action on the ventral tegmental area and influence the firing of NE neurons in the locus ceruleus. Serotonergic (5-HT) projections from the raphe nucleus extend to the ventral tegmental area and the nucleus accumbens. The figure shows the proposed sites of action of the various drugs of abuse in these circuits. *Abbreviations*: DA, dopamine; GLU, glutamatergic; GABA, γ-aminobutyric acid; NE, norepinephrine. *Source*: From Ref. 17.

contributing to addiction, helps enormously in understanding risk and the factors contributing to risk (Fig. 2) (19). Moreover, this model helps us understand that addiction may not be an all-or-none phenomenon, but rather a continuum that could develop in any patient given the right combination of drug, psychosocial circumstance, and genetic predisposition.

LONG-TERM OPIOID EFFICACY, SIDE EFFECTS, AND COMPLICATIONS

Alternatives to opioids are limited not only by the fact that, unlike most of the opioids, they have a ceiling effect (a dose at which no further analgesia is attained, or side effects limit utility), but also by the fact that their side effects can cause serious harm. For example, the gastric effects of nonsteroidal anti-inflammatory drugs (NSAIDs) can result in fatal bleeding, and because of this risk, opioids may be a safer option, for example, when treating degenerative arthritis. Because of the clear efficacy and relative safety of opioids during the treatment of acute and terminal cancer pain, the treatment was extended to patients with chronic noncancer (nonterminal) pain. This has given the medical community an opportunity to assess the value of the treatment—both its risks and its benefits. The addiction issue is clearly of paramount importance when assessing the appropriateness of opioid treatment for chronic pain, yet it cannot be considered in isolation. Addiction and other risks must be balanced against the positive effects and potential benefit of

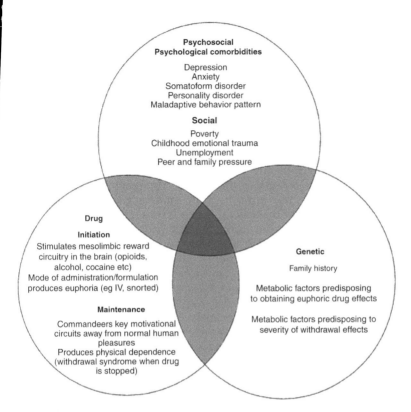

FIGURE 2 The three domains of addiction. *Source*: From Ref. 19.

opioid-induced pain relief in restoring autonomy, dignity, independence, function, and quality of life. Like most medical decisions, the decision to treat or not hinges on a complex balance between benefit and risk, for which there is no formula, and which must be judged for each individual patient.

ANALGESIC EFFICACY

One argument that has been used against using opioids for chronic pain is that chronic pain conditions may not be opioid sensitive. Uncertainty about the opioid responsiveness of broad categories of chronic pain complaints such as arthritic pain, musculoskeletal pain, neuropathic pain, and fibromyalgia led investigators to conduct randomized controlled trials (RCTs) that have convincingly established that opioids provide superior analgesic efficacy when compared to placebo and established treatments (usually NSAIDs) for a number of chronic pain conditions (20–37). Conditions studied in the published RCTs include musculoskeletal pain, neuropathic pain, and arthritis. The randomized trials were conducted for up to a maximum of 32 weeks (24). It is noteworthy that the more recent of these trials have assessed opioids for chronic neuropathic pain conditions, which, of all the chronic pain conditions, were traditionally considered nonopioid responsive. The apparent nonresponsiveness of neuropathic pain, and the fact that many chronic pain conditions likely have a neuropathic component, has been used as an argument against using opioids for chronic pain. However, the recent RCTs establish firmly that neuropathic pain is, in fact, opioid responsive, even though larger than normal doses may be required; in other words, the dose response curve is shifted to the right (26,30,33–37). Published RCTs confirm the opioid responsiveness of several chronic pain conditions, but because they are conducted only over short periods, they leave to question whether analgesic efficacy is sustained in the long-term.

Long-term analgesic efficacy is more difficult to assess, not least because the factors that influence analgesic effect over time are complex. These include: development of tolerance, development of opioid-induced hyperalgesia, and psychological factors such as changes in the placebo component. Reports in the literature comprise case and case series reports, surveys (38) and open-label follow-up studies in association with some RCTs (39). These report treatment durations of up to six years. The general finding is that patients attain satisfactory analgesia using moderate nonescalating doses (up to 195 mg morphine equivalence per day), often accompanied by an improvement in function, and minimal risk of addiction. As a point of discussion, it must be remembered that the studies contributing to this support of chronic opioid therapy are considered weak for the accepted reason that the reporters of case series may be biased toward the reported treatments, and likely carry out the treatments with unusual care (The latter is particularly relevant to chronic opioid therapy, which requires considerable dedication, patience, and caution in order to be successful) (14). Existing open-label follow-up studies suggest that the failure rate of chronic opioid therapy may be higher than was previously thought. The authors of a recent meta-analysis of chronic opioid therapy systematically assessed available follow-up studies and found a 56% drop out rate (39). Although these reviewers were unable to distinguish drop out due to inadequate analgesia from drop out due to unacceptable side effects, the high noncompletion rate does seem at odds with the high success rates reported in observational studies. Further study is needed to determine how many, and particularly which, patients respond well to long-term opioid therapy in terms of analgesic efficacy.

Anecdotally, as more patients are treated with opioids (40,41), more patients present to physicians with severe pain despite opioid treatment—sometimes despite high-dose opioid treatment (42,43). Several authors have reported that weaning these patients off opioids results in an improved sense of well-being and no change in pain; sometimes pain has even been found to improve (44,45). Mechanisms for failed opioid analgesia could be related to rampant tolerance or to opioid-induced hyperalgesia (42,46). It is now understood that repeated administration of opioids results not only in the development of tolerance (a desensitization process), but also leads to a pronociceptive process (sensitization); thus pharmacological tolerance and induced hyperalgesia are seen to coexist, just as analgesia and hyperalgesia coexist, although one may predominate over the other (42). The clinical quandary is obvious: increasing doses could improve or worsen pain. A great deal of uncertainty remains regarding whether opioid dose, length of treatment, or drug choice influences the development of hyperalgesia. Additionally, the exact clinical circumstances in which opioid-induced hyperalgesia interferes is uncertain. Nevertheless, whether it is hyperalgesia, tolerance, or other factors (including psychological factors) that interfere, it has become clear that open-ended dose escalation often fails to sustain analgesic efficacy, and the premise that tolerance can always be overcome by dose escalation is now questioned (38). It is also clear that good analgesic efficacy is not always sustained over time, and that there are clinical situations in which pain and well-being can be improved by weaning rather than continuing opioid treatment.

FUNCTION AND QUALITY OF LIFE

Many medical practitioners and experts believe that improvements in function and in quality of life are needed for long-term opioid treatment to be deemed a success, although a few believe that good pain relief, regardless of other markers of successful treatment, is enough to justify continued opioid treatment. There is little consensus on this issue. It is surprising then, given the importance of this debate, to find that the literature provides limited evidence on nonanalgesia-related outcomes. Some randomized trials combine assessments of pain relief with assessment of function, but the focus of these assessments tends to vary with the primary interest of investigators. For example, they may use the Fries Index of functions of daily living, the Ritchie score of joint tenderness, the Grip Strength Score for patients with arthritis (21), sleep indices (24,27,29), or the brief pain inventory (29). Such variability in measurement instruments precludes making an overall assessment, and while some investigators demonstrate improvements in these limited measures of function, others find no difference. Observational trials contribute little in the way of assessment of function, and although some report improvements in broad measures such as ability to perform activities of daily living and return to work, others do not comment on this issue. Few opioid trials measure quality of life, which is again surprising given the importance of this factor and the fact that there are several validated measurement instruments available. This is certainly an area for future research.

Several studies have looked specifically at cognitive function, including the ability to drive and operate machinery while on opioids. These factors are obviously critical in terms of whether opioid-treated patients should be encouraged to return to work, to normal daily activities, and in particular, to driving. These studies have found that cognitive function, manual dexterity, and reaction times are maintained at normal levels provided a stable dose of opioid is used (47–50). This may not be true when dosing is irregular or escalates (47).

SIDE EFFECTS

Opioid side effects are well known and include respiratory depression, nausea, sedation, euphoria or dysphoria, constipation, and itching. With chronic use, most side effects subside, because tolerance seems greater to side effects than to analgesic effects. Constipation is an exception, and there appears to be no tolerance to the direct slowing effects of opioids on the bowel, and accordingly constipation remains a high risk and usually requires treatment. Serious constipation and bowel obstruction may even be life threatening. The more likely threat to life, however, is respiratory depression; even though the likelihood of this occurring is reduced during chronic use, it may still occur, especially when a regime is changed or when an opioid is not used as directed. Death due to respiratory depression and sedation may arise during end of life care, and ethical issues related to providing relief from pain and suffering at the risk of hastening death at the end of life present difficult ethical dilemmas that are discussed elsewhere in this book.

HORMONAL AND IMMUNE EFFECTS

Long-term opioid use results in clinically relevant suppression of both hypothalamo-pituitary-adrenal and -gonadal axes, with suppression in luteininzing hormone, follicle-stimulating hormone, testosterone, estrogen, and cortisol (51–53). These effects have been demonstrated in addicts, past addicts treated with methadone maintenance (51) and more recently, in opioid-treated chronic pain patients (52). The effects are most prominent in patients treated with intrathecal opioids (54–56). The gonadal effects can result in male and female infertility and decreased libido, drive, and aggression. Clinically, testosterone deficiency is the most frequently manifest of the deficiencies, and male patients can benefit from testosterone replacement (55,57). Although the suppressive effect of opioids on the endocrine system seems clear, determining the exact contribution to health of these effects is not straightforward. Most chronic pain patients present with complex medical and psychosocial histories, and many have underlying neuroendocrine derangements, either because of coexisting medical illness, or because of the effects of their treatment. Chronic pain and depression often coexist, and both are associated with disturbances in the hypothalamic-pituitary-adrenal axis. Thus, even knowing the likely direct effects of opioids on endocrine function, their exact clinical relevance in an individual patient is not clear.

Opioid drugs may affect immunity through their neuroendocrine effects, or through direct effects on the immune system. Preclinical research convincingly demonstrates that opioids alter the development, differentiation, and function of immune cells. Moreover, opioid receptors have been found to exist on immune cells (58,59). Bone marrow progenitor cells, macrophages, natural killer cells, immature thymoctyes, and T cells and B cells are all affected. Evidence of immune modulation in humans is limited, but opioids have been shown to exacerbate immunosuppression in HIV patients, which suggests that prolonged opioid use may affect the immune system, at least in immunocompromised persons (60). There are no studies of immune function in patients receiving long-term opioid therapy for chronic pain. However, the direct evidence that opioids impair immune function in susceptible individuals is of concern. Pain itself can suppress immune function, so patients receiving prolonged opioid therapy without good pain relief are probably the most vulnerable.

SUMMARY OF THE EVIDENCE SUPPORTING LONG-TERM OPIOID USE

Many years of clinical use of opioids for pain made it clear that opioids are strong and effective analgesics. Randomized trials were conducted specifically to assess whether chronic pain conditions such as fibromyalgia, arthralgia, and neuralgia (conditions that were often considered nonresponsive to opioids), could be effectively treated with opioid. The randomized trials confirm the sensitivity to opioids of several common chronic pain conditions and demonstrate that a short course of treatment (up to 32 weeks) using moderate doses (up to 180 mg morphine or equivalent) is effective.

To assess other questions—the many issues that determine whether opioid treatment can be continued as chronic therapy—it is necessary to turn to less satisfactory sources of evidence. Here, the existing published literature yields only limited information. With regard to sustained analgesic efficacy, many authors report (in case reports and case series) prolonged and satisfactory analgesia for up to six years using moderate doses of opioid (up to 195 mg morphine or equivalent) (38). Yet others report that failed patients improve when taken off opioids.

It seems that in these patients at least, there is virtually no analgesic effect, because treatment discontinuation results in no change in pain (44,45). Reports of difficulty controlling acute pain when it arises in opioid-treated or opioid-using patients also suggest that either tolerance or hyperalgesia are interfering with analgesic efficacy (61). Sustained analgesic efficacy, and the reliability of dose escalation to overcome tolerance, must be questioned.

The next question is whether chronic opioid treatment improves not just a simple pain score, but broader outcomes such as function (ability to work and perform normal daily activity) and quality of life. Whether such improvements are necessary in order to deem chronic opioid therapy a success is an issue that is much debated, but these broader outcomes could be considered paramount. Yet evidence on these outcomes is extremely limited. Is this paucity of evidence due to a tendency to rely too heavily on randomized trials in this era of evidence-based medicine and evidence hierarchies? The conduct of controlled trials over prolonged periods is logistically difficult, especially for chronic pain patients. Randomized trials generally select atypical (ideal) patients who are (i) willing to be randomized out of opioid therapy and (ii) motivated to improve. These factors alone place significant limitations on the ability of randomized trials to assess chronic opioid therapy. We lack well-structured and well-conceived multicenter observational studies. This deficiency has been widely recognized in the pain community, and several groups are now in the process of developing simple measurement tools that may help stratify risk, identify deterioration in life measures, and record important outcomes in a standardized manner for future incorporation in multicenter studies (62–66).

Although data regarding common side effects and complications are available from the published trials and reports already described, these suggesting that side effects such as nausea, dysphoria, sedation, and constipation can significantly interfere with treatment (39) the more insidious complications or liabilities are assessed by a separate literature. These include hormonal and immune effects, and addiction. Studies in opioid addicts, methadone-treated recovering addicts, and more recently opioid-treated chronic pain patients, clearly demonstrate clinically significant hormonal changes (51,52,55,57). Immune changes have also been demonstrated but these have uncertain clinical significance (60). The clinical question is whether these effects, independent of other more direct opioid effects, contribute to the general poor psychological and physical health of opioid-treated patients. The complexity of interactions among psychological, neuroendocrine, and immune factors defies understanding, but it seems important, at least, to be able to identify any changes that may be amenable to treatment or improved by opioid dose adjustment. The studies of these issues are in their infancy, but the medical community has been alerted to the potential of these opioid effects to cause deteriorations in the health of patients on opioids.

Finally, on the question of addiction and its prevalence during the treatment of pain with opioids, the literature is uncertain. While extremes of addiction and freedom from addiction may seem apparent, it remains difficult to determine whether the patients who fall between the extremes are addicted or not. There are no satisfactory definitions of iatrogenic opioid addiction, and the lack of an accepted incidence stems from this lack of agreed definition. The published rate lies between 5% in some practice settings and 19% in others, but as stated earlier, these figures can only be interpreted as reflecting addiction as defined by the person reporting—not by a generally agreed definition. Until or unless medical science advances to the point of identifying a marker of addiction, either through advanced imaging or through genetic profiling, addiction can only be regarded as a continuum—a risk that could theoretically arise in any patient given the right combination of drug, psychosocial situation, and genetic predisposition.

DISCUSSION

During the 20th century, the effectiveness and relative harmlessness of opioid therapy for acute and cancer pain were firmly established, and ethical struggles related to opioid use were drawn away from these relatively straightforward[b] realms of opioid treatment. Opioid treatments for acute and terminal cancer pain are consistent with popular biomedical ethical principles (67). **Autonomy**: Choice can be open because of a low likelihood of harm and virtually no risk of problematic addiction. **Beneficence**: No other currently available systemic treatment has equivalent analgesic efficacy. **Nonmaleficence**: The treatment is generally safe, provided care is taken with regard to the potentially dangerous side effects of respiratory depression and suppression of bowel mobility; the harmful effects of pain are avoided; problematic addiction virtually never arises. **Justice**: There is no rational reason to deny treatment.

Opioid treatment of chronic, long-term pain, on the other hand, is associated with overwhelming ethical dilemmas with regard to each of these principles, and these are primarily related to addiction. Even though addiction arises in only a minority of patients during opioid treatment of chronic pain, at present there is no reliable means of either predicting or identifying addiction in opioid-treated pain patients, thus the addiction risk must be considered in all patients[c] (68,69).

Addiction is a miserable state. It tends to be associated with secrecy and shame. It pervades the personality and core values of the sufferers, thereby destroying their lives. When an illegal substance is involved, the situation is made worse when the sufferers are driven to commit crime to obtain the substance, and often find themselves at the mercy of ruthless traders who take advantage of their addictive state. Opioid addiction differs from all other drug addictions. Uniquely, the drugs act via an endogenous system that consists of receptors and endogenous ligands that are themselves opioids. Not only does this mean that opioid

---

[b] Except end of life issues.
[c] These distinctions may seem simplistic, especially to clinicians treating pain, who will understand that acute, chronic, and cancer pain readily merge, even in a single individual. Nevertheless, the idea that chronic pain should be considered as a separate entity remains a useful basis for thought that attempts to preserve the progress made by pain advocates toward balancing the need for opioids for the relief of pain against the need for opioid controls. Fear mongering about addiction inhibited opioid treatment of pain and significantly hampered pain relief, particularly in the United States, throughout much of the twentieth century. Kathleen Foley nicely encapsulates the problem with a clinical anecdote which, as she says, captures the reality of the undertreatment of pain which is one of the serious, unintended consequences of the war on drugs. She quotes one of her patients: *"I would rather be in pain than be considered an addict."* Yet considering our recent state of knowledge about the prevalence and mechanisms of addiction, it would seem as damaging to patients to hide what is understood about addiction during chronic pain treatment, because it has been making them fearful of addiction during treatment of acute and terminal cancer pain. The least harm is done through honest appraisal, with every effort to remove emotional and irrational rhetoric from pain and opioid advocacy.

euphoria—the assumed trigger of opioid addiction—can be achieved without exogenous drugs, but also that endogenous opioid mechanisms are involved in other addictions, e.g., alcohol addiction (70–72). Opioids are the only drugs with an important medical indication that are so strongly addictive that they have come under regulatory scrutiny; physicians bear the burden of prescribing these necessary drugs within legal constraints. Moreover, opioid addiction is the only addiction that has been found responsive to maintenance treatment. The effectiveness of opioid maintenance for opioid craving, established by Nyswander, Dole, and Kreek in the 1960s (4) has now been validated by over 30 years of successful use. As Vincent Dole says: "The typical heroin addict is a gentle person, trapped in chemical slavery, pathetically grateful for understanding and effective treatment" (73). Addicted patients maintained on opioids (traditionally methadone) are seen to have improved social functioning, often operating normally in society and in the workplace, sometimes at a high level. They also have a lower recidivism rate than nontreated addicts (74). Failed opioid maintenance (which seems to occur in 10% to 25% of those in methadone programs) (75) is thought to occur because of a predominance of craving for the paraphernalia, depravity, and other associations of opioid use, over that for the drug itself. If this is true, opioid treated pain patients will be less likely to fail maintenance treatment because they will not have been exposed to the excitements of illicit opioid use and procurement. A parallel between the principles of opioid maintenance for pain and those for addiction emerges, wherein both involve careful selection and follow up. The chief difference is that for the former, principles of care are recommended, whereas for the latter, they are mandated. Comparison of the recommended guidelines for opioid treatment of chronic pain (38,76) and the principles of opioid treatment for addiction (77,78) amply supports the contention that little separates them. One could argue, then, that if problematic behaviors arise during opioid treatment of chronic pain, the best approach is for the treating physician to continue careful maintenance treatment.

The argument for opioid treatment of pain states that opioids are indispensable for the treatment of pain and suffering (69). This argument is further supported knowing that uncontrolled pain may have deleterious physical (79–81) and psychological sequelae; persistent pain destroys the individual's autonomy and dignity and compromises the person's decision-making capacity. But the argument for opioid treatment always occurs against a backdrop of concerns about addiction. The "principle of balance" recognizes that opioids are indispensable, that they may also be abused, and that efforts to address abuse should not interfere with legitimate medical practice and patient care (82,83). Yet in the case of chronic pain treatment, on the one hand we may see analgesic efficacy diminishing over time (38,39,44,45) and on the other, addressing abuse may involve complex and far-reaching considerations that inevitably interfere. The question of whether to accept the addiction risk is complicated by the fact that sustained analgesic efficacy is not guaranteed, not least because addiction risk is markedly increased once treatment is begun. This is yet another argument for caution in selecting and managing chronic opioid treatment.

Traditional medical ethics have focused on ensuring that the power of physicians is used benevolently. Physicians have taken a paternalistic role based on their superior knowledge and status, with the patients being vulnerable and passive partners in physician–patient relationships. Contemporary medical ethics have had to adapt to the political philosophy that now guides liberal states such as the United States. The philosophy of liberalism is described as "a political philosophy based in belief in progress, the essential goodness of man, and autonomy of the individual and standing for the protection of political and civil liberties" (84). The physician is no longer seen as all powerful or the chief decision maker in an active–passive relationship, but instead enters a guidance-cooperation relationship, whereby the patient is the chief decision-maker, guided by the physician (85). The patient assumes the right to self-determination. The need to reformulate medical ethics became urgent in the 20th century because the rapidly evolving biomedical sciences threatened the presumptions of life itself. This culminated in the writing of a patients' charter adopted by the U.S. Advisory Commission on Consumer Protection and Quality in the Health Care Industry in 1998 (86). Many health plans now incorporate the charter's principles. Participation in treatment decisions is considered a right: "You have the right to know your treatment options and to participate in decisions about your care. Parents, guardians, family members, or other individuals that you designate can represent you if you cannot make your own decisions." Yet the ethical context must continue to acknowledge the reality of the physician's superior knowledge that forms the basis for maintaining the tenets of duty and selflessness on the part of the physician. When the patient is considered incompetent, the guidance-cooperation model breaks down, and the relationship again relies on benevolent paternalism. Patients' right to pain treatment, including opioid treatment, has now been established, albeit after years of lobbying and political activism on the part of pain advocates, culminating in the enactment of so-called "intractable pain" statutes (87). "Controlled substances and, in particular, narcotic analgesics may be used in the treatment of pain experienced by a patient with a terminal illness or chronic disorder. These drugs have a legitimate clinical use and the physician should not hesitate to prescribe, dispense, or administer them when they are indicated for a legitimate medical purpose" (88).

Despite the established right of patients to receive opioid treatment for acute, terminal, and chronic pain, key ethical issues persist. The most intransigent of these during the treatment of chronic pain with opioids are centered on whether a patient at risk of developing addiction should embark on a course of chronic opioid treatment. Will addiction become a greater burden than pain? Who is in the better position to judge whether addiction will arise—the physician or the patient? Does the physician have the tools to identify a likely abuser? Does the physician perceive that the patient is incapable of self-determination either because of the pervasive effect of intractable pain, or because of the influence of past or present drug use? Then does the physician's presumption of the patient's incompetence compromise the patient's autonomy? (89). The complexity of these ethical issues, and the recognition of the uniqueness of these and other issues to the new field of pain medicine, made obvious the need for a specific charter of ethics for pain medicine. In 2005, a committee of the American Academy of Pain Medicine, including both physicians with ethical interests and ethicists with medical expertise, published an Ethics Charter for pain medicine (69,82). It had taken 10 years to finally progress beyond draft stage for this document, and it will likely need modification as the political and legal landscape changes. Nevertheless, the document represents an important advance in that it clearly and rationally delineates ethical dilemmas affecting the provision of pain treatment in an era in which the constraints of policies, laws, and medical enterprise complicate physicians' traditional moral priority to relieve pain and suffering.

Drug laws reflect the moral-political values of a country. In the United States and other liberal societies, the law respects individual freedom, and antidrug laws target the production, importation, and dissemination of drugs, not individual users. The aim of antidrug laws is to control illicit drug availability, thereby protecting the population, particularly its vulnerable sectors. Thus the laws aim to protect communal values. Communitarianism, so-called, has tended to be the province of political rather than traditional biomedical ethics, where the physician's primary duty is to the patient (90). But as medicine moves away from the model of highly individualist relationships between patients and their physicians, in which moral issues are decided within its partnerships and patients are protected by the tenets of the Hippocratic tradition "producing good for the patient and protecting that patient from harm" (91), it becomes necessary for public morality to constrain and modify medical ethics (92). Medical practice is thus increasingly directed by guidelines, regulations, and mandates, and less by the dictates of individual physicians. In keeping with this trend, and recognizing that the institution of drug regulations had a chilling effect on opioid treatment of pain, attempts are now being made to restore pain treatment through the introduction of guidelines and mandates (76,93,94). In 1998, the Federation of State Medical Boards promulgated guidelines for the use of controlled substances for the treatment of pain (76). Apart from disseminating the principles of careful opioid pain management, the goal of these guidelines was to remove misunderstandings on the part of both physicians and regulators about the legitimate role of opioids in outpatient pain treatment and to encourage physicians to prescribe opioids without fear of censure. A second effort to extend the reach of pain treatment was made when a consortium of pain bodies, believing that pain's visibility could improved by mandating the development of processes to increase provider accountability for the assessment and treatment of pain, solicited the involvement of the Joint Commission on Accreditation of Healthcare Organizations (JCAHO) (95). JCAHO pain standards were formally introduced into the accreditation process in 2001 (94). The aim of the JCAHO mandate was to raise awareness of the existence of pain and to encourage institutions to institute systems that ensure active pain management and education; there was never an intention that the mandate should be used specifically to encourage opioid treatment of pain. Nevertheless, it is impossible to separate opioid issues from pain issues, and right or wrong, the mandate is being used to ensure that opioid treatment is offered.

The preceding discussion has explored reasons supporting long-term opioid treatment for the relief of chronic pain, and reasons for carrying out such treatment carefully and selectively. If, then, the treatment is not suitable for all patients in pain, how should patients be selected for treatment? This presents among the most difficult moral and ethical decisions for physicians facing individuals with uncontrolled and debilitating pain, decisions that are made all the more difficult when legal considerations intervene. The easiest course would be to allow all patients needing treatment to start carefully managed opioid treatment, being prepared to wean if necessary. But when we know that the risk for individuals predisposed to addiction is increased by giving an addictive drug, does this make the risk of prescribing opioids unacceptable for certain patients, and do we have the means of identifying those at risk? At present, we do not, although a number of groups are developing measurement tools that might prove valuable in helping physicians stratifying risk (62–66). And even though it is supposed that known substance abusers are at greater risk than others, evidence to date suggests that these patients do not, in fact, present an increased risk when receiving opioids for the treatment of pain (96–98). It seems, therefore, that a history of substance abuse per se is not necessarily associated with problematic use during opioid treatment of pain. Yet a substance abuse history may constitute only one component of complex circumstances involving the social situation of both individual patients and their community. For example, physicians may find themselves deciding whether their patients are likely to abuse or divert on the basis of income, race, social status, criminal record, employment status, being perceived as a malinger or drug-seeker, or being known as a frequent drug offender. Physicians are either helplessly torn between legal obligation, duty to patients, and duty to the community; or, they may take the more comfortable position of considering only their moral duty to patients. Physicians may receive little guidance or training that helps them make troubling decisions regarding individual patients, despite the existence of guidelines, mandates, and ethical charters broadly recommending fair distribution and careful selection (82,99). Recognizing that the rapidly changing healthcare environment presents physicians with moral-ethical-legal conflicts with which they are ill-equipped to deal, hospitals and specialty bodies have begun developing ethics committees and forums to provide guidance on the specific aspects of individual cases that may not have been captured by the deductive model (82,90,100).

CONCLUSION

As well as imposing legal considerations on medical decisions regarding opioid use, drug regulations have had the effect of criminalizing and stigmatizing addiction in the minds of both care providers and patients. Addiction issues are so complex and uncertain that physicians have tended to compartmentalize opioid treatment for pain versus addiction. Those treating pain do not treat addiction, and, legally, are they not permitted to do so. Should addiction arise during the treatment of pain with opioids, the patient must seek specialty care. I will argue that it is this situation that has produced the most harm in terms of treating chronic pain with opioids. For the many reasons outlined in this chapter, the medical community has rightly embraced opioid therapy for chronic pain, but it has not fully accepted that opioid dependence—psychological as well as physical—will interfere, to an extent not yet fully defined. When problematic addiction arises, patients are too often abandoned to trail from physician to physician until they can receive the treatment they need, or worse still, obtain illicit supplies. Even if it is offered, they may not accept addiction or psychiatric treatment, either because of the stigma associated with such treatment, the restrictive nature of addiction programs (e.g., participants have difficulty keeping a regular work schedule), or the insurance and employment constraints associated with psychiatric treatment. Yet these patients, and those with less severe problematic behaviors that do not necessarily fulfill addiction criteria, above all, need continued careful care. Chronic opioid pain therapy must be embraced recognizing the complexity of the treatment and the uncertain addiction risk. The treatment must be carried out with care, as recommended in the literature (14,38,76). It is important to continue the process of education about the role of opioids in pain and addiction, not separating the two. Finally, we must continue to persuade the regulatory bodies to make addiction treatment less restrictive so that patients are not stigmatized and abandoned when they do become unmanageable in the hands of unwary but well-intentioned physicians treating pain[d]. In today's humane and liberal society, it is not

---

[d] There has already been improvement in the recent introduction to the U.S. of office-based addiction treatment. (Drug Addiction Treatment Act of 2000) (77).

ethical, legal or good medical practice to withhold long-term opioids from patients whose lives could be improved by the treatment. The key element, however, is that the treatment should improve patients' lives. Present evidence strongly suggests that the best way to do this is through a cautious, selective, and supportive approach.

REFERENCES

1. Horder TJ. Manufacture of Heroin. London: The Times, 1955:11e.
2. Anslinger H, Tompkins W. The Traffic in Narcotics. Library of congress catalog card number 536984. 1953.
3. Webb et al. v. United States 2 U.S. 9. 1919.
4. Dole VP, Nyswander M, Krekk MJ. Narcotic blockade. Arch Int Med 1966; 188:304–309.
5. Pert CB, Snyder SH. Opiate receptor binding of agonists and antagonists affected differentially by sodium. Mol Pharmacol 1974; 10:868–879.
6. Hughes I, Smith TW, Kosterlitz HW, Fothergitt FA, Morgan BA, Morris HE. Identification of two related pentapeptides from the brain with potent opiate agonist activity. Nature 1975; 258:577–579.
7. DHHS, SAMHSA. National Household Survey on Drug Abuse Main Findings. 1998:Series H-11.
8. DHHS, SAMHSA. National Survey on Drug Use and Health. www.oas.samha.gov, 2003.
9. Narita M, Kishimoto Y, Ise Y, Yajima Y, Misawa K, Suzuki T. Direct evidence for the involvement of the mesolimbic kappa-opioid system in the morphine-induced rewarding effect under an inflammatory pain-like state. Neuropsychopharmacology 2005; 30:111–118.
10. American Psychiatric Association. Diagnostic and Statistical Manual of Mental Disorders. 4th ed. Washington, DC: American Psychiatric Association, 1994.
11. Savage S, Covington EC, Ehit HA, Hunt J, Joranson D, Schnoll SH. Definitions related to the use of opioids for the treatment of pain : a consensus document from the American Academy of Pain Medicine:the American Pain Society and the American Society of Addiction Medicine, 2001.
12. Savage SR, Joranson DE, Covington EC, Schnoll SH, Heit HA, Gilson AM. Definitions related to the medical use of opioids: evolution toward universal agreement. J Pain Symptom Manage 2003; 26:655–667.
13. Porter J, Jick H. Addiction rare in patients treated with narcotics (letter). N Engl J Med 1980; 2:123.
14. Portenoy RK, Foley KM. Chronic use of opioid analgesics in nonmalignant pain: report of 38 cases. Pain 1986; 25:171–186.
15. U.S. Dept of Health and Human Services. Substance Abuse and Mental Health Services Administration, Office of Applied Studies. National Survey on Drug Use and Health, 2004. ICPSR04373-VI. Research Triangle Park. NC Research Triangle Institute, 2005. Ann Arbor, MI Inter-University Consortium for Political and Social Research 2006; 05–12.
16. Fishbain DA, Rosomoff HL, Rosomoff RS. Drug abuse, dependence and addiction in chronic pain patients. Clin J Pain 1992; 8:77–85.
17. Cami J, Farre M. Drug addiction. N Engl J Med 2003; 349:975–986.
18. Heit HA. Addiction, physical dependence, and tolerance: precise definitions to help clinicians evaluate and treat chronic pain patients [Review] [30 refs]. J Pain Palliat Care Pharmacother 2003; 17(1):15–29.
19. Ballantyne J. Pharmacology and practice of opioid drugs for visceral pain. In: Pasricha J, Gebhart G, eds. Chronic Abdominal and Visceral Pain: Theory and Practice. Boca Ratan, FL: CRC Press, 2006.
20. Kjaersgaard-Andersen P, Nafei A, Skov O, et al. Codeine plus paracetamol versus paracetamol in longer-term treatment of chronic pain due to osteoarthritis of the hip: a randomised, double-blind, multicentre study. Pain 1990; 43:309–318.

21. Moran C. MST continus tablets and pain control in severe rheumatoid arthritis. Br J Clin Res 1991; 2:1–12.
22. Arkinstall W, Sandler A, Groghnour B, Babul N, Harsanyi Z, Darke AC. Efficacy of controlled-release codeine in chronic nonmalignant pain: a randomized placebo-controlled clinical trial. Pain 1995; 62:168–178.
23. Moulin DE, Iezzi A, Amireh R, Sharpe WKJ, Boyd D, Merskey H. Randomized trial of oral morphine for chronic noncancer pain. Lancet 1996; 347:143–147.
24. Jamison RN, Raymond SA, Slawsby EA, Nedeljkovic SS, Katz NP. Opioid therapy for chronic noncancer back pain: a randomized prospective study. Spine 1998; 23:2591–2600.
25. Sheather-Reid RB, Cohen ML. Efficacy of analgesics in chronic pain: a series of n-of-1 studies. J Pain Symptom Manage 1998; 15:244–252.
26. Watson CPN, Babul N. Efficacy of oxycodone in neuropathic pain: a randomized trial in postherpetic neuralgia. Neurology 1998; 50:1837–1841.
27. Caldwell JR, Hale ME, Boyd RE, et al. Treatment of osteoarthritis pain with controlled release oxycodone or fixed combination oxycodone plus acetaminophen added to nonsteroidal antiinflammatory drugs: a double blind, randomized, multicenter, placebo controlled trial. J Rheumatol 1999; 26:862–869.
28. Peloso PM, Bellamy N, Bensen W, et al. Double blind randomized placebo-control trial of controlled release codeine in the treatment of osteoarthritis of the hip or knee. J Rheumatol 2000; 19:764–771.
29. Roth SH, Fleischmann RM, Burch RX, et al. Around-the-clock, controlled-release oxycodone therapy for osteosrthritis-related pain. Arch Intern Med 2000; 160:853–860.
30. Huse E, Larbig W, Flor H, Birbaumer N. The effect of opioids on phantom limb pain and cortical reorganization. Pain 2001; 90:47–55.
31. Caldwell JR, Rapoport RJ, Davis JC, et al. Efficacy and safety of a once-daily morphine formulation in chronic, moderate-to-severe osteoarthritis pain: results from a randomized, placebo-controlled, double-blind trial and an open-label extension trial. J Pain Symptom Manage 2002; 23:278–291.
32. Maier C, Hildebrandt J, Klinger R, Henrich-Eberl C, Lindena G. Morphine responsiveness, efficacy and tolerability in patients with chronic nontumor associated pain—results of a double-blind placebo-controlled trial (MONTAS). Pain 2002; 97:223–233.
33. Raja SN, Haythornthwaite JA, Pappagallo MClark MR, et al. A placebo-controlled trial comparing the analgesic and cognitive effects of opioids and tricyclic antidepressants in postherpetic neuralgia. Neurology 2002; 59:1015–1021.
34. Gimbel JS, Richards P, Portenoy RK. Controlled-release oxycodone for pain in diabetic neuropathy: a randomized controlled trial [see comment]. Neurology 2003; 60(6):927–934.
35. Morley JS, Bridson J, Nash TP, Miles JB, White S, Makin MK. Low-dose methadone has an analgesic effect in neuropathic pain: a double-blind randomized controlled crossover trial. Palliat Med 2003; 17:576–587.
36. Rowbotham MD, Twilling L, Davies PS, Reisner L, Taylor K, Mohr D. Oral opioid therapy for chronic peripheral and central neuropathic pain. N Engl J Med 2003; 348:1223–1232.
37. Watson CPN, Moulin D, Watt-Watson J, Gordon A, Eisenhoffer J. Controlled-release oxycodone relieves neuropathic pain: a randomized controlled trial in painful diabetic neuropathy. Pain 2003; 105:71–78.
38. Ballantyne JC, Mao J. Opioids for chronic pain. N Engl J Med 2003; 349:1943–1953.
39. Kalso E, Edwards J, Moore R, McQuay H. Opioids in chronic noncancer pain: systematic review of efficacy and safety. Pain 2004; 112:372–380.
40. Gilson A, Ryan K, Joranson D, Dahl J. A reassessment of trends in the medical use and abuse of opioid analgesics and implications for diversion control. J Pain Symptom Manange 2004; 28:176–188.
41. U.S. Drug Enforcement Administration. Automation of Reports and Consolidated Orders System (ARCOS); http://www.deadiversion.usdoj.gov/arcos/retail_drug_-summary/index.html.

42. Mao J. Opioid induced abnormal pain sensitivity: implications in clinical opioid therapy. Pain 2002; 100:213–217.
43. Mercadante S. Opioid rotation for cancer pain. Cancer 1999; 86:1856–1866.
44. Schofferman J. Long-term use of opioid analgesics for the treatment of chronic pain of nonmalignant origin. J Pain Symptom Manage 1993; 8:279–288.
45. Harden RN. Chronic opioid therapy: another reappraisal. APS Bull 2002; 12(1).
46. Mao J, Price DD, Mayer DJ. Mechanisms of hyperalgesia and opiate tolerance: a current view of their possible interactions. Pain 1995; 62:259–274.
47. Bruera E, Macmillan K, Hanson J, MacDonald N. The cognitive effects of the administration of narcotic analgesic in patients with cancer pain. Pain 1989; 39:13–16.
48. Vainio A, Ollila J, Matikainen E, Rosenberg P, Kalso E. Driving ability in cancer patients in patients receiving long-term morphine analgesia. Lancet 1995; 346:667–670.
49. Galski T, Willimas B, Ehle HT. Effects of opioids on driving ability. J Pain Symptom Manage 2000; 19:200–208.
50. Haythornthwaite JA, Menefee LA, Quatrano-Piacentini AL, Pappagalla M. Outcome of chronic opioid therapy for noncancer pain. J Pain Symptom Manage 1998; 15:185–194.
51. Mendelson JH, Meyer RE, Ellingboe J, Mirin SM, McDougle M. Effects of heroin and methadone on plasma cortisol and testosterone. J Pharmacol Exp Ther 1975; 195:296–302.
52. Daniell HW. Hypogonadism in men consuming sustained-action oral opioids. J Pain 2002a; 3:377–384.
53. Lee C, Ludwig S, Duerksen D. Low serum cortisol associated with opioid use-case report and review of literature. Endocrinologist 2002; 12:5–8.
54. Paice JA, Penn RD, Shott S. Intraspinal morphine for chronic pain: a retrospective, multicenter study. J Pain Symptom Manage 1996; 11:71–80.
55. Finch PM, Roberts LJ, Price L, Hadlow NC, Pullan PT. Hypogonadism in patients treated with intrathecal morphine. Clin J Pain 2000; 3:251–254.
56. Abs R, Verhelst J, Maeyaert J, Van Buyten JP, et al. Endocrine consequences of long-term intrathecal administration of opioids. J Clinic Endocrinol Metab 2000; 85:2215–2222.
57. Daniell HW. Narcotic-induced hypogonadism during therapy for heroin addiction. J Addict Dis 2002b; 21:47–53.
58. Roy S, Loh HH. Effects of opioids on the immune system. Neurochem Res 1996; 21:1375–1386.
59. Risdahl JM, Khanno KV, Peterson PK, Molitor TW. Opiates and infection. J Neuroimmunol 1998; 83:4–18.
60. Peterson PK, Sharp BM, Gekker G, Poroghese PS, Sannerud K, Balfour HH. Morphine promotes the growth of HIV-1 in human peripheral blood mononuclear cell cocultures. AIDS 1990; 4:869–873.
61. Mitra S, Sinatra RS. Perioperative management of acute pain in the opioid-dependent patient. Anesthesiology 2004; 101:212–227.
62. Chabal C, Erjavec MK, Jacobson L, et al. Prescription opiate abuse in chronic pain patinets: clinical criteria, incidence and predictors. Clin J Pain 1997; 13:150–155.
63. Compton P, Darakjian J, Miotto K. Screening for addiction in patients with chronic pain with "problematic" substance use: evaluation of a pilot assessment tool. J Pain Symptom Manage 1998; 16:355–363.
64. Passik SD, Kirsh KL, Whitcomb L, et al. A new tool to assess and document pain outcomes in chronic pain patients receiving opioid therapy. Clin Ther 2004; 26(4):552–561.
65. Adams LL, Gatchel RJ, Robinson RC, et al. Development of a self-report screening instrument for assessing potential opioid medication misuse in chronic pain patients. J Pain Symptom Manage 2004; 27(5):440–459.
66. Butler SF, Budman SH, Fernandez K, Jamison RN. Validation of a screener and opioid assessment measure for patients with chronic pain. Pain 2004; 112:65–75.
67. Beauchamp TL, Childress JF. Principles of Biomedical Ethics. 4th ed. Oxford: Oxford University Press, 1994:11.
68. Gourlay DL, Heit HA, Almahrezi A. Universal precautions in pain medicine: a rational approach to the treatment of chronic pain. Pain Med 2005; 6:107–112.

69. AAPM Council on Ethics. American Academy of Pain Medicine. Ethics Charter Available at: www.painmed.org/productpub/pdfs/EthicsCharter.pdf, 2005.
70. Oswald LM, Wand GS. Opioids and alcoholism. Physiol Behav 2004; 81:339–358.
71. Sinclair JD. Evidence about the use of naltrexone and for different ways of using it in the treatment of alcoholism. Alcohol Alcoholism 2001; 36:2–10.
72. Mangold DL, Peyrot M, Giggey P, Wand GS. Endogenous opioid activity is associated with obsessive-compulsive symptomology in individuals with a family history of alcoholism. Neuropsychopharmacology 2000; 22:595–607.
73. Dole VP. What we have learned from threee decades of methadone treatment. Drug Alcohol Rev 1994; 13:3–4.
74. Brecher EM, Editors of Consumer Reports Magazine. How well does methadone maintenance work? The Consumers Union Report on Licit and Illicit Drugs. Schaffer Library of Drug Policy. Available at: http://www.druglibrary.org/schaffer/Library/studies/cu/CU15/html. Accessed 1/8/2006.
75. Chambers CD, Babst DV, Warner A. Characteristics predicting long-term retention in methadone maintenance programs. Proceedings, Third Methadone Conference, 1970.
76. West JE, Aronoff G, Dahl JL, et al. Model guidelines for the use of controlled substances for the treatment of pain. A policy document of the Federation of State Medical Boards of the United States, Inc. Federation of State Medical Goards of the United States, Inc., Euless Texas 1998 [Abstr].
77. Waiver authority for physicians who dispense or prescribe certain narcotic drugs for maintenance treatment or detoxification treatment. Center for Substance Abuse Treatment, H.R., Rockville, MD, 2000; 4365:122–127 (Access at http://www.samhsa.gov/centers/csat/csat.html).
78. Fiellin DA, O'Connor PG. Office-based treatment of opioid-dependent patients. N Engl J Med 2002; 347:817–823.
79. Carr DB, Goudas LC. Acute pain. Lancet 1999; 353:2051–2058.
80. Kehlet H, Dahl JB. Anaesthesia, surgery, and challenges in postoperative recovery. Lancet 2003; 362:1921–1928.
81. Brennan TJ, Kehlet H. Preventive analgesia to reduce wound hyperalgesia and persistent postsurgical pain: not an easy path. Anesthesiol 2005; 103:681–683.
82. Dubois MY. The birth of an ethics charter for pain medicine. Pain Med 2005; 6:201–202.
83. Joranson DE, Gilson AM, Dahl JL, Haddox JD. Pain medicine, controlled substances, and state medical board policy: a decade of change. J Pain Symptom Manage 2002; 23:138–147.
84. Brennan TA. Just doctoring. Medical Ethics in the Liberal State. Berkeley and Los Angeles, CA: University of California Press 1991a:3 (Brennan quotes the Webster Dictionary definition of liberalism).
85. Szasz T, Hollender J. The basic model of the doctor–patients relationship. Arch Int Med 1956; 97:85–90.
86. Advisory Commission on Consumer Protection and Quality in the Health Care Industry. Patients' Rights and Responsibilities http://www.consumer.gov/qualityhealth/rights/htm, 1998.
87. Joranson DE, Gilson AM. State intractable pain policy: current status. APS Bull 1997; 7:7–9.
88. Drug Enforcement Administration. Physician's Manual. Alexandria, VA, 1990.
89. Opinions on Practice Matters, sec 8.081:222,223. Code of Medical Ethics, Current Opinions with Annotations, 2004–2005 ed. Chicago: American Medical Association, 2004.
90. Sullivan M. Ethical principles in pain management. Pain Med 2001; 2:106–111.
91. Veach RM. The Theory of Medical Ethics. New York: Basic Books, 1981:23.
92. Brennan TA. Just Doctoring. In: Medical Ethics in the Liberal State. Berkeley and Los Angeles, CA: University of California Press, 1991b:25.
93. Acute Pain Management: Operative or Medical Procedures and Trauma. Clinical Practice Guideline. AHCPR Pub No. 92–0032. Agency for Health Care Policy and Research, Public Health Service, U.S. Department of Health and Human Services, Rockville, MD, 1992.

94. Joint Commission on Accreditation of Healthcare Organizations. Pain management standards. Effective January 1, 2001; Available at: www.jcaho.org/standard/.
95. Dahl JL, Gordon DB. Joint Commission pain standards: a progress report. APS Bull 2002; 12:1–8.
96. Weaver MF, Schnoll SH. Opioid treatment of chronic pain in patients with addiction. J Pain Palliat Care Pharmacother 2002; 16:5–26.
97. Collins ED, Streltzer J. Should opioid analgesics be used in the management of chronic pain in opiate addicts? Am J Addict 2003; 12:93–100.
98. Newman RG. Analgesia and opiate addicts. Am J Addict 2004; 13:494.
99. Fields HL. Ethical standards in pain management and research. In: Fields HL, ed. Core Curriculum for Professional Education in Pain. Seattle: IASP Press, 1995:117–123.
100. Dubois MY. Why an "ethics" forum in pain medicine. Pain Med 2000; 1:105–106.

10 Current Legal Issues Regarding the Use of Controlled Substances for the Treatment of Pain

Jennifer Bolen

The Legal Side of Pain, Knoxville, Tennessee, U.S.A.

OVERVIEW OF CURRENT LEGAL/REGULATORY LANDSCAPE

The abuse and diversion of controlled prescribed drugs is increasing, especially in young adults (1). In response to the growing problem, law enforcement authorities and state licensing boards continue to investigate clinicians and their prescribing habits. While the propriety of certain investigations, at times, has been questionable and arguably contributory to the growing fear of prescribing controlled substances, clinicians need to stay current with legal/regulatory issues pertaining to the use of controlled substances to treat pain. By doing so, clinicians can conquer their fear issues and stay prepared for unexpected board inquiries and other legal challenges. Likewise, clinicians should strive to understand the fundamentals of the legal/regulatory landscape governing prescribing of controlled substances so they can make (and document) their response to patient issues while simultaneously providing quality medical care.

Since May 2004, there have been many changes in legal/regulatory materials governing the use of controlled substances to treat pain. Many of these changes relate to the U.S. Drug Enforcement Administration's (DEA's) development of policy statements on its expectations of DEA registrants, and include the Interim Policy Statement (IPS) on Dispensing Controlled Substances for the Treatment of Pain (November 2004; the IPS) (2) and the Clarification of Existing Requirements Under the Controlled Substances Act (CSA) for Prescribing Schedule II Controlled Substances (August 2005; the Clarification Statement) (3) Also, the Federation of State Medical Boards (FSMB) adopted a revised set of guidelines for prescribing pain medication and published them in a document called the Model Policy for the Use of Controlled Substances for the Treatment of Pain (May 2004; the Model Policy) (4) Clinicians should expect DEA to issue a Final Policy Statement and a revised Physician's Manual in 2006. DEA will use these items to explain its expectations relative to a registrant's issuance of prescriptions for controlled substances, in general, and to treat pain. Similarly, and based on the DEA and FSMB's actions, clinicians should expect their state licensing boards to update board regulations/rules and prescribing guidelines/position statements, spelling out the boundaries of proper prescribing and related documentation practices. Thus, clinicians should use this chapter to become familiar with the basic legal/regulatory materials and make necessary changes to their medical practices.

IDENTIFYING BASIC LEGAL/REGULATORY MATERIALS ON CONTROLLED SUBSTANCE PRESCRIBING

There are two basic levels of legal/regulatory authorities for controlled substance prescribing: federal and state governments and their agencies. Within the federal and state framework, there are three levels of legal/regulatory materials: laws, regulations, and guidelines/position statements (5).

Typically, laws are found in acts, codes, and/or statutes—federal or state. Examples include federal and state CSAs, and state Medical, Nursing, and Pharmacy Practice Acts, state Intractable Pain Treatment Acts, and state Electronic Prescription Monitoring Acts. Laws form the base of the legal/regulatory pyramid for prescribing controlled substances, in general, and for other legal/regulatory materials affecting pain management, such as controlled substance prescribing rules and regulations governing professional conduct.

Laws give permission to federal and state agencies to regulate the flow of controlled substances and, with respect to state licensing boards, to protect the public by setting minimum expectations/standards for the practice of medicine and use of controlled substances for pain management. Laws also contain penalty provisions (civil and criminal), which are enforceable through administrative or legal process.

Regulations (sometimes called "rules") explain a corresponding law and set additional boundaries based specifically on the monitoring/sponsoring agency's interpretation of the law. Examples include the Code of Federal Regulations (CFRs), which explains the CSA of 1970, and gives DEA oversight authority for the flow of controlled substances in the United States. The individual states also have regulatory codes explaining state CSAs and medical practice acts. States also have regulations governing the operation of licensing boards.

Regulations give agencies additional permission to establish guidelines or position statements that further explain the regulations. Unfortunately, however, some state laws and regulations prohibit state licensing agencies from establishing "explanatory" or "interpretive" materials. Thus, some state medical licensing boards such as the medical boards in Illinois and Wisconsin, do not have any authority to adopt controlled substance prescribing guidelines for pain management. Regulations have the force of law, meaning violating regulations normally results in sanctions, such as licensing suspension or revocation, in addition to civil fines and penalties. Some states have both regulations and rules.

Guidelines contain an agency's explanation or interpretation of a particular subject. Guidelines are not clinical care standards. Rather, agencies use guidelines to establish minimal expectations of licensees related to the specific subject matter. Typically, those who fail to follow guidelines may face administrative sanctions (licensing restrictions or educational orders) unless one can show good cause for the deviation from or failure to follow guidelines.

Despite these basic distinctions between laws and guidelines, lawyers use guidelines to establish the framework of civil and criminal lawsuits, including medical malpractice and wrongful death cases. Guidelines sometimes contain directives and language that are outdated and inconsistent with current clinical care standards. If you live in a state that lacks guidelines or has outdated guidelines, then you will want to look to the FSMB and its Model Policy (discussed below).

SPECIFIC FEDERAL LAWS AND REGULATIONS GOVERNING PRESCRIBING

CSA of 1970 is the primary body of federal law concerning several actions: administration, dispensing, manufacturing, and prescribing of controlled substances. Congress gave the DEA, a division of the U.S. Department of Justice, the authority to administer the CSA and monitor the flow of controlled substances in this country. Importantly, this authority does not include the ability to tell clinicians how to practice medicine or even decide what constitutes a legitimate medical purpose for the use of the controlled drugs. Congress left these last two matters to the states.

SCHEDULES AND CONTROLS

The CSA lists drugs (and chemicals, etc.) subject to DEA's control using five different schedules and miscellaneous provisions—Schedule I through Schedule V. Title 21, United States Code, Section 812, which describes the Schedules as follows: (i) Schedule I: (A) The drug or other substance has a high potential for abuse. (B) The drug or other substance has no currently accepted medical use in treatment in the United States. (C) There is a lack of accepted safety for use of the drug or other substance under medical supervision. (ii) Schedule II—(A) The drug or other substance has a high potential for abuse. (B) The drug or other substance has a currently accepted medical use in treatment in the United States or a currently accepted medical use with severe restrictions. (C) Abuse of the drug or other substances may lead to severe psychological or physical dependence. (iii) Schedule III—(A) The drug or other substance has a potential for abuse less than the drugs or other substances in schedules I and II. (B) The drug or other substance has a currently accepted medical use in treatment in the United States. (C) Abuse of the drug or other substance may lead to moderate or low physical dependence or high psychological dependence. (iv) Schedule IV—(A) The drug or other substance has a low potential for abuse relative to the drugs or other substances in schedule III. (B) The drug or other substance has a currently accepted medical use in treatment in the United States. (C) Abuse of the drug or other substance may lead to limited physical dependence or psychological dependence relative to the drugs or other substances in schedule III. (v) Schedule V—(A) The drug or other substance has a low potential for abuse relative to the drugs or other substances in schedule IV. (B) The drug or other substance has a currently accepted medical use in treatment in the United States. (C) Abuse of the drug or other substance may lead to limited physical dependence or psychological dependence relative to the drugs or other substances in schedule IV. The CSA contains the rationale for drug classification and establishes controls relating to those listed in each schedule, and the lower the schedule number, the greater the number of controls placed upon the drugs within the schedule. Thus, DEA imposes the greatest restrictions on drugs in Schedule I, which have no accepted medical use in the United States. DEA imposes the fewest restrictions on drugs in Schedule V, which do have accepted medical use in this country and are, at least in theory and the world of governmental drug scheduling, the least likely to be abused and cause dependence problems. For more information regarding these issues, the DEA's Pharmacist Manual (6) may serve as a valuable resource.

REGISTRANT RESPONSIBILITIES

When an individual obtains a federal drug registration number, DEA expects the registrant to follow federal controlled substances laws, regulations, and policies. DEA expects clinicians to administer, dispense, and prescribe controlled substances for a legitimate medical purpose while acting in the usual course of professional practice (7). DEA also expects clinicians to minimize the potential for the abuse and diversion of controlled substances by adhering to applicable legal/regulatory boundaries and by following current, accepted clinical care standards (2).[a]

THE CONTROLLED SUBSTANCES ACT OF 1970—
PRESCRIBING—RELATED SECTIONS

Visiting the DEA's Office of Diversion Control website and reading all the applicable sections of the CSA can be informative. The following section of the CSA relates directly to the act of prescribing: Title 21, United States Code, Section 829—Prescriptions. Section 829 contains the following federal legal requirements:

> Schedule II substances—(a) Except when dispensed directly by a practitioner, other than a pharmacist, to an ultimate user, no controlled substance in schedule II, which is a prescription drug as determined under the Federal Food, Drug, and Cosmetic Act, may be dispensed without the written prescription of a practitioner, except that in emergency situations, as prescribed by the Secretary by regulation after consultation with the Attorney General, such drug may be dispensed upon oral prescription in accordance with section 503(b) of that Act. Prescriptions shall be retained in conformity with the requirements of section 827 of this title. No prescription for a controlled substance in schedule II may be refilled (7).

> Schedule III and IV substances—(b) Except when dispensed directly by a practitioner, other than a pharmacist, to an ultimate user, no controlled substance in schedule III or IV, which is a prescription drug as determined under the Federal Food, Drug, and Cosmetic Act, may be dispensed without a written or oral prescription in conformity with section 503(b) of that Act. Such prescriptions may not be filled or refilled more than six months after the date thereof or be refilled more than five times after the date of the prescription unless renewed by the practitioner (8).

> Schedule V substances—(c) No controlled substance in schedule V that is a drug may be distributed or dispensed other than for a medical purpose (8).

> Nonprescription drugs with abuse potential—(d) Whenever it appears to the Attorney General that a drug not considered to be a prescription drug under the Federal Food, Drug, and Cosmetic Act should be so considered because of its abuse potential, he shall so advise the Secretary and furnish to him all available data relevant thereto (8).

CODE OF FEDERAL REGULATIONS ON PRESCRIPTIONS

CFR contains a great deal of information relevant to controlled substances. One may visit the DEA's Office of Diversion Control website and read the applicable sections of the CFR. The following sections of the CFR relate directly to the act of prescribing:

21 CFR § 1306.03—Persons entitled to issue prescriptions:

> (a) A prescription for a controlled substance may be issued only by an individual practitioner who is: (i) authorized to prescribe controlled substances by the jurisdiction in which he is licensed to practice his profession and (ii) either registered or exempted from registration pursuant to §§ 1301.22(c) and 1301.23 of this chapter. (b) A prescription issued

---

[a] Although the DEA used the term "dispensing" in the IPS, the DEA will apply its interpretation to other conduct, including administering and prescribing controlled substances to treat pain.

by an individual practitioner may be communicated to a pharmacist by an employee or agent of the individual practitioner (9).

21 CFR § 1306.04—Purpose of issue of prescription:

(a) A prescription for a controlled substance to be effective must be issued for a legitimate medical purpose by an individual practitioner acting in the usual course of his professional practice. The responsibility for the proper prescribing and dispensing of controlled substances is upon the prescribing practitioner, but a corresponding responsibility rests with the pharmacist who fills the prescription.

An order purporting to be a prescription issued not in the usual course of professional treatment or in legitimate and authorized research is not a prescription within the meaning and intent of section 309 of the Act (21 U.S.C. 829) and the person knowingly filling such a purported prescription, as well as the person issuing it, shall be subject to the penalties provided for violations of the provisions of law relating to controlled substances. (b) A prescription may not be issued in order for an individual practitioner to obtain controlled substances for supplying the individual practitioner for the purpose of general dispensing to patients. (c) A prescription may not be issued for the dispensing of narcotic drugs listed in any schedule for "detoxification treatment" or "maintenance treatment" as defined in Section 102 of the Act (21 U.S.C. 802) (7).

21 CFR § 1306.05—Manner of issuance of prescriptions (relevant part only):

(a) All prescriptions for controlled substances shall be dated as of, and signed on, the day when issued and shall bear the full name and address of the patient, the drug name, strength, dosage form, quantity prescribed, directions for use and the name, address, and registration number of the practitioner. A practitioner may sign a prescription in the same manner as he would sign a check or legal document (e.g., J.H. Smith or John H. Smith). Where an oral order is not permitted, prescriptions shall be written with ink or indelible pencil or typewriter and shall be manually signed by the practitioner. The prescriptions may be prepared by the secretary or agent for the signature of a practitioner, but the prescribing practitioner is responsible in case the prescription does not conform in all essential respects to the law and regulations. A corresponding liability rests upon the pharmacist who fills a prescription not prepared in the form prescribed by these regulations (10).

21 CFR § 1306.06—Persons entitled to fill prescriptions:

A prescription for controlled substances may only be filled by a pharmacist acting in the usual course of his professional practice and either registered individually or employed in a registered pharmacy or registered institutional practitioner (11).

21 CFR § 1306.07—Administering or dispensing of narcotic drugs:

(a) The administering or dispensing directly (but not prescribing) of narcotic drugs listed in any schedule to a narcotic drug dependent person for 'detoxification treatment' or 'maintenance treatment' as defined in section 102 of the Act (21 U.S.C. 802) shall be deemed to be within the meaning of the term 'in the course of his professional practice or research' in section 308(e) and section 102 (20) of the Act [21 U.S.C. 828(e)]: Provided, That the practitioner is separately registered with the Attorney General as required by section 303(g) of the Act [21 U.S.C. 823(g)] and then thereafter complies with the regulatory standards imposed relative to treatment qualification, security, records, and unsupervised use of drugs pursuant to such Act (12).

(b) Nothing in this section shall prohibit a physician who is not specifically registered to conduct a narcotic treatment program from administering (but not prescribing) narcotic drugs to a person for the purpose of relieving acute withdrawal symptoms when necessary while arrangements are being made for referral for treatment. Not more than one day's medication may be administered to the person or for the person's use at one time. Such emergency treatment may be carried out for not more than three days and may not be renewed or extended (12).

(c) This section is not intended to impose any limitations on a physician or authorized hospital staff to administer or dispense narcotic drugs in a hospital to maintain or detoxify a person as an incidental adjunct to medical or surgical treatment of conditions other than addiction, or to administer or dispense narcotic drugs to persons with intractable pain in which no relief or cure is possible or none has been found after reasonable efforts (12).

In summary, federal law recognizes a controlled substance prescription as valid if the clinician issues it (i) for a legitimate medical purpose, (ii) within the usual course of professional practice, and (iii) takes steps to minimize the potential for abuse and diversion of the drug prescribed (7). These three requirements make up the "substantive" requirements for a valid prescription. Clinicians must also meet "technical" requirements, such as correctly dating and signing each prescription, and including the correct dosing and quantity information and patient demographic material on the face of each prescription. State laws may add requirements such as writing the quantity in both numeric and spelled out version.

FEDERAL POSITION STATEMENTS AND CURRENT EVENTS

The following series of legal/regulatory materials have been issued (and in one instance retracted) by the DEA:

1. Prescription Pain Medications: Frequently Asked Questions and Answers—published on the DEA website in August 2004 and retracted by DEA in October 2004.[b]
2. IPS. Published in the Federal Register in November 2004. This document replaced the FAQ.
3. Clarification Statement. Published in the Federal Register in August 2005. This document "clarifies" the IPS and certain issues regarding Schedule II drugs.

Additional useful information may be obtained by reviewing the series of letters and comments about DEA's retraction of the FAQ and its decision to issue the IPS and Clarification Statement (13,14).

---

[b] Because DEA retracted the FAQ from its website, this document is no longer a viable authority for a discussion on federal legal/regulatory materials pertaining to the use of controlled substances for the treatment of pain. Take time to read a copy of the FAQ because it contains helpful information on clinical issues for pain management and ideas for monitoring patients. Although the DEA does not consider the FAQ a viable authority, many clinicians, especially those involved in writing the FAQ, believe the document is accurate and useful. I agree with this statement, but ethically I cannot cite it as legal authority for DEA's position on the issues I discuss in this chapter. You may find a copy of the FAQ by searching the Internet using these terms: DEA, FAQ, and Prescribing Pain Medications.

The Interim Policy Statement

In November 2004, following the publication and retraction of the FAQ, DEA published an IPS on dispensing controlled substances to treat pain (2).[c] The IPS covers four key areas of DEA concern about the use of controlled substances to treat pain, as discussed below. The IPS is an official statement of the DEA, meaning the agency will use it when performing agency functions relating to registrants and prescribed controlled substances.

The IPS and the DEA's Ability to Commence Investigations

DEA first used the IPS to remind registrants that it may initiate an investigation of a registrant at any time and for any reason without jumping through any "hoops (2)." This is not a new concept because DEA has the ability (and the responsibility) to investigate allegations that a registrant has failed to follow the federal law relating to controlled substances—from both an administrative and a criminal perspective. DEA's responsibility here is analogous to a state medical licensing board's responsibility to investigate allegations that a licensee has practiced medicine in a manner inconsistent with state minimum standards, etc.

DEA claimed "FAQ erroneously stated '[t]he number of patients in a practice who receive opioids, the number of tablets prescribed for each patient, and the duration of therapy with these drugs do not, by themselves, indicate a problem, and they should not be used as the sole basis for an investigation by regulators or law enforcement (2)." It is the DEA's position that these factors, while not "necessarily determinative," "may indeed be indicative of diversion (2)." In support of its position, DEA cited a federal case called United States versus Rosen (15) pointing out that the Rosen court summarized "certain recurring concomitance of condemned behavior:

1. An inordinately large quantity of controlled substances was prescribed.
2. Large numbers of prescriptions were issued.
3. No physical examination was given.
4. The physician warned the patient to fill prescriptions at different drug stores.
5. The physician issued prescriptions to a patient known to be delivering the drugs to others.
6. The physician prescribed controlled drugs at intervals inconsistent with legitimate medical treatment.
7. The physician involved used street slang rather than medical terminology for the drugs prescribed.
8. There was no logical relationship between the drugs prescribed and treatment of the condition allegedly existing.
9. The physician wrote more than one prescription on occasions in order to spread them out (16)."

DEA also used the IPS to reiterate a "longstanding legal principle—that the Government 'can investigate merely on suspicion that the law is being violated, or even just because it wants assurances that it is not (17).'" Thus, DEA believes the FAQ incorrectly suggests, "DEA must meet some arbitrary standard or threshold

---

[c] Although the DEA used the term "dispensing" in the IPS, the DEA will apply its interpretation to other conduct, including administering and prescribing controlled substances to treat pain.

evidentiary requirement to commence an investigation of a possible violation of the CSA (2)."

The Interim Policy Statement and "Do Not Fill" Prescriptions

DEA's second problem with the FAQ concerns the following language:

> Schedule II prescriptions may not be refilled; however, a physician may prepare multiple prescriptions on the same day with instructions to fill on different dates.[d]

According to the DEA, "the first part of this sentence is correct, as the CSA expressly states: 'No prescription for a controlled substance in schedule II may be refilled (2).[e]'" However, DEA used the IPS to say the CSA does not allow for the activity described in the italicized portion of the FAQ language above (2). Instead, in the IPS, DEA said that physicians who "prepare multiple prescriptions on the same day with instructions to fill on different dates (2)" are essentially "writing a prescription authorizing refills of a schedule II controlled substance, [and doing so] conflicts with one of the fundamental purposes of section 829(a) (2)."

To support its position, DEA refers to factors quoted in a federal criminal case, United States versus Rosen (16) and comments that "writing multiple prescriptions on the same day with instructions to fill on different dates is a recurring tactic among physicians who seek to avoid detection when dispensing controlled substances for unlawful (nonmedical) purposes (16)." DEA's reference to Rosen is weak because Rosen involved "postdated prescriptions" rather than "Do Not Fill" prescriptions, which are properly dated prescriptions containing instructions to the dispensing pharmacist about the dispensing period (18). Thus, DEA's position against "Do Not Fill" prescriptions is one that may actually promote abuse and diversion rather than minimize it (18).

The IPS and the Registrant's Responsibility to "Minimize the Potential for Abuse and Diversion"

DEA cited a third problem with the FAQ, claiming that the FAQ [allegedly] understates "the degree of caution that a physician must exercise to minimize the likelihood of diversion when dispensing controlled substances to known or suspected addicts (2)." DEA used the IPS to explain that registrants have "a responsibility to exercise a much greater degree of oversight to prevent diversion in the case of a known or suspected addict than in the case of a patient for whom there are no indicators of drug abuse (2)." Thus, DEA believes that physicians must "engage in additional monitoring of the patient's use of narcotics" when the physician "is aware that the patient is a drug addict and/or has resold prescription narcotics (2)." DEA also believes that the federal law prohibits physicians from "dispensing controlled substances with the knowledge that they will be used for a nonmedical purpose or that they will be resold by the patient (2)." DEA left the method of monitoring to the individual clinician and the states. The IPS contains a discussion of monitoring examples (2).

---

[d] To find the FAQ, conduct an Internet search using the following terms: DEA, FAQ, Prescription Pain Medications. The DEA retracted the FAQ from its website on or about October 6, 2004. Thus, there is no formal citation to the document available.
[e] See also 21 U.S.C. § 829(a).

The IPS and the DEA Registrant's Responsibility to "Seriously Consider"
any "Sincerely Expressed Concerns" by Family Members About a Patient
DEA's fourth criticism of the FAQ was that it "incorrectly minimized the potential significance of a family member or friend expressing concern to the physician that the patient may be abusing the pain medication (2)." In this regard, the FAQ states:

> Family and friends, or health care providers who are not directly involved in the therapy, may express concerns about the use of opioids. These concerns may result from a poor understanding of the role of this therapy in pain management or from an unfounded fear of addiction; they may be exacerbated by widespread, sometimes inaccurate media coverage about abuse of opioid pain medications (2).

DEA believes that "family members are not always determinative of whether the patient is engaged in drug abuse," but also stated that, "the above-quoted [FAQ] statement is incorrect to the extent it implies that physicians may simply disregard such concerns expressed to them by family members or friends (2)."

While "a family member or friend might be aware of information that the physician does not possess regarding a patient's drug abuse (2)," DEA also stated that

1. The addictive and sometimes deadly nature of prescription narcotic abuse,
2. The tremendous volume of such drug abuse in the United States, and
3. The propensity of many drug addicts to attempt to deceive physicians in order to obtain controlled substances for the purpose of abuse (2).

require physicians to "seriously consider any sincerely expressed concerns about drug abuse conveyed by family members and friends (2)." Unfortunately, DEA did not explain in the IPS its expectations regarding "sincerely consider" or "sincerely expressed concerns." Consequently, if a family member or friend contacts a physician about a patient's behavior regarding controlled substances, he/she should document the contact and do something that provides evidence that the matter has been addressed with the patient. While it is not necessary to discuss the third-party contact with the patient, it is necessary to take steps to minimize the potential for abuse and diversion of the controlled substances that are prescribed using follow-up visits, laboratory testing, psychological and substance abuse counseling, changes in the treatment plan, consultations, and referrals, to ensure the patient continues to benefit from the medications prescribed.

The August 2005 Clarification Statement

Following its publication of the IPS and its solicitation of comments regarding the IPS, in August 2005, the DEA issued a document entitled Clarification of Existing Requirements under the CSA on the Use of Schedule II Controlled Substances (the Clarification Statement) (3). DEA issued the Clarification Statement to respond to some of the comments made by the public about the IPS. In particular, DEA received many comments from patients who had been using schedule II controlled substances for several years and routinely saw their physician once every three months (3). DEA said that some of the individuals commenting on the IPS "were under the mistaken impression that, because of the [IPS], they now must begin seeing their physician every month (3)." In response to these comments, DEA stated: "the IPS did not state that patients must visit their physician's office every month to pick up a new prescription. There is no such requirement in the CSA or DEA regulations (3)." Significantly, however, DEA clearly stated that physicians who issue prescriptions for controlled substances must determine whether "there is a legitimate medical purpose for the patient to be prescribed that controlled substance and that the physician [has acted] in the usual course of professional practice (3)."

DEA recognizes that "schedule II controlled substances, by definition, have the highest potential for abuse, and are the most likely to cause dependence, of all the controlled substances that have an approved medical use (3)." Thus, DEA expects physicians to:

> use the utmost care in determining whether their patients for whom they are prescribing schedule II controlled substances should be seen in person each time a prescription is issued or whether seeing the patient in person at somewhat less frequent intervals is consistent with sound medical practice and appropriate safeguards against diversion and misuse (3)."

DEA also expects physicians to "abide by any requirements imposed by their state medical boards with respect to proper prescribing practices and what constitutes a bona fide physician-patient relationship (3).[f]"

What does this mean to medical practice? If a physician regularly sees a patient and issues him/her a prescription for a schedule II controlled substance (for a legitimate medical purpose and without seeing the patient in person), DEA believes it is proper to "mail the prescription to the patient or pharmacy (3)." The Clarification Statement also notes that the DEA regulations state:

> A prescription for a schedule II controlled substance may be transmitted by the practitioner or the practitioner's agent to a pharmacy via facsimile equipment, provided that the original written, signed prescription is presented to the pharmacist for review prior to the actual dispensing of the controlled substance, except as noted [elsewhere in this section of the regulations] (3).[g]

DEA therefore believes that the CSA allows registrants to fax a schedule II prescription to facilitate processing to the patient, "but only if the pharmacy receives the original written, signed prescription prior to dispensing the drug to the patient [and only if state law permits] (3)."

Neither the CSA nor the CFR contain "a specific limit on the number of days' worth of a schedule II controlled substance that a physician may authorize per prescription (3)." Some states, however, do impose specific limits on the amount of a schedule II controlled substance that may be prescribed and a physician must follow them as well, "so long as the state requirements do not conflict with or contravene the Federal requirements (3).[h]"

Again, DEA expects its registrants to issue controlled substance prescriptions for a legitimate medical purpose in the usual course of professional practice. And, "physicians and pharmacies have a duty as DEA registrants to ensure that their prescribing and dispensing of controlled substances occur in a manner consistent with effective controls against diversion and misuse, taking into account the nature of the drug being prescribed (3).[i]"

---

[f] Also see Title 21, United States Code, Section 823(f)(1), (4).
[g] Also see 21 CFR 1306.11(a).
[h] Title 21, United States Code, Section 903.
[i] Title 21, United States Code, Section 823(f).

DRUG ENFORCEMENT ADMINISTRATION AND A FINAL POLICY STATEMENT

DEA will issue a final policy statement on the use of controlled substances for the treatment of pain, and every physician who prescribes controlled substances should find a good source to help him/her stay current on these matters. In all cases, physicians and physician extenders must become familiar with existing federal and state legal/regulatory materials and be prepared to reevaluate their practices for compliance purposes.

STATE LEGAL/REGULATORY MATERIALS

State legal/regulatory materials have many parallels to the federal materials. For example, states have controlled substances laws (often called "Uniform CSAs" and found in state statutes), and most parallel the federal law. Most state controlled substances laws prohibit nonmedical use of controlled substances. Some states have additional Schedules for drugs that present regional issues of abuse and diversion, such as carisoprodol (Soma®) and tramadol (Ultram®). Some states have electronic prescription monitoring programs (sometimes called electronic prescription accountability acts), which, in many cases, provide clinicians with access to a database to determine whether a patient has obtained controlled substances from other sources within the state. Some states have Intractable Pain Treatment Acts and Patient Bill of Rights Acts making it legal for: (i) patients to request opioids for pain management; (ii) clinicians to treat intractable pain using high doses of opioids and/or unusual combinations of drugs, but only if the clinician follows the law making up these acts; and (iii) clinicians to refuse to treat patients with high doses or unusual combinations, as long as the refusing clinician points the patient in the direction of someone who does so (5).

Most states have Medical Practice Acts and corresponding regulations or rules governing the practice of medicine. When state licensing authorities grant health care professionals the privilege to practice, these authorities expect them to know and follow the licensing state's body of guidelines, laws, and regulations, including those related to controlled substances. Most state licensing authorities publish these materials on websites and in handbooks. Some state boards even use law examinations to encourage health care professionals to learn and follow legal/regulatory materials. The organization of and terminology used by state authorities to refer to these materials varies, and a detailed discussion of these matters is beyond the scope of this chapter. Clinicians should take time to identify and read their licensing state's legal/regulatory materials pertaining to the use of controlled substances to treat pain and medical record documentation requirements. It is important to note that the federal law sets the outer parameters for legal matters pertaining to controlled substances.

State licensing boards expect clinicians to "control the flow of drugs" within the framework outlined by federal and state materials, and according to accepted clinical standards. In the context of using controlled substances, especially opioids, for pain management, state licensing boards expect clinicians to take and document (i) the patient's history and a physical evaluation, (ii) an individualized treatment plan, (iii) informed consent and treatment agreement, (iv) periodic review or patient follow-up justifying the continued use of the controlled substances, and (v) relevant consultations and referrals (5). When a clinician loses control of his/her prescribing practices or fails to document the items above, he/she is inviting scrutiny from federal and state authorities [Additional discussion of staying in charge of your medical practice at (19,20)]. Most states have some form of regulation/rule and/or guideline/position statement on prescribing controlled substances to treat pain.

If a physician practices in a state that has specific legal/regulatory materials on prescribing controlled substances to treat pain, those materials should be reviewed carefully. After doing so, state materials should be used to perform a file review. A board's requirements/suggestions should be compared with one's documentation, and necessary improvements should be made. If practicing in a state that does not have specific legal/regulatory materials on prescribing controlled substances to treat pain, using the FSMB's Model Policy for the Use of Controlled Substances for the Treatment of Pain (Model Policy) (4) should be considered as a reference for proper documentation and prescribing boundaries. Finally, it is important to note that many of the states with legal/regulatory materials on prescribing controlled substances to treat pain use the FSMB's Model Policy or an earlier version called Model Guidelines for the Use of Controlled Substances for the Treatment of Pain (21).

THE FSMB'S MODEL POLICY FOR THE USE OF CONTROLLED SUBSTANCES FOR THE TREATMENT OF PAIN

This section contains general guidance and documentation recommendations based on the FSMB's Model Policy. The FSMB's Model Policy stresses the clinician's "professional and ethical responsibility . . . to assess patients' pain (4)." The Model Policy "is not intended to establish clinical practice guidelines nor is it intended to be inconsistent with controlled substance laws and regulations (4)." Clinicians should look to state materials and accepted and current clinical care standards when prescribing controlled substances to treat pain. Clinicians must also document medical records properly or risk administrative and legal sanctions. Medical record documentation must reflect a valid physician-patient relationship and the legitimate medical purpose justifying the use of controlled substances for pain.

Overview of the Model Policy

The Model Policy contains seven key compliance and documentation elements pertaining to the use of controlled substances for the treatment of pain. When comparing the Model Policy with a specific state's materials on the use of controlled substances for the treatment of pain, paying attention to differences in "directive" language (words telling you what you "shall," "must," "should," or "may" do) is recommended and provides a good idea of the board's boundaries on controlled substance prescribing and supporting documentation, and what the board expects a physician to do to provide quality medical care, thereby resulting in maintenance of one's license and controlled drug registration. As with most state legal/regulatory materials, including guidelines and position statements, key elements like those set forth above include basic instructions.

Evaluation of the Patient (History and Physical Examination) (22)
The Model Policy's first element suggests clinicians "should:

- evaluate the patient's medical history and perform a physical examination and document these efforts, including
- the nature and intensity of the patient's pain.
- the patient's current and past treatments for pain.
- underlying or coexisting diseases or conditions.
- the effect of the pain on the patient's physical and psychosocial function.
- the patient's history of substance abuse (including alcohol).
- the presence of one or more recognized medical indications for the use of a controlled substance (4)."

In addition to the Model Policy's suggestions, clinicians "should:

- verify the patient's self-report of medication usage with prior clinicians and attempt to do so prior to prescribing more than a couple of days' of that same medication to a new patient.
- talk to the patient about his/her reluctance to try a different medication or combination of medications and document their efforts in the patient's medical record. Sometimes the reluctance stems from a fear of addiction or simply the process of "change" in general. Other times, the reluctance stems from an abuse and/or diversion problem. In either case, the physician's role is to determine how the patient's reluctance plays into his/her medical history and the development of the treatment plan.
- review all documentation from prior prescribing health care providers and talk to that provider about the patient's case. Of course this implicates Health Insurance Portability and Accountability Act (HIPAA) issues, but your attorneys should be able to tell you that HIPAA permits communications between health care providers about the "treatment" of the patient, among other things such as "payment" and "health care options." This recommendation is especially important if a patient comes to you on high doses or combinations of controlled substances for pain management. This is just as important when a patient comes to you after having been discharged by the prior provider for whatever reason. Your job is to find out why the patient wants you to review his/her case, what the prior provider has documented about the patient's case, and what the answers to those questions mean in light of your obligations—ethical, legal/regulatory, and professional.
- request an initial drug screen (blood or urine) from a patient to verify patient self-reports and ensure proper patient assessment and selection in light of the physician's obligation to follow accepted clinical care standards and minimize the potential for abuse and diversion of controlled substances (23)."

If a patient needs high doses or unusual combinations of controlled substances, then documenting the legitimate medical reason for prescribing them to him/her is essential. It is important to evaluate and document each patient's case according to professional care standards, licensing board, and DEA registrant obligations.

Before prescribing controlled substances to treat pain, especially prior to prescribing them long-term, most states require clinicians to engage in a history and physical evaluation process designed to learn enough about the patient's pain history to make an informed clinical recommendation about future pain treatments. Clinicians should also consider interviewing the patient about past drug treatments that have been tried and failed or found to be inappropriate. It consideration should be made whether to use consultations and/or referrals with the patient early in the treatment relationship, especially if the patient has a history of substance abuse or coexisting psychological disorder. Finally, many states require clinicians to document the presence of one or more recognized medical indications for the use of a controlled substance. It is important to follow this last directive to meet the legitimate medical purpose standard.

Treatment Plan (22)

The Model Policy's second element states clinicians "should:

- use a written treatment plan.
- use the written treatment plan to state objectives that will be used to determine treatment success, such as pain relief and improved physical and psychosocial function.
- use the written treatment plan to indicate if any further diagnostic evaluations or other treatments are planned (4)."

After treatment begins, the Model Policy encourages clinicians to:

- adjust drug therapy to the individual medical needs of each patient, and
- realize that other treatment modalities or a rehabilitation program may be necessary depending on the etiology of the pain and the extent to which the pain is associated with physical and psychosocial impairment.

Clinicians should evaluate documentation to determine whether it shows a pattern of continued prescribing despite (i) pain levels that are always the same, (ii) a lack of improved functioning (on physical and psychosocial levels) according to treatment plan goals, and/or (iii) noncompliance with a treatment agreement or the treatment plan. Appropriate changes to patient evaluation and corresponding documentation to demonstrate compliance with one's state legal/regulatory materials or the Model Policy should be made. Finally, a treatment plan ought to be approached as a "work in progress." The physician's and patient's goals and ideas should serve as a starting point, followed by modification of the plan in response to the patient's progress (or lack thereof) toward the goals. Most importantly, this information should be documented in the patient's record.

Informed Consent and Treatment Agreements (22)

The Model Policy's third element suggests clinicians "should:

- discuss the risks and benefits of the use of controlled substances with the patient, persons designated by the patient or with the patient's surrogate or guardian if the patient is without medical decision-making capacity.
- require the patient to receive prescriptions from one physician and one pharmacy whenever possible (4)."

If the patient is at high risk for medication abuse or has a history of substance abuse, the Model Policy suggests clinicians "should:

- consider the use of a written agreement between physician and patient outlining patient responsibilities, including

1. urine/serum medication levels screening when requested;
2. number and frequency of all prescription refills; and

3. reasons for which drug therapy may be discontinued (e.g., violation of agreement) (4)."

The Model Policy reads as if "informed consent" and "agreement for treatment" are the same. In pain policy, they typically are; in the law, they are not. Fortunately, it is easy to correct informed consent and agreement for treatment forms to ensure that they incorporate the correct legal/regulatory elements. Before examining a practice's informed consent and agreement for treatment forms, this section should be considered carefully. Documents should be reorganized using the legal/regulatory distinctions between informed consent and treatment agreements, and key language from state materials.

Informed consent relates to a practitioner's ethical and, in most states, legal/regulatory obligation to discuss with the patient the risks, benefits, special issues, and treatment alternatives relating to the use of controlled substances. To increase one's chances of surviving legal challenges related to informed consent, the informed consent process should be documented carefully.

The concept of informed consent is not new [For more information on Informed Consent (24)]. Clinicians routinely use a general informed consent for documenting a physician-patient relationship and a specific informed consent prior to performing office procedures or surgery. The American Medical Association refers to informed consent as a "process" by which the clinician supplies the patient with information about the risks, benefits, special issues, and treatment alternatives, thereby aiding the patient in his/her decision-making process (25). Conversely, the Model Policy's language suggests that informed consent is a "should" do it process rather than a "must" do it obligation. This apparent conflict raises an important point: "policy-type" language usually refers to "minimum standards," which are distinct from accepted clinical standards of care and from legal/regulatory obligations imposed by the state.

An "agreement for treatment" is a document containing behavioral boundaries and office policies and limits relating to a patient's use of controlled substances for pain relief. At a minimum, a physician ought to consider using agreements for treatment with patients who have an active or past history of substance abuse. Additionally, their use should be considered with patients who live in an environment that presents a risk for abuse.

Agreements for treatment typically remain the same over the term of care with all patients and changes only when there is a need due to the patient's situation or when office policies change. Informed consent documents change relating to the drugs prescribed (much like they change with the procedures performed). Each drug brings with it different risks and benefits, its own set of special issues, and alternatives tied to the patient's overall medical condition. The clinician is ultimately responsible for explaining informed consent issues to the patient and a failure to do so may set the stage for a malpractice claim [For more information on Agreements for Treatment (26)].

Periodic Review (22)

The Model Policy's fourth element suggests that clinicians "should:

- periodically review the course of pain treatment and any new information about the etiology of the pain or the patient's state of health.
- remember that the continuation or modification of controlled substances for pain management therapy depends on (the physician's) evaluation of progress toward treatment objectives.

- remember that satisfactory response to treatment may be indicated by the patient's decreased pain, increased level of function, or improved quality of life.
- monitor the patient for objective evidence of improved or diminished function.
- consider information from family members or other caregivers in determining the patient's response to treatment, [subject to HIPAA considerations] (4)."

If the patient's progress is unsatisfactory, the Model Policy suggests that clinicians should "assess the appropriateness of continued use of the current treatment plan and consider the use of other therapeutic modalities (4)."

Most state licensing boards rightly give physicians discretion on the timing of periodic review based on the documented, individual circumstances of the patient's case. However, New Jersey and Louisiana use legal/regulatory tools to require clinicians to see chronic controlled substance users every 12 weeks at a minimum. Before deciding how frequently to see patients, the impact of the DEA's IPS on patient follow-up should be considered, particularly if the follow-up involves the issuance of a schedule II controlled substance. Checking one's licensing board to see how it interprets the IPS regarding the issuance of multiple schedule II prescriptions with "do not fill before" language on them in light of patient follow-up policies/regulations is prudent. Similarly, it is wise to determine the appropriate follow-up period and document the rationale for the method and timing of follow-up.

Many clinicians have "trouble" with their licensing board because of poor documentation and periodic review practices. In the most basic sense, periodic review is the clinician's avenue for determining whether controlled substances remain indicated in the patient's treatment plan. Periodic review thus encompasses patient monitoring, which is a challenging subject because most patients are compliant and are not a threat when it comes to handling controlled substances responsibly.

There are many ways to meet periodic review obligations. Determining what the state says about the matter and deciding how the language in one's specific state's legal/regulatory materials can be useful in establishing patient monitoring forms and office policies. Additionally, a physician should consider using language from these materials to advocate for patients when a health plan requests action or requests services that are inconsistent with clinical care standards and/or the state's legal/regulatory materials. For further guidance on periodic review, the article by Passik and Weinreb entitled The Four A's of Pain Treatment Outcomes (1998) (27) may be accessed. Finally, clear description of reasons for denying or increasing medications is an element of sound medical practice. By doing so, the practitioner will be better prepared to meet challenges to his/her prescribing habits—especially those that come from disgruntled patients.

Consultations and Referrals (22)

The Model Policy's fifth element suggests clinicians "should:

- be willing to refer the patient as necessary for additional evaluation and treatment in order to achieve treatment objectives.
- give special attention to those patients with pain who are at risk for medication misuse, abuse, or diversion (4)."

Accepted medical practice and current standards of care contemplate the use of consultations and referrals as necessary to achieve treatment objectives (23). In pain management, it may be necessary to recommend that a patient see someone trained in addiction medicine or qualified to address psychological components of pain. For example, if a patient has a history of substance abuse, it may be prudent to refer to another health care professional for evaluation to help construct a treatment plan that will address the patient's pain while controlling the drug supply. Unfortunately, however, not all health care benefit plans encourage these consultations or referrals. As a result, clinicians must decide how to address the patient's needs while balancing insurance plan allowances and regulatory guidelines with appropriate standards of care.

It is crucial to understand the state's position on consultations and referrals, because some state licensing boards require clinicians to use consultations and referrals when dealing with specific patient populations, especially those who have a history of substance abuse or other comorbid psychological disorders. The Model Policy contemplates the documentation efforts described above, and encourages clinicians to pay special attention to patients who may be at risk of medication misuse, abuse, or diversion (4,28).[j] It is important to remember, "the management of pain in patients with a history of substance abuse or with a comorbid psychiatric disorder may require extra care, monitoring, documentation, and consultation with or referral to an expert in the management of such patients (4)." For this reason, one should obtain documentation of all consultations and referrals directly from the health care provider. Upon receipt of these items, it is important to review them and determine whether the results support the continuation of the current treatment plan or a change relating both to the treatment in general and controlled substances specifically. After making a decision, physicians should document their rationale, along with the corresponding consultation/referral documentation in the patient's medical record.

A number of situations may require a consultation and/or a referral: (i) change in pain pattern or location; (ii) evidence of abuse, diversion, or addiction; (iii) neurological deficit; (iv) uncontrolled depression or anxiety; (v) new findings or imaging studies; and (vi) increasing pain despite increasing doses of medication. Patients reporting pain levels of "10" at every office visit also require closer attention. Careful documentation of the physician's own response to these patients and not forgetting to use consultations and referrals according to accepted medical practice is likely to reduce potential legal complications.

Typical Medical Records Required (29)

The Model Policy's sixth element concerns Medical Records (4,21). State licensing boards may require clinicians to follow stricter documentation requirements. Clinicians should review their licensing board requirements carefully and ensure compliance with all state pain policies, rules, and regulations on medical records. The Model Policy states that clinicians "should keep accurate and complete records to include:

1. the medical history and physical examination,
2. diagnostic, therapeutic, and laboratory results,
3. evaluations and consultations,
4. treatment objectives,
5. discussion of risks and benefits,

---

[j] For more information on aberrant drug-related behavior and addiction potentials in patients being treated with opioids for pain.

6. informed consent,
7. treatments,
8. medications (including date, type, dosage, and quantity prescribed),
9. instructions and agreements, and
10. periodic reviews.

Clinicians should keep these records current and maintain them in an accessible manner and ensure they are readily available for review (4)." In certain cases, both federal and state law prohibit clinicians from keeping certain types of documents in a patient's medical record, including documentation related to inquiries into state prescription monitoring databases and documentation related to current or past treatment for psychological disorders or substance abuse (30).

Compliance with Controlled Substance Laws and Regulations (22)
The Model Policy's seventh and final element is Compliance with Laws and Regulations. When prescribing controlled substances, clinicians must comply with all applicable laws and regulations, which most often means prescribing clinicians must:

1. Possess a valid current license to practice medicine in their licensing state(s);
2. Possess a valid and current controlled substances DEA registration for the schedules they prescribe;
3. Comply with applicable federal and state statutes, if they dispense drugs from their office; and
4. Comply with federal and state regulations, if they administer or dispense controlled substances for detoxification (as allowed by law) (4,31).

Regarding this final element, the Model Policy states: "[t]o prescribe, dispense or administer controlled substances, the physician must be licensed in the state and comply with applicable federal and state regulations (4)." Every provider should obtain and keep a copy of the DEA's Physician's Manual and Pharmacist's Manual (32) along with all relevant documents issued by state licensing boards on the use of controlled substances (for the treatment of pain or otherwise).

Additional Considerations
Clinicians must have a working knowledge of current terms used in legal/regulatory materials and clinical settings, especially those terms related to common risks associated with the use of controlled substances to treat pain. The terms below come from the FSMB's Model Policy, and state licensing boards may or may not use them. These terms and corresponding definitions should be compared with those used by one's state licensing board. Finding a way to incorporate these terms and definitions into the documentation used with patients for the informed consent and treatment agreement process is recommended (Fig. 1) (21,4).[k]

If a state's definitions are out of date, that state's licensing board should be encouraged to consider updating them. If the state uses definitions that appear to conflict with the Federation's definitions, checking with the licensing board and asking for clarification is probably best done through a professional medical

---

[k] There may be other definitions for these terms in medical literature. However, the FSMB adopted these definitions at the time it released its new Model Policy.

Key Term	FSMB Definition
Acute Pain	Acute pain is the normal, predicted physiological response to a noxious chemical, thermal or mechanical stimulus and typically is associated with invasive procedures, trauma and disease. It is generally time-limited.
Addiction	Addiction is a primary, chronic, neurobiologic disease, with genetic, psychosocial, and environmental factors influencing its development and manifestations. [Addiction] is characterized by behaviors that include the following: impaired control over drug use, craving, compulsive use, and continued use despite harm. Physical dependence and tolerance are normal physiological consequences of extended opioid therapy for pain and are not the same as addiction.
Chronic Pain	Chronic pain is a state in which pain persists beyond the usual course of an acute disease or healing of an injury, or that may or may not be associated with an acute or chronic pathologic process that causes continuous or intermittent pain over months or years.
Pain	An unpleasant sensory and emotional experience associated with actual or potential tissue damage or described in terms of such damage.
Physical Dependence	Physical dependence is a state of adaptation that is manifested by drug class-specific signs and symptoms that can be produced by abrupt cessation, rapid dose reduction, decreasing blood level of the drug, and/or administration of an antagonist. Physical dependence, by itself, does not equate with addiction.
Pseudoaddiction	The iatrogenic syndrome resulting from the misinterpretation of relief seeking behaviors as though they are drug-seeking behaviors that are commonly seen with addiction. The relief seeking behaviors resolve upon institution of effective analgesic therapy.
Substance Abuse	Substance abuse is the use of any substance(s) for non-therapeutic purposes or use of medication for purposes other than those for which it is prescribed.
Tolerance	Tolerance is a physiologic state resulting from regular use of a drug in which an increased dosage is needed to produce a specific effect, or a reduced effect is observed with a constant dose over time. Tolerance may or may not be evident during opioid treatment and does not equate with addiction.

FIGURE 1 Current legal issues for the treatment of pain. *Source*: From Ref. 21.

organization. Otherwise, a physician should use his/her state's definition, although the ethical obligation to abide by accepted, current standards of care, which is likely to include using appropriate and current definitions, should not be forgotten (22).

CONCLUSION

Clinicians must commit to understanding the interplay of law and medicine when it comes to the use of controlled substances to treat pain. The law is not designed to prevent the use of controlled substances to treat pain. The law sets forth boundaries within which clinicians must operate to preserve a medical license or DEA registration. It is important to understand the legal/regulatory materials in one's state and to assess how they actually protect those who prescribe within the state's legal/regulatory framework. Using key phrases from legal/regulatory materials in office forms is recommended, as is use of these phrases when writing health care plans to explain prescribing rationale. By using these phrases routinely and in connection with practices that meet or exceed accepted clinical care standards, clinicians are better prepared to demonstrate that they have minimized the potential for abuse and diversion of controlled substances, and prescribed for a legitimate medical purpose within the usual course of professional practice. None of these measures can stop the event of a board or DEA inquiry, but it can certainly help determine the outcome—in the physician's favor. Pain management is a process tied to the individual circumstances of each patient. A practitioner's clinical rationale and documentation must reflect this individuality within the legal/regulatory framework of controlled substances and their use to manage pain.

REFERENCES

1. The National Center on Addiction and Substance Abuse at Columbia University (CASA). Under the counter: the diversion and abuse of controlled prescription drugs in the U.S. 2005. Available at www.casacolumbia.org (Accessed January 23, 2006).
2. U.S. Drug Enforcement Administration. Interim policy statement on dispensing controlled substances for the treatment of pain. Fed Regist 2004; 60(220):67170–67172. Available at http://waisaccess.gpo.gov (DOCID:fr16no04–82) (Accessed January 10, 2006).
3. U.S. Drug Enforcement Administration. Clarification of existing requirements under the controlled substances act for prescribing Schedule II controlled substances. Fed Regist 2005; 70(165):50408–50409. Available at http://wais.access.gpo.gov (DOCID:fr26au05–139) (Accessed January 10, 2006). Also see Title 21, United States Code, Section 823 (f)(1), (4).
4. Federation of State Medical Boards. Model policy for the use of controlled substances for the treatment of pain 2004. Available at www.fsmb.org (Accessed January 10, 2006).
5. Bolen J. Taking back your turf: understanding the role of law in medical decision making in opioid management (Part I—overview). J Opioid Manage 2005; 1(3):125–129.
6. U.S. Drug Enforcement Administration. Pharmacist's manual: an informational outline of the controlled substances act of 1970. 2004. Available at http://www.deadiversion.usdoj.gov/pubs/manuals/pharm2/2pharm_manual.pdf.
7. 21 CFR 1306.04. Available at www.deadiversion.usdoj.gov.
8. Title 21, United States Code, Section 829, Prescriptions. Available at http://www.deadiversion.usdoj.gov/21cfr/21usc/829.htm (Accessed on 1/12/2006).
9. 21 CFR 1306.01. Available at www.deadiversion.usdoj.gov.
10. 21 CFR 1306.05. Available at www.deadiversion.usdoj.gov.
11. 21 CFR 1306.06. Available at www.deadiversion.usdoj.gov.
12. 21 CFR 1306.07. Available at www.deadiversion.usdoj.gov.
13. Clinicians will find a series of communications between the University of Wisconsin's Pain & Policy Studies Group and the DEA at http://www.medsch.wisc.edu/painpolicy/DEA/index.htm.
14. Bolen J. Commentary, DEA, Schedule II "Do Not Fill Prescriptions"—Disappointing Enforcement Activity, accepted for publication in Pain Medicine 2006; 7(1):80–85.
15. United States v. Rosen, 582 F.2d 1032, 1035–1036 (5th Cir. 1978).
16. Rosen, 582 F.2d at 1035–1036.
17. United States v. Morton Salt Co. 338 U.S. 632. 1950; 642–643.
18. Joranson DE. Intractable pain treatment laws and regulations. APS Bull 1995; 5(2): 1–3,15–17. Available at http://www.medsch.wisc.edu/painpolicy/publicat/95apsip.htm (Accessed January 23, 2006).
19. Bolen J. Using controlled substances to treat pain: who's in CHARGE? Pain Pract 2005; 15(2):89–91 (Opinion and Advice).
20. Bolen J. Don't Tie our Hands. SPS News September 2005; 6–8 (published by the Southern Pain Society).
21. Federation of State Medical Boards. Model guidelines for the use of controlled substances for the treatment of pain. 1998. Available at www.fsmb.org (Accessed January 10, 2006).

22. Bolen J, Crutchfield D. Prescribing controlled substances: key legal/regulatory considerations in pain management, a CME/CPE program for physicians and pharmacists. Eli Lilly and Company, published by McMahon Publishing Group (Released December 1, 2005, CME expires December 31, 2006).

23. Controlled Substances and Risk Management, Hans Hansen MD, Art Jordan MD, Jennifer Bolen JD. Weiner's Pain Management: A Practical Guide for Clinicians. 7th ed. Boswell, MA and Cole, BE: Taylor & Francis, 2005, ISBN: 0849322626.

24. Bolen J. Pain and the law: back to basics, part I—informed consent facilitates use of controlled substances, Pain Med News 2005; 3(4):10 (published by McMahon Publishing Group). Available at www.painmedicinenews.com.

25. American Medical Association. Informed consent. 1998. Available at http://www.ama-assn.org/ama/pub/category/4608.html (Accessed February 1, 2006).

26. Bolen J. Pain and the law: back to basics, part I—informed consent facilitates use of controlled substances, Pain Med News 2005; 3(4):10 (published by McMahon Publishing Group). Available at Bolen J. Pain and the law: back to basics, part II—a treatment agreement establishes boundaries with patients. Pain Med News 2005; 3(4):10 (published by McMahon Publishing Group). Available at www.painmedicinenews.com.

27. Passik SD, Weinreb HJ. Managing chronic nonmalignant pain: overcoming obstacles to the use of opioids. Adv Ther. 2000; 17:70–83.

28. Steven DP, Kenneth LK, Pain Med 2003; 4(2):186. Available at www.painandchemicaldependency.org/presentations/FRIDAY/GRANDBALLROOM/3passikaberrantbehaviors.pdf.

29. Bolen J, Crutchfield D. Prescribing controlled substances: key legal/regulatory considerations in pain management, a CME/CPE program for physicians and pharmacists. Eli Lilly and Company, McMahon Publishing Group (Released December 1, 2005, CME expires December 31, 2006).

30. Kentucky's rule relating to KASPER records, initial or periodic KASPER Report(s) should not be part of the patient's records and should not be released to the patient or a third party. Medical Board Guideline: Use of Controlled Substances for the Treatment of Pain; The Kentucky Board of Medical Licensure (Effective date: March 22, 2001).

31. Drug Abuse Treatment Act of 2000 (known as DATA 2000). Available at http://www.drugabuse.gov/NIDA_notes/NNVol17N4/Buprenorphine.html and http://buprenorphine.samhsa.gov/. American Society of Addiction Medicine, www.asam.org, and the American Academy of Addiction Psychiatry, www.aaap.org, for additional information on this topic.

32. DEA Diversion website. www.deadiversion.usdoj.gov and search manuals. As of July 7, 2004, the DEA has not released its updated version of the Physician's Manual. See also U.S. Drug Enforcement Administration. Pharmacist's manual: an informational outline of the controlled substances Act of 1970. 2004. Available at http://www.deadiversion.usdoj.gov/pubs/manualspharm2/index.htm. (Accessed January 10, 2006).

11 The Solution to the Medicinal Cannabis Problem

Ethan B. Russo

Department of Pharmaceutical Sciences, University of Montana, Missoula, Montana and Department of Medicine, University of Washington, Seattle, Washington, U.S.A.

OVERVIEW

Chronic pain affects a significant proportion of the American population. Given the tremendous public health challenges attendant to pain treatment in this country, it is clear that new and better approaches are necessary to supplement the current armamentarium of pharmaceutical and complementary modalities. A recent nationwide poll indicates that 19% of adult Americans, or 38 million people, suffer chronic pain, and 6% (12 million) have treated pain with cannabis (1,2). It appears that the cannabis plant may hold important therapeutic promise for the treatment of chronic pain, but its medical use has to this point been fraught with strident controversy that has persisted for almost a decade, with no resolution in sight. The voters of 10 states, some 70% to 80% of the public, and many doctors and scientists feel that seriously ill patients should not be prosecuted for using herbal cannabis (the scientific name for marijuana), while the federal government denies that there is scientific evidence to support such use of a crude plant substance. The Supreme Court has ruled in the 2005 case of Gonzales v. Raich that the federal government does have the power to regulate the intrastate noncommercial cultivation and possession of cannabis for personal medical use.

Is there a solution to the medicinal cannabis question? This author believes so, but such a solution must respect the same time-honored process that any prescription medicine must undergo to reach the U.S. market: proof of safety and efficacy through randomized clinical trials (RCTs) leading to Food and Drug Administration (FDA) approval. While the Supreme Court acknowledged the scientific basis for the belief that cannabis has medical value, Justice Breyer was specific in his direction that it should be subjected to standard procedures of regulatory scrutiny. This author's personal contact with hundreds of chronic pain patients in the United States and Europe leads him to believe that there are many "unheard voices" in this reservoir of despair that would readily accede to use of a safe and effective nonsmoked cannabis-based pharmaceutical, who would never consider current black market options, even if legalized.

What might be the characteristics of such a cannabis-derived prescription medicine? Firstly, it must be standardized, rendered uniform in consistency and quality, as for any pharmaceutical product. Next, it must have a suitable and practical delivery system that provides predictable dose increments and onset of effects, but that minimizes risks to patients, such as intoxication, dependency, or lung damage. Additionally, it must be controlled and regulated through the conventional pharmaceutical supply chain to ensure that it is used by people who are genuinely ill, not those seeking to abuse or divert the product.

All seriously ill patients seek to alleviate their suffering, but few wish to resort to obtaining their medications through unregulated and unlawful channels that are fraught with myriad dangers. Rather, patients prefer a safe and effective evidence-based pharmaceutical solution that their doctors can knowledgeably and confidently prescribe, that their pharmacies will supply, and that their health insurance or third party payers will cover.

It is very unlikely that crude herbal cannabis could ever fulfill these criteria or gain FDA-approval, for it is too variable strain-to-strain, may harbor disease-causing molds, bacteria, pesticides, or heavy metals, and is generally smoked, a delivery system that poses risks common to tobacco: cough, phlegm, bronchitis, and inhalation of potentially carcinogenic pyrolytic by-products.

Early efforts to produce cannabinoid-based pharmaceutical products have been disappointing. Since 1985, synthetic tetrahydrocannabinol (THC, the main psychoactive component of cannabis) has been available in the United States as an oral agent for nausea in cancer chemotherapy, and later, for treatment of Acquired Immune Deficiency Syndrome (AIDS) -wasting. However, its oral absorption is slow and variable, and many patients complain of feeling intoxicated or dysphoric during its usage. Some patients prefer crude herbal cannabis and claim that its added natural ingredients produce herbal synergy and are more effective than THC alone. Inhalation of cannabis, as in smoking or newer vaporizers, produces a rapid peak of activity that maximizes risk of intoxication and reinforcement that could promote possible dependency. Transdermal patches and rectal suppositories avoid pulmonary risks, but have yet to prove practical or reach late stage clinical trials.

An ideal delivery system for cannabis would have reliable intermediate onset, obviate smoking, allow dose titration, provide relief of symptoms, but yet be chemically definable and safe for physicians to prescribe. Recently, a promising approach meeting these criteria has advanced through clinical trials and been accepted for prescription in Canada. The product, called Sativex®, employs an oro-mucosal spray composed of complex cannabis extracts, whose effects begin in 15 to 40 minutes, maintaining a therapeutic window of symptom control without creating a "high" that many interviewed patients regard as an undesirable side effect. This product combines climate-controlled, greenhouse-grown unique cannabis chemovars with high expression of THC and cannabidiol (CBD), respectively. CBD is a nonpsychoactive cannabis component that reduces pain and inflammation in its own right, attenuates anxiety and intoxication from THC, while boosting THC's other beneficial effects. CBD, however, is virtually absent from North American black market cannabis strains. Efficacy for this cannabis profile in human clinical trials has been demonstrated in chronic neuropathic pain, spasms, spasticity, sleep disturbance and bladder problems of multiple sclerosis, intractable pain in cancer, and symptoms of rheumatoid arthritis in some 2000 patients with 1000 patient-years of exposure (3–12), more fully discussed subsequently. Interestingly, this has occurred with no tolerance developing to benefits, no dose escalation, and no evidence of drug dependency or withdrawal in patients taking the medicine for one to four years. Most importantly, after initial titration, patients have achieved effective symptom control without notable intoxication, thus increasing and enhancing activities of daily living, and sometimes allowing a previously debilitated patient to return to work or school. No reports of abuse or diversion of this cannabis-derived spray has occurred in clinical trials, long-term extension studies, or general prescription use. Thus, while it has been effective for patients, there is little to suggest that people "like it too much," or would seek it as an agent of drug abuse.

Thus, the solution to the medicinal cannabis problem rests with a pharmaceutical approach. The Institute of Medicine recognized the analgesic potential of cannabis in its 1999 report (13), but called for alternative delivery systems beyond smoking. This is the only manner in which regulatory standards for a cannabis-based medicine are attained, patient needs are met, the risks of abuse or diversion are significantly reduced, and crude plant material is not smoked. A properly investigated cannabis-based pharmaceutical can be approved by regulatory authorities without contravening the United Nations Single Convention or other related international treaties (14). The development of such a medicinal cannabis prescription will additionally promote open and mutual therapeutic relationship with physicians, and maintain honest and honorable standing with the laws of our nation.

ASPECTS OF FOOD AND DRUG ADMINISTRATION NEW DRUG APPLICATION

Most drugs of old were derived from plants, and the *National Formulary* and *U.S. Pharmacopoeia* formerly contained numerous botanical agents. However, pharmaceutical development has changed over the past 50 years because research has focused more on receptor function and computer modeling of potential therapeutic agents (15). Contemporaneously in the past two decades, the American public has become increasingly interested in natural health approaches, especially herbal treatments. This led in 1994 to the passage of the Dietary Supplement and Health Education Act, wherein such agents are treated more because foods for which "structure and function" claims are allowable. The FDA has no jurisdiction to regulate a dietary supplement until or unless a compelling danger to the public health by such a product is demonstrated. In order for a manufacturer to claim that an agent is useful in the treatment of a disease or condition, however, it must take that agent through the standard drug approval process, at which point the FDA does have jurisdiction and oversight. A potential prescription drug must apply first for Investigational New Drug (IND) status, and once it has fulfilled all criteria of safety, efficacy, and consistency (standardization), it may qualify for New Drug Approval (NDA).

Heretofore, many experts did not believe that a complex botanical (plant-based) product could ever become FDA approvable, partly because of inherent prejudices in favor of single molecule, synthetic medicines, and additionally because no clear mechanism existed for entering complex botanicals into the FDA process. The latter situation has clearly changed with the finalization in June 2004 of the FDA *Guidance for Industry Botanical Drug Products* monograph (16,17). To briefly summarize, this document provides a blueprint by which botanical agents, defined as finished products containing vegetable matter, may be approved as prescription drugs, "intended for use in diagnosing, mitigating, treating, or curing disease—" (p. 3). The Botanical Guidance permits some flexibility in the early stages of research. At the point of NDA submission, however, all conventional requirements must be fulfilled. Because botanicals represent combinations of components, particular attention is necessary to product composition, which may be defined through quality control methods including spectroscopic and chromato-graphic techniques, chemical assays of particular markers (e.g., THC or other phytocannabinoids), biological assays of activity, raw material and process controls in manufacture, and process validation with batch analysis. To qualify for NDA status, a botanical not previously designated "Generally Recognized As Safe" (GRAS) must demonstrate its safety and efficacy in randomized, double-blind and placebo-controlled or dose-response trials. A requirement for any significant home preparation or processing of the product by patients is considered undesir-able. In treatment of chronic conditions with such an agent, clinical exposure to it for 6 to 12 months in long-term safety-extension (SAFEX) studies is considered sufficient (16). A botanical agent administered by a nonoral route requires addition pharmacology and toxicology documentation before initiation of RCTs.

The *Botanical Guidance* (16) additionally indicates that a botanical raw material (or crude herb) becomes a botanical drug substance (BDS) upon its proces-sing through extraction, blending, addition of excipients, formulation and packaging in a defined, exacting and precisely defined manner. This material should be studied for its pharmacokinetic (PK) and pharmacodynamic effects. Nonbinding recommendations were also published that include rigorous bioas-says, and monitoring of heavy metal, pesticide, microbial, and fungal contamination. Additional long-term animal toxicity studies in two species will likely be required, as well as reproductive toxicity, genotoxicity, and carcinogeni-city documentation prior to NDA. Studies of effects in subjects with renal or hepatic insufficiency are additionally recommended.

POLITICS ASIDE: THE CASE FOR MEDICINAL CANNABIS IN TREATMENT OF PAIN

Historical Data

A body of literature dating back several thousand years supports the premise that cannabis preparations are effective in treatment of various kinds of pain. Much of this information is summarized in previous publications (18–23), and includes attestations addressing neuropathic, musculoskeletal, dermatological, gastrointes-tinal, visceral, obstetric, and gynecological pain conditions in innumerable cultures around the world. Many authors have eloquently supported the prospect of using such leads to "mine the past" for evidence for new drug discovery (24), but in the modern regulatory arena, such information counts for very little, indeed.

Modern Anecdotal Information

An increasing recognition of the analgesic and palliative potential of cannabis pre-parations has developed over the past generation. Entire books (25,26) have been devoted to support this premise. Such reports, however, are considered *anecdotal*. They, are of no force or effect for regulatory purposes, and do not constitute proof of safety and efficacy sufficient to allow FDA-approval of cannabis or any parti-cular cannabis preparation. Such proof can only be supplied in the form of appropriate RCTs with accompanying safety and standardization documentation.

A call has come from numerous quarters to reassign cannabis to Schedule II of the federal Controlled Substances Act (27–29). However, such a reclassification alone would not solve the current problem. If herbal cannabis were so rescheduled, what form should it take? How would it be standardized? Who would account for quality control, let alone liability attached to any attendant medical misadventures? In order for a Schedule II substance to be made available by prescription, it must be contained in one or more specific dosage forms, as is the case for opium. Each and every one of such dosage forms must pass FDA muster.

Outside the United States, national governmental efforts to provide standardized herbal cannabis to patients have not met with success. In The Netherlands, a government program supporting herbal cannabis has been poorly supported by its physicians, and in a survey reported in September 2005 (30), only 40 persons in that country were found to be using the government sponsored cannabis. Similarly, in Canada, where access to medicinal cannabis was court mandated for qualifying individuals with serious or life-threatening diseases, as of September 2005, only 850 patients qualified with documentation supplied by their physicians (31), and only 250 of those had purchased seeds or herbal cannabis from the government. This could be attributed in part to suggestions to physicians not to take part in the program by the Canadian Medical Association (32), and a refusal of Canada's sole malpractice insurance carrier to underwrite liability issues attendant to the recommendation of herbal cannabis. Similar patterns would likely eventuate in the United States were herbal cannabis available medically. The Dutch and Canadian programs have concluded it important to subject their herbal cannabis to gamma irradiation to reduce risks of microbiological deterioration, creating attendant controversy, because this processing technique has never been tested for safety with any smoked product.

Cannabis and the Scientific Method

The analgesic and palliative effects of cannabis and cannabinoid preparations have been amply reported over the past generation, and have similarly been reviewed at length in previous citations. In essence, these effects result from a combination of receptor and nonreceptor mediated mechanisms. THC and other cannabinoids exert many actions through cannabinoid receptors, G-protein coupled membrane receptors that are extremely densely represented in central (33), spinal (34,35), and peripheral (36) nociceptive pathways. Endogenous cannabinoids (endocannabinoids) even regulate integrative pain structures such as the periaqueductal gray matter (37). The endocannabinoid system also interacts in numerous ways with the endogenous opioid (38) and vanilloid (39) systems that also modulate analgesia, and with a myriad of other neurotransmitter systems such as the serotonergic, dopaminergic, glutamatergic, etc.,(20) pertinent to pain. Research has shown that the addition of cannabinoid agonists to opiates enhances analgesic efficacy markedly in experimental animals (40), helps diminish the likelihood of the development of opiate tolerance (41), and prevents opiate withdrawal (42). The current author has suggested that a clinical endocannabinoid deficiency may underlie the pathogenesis of migraine, fibromyalgia, idiopathic bowel syndrome and numerous other painful conditions that defy modern pathophysiological explanation or adequate treatment (43).

Thus, the theoretical basis for utilizing cannabis-derived medications in treatment of pain is on a very firm foundation. Until very recently, however, very few cannabinoid RCTs in the area of pain management had been performed. These will be reviewed in the following section.

PROS AND CONS OF MEDICINAL CANNABIS DELIVERY SYSTEMS

Synthetics

THC ("dronabinol")
After initial investigations of analgesic effects by Noyes et al. in the 1970s (44–46), THC, as Marinol®, was approved for treatment of chemotherapy-associated nausea in 1985, and AIDS wasting in 1992. Results from pain studies have been mixed. Marinol was employed in two studies of central and peripheral neuropathic pain with oral doses up to 25 mg without clear benefit on pain or allodynia, and with prominent side effects (47,48). In a similar study of two- to five-year duration showed early benefits on pain that were not maintained (49). In a Swedish study (50) of Marinol doses to up to 10 mg/d in 24 multiple sclerosis patients with central neuropathic pain, median numerical pain scale in final week was reduced in the Marinol group ($p = 0.02$), and median pain relief was improved over placebo ($p = 0.035$). Moreover, pure oral THC in isolation may induce intoxicating and sedative complaints (51), as well as dysphoria, perhaps attributable to metabolism of THC to 11-hydroxy-THC. An RCT of Marinol in 40 post-operative patients failed to demonstrate analgesic efficacy (51a). When queried in surveys comparing Marinol to whole cannabis products, most medical patients who have utilized both prefer herbal cannabis (20).

Other THC delivery forms are in early research stages. THC hemisuccinate suppositories are twice as bioavailable as oral THC (52–55), but have not been assayed in RCTs of pain, and may not prove to be acceptable as a delivery method by consumers in the United States. THC skin patches are currently under investigation, but available PK data (56,57) indicate that serum delivery attained to date is only a fraction of that required to produce therapeutic effects. The gradient required to obtain THC delivery transcutaneously ensures that a large residual fraction would be left in the patch, and represent a diversion risk upon disposal.

The development of an inhaled prescription form of THC poses significant challenges. Pure THC aerosols have been investigated since the mid-1970s, hampered by the physical properties of the molecule and its irritating and cough-inducing effect when employed in isolation (58). Some authorities posit that concomitant terpenoid and flavonoid components are necessary for local anesthetic and anti-inflammatory benefits (59). In a recent Phase I clinical trial designed to develop aerosol THC for acute migraine (60), coughing and intoxication were quite prominent in most subjects, even at lowest dose levels. Certain conditions with breakthrough or paroxysmal pain (e.g., acute muscle spasm, trigeminal neuralgia or cluster headache) might merit this approach, but such rapid dose delivery is unnecessary for treatment of many chronic pain conditions, and poses its own drawbacks (vide infra).

Nabilone
Nabilone, or Cesamet®, is a synthetic cannabinoid similar to THC, but 10-fold more potent, and assessed as having a lower "abuse potential" (61). It is available in the United Kingdom, Canada, Australia, some European countries, and just recently in the USA as an anti-emetic (62). Analgesic effects of this drug were noted in patients with neuropathic pain (63), but with prominent drowsiness and dysphoria.

Ajulemic acid
Ajulemic acid (CT-3) is synthetic cannabinoid derivative with analgesic and anti-inflammatory properties in animal models (64,65) that have advanced to Phase II

clinical trials. Ajulemic acid binds to the peroxisome proliferator-activated receptor gamma, involved in inflammatory mechanisms (66), and also suppresses monocyte interleukin-1beta production in vitro (67). Ajulemic acid seems to have promising anti-inflammatory and analgesic properties, but recent reports suggest that this agent does bind to CB_1, and could produce psychoactive effects (68). Clinical research is currently confined to treatment of interstitial cystitis.

Herbal Cannabis

Smoking

Despite the frequent anecdotal citations of cannabis as analgesic in patient surveys and in the lay press, few RCTs with smoked cannabis have been completed (69). Perhaps the first study to demonstrate analgesic efficacy was an examination of 50 subjects with Human Immunodeficiency Virus (HIV) -related neuropathic pain, in whom 13 of 25 who utilized cannabis noted a greater than 30% pain reduction versus placebo ($p = 0.04$) (70).

Efficacy alone, however, is not sufficient to attain NDA status. Smoked cannabis would face virtually insurmountable hurdles from a regulatory standpoint, but the obvious sequelae of the delivery system (smoking) would alone seem to limit prospects for FDA regulatory approval. Foremost among these are pulmonary sequelae, which have recently been recently extensively reviewed (71). It is inarguable that chronic smoking of cannabis produces increased cough, phlegm, bronchitic complaints, and even bronchoscopic and histological changes similar to those in tobacco smokers. Although the largest epidemiological study to date has failed to support an etiological link between cannabis smoking and development of cancer (72), this does not clear the path for FDA-approval in the United States. As the Botanical Guidance makes clear (16) (p. 43), "All parenteral, topical, inhalation, or other nonorally administered botanical products are considered to be drugs, not dietary supplements, and must be studied under an IND for any use." The presence of tars, polyaromatic hydrocarbons (PAH) and similar toxic components in cannabis smoke would seemingly preclude the possibility of FDA-approval irrespective of the above epidemiological findings. Specifically, it is doubtful that any botanical whose delivery system creates known or potential carcinogens would receive a green light for prescription usage.

Apart from pulmonary risks, the smoked route of cannabis administration has also raised alarms with respect to vascular sequelae (73), specifically the claim of an increase in risk of myocardial infarction in the hour after smoking (74), likely secondary to tachycardia. Additionally, a case of "cannabis arteritis" associated with smoking was recently reported (75).

Infectious disease risks associated with contamination of herbal cannabis (Fig. 1) by bacteria or fungal pathogens have also been reviewed (71), but have been further highlighted by a recent outbreak of meningococcal meningitis spread by sharing of joints in Vancouver, British Columbia (76). These other public health threats contribute to a body of evidence that would likely preclude FDA acceptance of smoked cannabis.

Cannabis smoking is relatively inefficient, with up to 70% of THC destroyed in the process of burning (77), and additional losses in sidestream smoke, with systemic THC bioavailability ranging from 10% to 27% (78,79).

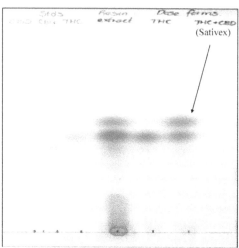

FIGURE 1   Thin-layer chromatography (TLC) of a sample of hashish (cannabis resin, or "soapbar") as obtained on the black market in the United Kingdom, compared to Sativex® oromucosal spray. Although the hashish, probably of Moroccan origin, contains both THC and CBD, adulterants including hair, dung, and petroleum distillates are common (TLC courtesy of Ian Flockhart, Applied Analysis, United Kingdom; other photos by Ethan Russo). *Abbreviations*: THC, tetrahydrocannabinol; CBD, cannabidiol.

Vaporization

A variety of devices have appeared on the black market in the last decade with the aim of mitigating smoking-associated sequelae of cannabis usage through vaporization of the herbal material to volatilize cannabis components without burning. Earlier devices failed to demonstrate compelling reductions in combustion products (80,81). More recently, studies with the Volcano® vaporizer (82) have begun. In a pilot study comparing use of the vaporizer to smoked national institute on drug abuse (NIDA) cannabis (83), the device markedly reduced carbon monoxide levels, and a majority of 18 subjects preferred it to smoking. However, results of laboratory analyses indicate that THCA, the herbal precursor of THC prior to heating, is incompletely decarboxylated to the active form even at the highest vaporizer temperature setting, and that the efficiency of delivery of pure THC is also incomplete at that level (84). Of greater concern, at the highest machine setting (corresponding to an air temperature of 230°C), 5% of yield of the vapor consisted of potentially carcinogenic PAH (85). While this technology has proven quite popular with cannabis consumers, the failure to eliminate potentially carcinogenic pyrolytic end products make it a virtual impossibility that it can pass regulatory scrutiny by the FDA in the current form. Furthermore, as a medical device, it lacks portability and convenience.

Oral Ingestion

Following oral administration of cannabis or cannabinoids, bioavailability is a primary issue, because absorption is erratic and far from complete unless a lipid carrier is employed (78) and often requires one to two hours or more. Such lengthy onset of action precludes ready dosage titration. Additionally, patients suffering from nausea or vomiting may be unable to employ this route of delivery. Some data have suggested that a "first pass effect" of hepatic metabolism occurs after oral usage, producing 11-hydroxy-THC, which may be more psychoactive than THC itself. It is clear that some patients are plagued by undesirable psychoactive effects even on dosages of 2.5 mg of THC-equivalent. Advantages of oral usage include a lack of pulmonary risk, and prolonged half-life compared to inhalation techniques.

Cannador

Cannador is an encapsulated oral cannabis extract that has been employed in several European studies. It is said to be standardized, but its THC:CBD ratios vary in published reports (86). In a large Phase III study of patients with spasticity in MS (CAMS) (87), there was failure to achieve statistically significant benefit on the Ashworth Scale. Nevertheless, an improvement was seen in the treatment group over placebo with respect to subjective pain associated with spasm ($p = 0.003$). In a subsequent long-term follow up, a statistically significant improvement in pain of cannabinoids versus placebo was also noted (88), but differences between Cannador and Marinol were not clear.

Cannador was also employed in two other recently reported pain RCTs. In a double-blind crossover study of postherpetic neuralgia versus placebo employing a maximal tolerable dose of Cannador in 26 subjects, no effect was noted on pain (89). In a study of 65 patients with postoperative pain (CANPOP) (90) without concomitant analgesics or opiates, 11/11 (100%) of subjects receiving 5 mg THC-equivalent required rescue medicine, while 15/30 (50%) receiving 10 mg THC-equivalent and 6/24 (25%) receiving 15 mg THC-equivalent did so. Most patients considered the psychoactive sequelae unpleasant or strange, but only 3/65 (4.6%) characterized feelings as "high" or "stoned." These results may indicate inadequate dosing via oral absorption, inadequate provision of CBD or the advisability of concomitant opiates in the postoperative pain trial.

Sativex®

An oromucosal spray (Fig. 1) known by the brand name of Sativex® is currently approved for prescription in Canada under a Notice of Compliance with conditions for treatment of central neuropathic pain in multiple sclerosis. It is a highly standardized medicinal product derived from the active components of two selected chemovars of *Cannabis sativa* plants grown under conditions of Good Agricultural Practice. One chemovar yields a high and reproducible proportion of Δ^9-THC [approximately 96% of total cannabinoids (91)], a psychoactive and analgesic component. The other chemovar yields primarily CBD [approximately 90% of total cannabinoids (91)], a nonpsychoactive, analgesic, and anti-inflammatory drug that also counteracts many adverse events (AEs) associated with THC (86). Sativex® is a blend of the THC-predominant extract (Tetranabinex®) and the CBD-predominant extract (Nabidiolex®) (92). Dried inflorescences of unfertilized female cannabis plants are extracted and processed under current Good Manufacturing Practice conditions to yield a botanical drug substance (BDS) of defined composition. The contents of the principle actives in the BDS are well controlled and reproducible from batch to batch, and represent some 70% (w/w) of the total (91). Minor cannabinoids are present (5–6%) (89). The remainder of the BDS consists of terpenes (6–7%, most GRAS), sterols (6%), triglycerides, alkanes,

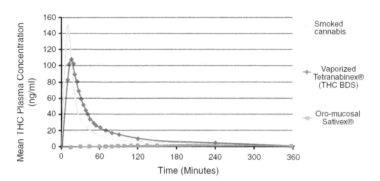

FIGURE 2 Comparison of pharmacokinetic peaks of Sativex® oromucosal spray containing 10.8 mg THC and 10 mg cannabidiol, vaporized Tetranabinex® with 6.65 mg THC (GWPK0114, data on file, GW Pharmaceuticals), and smoked cannabis from a cigarette containing an estimated 34 mg THC (78,79). Note that the mean THC plasma concentration with Sativex® never exceeds 2 ng/ml. *Abbreviations*: THC, tetrahydrocannabinol; BDS, botanical drug substance.

squalene, tocopherol, carotenoids, and other minor components (also GRAS) derived from the plant material (59), such that over 95% of components are characterized. The medicine is formulated into a spray for sublingual and oro-mucosal administration. Each 100 μL pump-action spray increment contains 2.7 mg of THC and 2.5 mg of CBD, the minor components, plus ethanol and propylene glycol excipients and peppermint flavoring. Detailed PK data on this material is available (93) (Fig. 2, purple trace). The preparation has onset of activity in 15 to 40 minutes, which allows patients to titrate dosing requirements according to their symptoms, with a very acceptable profile of AEs. Experience in well over 1000 patient-years of Sativex® exposure in over 2000 experimental subjects has been amassed in Phase II to III randomized, double-blind, placebo-controlled clinical trials herein discussed. A slight majority of subjects have had no previous recreational or medicinal cannabis exposure. All studies were performed in self-titration protocols with Sativex® added adjunctively to existing drug regimens in patients with intractable or uncontrolled symptoms. Sativex® has met all regulatory requirements for safety and quality (manufacturing consistency) of Health Canada, and the Medicines and Health Products Regulatory Agency in the United Kingdom.

In a Phase II clinical trial in 20 patients with intractable neurogenic symptoms (12), patients were treated with THC-predominant, CBD-predominant, and 1:1 preparation (Sativex®) in a double-blind crossover trial against placebo. Significant improvement was seen with both THC- and CBD-predominant extracts on pain (especially neuropathic) ($p < 0.05$). However, post hoc analysis revealed that overall symptom control was best with Sativex® ($p < 0.0001$), with less intoxication than with THC-predominant extract.

In another Phase II double-blind crossover study of intractable chronic pain (7), in 24 subjects who did not employ rescue medication, visual analogue scales (VAS) were 5.9 for placebo, 5.45 for CBD-predominant, 4.63 for THC-predominant, and 4.4 for Sativex® extracts ($p < 0.001$). Sleep was also most improved on the latter ($p < 0.001$). Of 28 subjects, 11 preferred Sativex® overall, while 14 found Tetranabinex and Sativex® equally satisfactory. For pain in the MS patients, Sativex® produced best results ($p < 0.0042$).

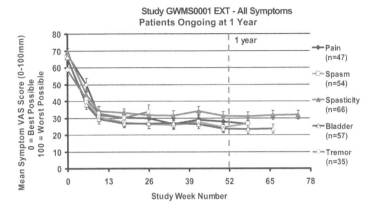

FIGURE 3 Graphic representation of VAS of various symptoms of multiple sclerosis in Sativex® patients (10) that continued in safety-extension studies for over one year. Note the continued decline in symptoms with extended usage. *Abbreviation:* VAS, visual analogue scales.

In a Phase III study of intractable pain associated with brachial plexus injury (3), roughly equivalent benefits were noted in Box Scale-11 pain scores with Tetranabinex ($p = 0.002$) and Sativex® extracts ($p = 0.005$).

On the basis of these results with oromucosal cannabis-based medicines, Professor Carlini of Brazil, a member of the International Narcotics Control Board, has stated (94) (p. 463), "However, any possible doubts that might exist on whether or not Δ^9-THC is an useful medicine for MS symptoms, were removed by the results obtained in four very recent randomized, double-blind, placebo-controlled trials."

In a controlled double-blind clinical trial of intractable central neuropathic pain (9), 66 MS subjects showed mean Numerical Rating Scale analgesia favoring Sativex® over placebo ($p = 0.009$), with sleep disturbances scores also improved ($p = 0.003$).

In a Phase III double-blind placebo-controlled trial of peripheral neuropathic pain with allodynia (95), Sativex® produced highly statistically significant improvements in pain levels ($p = 0.004$) with additional benefit on dynamic allodynia ($p = 0.042$) and sleep disturbance ($p = 0.001$) measures.

In a SAFEX study of Phase III double-blind placebo-controlled trial in 160 subjects with various symptoms of MS (10), 137 patients elected to continue on Sativex® (11). On VAS of symptoms, rapid declines were noted over the first 12 weeks in pain ($n = 47$) with slower sustained improvements for more than one year (Fig. 3).

A dedicated Phase II double-blind, randomized placebo-controlled parallel group study of 56 rheumatoid arthritis patients with Sativex® was recently undertaken in the United Kingdom over a period of five weeks (4). Nocturnal treatment was initiated with a single spray each evening (2.7 mg THC + 2.5 mg CBD) and titrated upward every other night according to need to a maximum of six sprays per evening (16.2 mg THC +15 mg CBD), after which stable dosing was pursued for a minimum of three weeks. In the final treatment week, many study measures favored Sativex® over placebo: morning pain on movement ($p = 0.044$), morning pain at rest

($p = 0.018$), quality of sleep ($p = 0.027$), 28-joint disease activity score (DAS28) ($p = 0.002$) measure of disease activity ($p = 0.002$), and short-form McGill pain questionnaire (SF-MPQ) pain at present ($p = 0.016$).

Finally, the recently announced results of a Phase III study comparing Sativex®, THC-predominant extract, and placebo in intractable pain due to cancer unresponsive to opiates (6) with strong neuropathic pain components, demonstrated that Sativex® produced highly statistically significant improvements in analgesia ($p = 0.0142$), while the Tetranabinex failed to do so in this trial, confirming the key importance of the inclusion of CBD in the Sativex® preparation. In January 2006, the FDA approved an investigational new drug application for phase III studies of Sativex® in the USA in intractable cancer pain unresponsive to optimized opiate therapy.

Analysis of sleep parameters in seven Phase II and III trials of MS and neuropathic pain and two corresponding SAFEX studies to date demonstrate significant to highly statistically significant and durable benefits of Sativex® on this important clinical symptom (96).

Common AEs of Sativex® acutely in RCTs have included complaints of bad taste, stinging, dry mouth, dizziness, nausea or fatigue, but these rarely necessitate discontinuation, and are less common in regular usage (vide infra).

Sativex® contains no known potentially carcinogenic components. Sativex®, Nabidiolex, and Tetranabinex have failed to produce genotoxicity or mutagenicity in rodent tests (97). CBD (and THC) have proven cytotoxic for glioma cells, while cytoprotective for normal brain cells (98).

While no "head-to-head" comparisons of Sativex® to Marinol or smoked THC have been performed in RCTs, examination of respective AE profiles is possible. The issue of central neuropathic pain in MS has been studied with Marinol ($N = 24$) (50), and Sativex® ($N = 33$) (9) with positive benefits in each ($p = 0.02$ and $p = 0.009$, respectively). However, it is interesting to compare the AEs in the two trials (Fig. 4A and B) and note that these generally favor Sativex®, despite the fact that less than or equal to 10 mg of THC was employed in the Marinol trial (50), while a mean of 25.9 mg of THC-equivalent was utilized by Sativex® patients (9).

A series of studies have been done in the Netherlands and Canada examining survey reports of AEs in patients, who have employed herbal cannabis in legal programs in those countries. Although these smoked cannabis studies were not placebo-controlled RCTs, again a comparison of attributable AEs to self-selected patients in Sativex® SAFEX studies is possible, including those with multiple symptoms of MS ($N = 137$) (GWMS0001 SAFEX) continuing on from a previous study (10), and a composite of various studies above reviewed with central or peripheral neuropathic pain ($N = 507$) (GWNP0101 SAFEX), all of whom took Sativex® for more than a year, and up to four years in some subjects.

In Canada, the effects of government supplied herbal cannabis in the Marihuana Medical Access Regulations (MMAR) program was studied in 30 chronic pain subjects (99), half of whom had previously used black market supplies. Some may have continued to do so. MMAR cannabis had a THC content of 9.63% to 13.89%, with CBD undetectable. Average daily dose employed was 2.75 g, and 28/30 (93.3%) of subjects smoked as their delivery technique. A comparison of AE profiles (Fig. 5A and B) reveals dizziness as the sole parameter favoring MMAR material, while results otherwise clearly favored Sativex®, especially parameters pertaining to sedation and appetite. It should be emphasized that certain Sativex® patients crossed over from placebo to Sativex® in the

Adverse Event	Marinol (THC ≤10 mg/d)	Sativex (mean THC 25.9 mg/d)
Dizziness	58%	52%*
Somnolence	46**	9
Fatigue	4	6
Feeling drunk	8	3
Dry mouth	13	12
Nausea	13	9
Headache	25**	3

* Incidence is higher than in other clinical trials   ** Difference appears significant

(A)

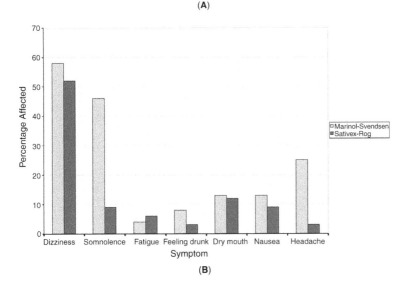

(B)

FIGURE 4 **(A)** Table and **(B)** graphic representation of adverse effects of Marinol (40) (*N* = 24) versus Sativex® (9) (*N* = 33) in respective randomized clinical trials in treatment of neuropathic pain in multiple sclerosis. *Abbreviation*: THC, tetrahydrocannabinol.

SAFEX studies, and thus, certain early AE were noted prior to the development of tolerance.

The Dutch Office of Medicinal Cannabis has previously allowed prescription by physicians and distribution through pharmacies of two proprietary herbal cannabis strains provided as herbal material: SIMM 18 with THC 13.7% and CBD 0.7%, and Bedrocan with THC 18% and CBD 0.8%. Results in 200 subjects (60.9% of whom previously employed black market supplies), the majority of whom employed cannabis for pain, were analyzed by the PHARMO Institute (100): 73.5% used cannabis in tea [!], 20.5% smoked with tobacco, 6.5% vaporized, 5.5% smoked with a waterpipe, and 7% used other means (oral). Examination of comparative AE profiles (Fig. 6A and B) reveals that nausea was marginally

Programme	MMAR-PPS	GWMS0001	GWNP0102
N =	30	137	507
Adverse Event	% affected	% affected	% affected
Fatigue	20	8	9.1
Lethargy	10	5.1	3
Appetite ↑	60	0.7	1
Dizziness	3.3	15.3	27
Anxiety	6.7	0.7	2
Palpitations	3.3	0	1.4
Tachycardia	13.3	0	0.6
Confusion	6.7	0	0
Weight gain	23.3	stable	stable

(A)

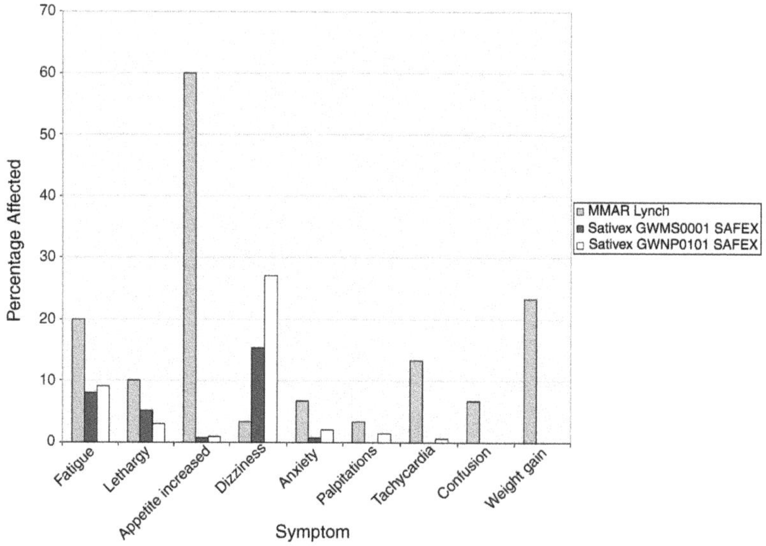

(B)

FIGURE 5 (A) Table and (B) graphic representation of AE reported with smoked cannabis in chronic pain patients in the Canadian MMAR program (99) ($N=30$) versus Sativex® SAFEX studies of MS ($N=137$) and central and peripheral neuropathic pain ($N=507$). *Abbreviations*: AE, adverse event; MMAR, Marijuana Medical Access Regulations; SAFEX, safety-extension.

reported more frequently in Sativex® patients (perhaps as a function of ethanol in the preparation), while most other side effects were notably more common with crude cannabis.

Another company, Maripharm, previously supplied herbal cannabis to Dutch pharmacies, and this material had a content of 10.2% THC with CBD less than 1%. Some 107 subjects with predominantly chronic pain and neurological conditions employed this material, primarily via smoking (101). Comparison of AEs reported in the article (Fig. 7A and B) clearly favors Sativex® with respect to dry mouth and cognitive seque-lae. Additional AEs were also analyzed in online material (102), and can be compared to Sativex® (Fig. 8A and B). In every instance, the AE profile markedly favors Sativex®.

Adverse Event	% Reporting	Mild	Moderate	Severe
Languor/Dullness	42.5	52.1	41.7	6.3
Dry Mouth	38.1	55.8	23.3	20.9
Giddiness	33.6	73.7	15.8	10.5
Muscle weakness	31.9	38.9	44.4	16.7
Hunger	25.2	26.7	40.0	33.3
Feeling hot or cold in hands or feet	23.5	42.9	32.1	25.0
Red eyes	16.0	63.2	21.1	15.8
Disorientation to time or place	15.1	44.4	50.0	5.6
Airway irritation	14.3	64.7	29.3	5.9
Better hearing	11.8	64.3	21.4	14.3
Improved color vision	10.9	46.2	30.8	23.1
Confusion	10.9	69.2	23.1	7.7
Tachycardia	10.9	46.2	30.8	23.1
Nausea	9.2	63.6	27.3	9.1
Headache	8.4	100.0	0	0
Anxiety/Panic	5.0	67.0	33.0	0
Insomnia	5.0	66.7	16.7	16.7
Agitation	4.2	60.0	40.0	0
Delusion	3.4	50.0	25.0	25.0
Excitability	3.4	50.0	50.0	0

(A)

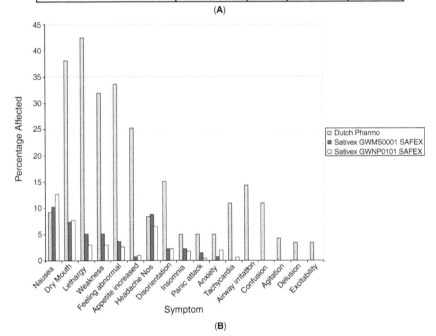

(B)

FIGURE 6 (**A**) Table of AE reported in the PHARMO study (100) of cannabis from Dutch pharmacies (*N* = 200), with (**B**) graphic comparison to AE in Sativex® SAFEX studies of MS (*N* = 137) and central and peripheral neuropathic pain (*N* = 507). *Abbreviations:* AE, adverse event; SAFEX, safety-extension.

Two conclusions are possible in consideration of these results:

1. Sativex® allows attainment of higher daily doses of oral THC, probably due to oromucosal delivery and the actions of CBD.
2. The AEs attributable to Sativex® are significantly less frequent than those reported with other delivery systems of standardized herbal cannabis.

Programme	Maripharm-Gorter	Sativex GWMS0001	Sativex GWNP0101
N =	107	137	507
Symptom	% Affected	% Affected	% Affected
Dry mouth	27.4	7.3	7.7
Lethargy	13.9	5.1	3
Feeling abnl	10.6	3.6	2.6
Dist. in attn.	11.7	5.1	3.2
Euphoric mood	13.3	0.7	4.3

(A)

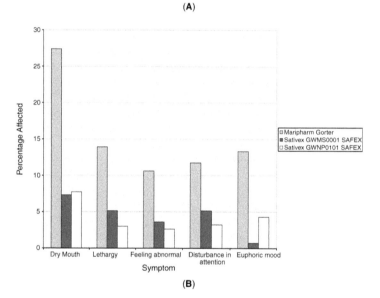

(B)

FIGURE 7 (**A**) Table and (**B**) graphic representation of AE reported in the study of Maripharm cannabis from Dutch pharmacies (N = 107) (101), in comparison to AE in Sativex® SAFEX studies of MS (N = 137) and central and peripheral neuropathic pain (N = 507). *Abbreviations:* AE, adverse event; SAFEX, safety-extension.

SATIVEX® AND MEDICINAL CANNABIS CONTROVERSIES

Herbal Synergy: Does It Exist?

The contributions of cannabis components beyond THC to its medicinal effects has been widely debated (103,104) with some authors supporting the concept of herbal synergy (59,105,106), the likes of which has been convincingly demonstrated for endocannabinoids via "the entourage effect" of active and seemingly inactive metabolites (107,108). Such synergy would be apparent under conditions in which the activity of a minor component complemented the major, diminished the AE profile, or otherwise contributed to a preparation's stability or efficacy. The case in support of CBD as a synergist to THC has recently been examined in detail (86). To enumerate just a few examples, CBD displays antianxiety effects (109), is antipsychotic in high

Programme	Maripharm	GWMS0001	GWNP01001
N =	107	137	507
Symptom	% affected	% affected	% affected
Eye irritation	11.8	0	0.2
Feeling high	38.8	3.6	4.9
STM loss	27.2	4.4	1.4
Sleepiness/Som	38.7	5.8	7.9
Hunger	32.4	0.7	1
↓ Concntrn/ Attn	30.1	5.1	3.2
↓Motvtn/ Interest	19.6	0.7	0
Anxiety	14.4	0.7	2
Euphoria	24.7	0.7	4.3
Depression	18.1	0.7	1.6
Dry mouth	59.9	7.3	7.7
↓ Coordination	26	0.7	0.4

(A)

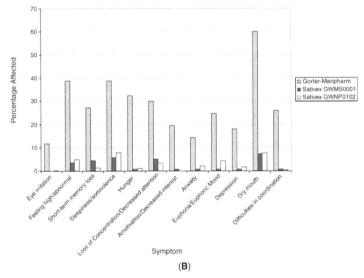

(B)

FIGURE 8 (**A**) Table and (**B**) graphic representation of supplemental AE reported in the study of Maripharm cannabis from Dutch pharmacies ($N = 107$) (101), in comparison to AE in Sativex® SAFEX studies of MS ($n = 137$) and central and peripheral neuropathic pain ($N = 507$). *Abbreviations:* AE, adverse event; SAFEX, safety-extension; STM, short-term memory.

doses (110,111), inhibits metabolism of THC to the possibly more psychoactive 11-hydroxy-THC (112), inhibits glutamate excitotoxicity, displays antioxidant effects (113), and has anti-inflammatory and immunomodulatory activity in its own right (114). CBD and perhaps other cannabis components (59) are synergistic to THC (115) by virtue of potentiation of benefits, attenuation of side effects, summation, and the provision of PK and metabolic advantages. To do so, however, sufficient quantities of CBD must be present, and this was a prime motivator behind the composition of Sativex® as a blend of two chemovars, because individual cannabis plants do not naturally contain high percentages of both cannabinoids simultaneously (116). In contrast, North American strains of cannabis are virtually devoid of CBD (117,118).

Pharmacokinetics and Cannabinoid Dose Titration

It has previously been mentioned that phytocannabinoids are lipid soluble and oral absorption is slow and erratic. Cannabis users occasionally allege in press interviews that the smoking of cannabis allows easy dose titration due to its rapid onset (Fig. 2), but this method also produces extremely high serum (and presumably brain) levels. Such high serum levels are, of course, the goal of recreational usage, but inappropriate and unnecessary for therapeutic applications (Fig. 2), because intoxication is an undesirable side effect for most patients, who are merely seeking pain relief. In fact, outside of early dosage titration, most Sativex® patients experience no "high" and report subjective intoxication levels on VAS that are in the single digits out of 100 (Fig. 9), indistinguishable from placebo (11). The Sativex® research program to date has debunked the notion that noticeable psychoactive effects are necessary for symptomatic benefits to be realized from a cannabis-derived medicine.

Anti-inflammatory Drugs and Cyclo-Oxygenase Inhibition

Current concern has been prominent in relation to morbidity and mortality associated with nonsteroidal anti-inflammatory drugs, wherein older cyclooxygenase (COX-1) agents may predispose to gastric ulceration and hemorrhages, while newer COX-2 agents have been associated with increased risk of myocardial infarction and cerebrovascular accidents (119,120). Recent study has demonstrated, however, that the anti-inflammatory and analgesic effects of Tetranabinex (high THC) and Nabidiolex (high CBD) extracts must occur via independent mechanisms, because they produce no COX inhibition of either isozyme at relevant pharmaceutical concentrations (121).

Blinding in Cannabis Randomized Clinical Trials

The issue of adequacy of blinding in RCTs of psychoactive drugs has frequently been called into question. However, all information to date supports the preservation of blinding in Sativex® studies. Sativex® and its placebo are identical in appearance, color, taste, and inclusion of peppermint flavoring. Approximately

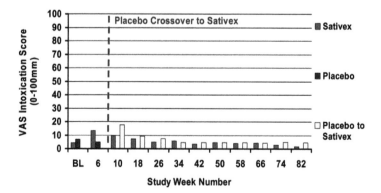

FIGURE 9 Visual analogue scores of intoxication of Sativex® versus placebo in MS patients (10) with various symptoms. safety-extension subjects were followed subsequently, and placebo subjects then titrated onto Sativex®. Note that after early titration, their intoxication scores are similarly indistinguishable from placebo.

40% to 50% of RCT participants have had prior experience of cannabis whether recreationally or therapeutically, but post hoc analysis of patients in two studies (8,9) reveals no differences in efficacy or AE profile in cannabis-experienced versus cannabis-naïve subjects. Furthermore, this analysis also showed that Sativex® had differential efficacy in various MS symptoms (122). If those patients achieving efficacy in one symptom had thereby become unblinded, one would anticipate that their other symptoms would also have improved. It was also noted that there was no difference in efficacy among previously cannabis-naïve or experienced patients, who experienced dizziness as an AE. Intoxication issues in the RCTs have been previously addressed (11).

Cannabis, Drug Abuse Liability and Drug Enforcement Administration Scheduling

Recreational cannabis abuse and dependence remain hot-button issues, with recent description of the elements of a cannabis withdrawal syndrome (123), while other authorities questioned its validity (124). The addictive potential of a drug is determined by its degree of intoxication, reinforcement, tolerance, withdrawal, and dependency. Drug abuse liability (DAL) is further determined by historical rates of an agent's abuse and diversion.

When enacting the Controlled Substances Act, Congress placed herbal cannabis in Schedule I, which is reserved for drugs that are considered to be addictive or dangerous, have severe abuse potential, and lack any recognized medical use. Upon its FDA-approval in 1985, Marinol was transferred to Schedule II, the category for drugs with high abuse potential and liability to produce dependency, but certain recognized medical uses. After subsequent study showed little abuse or diversion of the product (51), Marinol was reassigned in 1999 to Schedule III, a category denoting a lesser potential for abuse or lower dependency risk.

Intoxication is the primary purpose of recreational cannabis smoking, and remains a likely sequela of therapeutic usage of smoked herbal materials. It has similarly been a pitfall of Marinol therapy (51). As previously noted, in contrast, intoxication has been occasionally encountered in Sativex® RCTs early in dose titration, but is rarely problematic in long-term usage (Fig. 9).

The reinforcement properties of a drug are mediated in part by the rapidity of its delivery (125). Sativex® onset of effects is 15 to 40 minutes, with peak activity in a few hours. This is considerably slower than most drugs of highest abuse potential. CBD attenuates THC intoxication effects (86), and certainly may lower DAL potential.

Information from Sativex® RCTs and SAFEX studies does not indicate any particular reinforcement or euphoria (11).

A marked degree of tolerance is seen in a wide variety of measures of initial cannabinoid intoxication: tachycardia, hypothermia, orthostatic hypotension, dry mouth, ocular injection, intraocular pressure decreases, etc. (126). In well over 1000 patient-years of experience, no dose tolerance to Sativex® has been observed, however, and therapeutic efficacy is maintained for all symptoms studied to date (Fig. 3). In SAFEX studies in MS and peripheral neuropathic pain, Sativex® doses have been stable or even decreased after months to years of administration (11) (Fig. 10). Simultaneously, symptomatic pain control is maintained (11) (Fig. 11) with slow continued improvement.

In contrast to withdrawal effects reported in some long-term recreational cannabis users (127), in a cohort of 24 volunteers with MS who abruptly stopped

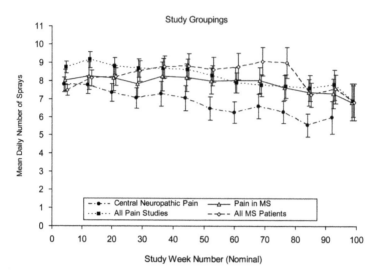

FIGURE 10   Mean daily sprays of Sativex® employed in GWNP0101 safety-extension studies of central and peripheral neuropathic pain ($N = 507$). Note that daily dosing required to produce pain control is stable or even declines slightly over the course of two years.

Sativex® after more than a year of continuous administration, no significant evidence for a formal withdrawal syndrome was observed. Rather, patients suffered recrudescence of symptoms after 7 to 10 days, but easily retitrated to prior dosages with renewed efficacy (11).

The above appears to show that Sativex® has a lower dependency risk than herbal cannabis, due to slower onset, low therapeutic dosages, virtual absence of

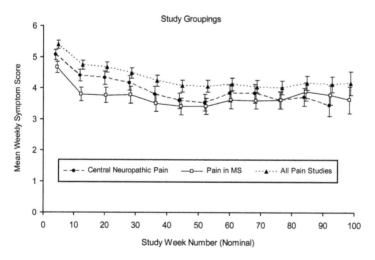

FIGURE 11   Box scale-11 numerical rating scales of central and peripheral neuropathic pain patients in GWNP0101 safety-extension subjects taking Sativex® for two years (N-507). Note that no tolerance develops and a slow, steady decline in pain levels results.

intoxication in regular therapeutic application, and lack of observed withdrawal even after prolonged usage. Finally, no known abuse or diversion incidents after Sativex® usage have occurred to date (as of August 2006). Formal postmarketing surveillance in Canada and DAL studies are planned as part of the U.S. regulatory approval process. Sativex® is expected to be placed in Schedule IV of the Misuse of Drugs Act in the United Kingdom upon its marketing approval in that country.

Cognitive Issues

A detailed analysis of cognitive factors surrounding cannabis-derived medicines is beyond the scope of this chapter. The cognitive impact of cannabis use has been previously reviewed (128,129). The issue has been less studied in therapeutic contexts with cannabis-based medicines. It has been reported that the effects on memory of heavy chronic recreational cannabis seem to diminish with a few weeks' abstinence without residua (130).

Components of the Halstead-Reitan battery have been performed in two Sativex® studies. In neuropathic pain with allodynia (8), no changes were seen versus placebo. In central neuropathic pain in MS (9), four of five measures showed no significant differences. The Selective Reminding Test did not change significantly on Sativex® over the course of the trial, but placebo patients did register an unexpected improvement ($p = 0.009$).

Depression and anxiety have been posited as sequelae of recreational cannabis usage (129), but slight improvements were noted with Sativex® in MS patients with central neuropathic pain (9) on Hospital Anxiety and Depression Scales, although these did not attain statistical significance. Examinations of long-term AE profiles in the figures also indicate little liability for mood disorders for this preparation.

The debate about an etiological role for cannabis in psychosis continues (129). If such an association exists [which is not supported by epidemiological data (131)], it would logically have some relation to dose, with a greater liability with chronic high dose exposure. The lower serum levels of Sativex® in therapeutic usage, coupled with the antipsychotic properties of CBD (132), would hopefully minimize such risks. Sativex® RCTs to date have excluded children and adolescents and anyone with a history of serious mental disorder. Once more, the long-term AE profile of Sativex® would seem to indicate few symptoms of paranoia, thought disorder, or similar changes.

Immune Function

Deleterious effects of cannabinoids on immune function have frequently been claimed in the literature, but generally these effects are noted in experimental animals exposed to 50 to 100 times the psychoactive dose (133). No changes in white blood cell, CD4 or CD8 cell counts were noted in small group of patients, who had used herbal cannabis therapeutically for over 20 years (128). A recent study of MS patients in the CAMS trial with Cannador showed no effects on major immune parameters (134), nor were any seen with smoked cannabis in a short-term RCT in HIV patients (135). Hematological parameters have been normal in all Sativex® RCTs to date, with no indication of anergy or hyperimmune sequelae.

Cannabinoid-Drug Interactions

Certainly, a risk of additive sedative effects may be possible with cannabinoids and other such drugs (18). In Sativex®, these sedative influences are actually counteracted by CBD (136). While there have been concerns about cannabinoid interference in metabolism of other drugs, particularly the effect of CBD on hepatic cytochrome P450 complex, no such changes were observed in a study of Sativex®, Tetranabinex and Nabidiolex at relevant concentrations in an experimental protocol (137). Thus, Sativex® should be safe to use in conjunction with fentanyl and other such drugs. In practice, Sativex® has been employed as an adjunctive medicine in complex intractable pain patients on regimens including the full range of opiates, tricyclic antidepressants, anticonvulsants, etc., without evidence of untoward drug-drug interactions.

Driving Safety

The issue of driving safety and drug use is an important topic in modern public health. While it is well established that significant alcohol intake impairs the ability to properly operate a motor vehicle, and that blood ethanol levels may accurately assess inherent risks, such relationships with cannabis usage, particularly in a recreational context, are much more problematic. While some retrospective studies of motor vehicle accidents or road crashes have claimed an etiological relationship to cannabis usage, others (138) have not supported a valid link, unless cannabis was concomitantly employed with alcohol. In a recent comprehensive review (139), the weight of evidence was interpreted to support a very low risk for cannabis in such accidents, and one less than that associated with many common therapeutic medications including benzodiazepines and older antihistamine formulations (140). A recent conference report also supports these findings (141).

The matter is further complicated when consideration turns to driving and medicinal cannabinoid usage. In the situation of Marinol, the information provided by the manufacturer to physicians indicates (142) (p. 5), "Patients receiving MARINOL capsules should be specifically warned not to drive, operate machinery, or engage in any hazardous activity until it is established that they are able to tolerate the drug and to perform such tasks safely."

The Sativex® Product Monograph in Canada states (143) (p. 8):

> "SATIVEX® may impair the mental and/or physical abilities required for certain potentially hazardous activities such as driving a car or operating machinery. Patients should be warned not to drive or engage in activities requiring unimpaired judgment and coordination. Patient should also be cautioned about the additive/synergistic effects of SATIVEX® with other CNS depressants, including opioids, GABA inhibitors, sedative/hypnotics, and alcohol."

Specific testing of the effects of Sativex® upon driving skills has not yet been undertaken, but other factors may have bearing on the issue. While THC forms a key component of Sativex®, the presence of almost equal amounts of the non-psychoactive CBD may serve to counteract intoxication and other side effects (86,144,145), as was specifically observed in a Phase I trial of Sativex® in normal subjects, in which CBD exerted alerting effects on sleep and eliminated counterbalanced residual THC effects the morning following nocturnal administration (136). Neuropsychological testing in peripheral neuropathic pain patients (8) and in multiple sclerosis patients with central pain (9) (vide supra) supports the concept that few perceptual or cognitive changes of note are observed with Sativex®. Finally, post hoc analysis of SAFEX patients with MS taking Sativex® for over one year indicate that in the 73% of 119 subjects completing a questionnaire, 59% noted an improvement in total disability, 63% improved in at least one activity, 20% reported a decreased need for equipment or assistance, 95% noted positive changes in General Life Benefits, and 12% to 32% of caretakers noted easier administration to demands of activities of daily living.

A new report by an expert panel (147) provides a comprehensive analysis of the issue of cannabinoids and driving. Among other recommendations, it suggests utilization of scientific standards to assess driving ability, such as roadside sobriety tests, as opposed to per se standards that may include measurement of inactive cannabinoid metabolites that serve as markers of past usage without providing accurate commentary upon a driver's actual driving ability status. In an effort to provide some framework for measuring putative impairment by cannabis that would be accessible to law enforcement, the panel did endorse the validity of measures of THC itself (146) (p. 7):

> "Based on the results of culpability studies and from meta-analyses of experimental studies, per se laws for DUIC (driving under the influence of cannabis) should specify a legal limit for THC in blood serum of 7 to 10 ng/mL as a reasonable choice for determining relative impairment by cannabis. This corresponds to THC concentration in whole blood—the parameter commonly used in U.S. jurisdictions- or 3.5 to 5 ng/mL."

Of note, no studies demonstrated relevant impact of cannabis on driving skills at plasma levels below 5 ng/ml of THC.

It is thus interesting to compare PK values of THC obtained by smoking and those from Sativex® (equivalent to four rapid oromucosal sprays) (Fig. 2), in which THC levels remained below this threshold. GW Pharmaceuticals hopes to collaborate with Bayer HealthCare in Canada in the performance of actual driving tests on patients with neuropathic pain before and after stabilization on Sativex® to better ascertain its effects, and appropriate advice that physicians should provide regarding this important issue.

CONCLUSIONS

The need for useful additional medicines in treatment of chronic pain conditions is clear, and the data supporting a role for certain cannabis-based drugs in such treatment is compelling. An evident path for approval of such drugs by the FDA has been provided in the form of the *Botanical Guidance* (16). With its approval in Canada, Sativex® is the only cannabis-based medicine to date that has provided the necessary evidence-based data on safety, clinical efficacy, and product quality and consistency to pass regulatory muster. The same cannot necessarily be said for other preparations that lack equivalent efficacy and especially, safety data. Upon successful completion of additional clinical trials and other regulatory safety mandates, Sativex® or other agents that provide an equivalent level of scientific support may soon be added to the available armamentarium of treatment options to treat chronic pain in the United States, to the likely mutual benefit of patients and their caregivers.

REFERENCES

1. ABC News, USA Today, Stanford Medical Center Poll. Broad experience with pain sparks search for relief. May 9 2005.
2. http://abcnews.go.com/images/Politics/979a1TheFightAgainstPain.pdf.
3. Berman JS, Symonds C, Birch R. Efficacy of two cannabis based medicinal extracts for relief of central neuropathic pain from brachial plexus avulsion: results of a randomised controlled trial. Pain 2004; 112(3):299–306.

4. Blake DR, Robson P, Ho M, Jubb RW, McCabe CS. Preliminary assessment of the efficacy, tolerability and safety of a cannabis-based medicine (Sativex) in the treatment of pain caused by rheumatoid arthritis. Rheumatology (Oxford) 2006; 45(1):50–52.

5. Brady CM, DasGupta R, Dalton C, Wiseman OJ, Berkley KJ, Fowler CJ. An open-label pilot study of cannabis based extracts for bladder dysfunction in advanced multiple sclerosis. Mult Scler 2004; 10:425–433.

6. Johnson JR, Potts R. Cannabis-based medicines in the treatment of cancer pain: a randomised, double-blind, parallel group, placebo controlled, comparative study of the efficacy, safety and tolerability of Sativex and Tetranabinex in patients with cancer-related pain. Paper presented at British Pain Society, Edinburgh, Scotland, March 8–11, 2005.

7. Notcutt W, Price M, Miller R, et al. Initial experiences with medicinal extracts of cannabis for chronic pain: results from 34 "N of 1" studies. Anesthesia 2004; 59:440–452.

8. Nurmikko TJ, Serpell MG, Hoggart B, Toomey PJ, Morlion BJ. A multicenter, double-blind, randomized, placebo-controlled trial of oromucosal cannabis-based medicine in the treatment of neuropathic pain characterized by allodynia. Neurology 2005; 64(6 suppl 1):A374.

9. Rog DJ, Nurmiko T, Friede T, Young C. Randomized controlled trial of cannabis based medicine in central neuropathic pain due to multiple sclerosis. Neurology 2005; 65(6):812–819.

10. Wade DT, Makela P, Robson P, House H, Bateman C. Do cannabis-based medicinal extracts have general or specific effects on symptoms in multiple sclerosis? A double-blind, randomized, placebo-controlled study on 160 patients. Mult Scler 2004; 10(4):434–441.

11. Wade DT, Makela PM, House H, Bateman C, Robson PJ. Long-term use of a cannabis-based medicine in the treatment of spasticity and other symptoms in multiple sclerosis. Mult Scler. In press.

12. Wade DT, Robson P, House H, Makela P, Aram J. A preliminary controlled study to determine whether whole-plant cannabis extracts can improve intractable neurogenic symptoms. Clin Rehabil 2003; 17:18–26.

13. Joy JE, Watson SJ, Benson JA Jr. Marijuana and medicine: assessing the science base. Washington, DC: Institute of Medicine, 1999.

14. Mead A. International control of cannabis: changing attitudes. In: Guy GW, Whittle BA, Robson P, eds. Medicinal Uses of Cannabis and Cannabinoids. London: Pharmaceutical Press, 2004:369–426.

15. Russo EB. Handbook of Psychotropic Herbs: A Scientific Analysis of Herbal Remedies for Psychiatric Conditions. Binghamton, NY: Haworth Press, 2001.

16. Food and Drug Administration. Guidance for industry: botanical drug products. In: Services UDoHaH, ed. US Government. 2004:48.

17. http://www.fda.gov/cder/guidance/4592fnl.pdf.

18. Russo EB. The role of cannabis and cannabinoids in pain management. In: Cole BE, Boswell M, eds. Weiner's Pain Management: A Practical Guide for Clinicians. 7th ed. Boca Raton, FL: CRC Press, 2006:823–844.

19. Russo EB. Cannabis in India: ancient lore and modern medicine. In: Mechoulam R, ed. Cannabinoids as Therapeutics. Basel, Switzerland: Birkhäuser Verlag, 2005:1–22.

20. Russo EB. Hemp for headache: an in-depth historical and scientific review of cannabis in migraine treatment. J Cannabis Ther 2001; 1(2):21–92.

21. Russo EB. History of cannabis as medicine. In: Guy GW, Whittle BA, Robson P, eds. Medicinal Uses of Cannabis and Cannabinoids. London: Pharmaceutical Press, 2004:1–16.

22. Mechoulam R. Cannabinoids as therapeutic agents. Boca Raton, FL: CRC Press, 1986.

23. Russo E. Cannabis treatments in obstetrics and gynecology: a historical review. J Cannabis Ther 2002; 2(3–4):5–35.

24. Riddle JM. Historical data as an aid in pharmaceutical prospecting and drug safety determination. J Altern Complement Med 1999; 5(2):195–201.

25. Randall RC. Muscle spasm, pain & marijuana therapy: testimony from federal and state court proceedings on marijuana's medical use in the treatment of multiple sclerosis, paralysis, and chronic pain. Washington, DC: Galen Press, 1991.

26. Grinspoon L, Bakalar JB. Marihuana, the forbidden medicine. Rev. and expanded. New Haven: Yale University Press, 1997.
27. Last resorts and fundamental rights: the substantive due process implications of prohibitions on medical marijuana. Harv Law Rev 2005; 118(62):1985–2006.
28. Gostin LO. Medical marijuana, American federalism, and the Supreme Court. JAMA 2005; 294(7):842–844.
29. Okie S. Medical marijuana and the Supreme Court. N Engl J Med 2005; 353(7):648–651.
30. Janse A, Breekveldt-Postma N, Erkens J, Herings R. Medicinal cannabis in the Netherlands. Paper presented at International Association for Cannabis as Medicine, Leiden, Netherlands, September 9, 2005.
31. Déry L. Canadian Medical Marijuana Research Program: main purpose and accomplishments. Paper presented at International Association for Cannabis as Medicine, Leiden, Netherlands, September 9, 2005.
32. Sibbald B. New medicinal marijuana rules ease onus on physicians. CMAJ 2005; 173(5):473.
33. Richardson JD, Aanonsen L, Hargreaves KM. SR 141716A, a cannabinoid receptor antagonist, produces hyperalgesia in untreated mice. Eur J Pharmacol 1997; 319(2–3): R3–R4.
34. Richardson JD, Aanonsen L, Hargreaves KM. Hypoactivity of the spinal cannabinoid system results in NMDA-dependent hyperalgesia. J Neurosci 1998; 18(1):451–457.
35. Richardson JD, Aanonsen L, Hargreaves KM. Antihyperalgesic effects of spinal cannabinoids. Eur J Pharmacol 1998; 345(2):145–153.
36. Richardson JD, Kilo S, Hargreaves KM. Cannabinoids reduce hyperalgesia and inflammation via interaction with peripheral CB1 receptors. Pain 1998; 75(1):111–119.
37. Walker JM, Huang SM, Strangman NM, Tsou K, Sanudo-Pena MC. Pain modulation by the release of the endogenous cannabinoid anandamide. Proc Natl Acad Sci 1999; 96(21):12198–12203.
38. Welch SP, Eads M. Synergistic interactions of endogenous opioids and cannabinoid systems. Brain Res 1999; 848(1–2):183–190.
39. Bisogno T, Hanus L, De Petrocellis L, et al. Molecular targets for cannabidiol and its synthetic analogues: effect on vanilloid VR1 receptors and on the cellular uptake and enzymatic hydrolysis of anandamide. Br J Pharmacol 2001; 134(4):845–852.
40. Cichewicz DL, Martin ZL, Smith FL, Welch SP. Enhancement of mu opioid antinociception by oral delta9-tetrahydrocannabinol: dose-response analysis and receptor identification. J Pharmacol Exp Ther 1999; 289(2):859–867.
41. Cichewicz DL, Haller VL, Welch SP. Changes in opioid and cannabinoid receptor protein following short-term combination treatment with delta (9)-tetrahydrocannabinol and morphine. J Pharmacol Exp Ther 2001; 297(1):121–127.
42. Cichewicz DL, Welch SP. Modulation of oral morphine antinociceptive tolerance and naloxone-precipitated withdrawal signs by oral Delta 9-tetrahydrocannabinol. J Pharmacol Exp Ther 2003; 305(3):812–817.
43. Russo EB. Clinical endocannabinoid deficiency (CECD): can this concept explain therapeutic benefits of cannabis in migraine, fibromyalgia, irritable bowel syndrome and other treatment-resistant conditions? Neuroendocrinol Lett 2004; 25(1–2):31–39.
44. Noyes R Jr., Baram DA. Cannabis analgesia. Compr Psychiatry 1974; 15(6):531–535.
45. Noyes R Jr., Brunk SF, Avery DAH, Canter AC. The analgesic properties of delta-9-tetrahydrocannabinol and codeine. Clin Pharmacol Ther 1975; 18(1):84–89.
46. Noyes R Jr., Brunk SF, Baram DA, Canter A. Analgesic effect of delta-9-tetrahydrocannabinol. J Clin Pharmacol 1975; 15(2–3):139–143.
47. Attal N, Brasseur L, Guirimand D, Clermond-Gnamien S, Atlami S, Bouhassira D. Are oral cannabinoids safe and effective in refractory neuropathic pain? Eur J Pain 2004; 8(2):173–177.
48. Clermont-Gnamien S, Atlani S, Attal N, Le Mercier F, Guirimand F, Brasseur L. Utilization thérapeutique du delta-9-tétrahydrocannabinol (dronabinol) dans les douleurs neuropathiques réfractaires. [The therapeutic use of D9-tetrahydrocannabinol (dronabinol) in refractory neuropathic pain]. Presse Med 2002; 31(39 pt 1): 1840–1845.

49. Rudich Z, Stinson J, Jeavons M, Brown SC. Treatment of chronic intractable neuropathic pain with dronabinol: case report of two adolescents. Pain Res Manag 2003; 8(4):221–224.

50. Svendsen KB, Jensen TS, Bach FW. Does the cannabinoid dronabinol reduce central pain in multiple sclerosis? Randomised double blind placebo controlled crossover trial. BMJ 2004; 329(7460):253.

51. Calhoun SR, Galloway GP, Smith DE. Abuse potential of dronabinol (Marinol). J Psychoactive Drugs 1998; 30(2):187–196.

51a. Buggy DJ, Toogood L, Maric S, Sharpe P, Lambert DG, Rowbotham DJ. Lack of analgesic efficacy of oral delta-9-tetrahydrocannabinol in postoperative pain. Pain 2003; 106(1–2):169–172.

52. Broom SL, Sufka KJ, Elsohly MA, Ross RA. Analgesic and reinforcing properties of delta9-THC-hemisuccinate in adjuvant-arthritic rats. J Cannabis Ther 2001; 1(3–4): 171–182.

53. Brenneisen R, Egli A, Elsohly MA, Henn V, Spiess Y. The effect of orally and rectally administered delta 9-tetrahydrocannabinol on spasticity: a pilot study with 2 patients. Int J Clin Pharmacol Ther 1996; 34(10):446–452.

54. Elsohly MA, Little TL Jr., Hikal A, Harland E, Stanford DF, Walker L. Rectal bioavailability of delta-9-tetrahydrocannabinol from various esters. Pharmacol Biochem Behav 1991; 40(3):497–502.

55. Mattes RD, Engelman K, Shaw LM, Elsohly MA. Cannabinoids and appetite stimulation. Pharmacol Biochem Behav 1994; 49(1):187–195.

56. Challapalli PV, Stinchcomb AL. In vitro experiment optimization for measuring tetrahydrocannabinol skin permeation. Int J Pharm 2002; 241(2):329–339.

57. Brenneisen R. Pharmacokinetics. In: Grotenhermen F, Russo E, eds. Cannabis and Cannabinoids: Pharmacology, Toxicity and Therapeutic Potential. Binghamton, NY: Haworth Press, 2001.

58. Tashkin DP, Reiss S, Shapiro BJ, Calvarese B, Olsen JL, Lodge JW. Bronchial effects of aerosolized delta 9-tetrahydrocannabinol in healthy and asthmatic subjects. Am Rev Respir Dis 1977; 115(1):57–65.

59. McPartland JM, Russo EB. Cannabis and cannabis extracts: greater than the sum of their parts? J Cannabis Ther 2001; 1(3–4):103–132.

60. Miller J, Meuwsen I, ZumBrunnen T, de Vries M. A Phase I evaluation of pulmonary dronabinol administered via a pressurized metered dose inhaler in healthy volunteers. Paper presented at American Academy of Neurology, Miami Beach, FL, April 14, 2005.

61. British Medical Association. Therapeutic uses of cannabis. Amsterdam: Harwood Academic Publishers, 1997.

62. Grotenhermen F. Definitions and explanations. In: Grotenhermen F, Russo E, eds. Cannabis and Cannabinoids: Pharmacology, Toxicology and Therapeutic Potential. Binghamton, NY: Haworth Press, 2001.

63. Notcutt W, Price M, Chapman G. Clinical experience with nabilone for chronic pain. Pharmaceutical Sci 1997; 3:551–555.

64. Burstein SH. The therapeutic potential of ajulemic acid (CT3). In: Grotenhermen F, Russo E, eds. Cannabis and Cannabinoids: Pharmacology, Toxicology and Therapeutic Potential. Binghamton, NY: Haworth Press, 2001.

65. Burstein SH. Ajulemic acid (CT3): a potent analog of the acid metabolites of THC. Curr Pharm Res 2000; 6(13):1339–1345.

66. Liu J, Li H, Burstein SH, Zurier RB, Chen JD. Activation and binding of peroxisome proliferator-activated receptor gamma by synthetic cannabinoid ajulemic acid. Mol Pharmacol 2003; 63(5):983–992.

67. Zurier RB, Rossetti RG, Burstein SH, Bidinger B. Suppression of human monocyte interleukin-1beta production by ajulemic acid, a nonpsychoactive cannabinoid. Biochem Pharmacol 2003; 65(4):649–655.

68. Dyson A, Peacock M, Chen A, et al. Antihyperalgesic properties of the cannabinoid CT-3 in chronic neuropathic and inflammatory pain states in the rat. Pain 2005; 116(1–2):129–137.

69. Campbell FA, Tramber MR, Carroll D, Reynolds DJM, Moore RA, McQuay HJ. Are cannabinoids an effective and safe option in the management of pain? A qualitative systematic review. BMJ 2001; 323(7 July):1–6.
70. Abrams DI, Jay CA, Vizoso H, et al. Smoked cannabis therapy for HIV-related painful peripheral neuropathy: results of a randomized, placebo-controlled clinical trial. Paper presented at International Association for Cannabis as Medicine, Leiden, Netherlands, September 9, 2005.
71. Tashkin DP. Smoked marijuana as a cause of lung injury. Monaldi Arch Chest Dis 2005; 63(2):93–100.
72. Morgenstern H, Greenland S, Zhang Z-F, Cozen W, Mack TM, Tashkin DP. Marijuana use and cancers of the lung and upper aerodigestive tract: results of a case-control study. Paper presented at Symposium on the Cannabinoids, 2005:Clearwater, FL, June 26, 2005.
73. Roth MD. Marijuana and your heart. Nature 2005; 434(7 April):708–709.
74. Mittleman MA, Lewis RA, Maclure M, Sherwood JB, Muller JE. Triggering myocardial infarction by marijuana. Circulation 2001; 103(23):2805–2809.
75. Combemale P, Consort T, Denis-Thelis L, Estival JL, Dupin M, Kanitakis J. Cannabis arteritis. Br J Dermatol 2005; 152(1):166–169.
76. Zanocco V. Meningococcal cases linked by sharing joints. http://www.vch.ca/news/docs/2005_04_07_mening_joints.pdf. Accessed April 8.
77. Dussy FE, Hamberg C, Luginbuhl M, Schwerzmann T, Briellmann TA. Isolation of Delta9-THCA-A from hemp and analytical aspects concerning the determination of Delta9-THC in cannabis products. Forensic Sci Int 2005; 149(1):3–10.
78. Grotenhermen F. Clinical pharmacokinetics of cannabinoids. J Cannabis Ther 2003; 3(1):3–51.
79. Huestis MA, Henningfield JE, Cone EJ. Blood cannabinoids. I. Absorption of THC and formation of 11-OH-THC and THCCOOH during and after smoking marijuana. J Anal Toxicol 1992; 16(5):276–282.
80. Gieringer D. Waterpipe study. Bull Multidisciplinary Assoc Psychedel Stud 1996; 6:59–63.
81. Gieringer D. Why marijuana smoke harm reduction? Bull Multidisciplinary Assoc Psychedel Stud 1996; 6(64–66).
82. Russo EB, Stortz M. An interview with Markus Storz: June 19, 2002. J Cannabis Ther 2003; 3(1):67–78.
83. Abrams DI, Vizoso H, Shade SB, Jay C, Kelly ME, Benowitz N. Vaporization as a smokeless cannabis delivery system: a pilot study. Paper presented at International Association of Cannabis as Medicine, Leiden, Netherlands, September 10, 2005.
84. Hazekamp A, Ruhaak R, Zuurman L, van Gerven J, Verpoorte R. Evaluation of a vaporizing device (volcano) for the pulmonary administration of tetrahydrocannabinol. J Pharm Sci 2006; 95(6):1308–1317.
85. Gieringer D, St. Laurent J, Goodrich S. Cannabis vaporizer combines efficient delivery of THC with effective suppression of pyrolytic compounds. J Cannabis Ther 2004; 4(1):7–27.
86. Russo EB, Guy GW. A tale of two cannabinoids: the therapeutic rationale for combining tetrahydrocannabinol and cannabidiol. Medical Hypotheses 2006; 66(2):234–246.
87. Zajicek J, Fox P, Sanders H, et al. Cannabinoids for treatment of spasticity and other symptoms related to multiple sclerosis (CAMS study): multicentre randomized placebo-controlled trial. Lancet 2003; 362(9395):1517–1526.
88. Zajicek JP, Sanders HP, Wright DE, et al. Cannabinoids in multiple sclerosis (CAMS) study: safety and efficacy data for 12 months follow up. J Neurol Neurosurg Psychiatry 2005; 76(12):1664–1669.
89. Ernst G, Denke C, Reif M, Schnelle M, Hagmeister H. Standardized cannabis extract in the treatment of postherpetic neuralgia: a randomized, double-blind, placebo-controlled crossover study. Paper presented at International Association for Cannabis as Medicine, Leiden, Netherlands, September 9, 2005.
90. Holdcroft A, Maze M, Dore C, Tebbs S, Thompson S. A multicenter dose-escalation study of the analgesic and adverse effects of an oral cannabis extract (Cannador) for postoperative pain management. Anesthesiology 2006; 104(5):1040–1046.

91. Potter D. Growth and morphology of medicinal cannabis. In: Guy GW, Whittle BA, Robson P, eds. Medicinal Uses of Cannabis and Cannabinoids. London: Pharmaceutical Press, 2004:17–54.

92. de Meijer E. The breeding of cannabis cultivars for pharmaceutical end uses. In: Guy GW, Whittle BA, Robson P, eds. Medicinal Uses of Cannabis and Cannabinoids. London: Pharmaceutical Press, 2004:55–70.

93. Guy GW, Robson P. A Phase I, double blind, three-way crossover study to assess the pharmacokinetic profile of cannabis based medicine extract (CBME) administered sublingually in variant cannabinoid ratios in normal healthy male volunteers (GWPK02125). J Cannabis Ther 2003; 3(4):121–152.

94. Carlini EA. The good and the bad effects of (−) trans-delta-9-tetrahydrocannabinol (Delta (9)-THC) on humans. Toxicon 2004; 44(4):461–467.

95. Nurmikko TJ, Serpell MG, Hoggart B, Toomey PJ, Morlion BJ. A multicenter, double-blind, randomized, placebo-controlled trial of oro-mucosal cannabis-based medicine in the treatment of neuropathic pain characterized by allodynia. Paper presented at American Academy of Neurology, Miami Beach, FL, April 14, 2005.

96. Russo EB. Sativex cannabis based medicine maintains improvements in sleep quality in patients with multiple sclerosis and neuropathic pain. Paper presented at American Academy of Neurology, Miami Beach, FL, April 12, 2005.

97. Stott CG, Guy GW, Wright S, Whittle BA. The genotoxicology of Sativex. Paper presented at Conference on the Cannabinoids, Clearwater, FL, June, 2005.

98. Massi P, Vaccani A, Ceruti S, Colombo A, Abbracchio MP, Parolaro D. Antitumor effects of cannabidiol, a nonpsychotropic cannabinoid, on human glioma cell lines. J Pharmacol Exp Ther 2004; 308(3):838–845.

99. Lynch ME, Young J. Report on a case series of patients using medicinal marijuana marijuana for management of chronic pain under the Canadian Medical Marijuana Access Regulations. Paper presented at Symposium on the Cannabinoids, Clearwater, FL, 2005.

100. Janse AFC, Breekveldt-Postma NS, Erkens JA, Herings RMC. Medicinal gebruik van cannabis: PHARMO Instituut [Institute for Drug Outcomes Research]. April 2004.

101. Gorter RW, Butorac M, Cobian EP, van der Sluis W. Medical use of cannabis in the Netherlands. Neurology 2005; 64(5):917–919.

102. http://www.neurology.org/cgi/content/full/64/5/917/DC1.

103. Wachtel SR, ElSohly MA, Ross RA, Ambre J, de Wit H. Comparison of the subjective effects of delta9-tetrahydrocannabinol and marijuana in humans. Psychopharmacology 2002; 161:331–339.

104. Ilan AB, Gevins A, Coleman M, ElSohly MA, de Wit H. Neurophysiological and subjective profile of marijuana with varying concentrations of cannabinoids. Behav Pharmacol 2005; 16(5–6):487–496.

105. Wilkinson JD, Whalley BJ, Baker D, et al. Medicinal cannabis: is delta9-tetrahydrocannabinol necessary for all its effects? J Pharm Pharmacol 2003; 55(12):1687–1694.

106. Williamson EM. Synergy and other interactions in phytomedicines. Phytomedicine 2001; 8(5):401–409.

107. Ben-Shabat S, Fride E, Sheskin T, et al. An entourage effect: inactive endogenous fatty acid glycerol esters enhance 2-arachidonoyl-glycerol cannabinoid activity. Eur J Pharmacol 1998; 353(1):23–31.

108. Mechoulam R, Ben-Shabat S. From gan-zi-gun-nu to anandamide and 2-arachidonoyl-glycerol: the ongoing story of cannabis. Nat Prod Rep 1999; 16(2):131–143.

109. Zuardi AW, Shirakawa I, Finkelfarb E, Karniol IG. Action of cannabidiol on the anxiety and other effects produced by delta 9-THC in normal subjects. Psychopharmacology 1982; 76(3):245–250.

110. Zuardi AW, Morais SL, Guimaraes FS, Mechoulam R. Antipsychotic effect of cannabidiol [letter]. J Clin Psychiatry 1995; 56(10):485–486.

111. Leweke FM, Koethe D, Gerth CW, et al. Cannabidiol as an antipsychotic: a double-blind, controlled clinical trial on cannabidiol vs. amisulphide in acute schizophrenia. Paper presented at Symposium on the Cannabinoids, Clearwater, FL, June 26, 2005.

112. Bornheim LM, Grillo MP. Characterization of cytochrome P450 3A inactivation by cannabidiol: possible involvement of cannabidiol-hydroxyquinone as a P450 inactivator. Chem Res Toxicol 1998; 11(10):1209–1216.
113. Hampson AJ, Grimaldi M, Lolic M, Wink D, Rosenthal R, Axelrod J. Neuroprotective antioxidants from marijuana. Ann NY Acad Sci 2000; 899:274–282.
114. Malfait AM, Gallily R, Sumariwalla PF, et al. The nonpsychoactive cannabis constituent cannabidiol is an oral antiarthritic therapeutic in murine collagen-induced arthritis. Proc Natl Acad Sci USA 2000; 97(17):9561–9566.
115. Whittle BA, Guy GW, Robson P. Prospects for new cannabis-based prescription medicines. J Cannabis Ther 2001; 1(3–4):183–205.
116. de Meijer EP, Bagatta M, Carboni A, et al. The inheritance of chemical phenotype in *Cannabis sativa* L. Genetics 2003; 163(1):335–346.
117. ElSohly MA, Ross SA, Mehmedic Z, Arafat R, Yi B, Banahan BF III. Potency trends of delta9-THC and other cannabinoids in confiscated marijuana from 1980–1997. J Forensic Sci 2000; 45(1):24–30.
118. Mehmedic Z, Martin J, Foster S, ElSohly MA. Delta-9-THC and other cannabinoids content of confiscated marijuana: potency trends, 1993–2003. Paper presented at International Association of Cannabis as Medicine, Leiden, Netherlands, September 10, 2005.
119. Fitzgerald GA. Coxibs and cardiovascular disease. N Engl J Med 2004.
120. Topol EJ. Failing the public health—rofecoxib, Merck, and the FDA. N Engl J Med 2004; 351(17):1707–1709.
121. Stott CG, Guy GW, Wright S, Whittle BA. The effects of cannabis extracts Tetranabinex & Nabidiolex on human cyclooxygenase (COX) activity. Paper presented at Symposium on the Cannabinoids, Clearwater, FL, June 27, 2005.
122. Wright S. GWMS001 and GWMS0106: maintenance of blinding. London: GW Pharmaceuticals, 2005.
123. Budney AJ, Hughes JR, Moore BA, Vandrey R. Review of the validity and significance of cannabis withdrawal syndrome. Am J Psychiatry 2004; 161(11):1967–1977.
124. Smith NT. A review of the published literature into cannabis withdrawal symptoms in human users. Addiction 2002; 97(6):621–632.
125. Samaha AN, Robinson TE. Why does the rapid delivery of drugs to the brain promote addiction? Trends Pharmacol Sci 2005; 26(2):82–87.
126. Jones RT, Benowitz N, Bachman J. Clinical studies of cannabis tolerance and dependence. Ann NY Acad Sci 1976; 282:221–239.
127. Solowij N, Stephens RS, Roffman RA, et al. Cognitive functioning of long-term heavy cannabis users seeking treatment. JAMA 2002; 287(9):1123–1131.
128. Russo EB, Mathre ML, Byrne A, et al. Chronic cannabis use in the Compassionate Investigational New Drug Program: an examination of benefits and adverse effects of legal clinical cannabis. J Cannabis Ther 2002; 2(1):3–57.
129. Fride E, Russo EB. Neuropsychiatry: Schizophrenia, depression, and anxiety. In: Onaivi E, Sugiura T, Di Marzo V, eds. Endocannabinoids: The Brain and Body's Marijuana and Beyond. Boca Raton, FL: Taylor & Francis, 2006:371–382.
130. Pope HG Jr., Gruber AJ, Hudson JI, Huestis MA, Yurgelun-Todd D. Neuropsychological performance in long-term cannabis users. Arch Gen Psychiatry 2001; 58(10):909–915.
131. Degenhardt L, Hall W, Lynskey M. Testing hypotheses about the relationship between cannabis use and psychosis. Drug Alcohol Depend 2003; 71(1):37–48.
132. Zuardi AW, Guimaraes FS. Cannabidiol as an anxiolytic and antipsychotic. In: Mathre ML, ed. Cannabis in Medical Practice: A Legal, Historical and Pharmacological Overview of the Therapeutic Use of Marijuana. Jefferson, NC: McFarland, 1997:133–141.
133. Cabral G. Immune system. In: Grotenhermen F, Russo EB, eds. Cannabis and Cannabinoids: Pharmacology, Toxicology and Therapeutic Potential. Binghamton, NY: Haworth Press, 2001:279–287.
134. Katona S, Kaminski E, Sanders H, Zajicek J. Cannabinoid influence on cytokine profile in multiple sclerosis. Clin Exp Immunol 2005; 140(3):580–585.
135. Abrams DI, Hilton JF, Leiser RJ, et al. Short-term effects of cannabinoids in patients with HIV-1 infection. A randomized, placebo-controlled clinical trial. Ann Intern Med 2003; 139:258–266.

136. Nicholson AN, Turner C, Stone BM, Robson PJ. Effect of delta-9-tetrahydrocannabinol and cannabidiol on nocturnal sleep and early morning behavior in young adults. J Clin Psychopharmacol 2004; 24(3):305–313.

137. Stott CG, Guy GW, Wright S, Whittle BA. The effects of cannabis extracts Tetranabinex and Nabidiolex on human cytochrome P450-mediated metabolism. Paper presented at Symposium on the Cannabinoids, Clearwater, FL, June 27, 2005.

138. Movig KL, Mathijssen MP, Nagel PH, et al. Psychoactive substance use and the risk of motor vehicle accidents. Accid Anal Prev 2004; 36(4):631–636.

139. Hadorn D. A review of cannabis and driving skills. In: Guy GW, Whittle BA, Robson P, eds. Medicinal Uses of Cannabis and Cannabinoids. London: Pharmaceutical Press, 2004:329–368.

140. Verster JC, Volkerts ER. Antihistamines and driving ability: evidence from on-the-road driving studies during normal traffic. Ann Allergy Asthma Immunol 2004; 92(3): 294–303; quiz 303–295, 355.

141. Soderstrom CA, Dischinger PC, Kufera JA, Ho SM, Shepard A. Crash culpability relative to age, and sex for injured drivers using alcohol, marijuana or cocaine. Paper presented at Association for the Advancement of Automotive Medicine, Cambridge, MA, September 12–14, 2005.

142. Pertwee RG. The pharmacology and therapeutic potential of cannabidiol. In: DiMarzo V, ed. Cannabinoids. Dordrecht, Netherlands: Kluwer Academic Publishers, 2004.

143. http://www.solvaypharmaceuticals-us.com/static/wma/pdf/1/3/1/9/Marinol5000 124ERev52003.pdf.

144. http://www.bayerhealth.ca/display.cfm? Object_ID=272&Article_ID=121&expand Menu_ID=53&prevSubItem=5_52.

145. Pertwee RG. Cannabidiol as a potential medicine. In: Mechoulam R, ed. Cannabinoids as Therapeutics. Basel, Switzerland: Birkhäuser Verlag, 2005:47–65.

146. Grotenhermen F, Leson G, Berghaus G, et al. Developing Science-Based Per Se Limits for Driving Under the Influence of Cannabis (DUIC). Findings and Recommendations by an Expert Panel. Hürth, Germany: Nova-Institut, 2005.

12 Ethical Issues in Pain Management: Disability Assessment and Determination

Jaye E. Hefner

Department of Physical Medicine and Rehabilitation, Spaulding Rehabilitation Hospital, and Department of General Internal Medicine, Massachusetts General Hospital, Harvard Medical School, Boston, Massachusetts, U.S.A.

INTRODUCTION

Ethical Issues in Pain

Treating physicians are often asked to complete paperwork to determine disability for their patients. Usually, this treating physician is a primary care doctor with little understanding of the process of disability determination. The patient often presents with long-standing, chronic pain complaints that preclude the individual from continuing or obtaining gainful employment. The treating physician may be inexperienced with pain management and pain pathophysiology and therefore may be under treating pain from the onset. In addition, there is growing controversy regarding how chronic pain is treated and managed in the primary care setting (1,2).

Physicians are traditionally trained to be patient advocates. When presented with disability forms, the vast majority of primary care physicians do not understand the process of disability determination. Often the physicians who hold true to patient advocacy will complete the forms in a positive, nonobjective fashion. However, there are a number of physicians who do not believe chronic pain is a reason for disability and therefore either refuse to fill out the forms or do so in a fashion in which only a denial can take place.

The combination of these factors such as lack of training and understanding of a disability determination, increasing scrutiny of regulatory bodies, growing controversy regarding how chronic pain is treated and managed in the primary care setting, the desire to preserve the doctor–patient relationship and remain the patient's advocate, and the physician's own personal bias of governmental support often leads to ethical conflicts that may influence not only the disability determination, but also patient care.

This chapter is designed for the treating physician who is asked to complete a disability determination for the patients. The definition and historical perspective of disability are presented as well as the prevalence and economic burden to our society. Descriptions of the most common objective measures are illustrated and the processes of the most common agencies determining disability are described. Lastly, thoughts on the ethical considerations of chronic pain and disability determination are listed.

Definition of Disability

The international classification of functioning (ICF), disability, and health approved in 2001 by the World Health Organization, defines disability as an umbrella term for impairments, activity limitations or participation restrictions, framing an individual's functioning and disability as a dynamic interaction between health conditions and contextual factors, including environmental and personal attributes (3).The roots of disability, however, have long become embedded into societies as the concepts of employment and work developed. As societies developed and people labored to earn a wage, there obviously existed individuals in every community who were physically incapable of performing manual labor. Thus, the concept of communal support of the incapacitated developed. However, just as it exists today, there is an age-old desire to determine who is deserving of support and thus truly disabled and unable to work.

Traditionally, there have been two models or concepts of disability: the medical model and the social model. In the medical model, the focus is on the medical problem or underlying condition that is causing the disability. Medical care surrounding the disability is considered the main issue. Practicing clinicians are often asked to determine disability status for their patients based on the medical model. In addition, during office visits, treating physicians will often focus on disability care instead of preventive or wellness care for their primary care patients with disabilities. The focus and goal is to return a patient to normal functioning instead of leaving them with what is deemed as abnormal function.

The social model was developed in response to the medical model. If medical care is unable to return an individual to normal functioning, isolation and exclusion from society could occur. However, if the only barrier to full participation in society is a change in the social environment, then no disability would exist. Unlike the medical model, which focuses entirely on the underlying physical condition, the social model focuses on the environment. In the social model, the problem is neither the person who has the disability nor the medical condition, but rather the nonaccommodating environment.

Fortunately, the ICF integrates both the medical and the social model of disability and creates a "biopsychosocial" synthesis of different perspectives on health (3).

The ICF identifies three inter-related concepts:

1. Impairments are problems in body function or structure such as a significant deviation or loss.
2. Activity is the execution of a task or action by an individual.
3. Participation is involvement in a life situation.

ICF definition allows not only for a physical or mental impairment but also states that the function and participation of an individual should be considered when determining if disability exists (3).

Unfortunately, the definitions of disabilities used to determine if an individual will be compensated and supported vary and are numerous. These definitions also primarily reside in the medical model and do not incorporate the contribution of the environment to the severity of the disability. The social security administration (SSA) defines disability as "the inability to engage in any substantial, gainful activity by reason of a medically determinable physical or mental impairment(s), which can be expected to result in death or which has lasted or can be expected to last for a continuous period of not less than 12 months" (4). The SSA defines a medically determinable impairment as "an impairment that results from anatomical, physiological, or psychological abnormalities that can be shown by medically acceptable clinical and laboratory diagnostic techniques. A physical or mental impairment must be established also by medical evidence consisting of signs, symptoms, and laboratory findings—not only by the individual's statement of symptoms." (4).

The American Medical Association (AMA) defines impairment as a loss, loss of use, or derangement of any body part, organ system, or organ functions. Impairment differs from disability, which is an alteration of an individual's capacity to meet personal, social or occupational demands, or statutory or regulatory requirements because of impairment. The AMA Guides also discusses the importance of evaluating motivation as a potential connecting link between impairment and disability (5).

Despite attempts to standardize the process and definition, no single government or medical entity has been able to agree on a single definition that would incorporate the medical and social model to objectively determine the extent and duration an individual should be compensated for being unable to maintain gainful employment.

Causes of Disabilities

In general, there are three major life stages of disabilities, each with a different prevalence of underlying disease state. Ages birth to 17 years present with disabilities related to birth defects and childhood diseases and disorders that primarily affect school attendance and performance. Ages 18 to 69 years present with catastrophic accidents or development of major medical illnesses. There is a male predominance in this age group. The elderly, ages 70 years and beyond, present with chronic, end-stage medical disease, most commonly, arthritis.

Occupational injuries and chronic health conditions primarily contribute to work disability. Over the past 20 years, the number of reported occupational injuries and illnesses generally has decreased, but the impact of these injuries and illnesses has increased greatly. In 1972, for every 100 full-time workers, there were 10.9 occupational injuries or illnesses reported. In 1994, the incidence rate had dropped to 8.4 per 100 workers. While the incidence rate of reported occupational injuries and illnesses dropped from 1972 to 1991, the lost workdays per 100 workers increased from 47.9 to 86.5 (6).

The national health interview survey (NHIS) provides information about which chronic health conditions most frequently cause work limitation. Respondents to the NHIS are asked to specify "the main cause of work impairment." Back disorders are the most frequent causes of work limitation among people 18 to 69 years old. It is estimated that almost four million people experience work limitations that primarily are caused by back disorders, representing 21.1% of all conditions, followed by heart disease, osteoarthritis, and related disorders, diseases of the respiratory system, mental disorders, orthopedic impairments of lower extremities, and diabetes (7).

Prevalence

An estimated 19.4% of noninstitutionalized civilians in the United States, totaling 48.9 million people, have a disability. Almost half of these people can be considered to have a severe disability (8). This translates to one in five people in the United States experiencing a disability in the lifetime. An estimated 15% or 37.7

million noninstitutionalized U.S. residents, have an activity limitation. Of these, 11.5 million people are unable to perform a major activity, 14.3 million people are limited in the kind or amount of major activity they can perform, and 11.9 million are limited in activities other than a major activity they can perform (8).

Activities considered major, by age group, are:

Children under age of five years: playing;

Persons 5 to 17 years: attending school;

Persons 18 to 69 years: working or keeping house;

People aged 70 years and over: ability to care for oneself (bathing, eating, dressing, or getting around the home), and one's home (doing household chores, doing necessary business, shopping, or getting around for other purposes) without another person's assistance.

The nationally distributed current population survey (CPS) asks specifically about work disability, a condition that limits the kind or amount of work that can be done, or a severe work disability, a condition that prevents work. According to this definition, 17.2 million people, or 9.9% of the 1998 working-age U.S. population ages 16 to 64 years old, had a disability that prevented or limited work. It was estimated that 11.3 million, or 65.8% of the 17.2 million people with a work disability as measured by the CPS, were severe and unable to perform any work (9).

Economic Burden

The economic burden of disability to society is costly. The SSA has two insurance programs that provide benefits to working-age individuals with disabilities: Social Security Disability Insurance (SSDI) and Supplemental Security Income (SSI). In recent years, participation by working-age people in Social Security disability programs has grown from less than four million people in 1985 to 6.6 million people in 1995. The inflation-adjusted cost of cash benefits rose to 66% from $23 billion in 1985 to $53 billion in 1994. In addition, the cost of providing Medicare and Medicaid to these beneficiaries was approximately $48 billion annually. Thus, the cost of cash benefits and health care benefits for disabled beneficiaries in 1994 was $101 billion (10).

An estimated 96.1 million employees were insured by Workers' Compensation in 1993. From 1983 to 1993, disability compensation payments grew from $10.4 million to $23.4 million while compensation payments to survivors rose only slightly from $1.5 million to $1.9 million over the same period. Workers' compensation disability payments more than doubled between 1983 and 1993 (11).

ASSESSMENT AND DETERMINATION OF DISABILITY

Who Determines if an Individual Is Disabled or Not?

Clinicians often believe they are being asked to make an assessment or to make a determination of whether or not their patient can work, i.e., are disabled. This is usually at the request of a private insurance company or the SSA. However in all cases, the physician being asked to provide the documentation for the disability determination is not being asked to determine if an individual can return to work. Rather, the documenting physician, whether that doctor is the treating physician or an independent physician, is being asked to provide documentation of impairment.

Although not ideal because of potential conflicts of interest within the doctor–patient relationship, the treating physician is often the individual asked to perform the determination. In fact, the SSA believes that the most reliable information comes from the physician who knows the patient best. Unfortunately, these practicing clinicians generally have little or no understanding of the process of disability determination. In addition, they have neither been trained to perform an independent medical examination (IME) nor do they understand how to document their findings. They are often not reimbursed for either their time spent with the patient or completing the paperwork.

Understanding the Process
The IME and documentation that may be provided by the treating physician is but one part of a disability determination. There are both medical and nonmedical components. The physician who performs the IME or provides the documentation must communicate in writing their findings in a language that can be interpreted by nonmedical, often legal, personnel. The documenting physician, whether the treating physician or the independent medical examiner, does not determine disability or the ability to work. Rather the documentation is interpreted and used by the courts, the SSA, private insurance companies, and attorneys to determine the ability to work and the degree of compensation allowed.

Without proper training in occupational medicine, functional assessment, and pain determination, the treating physician often does not provide proper documentation of the functional assessment, the impairment and the impact of the chronic pain syndrome. While a patient applying for disability ideally would be referred for an IME, the treating physician may try to incorporate and document as much objective evidence into the physician's determination as possible.

DISABILITY ASSESSMENT TOOLS

A series of steps can guide a physician through the process of determining functional assessment and linking it to the qualifying medical disease. Whether making a determination for private insurance or Social Security, objectivity can be added through the use of validated functional and pain disability assessment tools as well as making a determination of motivation, which the American Medical Guides note as a connecting link between impairment and disability (5).

It is important however, to note the importance of the AMA's statement in the Guides to the Evaluation of Permanent Impairment, Fifth Edition, which states that "the Guides are not intended to be used for direct estimates of work disability. Impairment percentages derived according to the Guides criteria do not measure work disabilities. Therefore, it is inappropriate to use the Guides' criteria or ratings to make direct estimates of work disability." (5). Although adding objective information to the disability determination is important, none of these functional assessment tools can be used for direct estimates of disability. They merely serve as part of the medical component of a comprehensive assessment that will occur for determination of overall disability, which is beyond the scope of physician assessment.

Functional Assessment Questionnaires
There are at least 10 validated low-back functional assessment questionnaires available for physicians and other health care providers (12–21). Davidson and Keating compared the modified Oswestry Disability Questionnaire, the Quebec Back Pain Disability Scale, the Roland–Morris Disability Questionnaire, the

Waddell Disability Index, and the physical health scales of the Medical Outcomes Study 36-Item Short-Form Health Survey (SF-36) for reliability and responsiveness. They found the measurements obtained with the modified Oswestry Disability Questionnaire, the Quebec Back Pain Disability Scale, and the SF-36 Physical Functioning scale were the most reliable and had sufficient sensitivity to reliably detect improvement or worsening in most patients (22).

There are at least four validated upper extremity functional assessment questionnaires available for physicians and other health providers (23–26).

In addition to these measures, there are numerous disease-specific functional assessment tools available for clinicians to utilize to add objectivity to their disability determination documentation.

Pain Disability Assessment Instruments

While the disability assessment may include questions related to pain, it is often useful to use a separate instrument to assess disability pain. There are at least three validated instruments for health providers to assess pain disability (27–29).

GUIDES TO DISABILITY DETERMINATION

Social Security Disability

The SSA provides a guide book for treating physicians, medical consultants, and claimants known as the Blue Book (4). The disability evaluation under social security has been prepared to provide physicians and other health care professionals with an understanding of the disability programs administered by the SSA. It explains how each program works, and the kinds of information a health professional can furnish to help ensure sound and prompt decisions on disability claims. The blue book is available in on-line (30).

Social security uses a five-step process to determine if an individual with chronic pain as disability would qualify for SSDI (4,30).

The first step determines whether an individual is working (engaging in substantial gainful activity) according to the SSA definition, who is earning more than $810 a month as an employee.

The second step involves determining whether the chronic pain disability is severe enough to significantly limit one's ability to perform basic work activities needed to perform most jobs. For example, walking, standing, sitting, lifting, pushing, pulling, reaching, carrying or handling, seeing, hearing, and speaking, understanding/carrying out and remembering simple instructions, use of judgment, responding appropriately to supervision, coworkers and usual work situations, and dealing with changes in a routine work setting.

Step three states that the SSA is required to consider pain and the limitations imposed by pain in the adjudication of a disability claim. However, before pain may be considered, a medically determinable severe impairment must be established by medically acceptable clinical and laboratory diagnostic techniques. Once a medically determinable severe impairment is established, the impairment must reasonably be expected to produce the pain.

The SSA is required to evaluate the intensity, persistence, and functionally limiting effects of the pain, i.e., how the pain affect the individual's ability to perform basic work activities. As pain symptoms sometime suggest a greater severity of impairment than can be demonstrated through objective medical evidence alone, the adjudicator is required to carefully consider the individual's statements about the pain with the rest of the relevant evidence in the case record. An individual's statement about the intensity and persistence of pain or about the effect the pain has on the ability to work may not be disregarded solely because they are not substantiated by objective medical evidence.

The following factors are to be considered by the SSA in the assessment of pain:

1. The individual's daily activities
2. The location, duration, frequency, and intensity of the individual's pain (or other symptoms)
3. Factors that precipitate and aggravate the symptoms
4. The type, dosage, effectiveness, and side effects of any medication the individual takes or has taken to alleviate pain (or other symptoms)
5. Treatment, other than medication, the individual receives or has received for relief of pain (or other symptoms)
6. Any measures other than treatment the individual uses or has used to relieve pain (or other symptoms)(e.g., lying flat on back, standing for 15 to 20 minutes every hour, or sleeping on a board)
7. Any other factors concerning the individual's functional limitations and restrictions due to pain (or other symptoms)
8. Pain, if present, is a symptom that must be addressed in the adjudication of all disability claims.

The fourth step explores the ability of an individual to perform work that has been done in the past despite chronic pain disability. If the SSA finds that a person can perform the past work, benefits are denied. If the person cannot, then the evaluation proceeds to the fifth and final step.

The fifth step looks at age, education, work experience, and physical/mental condition to determine what other work, if any, the person can perform. To determine disability, SSA enlists vocational rules, which vary according to age. For example, if a person is

1. Under the age of 50 years and, as a result of the symptoms of chronic pain, unable to perform what SSA calls sedentary work, then SSA will reach a determination of disabled. Sedentary work requires the ability to lift a maximum of 10 pounds at a time, sit six hours and occasionally walk and stand two hours per eight-hour day.
2. Age 50 years or older and, due to chronic pain disability, limited to performing sedentary work but has no work-related skills that allow him/her to do so, SSA will reach a determination of disabled.
3. Over the age of 60 years and, due to chronic pain disability, unable to perform any of the jobs performed in the last 15 years, SSA will likely reach a determination of disabled.
4. Any age and, because of chronic pain, has a psychological impairment that prevents even simple, unskilled work, SSA will reach a determination of disabled (4).

American Medical Association Guides

The AMA Guides link impairment, disability, and motivation. Depending on motivational factors, impairment may lead to total or minimal disability. The fourth and fifth editions of the AMA Guides state that chronic pain is a medical, not a psychiatric, disorder and may involve any one or more of the following:

1. Altered perceptions and maladaptive behaviors.
2. Cannot be validated objectively or measured.
3. Objective findings and subjective complaints may be disproportionate.
4. There may be no on-going nociception.

The Guide takes the position that pain is not an impairment, but rather should trigger assessments with regard to ability to function and carry out daily activities (5,31).

The Guides Chapter on chronic pain makes three assumptions.

1. Pain is influenced significantly by psychosocial factors.
2. There may be no direct correlation between pain and mechanical dysfunction.
3. Pain may impact a patient's ability to perform activities of daily living (ADLs).

The pain chapter may be used if the patient meets all of the following criteria:

1. The symptoms or physical exam findings match a known medical condition.
2. The patient's presentation is typical of the diagnosed condition.
3. The diagnosed condition is accepted widely as having a well-defined pathophysiologic basis.

Specific guidelines are provided regarding when to use and not use the pain chapter to evaluate pain-related impairments (5).

THE IMPACT OF CHRONIC PAIN ON DISABILITY DETERMINATION

For disability assessments, individuals may be asked to perform various physical tasks including standing, bending, walking, squatting, and sitting. The ability to perform these tasks depends on many factors beyond physical functioning. These factors include: cognitive status and judgment, vision, balance and coordination, endurance and fitness, strength and mobility, agility, overall health status, and pain level. Pain levels may also vary widely on a daily basis, making it possible to stand or sit for prolonged periods of time one day and not on the next.

Chronic pain is one condition in which it may be advantageous for the treating physician to also be the physician performing the assessment. Treating physicians may or may not be the primary physician responsible for pain management. Nonetheless, the treating physician has the opportunity to evaluate the patient over the course of months and sometimes years, during which time the pain intensity and functional ability may fluctuate. A treating physician may have the unique perspective of knowing the potential influence of the pain intensity on function the day the assessment is to be performed.

Just as pain intensity may change over time, pain behavior may also change. Pain behavior is often learned and can be goal oriented. As stated previously, the AMA Guides suggest that motivation should be assessed when determining disability (5). An examiner who meets an individual patient for a disability assessment on a one-time-only basis may be deficient in certain medical, family, and social history, and may have to use a variety of questions in assessing chronic pain (32–34).

SUMMARY

There is no widely accepted definition of disability. The ICF, Disability, and Health best defines it as an umbrella term for impairments, activity limitations or participation restrictions, framing an individuals' functioning, and disability as a dynamic interaction between health conditions and contextual factors, including environmental and personal attributes (3). The journals of physical medicine and rehabilitation, occupational rehabilitation, and pain research, to name a few, contain a breath of information on functional assessments and pain determination. Unfortunately, this important body of literature is not usually accessed and read by many treating physicians who will be asked to document impairments and the impact of chronic pain on these impairments.

This chapter gives weight to the increasing economic and social burden of disability. As early as the 1990s, the phrase "disability epidemic" entered into the medical literature (35). A recent review of national U.S. data pertaining to office-based opioid prescriptions for chronic noncancer pain also reveals that a "pain epidemic" may be present as well (36). Clearly, this is concern for a medical community faced with increasing numbers of patients for whom they may be least trained to provide care.

The combination of the following factors often leads to an unsatisfactory process for both physicians and patients: the lack of physician training and education with independent medical examinations and the medical terminology used in the documentation, the lack of standardization of the definition and process, the potential compromise of the doctor–patient relationship when the traditional advocacy role of the physician should not be assumed, and the lack of understanding of both the patient and the physician that the role of the physician is one of documenting impairments and not assessing or determining the ability or inability to work.

Physicians also have many preconceived ideas about chronic pain, which may influence their objectivity in the disability determination process. A study by Turk et al., showed prescription of opioids by U.S. physicians was best predicted by a patients' observed pain behavior and not by pain severity or degree of physical findings that explained their pain (37). As cited previously, there is growing controversy regarding how chronic pain is treated and managed in the primary care setting. It has been suggested that prescribing opioids on the basis of pain behavior could provide a source of reinforcement for the pain behavior (38).

Physicians also may believe that patients exhibit more pain behavior and make less effort than is possible when they are undergoing a disability determination exam. In a similar fashion to receiving pain medication, there would be reinforcement for behavior in achieving a positive disability determination. Hence, many physicians are in conflict with their role as a patient advocate and their perceived role as the determiner of the patient's ability or inability to work.

Understanding the basic process of disability determination is the first step for many treating physicians. There are many readily available resources, such as the Blue Book from the SSA and the AMA Guides, for the unfamiliar treating physician to review. The most important concept is that these physicians are not solely determining disability. Rather, their role is one of fully assessing a patient and providing ample documentation that will then be used, along with other medical and nonmedical documents, by independent medical and nonmedical personnel for final disability determination.

Many physicians simply lack the experience or knowledge to perform such an assessment and therefore provide inadequate or incorrect documentation. In addition, as advocates for our patients, many treating physicians confuse their role in this process and provide only the documentation that would support the disability determination. In some rare cases, physicians may chose to word the documentation such that the disability determination will result is denial.

Adding objectivity to the examination process by using evidence-based, validated functional assessment tools, pain scales, and pain questionnaires may help the treating physician produce an unbiased, factual representation of the patient's true functional capability. Doing so constitutes ethical medical practice. In addition, many patients would benefit from referral to multidisciplinary pain centers and vocational rehabilitation. As Dr. Schatman's Chapter| in this book reveals, however, referral for multidisciplinary treatment of chronic pain is becoming progressively less of an option. A referral for an IME should be offered to all patients, especially when the doctor–patient relationship may be compromised by differing views of disability and return to work status.

Physicians should explain the process of disability determination to their patients and provide the most unbiased documentation possible. When considering chronic pain as part of the disability documentation, the treating physician must have adequate experience and training in assessing the impact of pain on function. The physician should feel comfortable with the patient's efforts at pain management, and recognize the presentation of pain behavior and assess it over time.

There are many ethical questions surrounding determination of disability from medical and mental conditions, not to mention the addition of chronic pain as a modifying factor. Expanding one's knowledgebase and working with allied health professionals and the legal system will help guide the inexperienced treating physician through the process and improve overall satisfaction with the process. Those physicians with excessively high, or low, favorable determinations should also seek help from existing resources. Patients benefit from referrals to specialists in this area, which include comprehensive pain centers, physical medicine and rehabilitation evaluations and treatments, vocational rehabilitation, and an independent medical examination.

REFERENCES

1. Stein C. What's wrong with opioids in chronic pain? Curr Opin Anesthesiol 2000; 13:557–559.
2. Ballantyne JC, Mao J. Medical progress: opioid therapy for chronic pain. N Engl J Med 2003; 349:1943–1953.
3. World Health Organization. International Classification of Impairments, Disability, and Health. Geneva, 2001.
4. United States Social Security Administration. Office of Disability. Disability evaluation under social security, SSA pub. no. 64–039, 2005.
5. Cocchiarella L, Anderson GBJ. American Medical Association: Guides to the Evaluation of Permanent Impairment. 5th ed. American Medical Association, 2001:565–592.
6. Bureau of Labor Statistics. Occupational injuries and illnesses in the United States, by industry, 1987. U.S. Department of Labor, Bulletin 2328. Washington, D.C.: U.S. Government Printing Office, 1989.
7. LaPlante MP, Carlson D. Disability in the United States: prevalence and causes. disability statistics report 7, Washington, D.C.: U.S. Department of Education, National Institute on Disability and Rehabilitation Research, 1992.

8. Kraus L, Stoddard S, Gilmartin D. Chartbook on Disability in the United States, 1996: An Infouse Report. Washington, DC: U.S. National Institute on Disability and Rehabilitation Research.
9. Stoddard S, Jans L, Ripple J, Kravs L. Chartbook on work and Disability in the United States 1998. An Info use Report. Washington, D.C.: National Institute on Disability and Rehabilitation Research, 1998.
10. General Accounting Office, Social Security Administration, April 1996.
11. Social Security Administration. Annual Statistical Supplement to the Social Security Bulletin. Baltimore: U.S. Department of Health and Human Services, 1996.
12. Fairbank JCT, Davies JB. The Oswestry low back pain disability questionnaire. Physiotherapy 1980; 66:271–273.
13. Kopec JA, Esdaile JM, et al. The Quebec back pain disability scale: conceptualization and development. J Clin Epidemiol 1996; 49:151–161.
14. Manniche C, Asmussen K, et al. Low back pain rating scale: validation of a tool for assessment of low back pain. Pain 1994; 57:317–326.
15. Gottlieb H, Strite LC, et al. Comprehensive rehabilitation of patients having chronic low back pain. Arch Phys Med Rehabil 1977; 58:101–108.
16. Bolton JE, Breen AC. The Bournemouth Questionnaire: a short-form comprehensive outcome measure-I: psychometric properties in back pain patients. J Manipulative Physiol Ther 1999; 22:503–510.
17. Ruta DA, Garratt AM, et al. Developing a valid and reliable measure of health outcome for patients with low back pain. Spine 1994; 19:1887–1896.
18. Stratford PW, Binkley JM, et al. Development and initial validation of the Back Pain Functional Scale. Spine 2000; 25:2095–2102.
19. Waddell G, Main CJ. Assessment of severity in low-back disorders. Spine 1984; 9:204–208.
20. Roland M, Morris R. A study of the natural history of low-back pain. Part I: Development of a reliable and sensitive measure of disability in low-back pain. Spine 1983; 8:141–144.
21. Ware JE Jr, Sherbourne CD. The MOS 36-Item Short-Form Health Survey (SF-36), Conceptual framework, and item selection. Med Care 1992; 30:473–483.
22. Davidson M, Keating JL. A comparison of five low-back disability questionnaires: reliability and responsiveness. Phys Ther 2002; 82:8–24.
23. Pransky G, Feuerstein M, et al. Measuring functional outcomes in work-related upper extremity disorders. JOEM 1997; 39:1195–1202.
24. Chung KC, Pillsbury MS, et al. Reliability and validity testing of the Michigan Hand Outcomes Questionnaire. J Hand Surgery 1998; 23A:575–587.
25. Hudak PL, Amadio PC, Bombardier C. Development of an upper extremity outcome measure: the DASH (disabilities of the arm, shoulder, and hand). Am J Indust Med 1996; 29:602–608.
26. Lord JP, Portwood MM, et al. Upper extremity functional rating for patients with Duchenne muscular dystrophy. Arch Phys Med Rehabil 1987; 68:151–154.
27. Melzack R. The McGill Pain Questionnaire: Major properties and scoring methods. Pain 1975; 1:277–299.
28. Chibnall JT, Tait RC. The Pain Disability Index: factor structure and normative data. Arch Phys Med Rehabil 1994; 75:1082–1086.
29. Richards JS, Nepomuceno C, et al. Assessing pain behavior: the UAB pain behavior scale. Pain 1982; 14:393–398.
30. www.ssa.gov/disability.
31. American Medical Association. Guides to the Evaluation of Permanent Impairment (4th edi.), 1994:565–592.
32. Turk DC. Evaluation of pain and disability. J Disabil 1991; 2:24–43.
33. Hebben N. Toward the assessment of clinical pain in adults: evaluation and treatment of chronic pain. Williams and Wilkins 1992:384–393.
34. Turk DC, Rudy TE. Persistent pain and the injured worker: integrating biomechanical, psychosocial, and behavioral factors in assessment. J Occup Rehab.
35. Aronoff GM. Chronic pain and the disability epidemic. Clin J Pain 1991; 7:330–338.

36. Caudill-Slosberg MA, Schwartz LM, Woloshin S. Office visits and analgesic prescriptions for musculoskeletal pain in the US: 1980 vs. 2000. Pain 2004; 109:514–519.
37. Turk DC, Okifuji A. What factors affect physicians' decisions to prescribe opioids for chronic noncancer pain? Clin J Pain 1997; 13:330–336.
38. Fordyce WE. Opioids and treatment targets. APS Bull 1991; 1:276–283.

Pain Management and Managed Care: Managing the System

David L. Trueman

Columbia University School of Law, New York, New York, U.S.A.

INTRODUCTION

Managed care has impacted tremendously on the delivery of health care treatment. Effective medical management of patients, which had always been solely within the province of an individual's physician, has now been disrupted by a system that often compromises necessary care. The treatment of individuals with severe pain, particularly chronic pain, has been significantly influenced by the cost-containment goals of managed care and its interjection in the health care system. Managing the managed care system is complex, troubling, and difficult. Both patients and their health care professionals need to understand the system and how to cope with its challenges to the provision of necessary and appropriate treatment.

The purpose of this chapter is simple: to help the pain management health care professional understand and deal with the managed care system. The chapter attempts to provide the health care professional with an understanding of managed care and the process by which it operates and concludes with a cautionary tale and some suggestions for working within the managed care system. While most of the chapter refers to health care professionals in general as opposed to chronic pain practitioners specifically, all recommendations are appropriate for professionals dedicated to the management of chronic pain conditions. Specific situations regarding cases of chronic pain management will be discussed.

PAIN MANAGEMENT AND MANAGED CARE

Pain management is of tremendous importance, since it is estimated that the majority of adults have experienced chronic or recurrent pain during the past year, and that one member of almost every other household experiences chronic pain (1). Additionally, almost all individuals will experience acute pain in the form of injuries resulting from athletic activities or accidents, as well as pain subsequent to surgery. However, there are significant concerns that pain is being undertreated, and the need for a comprehensive public and legal policy has been repeatedly articulated (2). Studies have demonstrated continued inadequacies in the treatment of patients most likely to suffer from chronic and acute pain, including terminally ill patients, cancer patients, nursing home residents, the elderly, including those with arthritis and fibromyalgia, and patients in hospital settings where pain is expected, such as the emergency room and postoperative settings (3). A number of causes for the undertreatment of pain have been reported, including fear of regulatory scrutiny, concerns about law enforcement, worry about iatrogenic addiction, medical malpractice lawsuits, and inadequate education and training regarding pain management (4).

Further compounding the problem is the failure of managed care to articulate a coherent pain management policy and the failure to understand the need to support a multidimensional approach to pain. Managed care's often myopic view of pain management and its goal of cost containment have impacted negatively on the ability of individuals to receive appropriate care for their pain. Indeed, a research study conducted for The Journal of the American Physical Therapy Association has indicated that only one-third of managed care organizations had a formalized mechanism for identifying members with chronic pain, and less than one-fifth of those entities systematically utilized clinical practice guidelines (5).

The problem begins both with managed care's goal of reducing health care costs and with its conceptualization of pain. Managed care fails to view pain as part of a complex system and does not promote a commitment to a broad-based assessment and treatment of the entire being. Doing so, of course, would potentially entail more in-depth diagnostic assessment, utilization of pain management specialists, and the provision of related services, such as physical therapy and psychotherapy or behavior therapy, effective for treating pain but requiring a commitment to on-going financial support. Indeed, for many patients with chronic pain, the psychological and behavioral management of their pain is an essential component of the most effective treatment. Instead, managed care companies tend to perceive pain as limited and in need of the cheapest and easiest method of intervention, typically the prescription of pain-relieving medication.

An additional problem is that under managed care, available drugs are limited to those specified on managed care drug formularies. In a formulary, the managed care entity will only pay for certain drugs and will not provide medications as written unless the type of drug is not on the formulary. Patients can obtain approval for nonformulary drugs if it can be demonstrated that there is a specific need for the nonformulary drug and the formulary drug will cause harm, either by its very nature, or by its ineffectiveness. Although formularies have achieved cost containment and changes in the behavior of physicians prescribing medications, while at the same time maintaining quality of care, these changes have primarily occurred in inpatient settings. Physicians in outpatient settings and their patients identify less success in the use of formularies and their medications, with cost containment much more limited. Additionally, these critics further identify that the development of formularies may be based more on financial alliances between pharmaceutical companies and the insurance industry rather than effective patient care (6).

Furthermore, critics complain that insurance companies and managed care organizations repeatedly fail to approve care which should have been approved in the first place. Carriers recognize that some segment of those patients will fail to follow through on appeals, not have the energy or health to fight the denials, or not have the funds to either pay an attorney or pay for the care initially and then appeal to a court subsequent to receiving care. When all of these concerns are viewed together, it is apparent that managed care is a system that presents significant problems for the effective treatment of individuals with pain, particularly chronic pain.

THE HEALTH CARE SYSTEM AND MANAGED CARE

The Health Care System and the Need for Cost Containment

Health care costs comprise the single greatest expense in this country, with 15.3% of the gross national product of the United States devoted to health care in 2003; this is expected to rise to 18.7% in 10 years (7). The concern, obviously, is that the country will not be able to support paying for the care of its citizens. Due to this considerable rise in health care costs, the financing and delivery of health care have dramatically changed. Prior to 1980, there were few, if any, obstacles to patients obtaining all physician-recommended care. Payment for most health care was provided through a system that retrospectively reimbursed patients, paying a significant percentage of the costs of care, either directly to the doctors or to the patients themselves in the form of reimbursement. The financing was provided primarily by traditional indemnity insurance, which was usually given to employees as a benefit of their employment. Health care coverage was obtained at one's place of employment, or through governmental initiatives, such as Medicare and Medicaid.

However, with the dramatic increase in health care costs the system had to change, and "managed care" forms a vast aspect of that metamorphosis. Since managed care is so pervasive, it is critical that all health care professionals understand the current health care system and its managed care components. This is especially true for those practicing in areas that are most vulnerable to cost-cutting efforts, notably the types of conditions in which subjective experience is an essential element of the problem, such as mental health and psychiatric treatment, physical therapy, and pain management.

Funding Health Care: Insurance, Managed Care, Medicare, and Medicaid

At the heart of the provision of medical care is the funding of that care. Medical care can be extraordinarily expensive and, unless one is able to fully pay for one's own health care services without undue hardship, some solution must be found to protect the individual from potentially ruinous expenditures. Payment by a third party for the costs of health care can occur in one of two ways: (i) the individual (or the individual's employer) enters into an agreement with an insurance company to accept the risk of the health care expenditures in exchange for some payment for the acceptance of that risk or (ii) the health care is funded or subsidized by the government.

Insurance

Insurance is a risk-shifting system; with insurance, individuals (or their employers) pay premiums of limited cost so as to avoid the potential of paying significant sums for some subsequent loss or need. Individuals, in essence, are indemnified against loss. Traditionally, all insurance was the same; if one paid the premiums and incurred losses covered under the policy, the insurance company would reimburse consistent with the provisions of the policy. Health care insurance was not significantly different; with traditional indemnity health insurance, individuals or their employers paid insurers a monthly premium which covered the "loss," i.e., the need to pay for health care.

In the traditional indemnity insurance system, individuals were free to select the physician or hospital of their choice. There were no real questions regarding the type of care; once treatment was received, the insurance company paid for that care as long as the health care provider indicated that the services were necessary for the patient.

With traditional indemnity insurance, individuals paid an annual deductible, generally of a limited amount. After the annual out-of-pocket amount was reached, the insurer paid a percentage (usually 80%) of what it determined was the "usual and customary" charges for the medical care. Generally, there were not many questions regarding the cost of care being above the usual and customary amounts. With most indemnity plans, the insured paid the physician directly and received reimbursement less than the co-payment. As noted, reimbursement was typically 80%, with the patient paying the other 20% as a co-payment. Hospital bills, which, of course, were more significant, were paid by the insurance company, often at the rate of 100%.

Indemnity plans had a cap on the amount an individual would have to pay out-of-pocket in any given year. When the combined deductible and co-insurance expenses reached a certain amount, the company paid 100% of all medical claims. Plans also had a maximum amount they would pay for health care in a year as well as in a lifetime. Individuals wishing to have coverage beyond that amount, usually over one million dollars, would purchase "catastrophic" health insurance policies.

Some individuals are fortunate to have such policies today, although this number is decreasing. Companies currently do not generally write traditional indemnity insurance, and most policies in existence have been in effect for many years. Although insurance policies still retain the same financing structure—reimbursement of usual and customary charges and insured's deductible and co-payment fees—there are dramatic differences in current health care policies.

Medicare and Medicaid

Medicare is a federally funded health insurance program for individuals 65 years or older, those under 65 years with certain disabilities, and individuals of all ages with end-stage renal disease (permanent kidney failure requiring dialysis or a kidney transplant). Medicare is comprised of various "Parts" which includes Part A Hospital Insurance, Part B Medical Insurance, and Part D Prescription Drug Coverage. Part A covers inpatient care in hospitals, critical care facilities, and skilled nursing facilities, but excludes custodial or long-term care. Medicare also covers hospice care and some home health care. Most individuals do not have to pay a premium for Part A because either they or spouses have already paid for it through payroll taxes during their working lifetime. Part B is a medical insurance program similar to a traditional indemnity insurance plan. Individuals pay a monthly premium for Part B that covers medical services and supplies that are medically necessary. Part D, which went into effect on January 1, 2006, is a prescription drug program available to everyone with Medicare. Individuals may pay a monthly premium that reduces prescription drug costs. Private companies provide the coverage, and individuals choose a drug plan and monthly premium.

Medicaid is a program managed by individual states and jointly funded by the federal government and states to provide health care insurance for individuals with limited income and resources. Medicaid is a need-based program, and is only available to individuals and families who meet certain financial requirements. This program pays health care providers directly for their services, and Medicaid recipients may have to pay a small deductible. Medicaid is a state-administered program, and each state establishes its own guidelines regarding both eligibility and payment for services.

HEALTH INSURANCE TODAY: THE ADVENT OF MANAGED CARE

Most health care policies in this country for individuals under 65 years are provided by employers as part of an employee's benefits package. Employers pay for some or all of the costs of providing the health insurance payment. Some employers contract with insurance companies that provide both administrative services for the plan and assume the risk of loss or coverage. Other companies provide self-funded plans that, although utilizing an insurer to administer the plan and provide all managing of care, do not pass on the risk to an insurer and place their own funds in a trust for the payment of the medical care of their employees.

Due to the dramatic increases in health care costs, all employer-provided health insurance today attempts to cope with those more substantial costs by "managing care." Additionally, the great majority of privately purchased plans, as well as a significant portion of Medicare and Medicaid, also constitute manage care. This "managing" of care is, essentially, an attempt to reduce the costs in the health care system by limiting payment for health care services and by limiting the services themselves, either in total or by the professionals who are eligible to provide those services. It is important to note that "managed care" is a general term for a variety of mechanisms employed by insurance companies and other corporate entities to "control" health care costs, this perceptive does not take into account Medicare and Medicaid, which are not part of the managed care system. However, there are Medicare and Medicaid managed care plans which do operate in the same manner as other managed care enterprises, and that the companies engaged in this process are almost all for-profit enterprises, with the management of health care costs integrally related to the enhancement of profits.

Managed Care "Cost Containment"
Managed care is the attempt to reduce health care costs primarily through the use of two mechanisms: (i) cost-containment financial arrangements with providers; (ii) reduction in the provision of care to patients.

Contractual Cost-Containment Arrangements with Providers
There are two methods of cost containment that managed care entities have established with providers: (i) capitation and the use of incentive programs to reduce referrals and (ii) discounted fees for service.

Capitation is the payment of a flat fee per patient (covered life, in insurance company terms) per period of time, such as a month. This is an arrangement usually made with primary care physicians. This type of agreement is common in the provision of primary care, as these physicians are likely to provide services for almost all covered individuals. This high volume drives the interests of both the companies that desire to reduce their risk of payment for large numbers of insureds as well as primary care physicians, who are guaranteed a certain income.

Pursuant to these capitation arrangements, the physician will only receive the set sum of money from the managed care entity for the entire group of patients under that company's plan. Obviously, the time which the physician spends will be dependent on the number of patients requiring treatment during the capitation period. The physician incurs the risk of needing to provide more care than can be comfortably provided, given the physician's schedule.

Capitation has been criticized as a mechanism that may lead to poorer patient care and as establishing an incentive for physicians to undertreat their patients. For example, in Jones versus Chicago Limited HMO, Inc., 191 Ill.2d 278 (Ill. 2000), the mother of a child whose disabling meningitis should have been diagnosed by the pediatrician who did not have time to see the child, successfully sued the HMO because it had assigned 650 patients to him. This risk can occur in a number of ways: physicians may spend less time with their patients, diagnosing and treating their patients by telephone or internet; physicians may utilize the services of physician assistants or nurses who may not be qualified to diagnose or treat many of the presenting problems; and patients may experience greater wait time, for both obtaining an appointment and waiting at the doctor's office. All of these problems may predictably lead to the failure on the part of the physician to adequately diagnose and treat the patient. Another problem, generated particularly by the additional wait time, is that patients may be more reluctant to seek care, tend to fail to make necessary appointments and experience an exacerbation of symptoms and illness.

In addition, many companies provide additional "incentive arrangements" whereby the primary care physician (PCP) or physician group is subject to either a "withhold" or a "bonus." A "withhold" is an agreement that some portion of the capitated amount will be withheld if excessive referrals are made for diagnostic testing, to specialist providers, or for hospitalization. A "bonus" is the provision of some additional percentage, if referrals are kept below a certain point. Often, these arrangements entail approximately 10% of the gross capitated amount. Obviously, such arrangements raise issues regarding whether the quality of medical services can be maintained and introduces into the system an element of doubt about the motives of health care professionals (8).

The second method of managing the financial aspect of payment to providers is "discounted fee for service," which entails enlisting physicians to be part of a panel of in-network providers who agree to accept lower fees than they would normally charge. Costs for the use of these "in-network" providers are thereby reduced for the insurance companies, while the in-network providers are guaranteed an advantage over those who are not on the panel. These contractual providers are typically specialists, including diagnostic entities, and are not generally primary care physicians. The advantage for patients is that they pay a very limited co-pay ($5–$15) to visit an in-network physician. Depending on the plan, visiting an out-of-network health care professional will limit reimbursement, with some plans not allowing for any payment of these providers. As a result of becoming a network provider and accepting a lower fee, the health care professional is on the provider list from which almost all patients select their doctors. Additionally, should a patient request a referral from the managed care organization, the referral would almost uniformly be from the company's provider list.

Utilization Review and Reduction of Care to Patients

The second method by which managed care entities reduce costs is by delimiting the care provided to patients, typically through precertification reviews of requests for treatment. Utilization review allows the company to prospectively (or concurrently, for patients in hospitals) analyze the medical recommendations of patients' doctors and then contain costs through denials of approval for treatment. This is a controversial procedure which, critics claim, substitutes the medical judgment of the case reviewers, and ultimately, the medical director, for that of the patient's doctor. However, managed care companies repeatedly claim that these "medical necessity" determinations are administrative, not medical, determinations, and the success of that argument has allowed companies to avoid liability with great frequency. Generally, the avoidance of liability is based on preemption due to the Employee's Retirement Income Security Act (ERISA) a federal law which has provided a loophole by which managed care organizations have avoided liability for their medical decision-making in the context of utilization review. Cases demonstrating this principle are legion. Corcoran versus United Health Care, 965 F.2d 1321 (5th Circ. 1992), is the seminal case that identified that although medical decisions enter into precertification determinations, the precertification process is administrative thereby foreclosing a chance of recovery based on medical negligence. The U.S. Supreme Court recently affirmed this principle in Aetna Health, Inc. versus Davila, 540 U.S. 200, 124 S.Ct. 2488 (2004).

In a related attempt to reduce the outlay of money for treatment, managed care organizations have begun to utilize precertification telephone lines. For companies utilizing this gate-keeping function, the insured is either required or urged to call a managed care entity's telephone line, whereby the patient will speak with a physician's assistant or a nurse prior to contacting the patient's own doctor. Some companies use these for emergency care while others use them for all situations. It seems clear that if doctors are not staffing these lines, the quality of care is called into question. This practice also raises issues of potential liability for the managed care companies. The functioning of these dedicated lines has been analogized to the provision of care, and not merely to an insurance determination. However, the use of these lines presents problems for companies and has led to successful suits by patients. For example, in Shannon versus McNulty, 718 A.2d 828, 836 (Pa. Super. Ct. 1998), the court, in deciding on behalf of a woman who had lost her baby due to delays by the company and bad advice when she called in to the company, the court stated that, "[w]hen a benefits provider ... interjects itself into the rendering of medical decisions affecting a subscriber's care, it must do so in a medically reasonable manner."

Ultimately, the greatest change brought about by the managed care system is the alteration of the patient-physician relationship. Physicians and their patients are no longer able to make unhindered decisions regarding what is the best choice of care. Managed care inserts itself into the delivery of health care by requiring review of other than routine care before it is provided, what diagnostic procedures will be paid, which specialists may be utilized, and how long individuals may be hospitalized.

Health Care Arrangements, Health Maintenance Organizations, and Health Care Insurance

A variety of terms have evolved that describe the manner in which health care is delivered within the managed care system. The term most recognized by the public is "HMO," which refers to a structure that can entail almost any arrangement by which a corporate entity provides health care services, and often is used interchangeably with any managed care enterprise. A number of distinctions can be made regarding this term. An HMO can be a structure by which individuals obtain care as well as an enterprise whereby the organization directly provides care.

Patients can receive treatment at an HMO facility; this is frequently referred to as a "closed model HMO" or "staff HMO" and refers to situations in which the organization hires physicians who also serve as gate-keepers to further service. Additionally, utilization review is conducted, and the medical director is the individual ultimately responsible for approval of care. In this case, the HMO serves as both a precertifier of care as well as the employer of the physicians who actually provide the treatment. In the most restrictive arrangement, both primary care and specialist physicians work at HMO facilities. Less restrictive arrangements involve primary care physicians as staff doctors and specialists on panels, although they function in their own offices.

An "independent practice association" (IPA) is a partnership or corporation usually comprised of independent practicing physicians. The association contracts directly with each independent physician with regard to the terms of employment and methods of payment. The physicians utilize their own offices and facilities to consult with patients. The managed care organization typically pays a capitated rate for each covered life to the IPA, which then pays the physician on a fee-for-service basis.

A "preferred provider organization" (PPO) is a group of providers that have organized to offer services to managed care entities, usually for a discounted fee. PPOs compete with HMOs and provide an alternative mechanism by which physicians can compete with network doctors. In a PPO, physicians, hospitals, and other providers contract to administer services on a predetermined fee-for-service basis. PPOs generally dictate strict utilization management that limits the care delivered to patients and erects financial disincentives for patient to receive care from out-of-network doctors. However, unlike the arrangement in an HMO, the PPO physicians are not constrained by financial incentives to voluntarily minimize referrals for diagnostic evaluations, hospitalization, and other treatment. In this sense, PPOs can be considered more ethically sound than are HMOs.

In some plans, patients can select a "Point of Service" option which allows them to utilize the services of out-of-network providers. The advantage, of course, is that the patients may select any physician of their wishes. For this choice, patients essentially pay a premium in the form of a high deductible, as great as $10,000, and a significant co-pay, sometimes rising to the level of 50% of the cost of the service. Unlike traditional indemnity plans, which only reviewed bills retrospectively and only to determine whether the fee was within usually and customary limits, point of service plans generally require the same precertification and utilization reviews of requested treatment as any other managed care plan.

OBTAINING TREATMENT IN THE MANAGED CARE SYSTEM

Managed care is, in essence, the rationing of health care. Through its utilization review mechanism, the insurer, not the physician, is the final decision maker, determining "medically necessary" care. This is in contrast to the traditional indemnity system in which the physicians determined what was medically necessary and the insurer retrospectively paid for that care. Since the public has not determined how care should be rationed, and rationing is currently determined solely by the insurance or managed care company, the best that can be done within such a system is to provide safeguards that hopefully will make the process work fairly and according to established rules.

Three mechanisms are available to accomplish the goal of providing safeguards within the system. The first entails state legislation mandating that certain standards of care be part of the health care contract. Treatment that has become mandatory in most states includes length of hospital stay after delivery of a baby, mastectomy reconstruction on both breasts, and a certain number of days of inpatient substance abuse hospitalization. In addition, many states require companies to allow patients to access any specialists they choose, to access the obstetrician-gynecologist of choice, and even to select a specialist as a primary care physician. Importantly, this legislation also mandates certain time frames for the review of patient requests for care and for the appeal of denials of these requests. All states provide for an expedited process for urgently needed care (9).

The second mechanism, enacted in the majority of states, allows individuals to appeal their denials to an independent external review agent who can overturn the determination of the managed care organization. These external reviews are generally binding and, if the patient wins, force the insurer to pay for the care. Although external reviews will be discussed below, it is essential that the practitioner knows the time frames related to external reviews and that if an individual fails to apply for an external review in the time frame established by the legislature, the opportunity for an appeal will be lost.

The third mechanism by which checks and balances of managed care is provided is by the availability of lawsuits against managed care entities, particularly, for wrongful denials or delays of care during the utilization review process. Although it is beyond the scope of this chapter to discuss litigation against companies for negligence in the utilization review process (10), majority of these suits are barred by a federal law, the ERISA 1974 which, by all accounts, was enacted to protect pensions. However, because of a loophole, ERISA has served as a shield for managed care organizations, serving to protect them from being sued for their actions during the utilization review process.

There exists considerable critical outrage in response to ERISAs technical loophole, through which a managed care or insurance company that wrongfully denies or delays necessary treatment, regardless of how egregious the conduct, cannot be held responsible for its actions. Even judges have had great difficulty with this result and have railed against this injustice. See, for example, Andrews-Clarke versus Travelers, 984 F. Suppl. 49 (D. Mass. 1997), in which the judge, in ruling that the wife of the decedent could not pursue her claim against the insurance company for egregious conduct in the utilization review process, stated that he "no choice but to pluck Diane Andrews-Clarke's case out of the state courts . . . and then, at the behest of Travelers and Greenspring, to slam the courthouse doors in her face and leave her without a remedy." After almost 20 years of judicial conflict over this issue, in 2004, the U.S. Supreme Court finally ruled on a case that stated that if an individual's health care plan is covered by ERISA, there will be absolutely no opportunity to sue the company for damages for injury or death due to wrongful denials or delays of care in the utilization review process. Interestingly, one of the cases that the Supreme Court considered pertained to pain management.

In Aetna Health, Inc. versus Davila (11), the Court finally decided the question of whether ERISA preempts claims for negligence or medical malpractice in the utilization review process. Davila represented two consolidated cases, both entailing suits by plaintiffs against their respective HMOs for alleged failure to act reasonably in the utilization review process in violation of duties imposed by a Texas statute (12). One of the plaintiffs, Juan Davila, had sued Aetna Health, Inc. for failing to approve payment for Vioxx. Although Mr. Davila's physician had recommended the pain medication for Davila's arthritis, the drug was not on the formulary, and Mr. Davila had to accept a substitute. Unfortunately, Mr. Davila suffered a severe reaction to the drug that required extensive treatments and hospitalization.

The Supreme Court ruled that ERISA preempted the claims. The Court failed to acknowledge the realities of the current health care system, treating it as if it were ruled by traditional indemnity insurance. The Court refused to acknowledge the reality of the intrusion of managed care into the health care delivery process and failed to take account of the position of the American Medical Association, other medical groups, state attorneys general, and state medical boards that have taken the position that utilization review is the practice of medicine (13). The Court, in essence, ruled that if a medical decision is part of an insurance process, such as utilization review, no matter how inherently medical the nature of the decision, it is considered purely an insurance administrative process and claims of wrongful conduct cannot be pursued.

The Supreme Court's decision in Davila seems to have ended any hope for plaintiffs to hold managed care organizations responsible for their actions in the utilization review process. The Court has, once and for all, directed that any changes in ERISA must come from Congress. However, Congress has repeatedly failed to act to amend ERISA and allows individuals to use the legal process in their states to address these issues. As always, an ounce of prevention is worth a pound of cure, and it is essential that patients and their health care professionals be prepared to take advantage of available internal and external appeals processes.

Obtaining Treatment Authorization: Initial Requests

Managed care's most significant alterations of the health care system is its intrusion into the physician-patient relationship and the use of utilization review to determine what medical care will be financed, and therefore, obtained. The argument that companies only approve payment for care is facile, at best. The failure to approve a treatment that is prohibitively expensive, such as high dose chemotherapy with autologous stem cell transplant, means that the care will not be provided. The process of utilization review entails an initial request for approval for care and, should that be denied, one or two levels of appeal. Routine treatment by a primary care physician generally does not require any contact with the company and can be provided in the doctor's office. There are exceptions, however, particularly in more restrictive HMOs. Diagnostic assessments, referrals to specialists, and hospital care are routinely reviewed by the managed care organization to determine whether the care is excluded from coverage from the policy and then, if available as a treatment, it is assessed to determine whether it is "medically necessary."

The first step in the process of obtaining care is a direct request by a health care professional to the managed care company. Only care that is within the parameters of the health care contract is eligible for approval. Certain treatments, such as those which are experimental or investigational, cosmetic surgery, and artificial insemination and fertilization procedures, are usually specifically excluded. In addition, there are limits to the availability of certain treatments. For example, inpatient mental health and substance abuse treatments are subject to yearly maximums, generally 30 days, and there are limits to outpatient physical therapy and outpatient mental health treatment.

If the treatment is not specifically excluded by the contract provisions, then it is eligible for consideration for approval. The stated standard by which care is considered is whether it is "medically necessary." However, that term has a different meaning to insurance carriers than the one given to it by treating physicians. Generally, if health care professionals recommend a certain type of care, it is medically necessary. Doctors do recommend treatment that may be considered cosmetic, but even those treatments are often necessary for an individual's psychological health. The companies' definition of "medically necessary" takes account of medical issues within the context of the cost of the care, focusing on profitability rather than on patient well-being. Doing so is certainly ethically suspect.

Decisions regarding requests for treatment must be made in a timely manner. Depending on state law, this can be within one, two, or three days of receiving the request and all relevant information. If the care requested is not urgent, then the company generally has 30 days from receipt of all necessary information to respond.

Obtaining Treatment Authorization: Internal Appeals

If the insurance company denies the physician's request for approval for treatment, there are a number of options available for the patient. Depending on the type of plan, the individual may have one or two internal appeals, or requests for the company to reconsider its denial. These internal appeals can be initiated by the patient or the physician, and entail requesting the company to review the clinical and objective data with the opportunity to submit additional material. Of course, simply asking the company to reconsider its denial without the submission of additional data limits the possibility of the company reversing its own decision. Accordingly, it is imperative that both the patient and the health care professional provide additional information for the appeal.

The need for an effective appeal is especially vital when the care needed is urgent. Most states mandate very limited time frames, usually 24 to 72 hours, for a company to consider urgent care requests. Additionally, patients do not need to obtain managed care approval for emergency room care; they will be reimbursed provided the emergency room visit would have appeared to the "reasonable" person to be necessary, and the visit is reported to the company in a timely manner.

The assistance of an attorney can be critical, since companies often respond very differently when an attorney is involved. Attorneys can "shape" the case, respond to the legal issues, and assist the patient's physician in documenting the medical-legal issues presented by the company's denial. Of course, legal assistance is expensive, but if a patient retains an attorney, the company understands that the patient is willing to finance an appeal and possibly a lawsuit. Conversely, the failure to retain an attorney may give the company the message that the patient will do little, if anything, to oppose the denial. This is critical since it is estimated that as many as 9% of requests for approval for medical care are denied by managed care organizations (14).

To maximize the possibility of an internal appeal reversing the denial, the patient and the health care professional must be focused and have a strong understanding of the issues. Appeals should provide additional support, including letters from the health care professional requesting the care as well as from other physicians. The appeal should specify the necessary care and directly oppose the reason for denial. If the denial states that the care is not medically necessary, the appeal should definitively state its necessity and great importance. Furthermore, when appropriate, the health care professional should state that treatment is essential, and that without such care the patient will suffer. The health care professional should, with as much precision as possible, delineate the benefits of the care and, with equal precision, outline what will happen to the patient if the care is not provided.

One of the greatest areas of contention relates to care that insurance companies consider to only "maintain" the patient. This is especially relevant to chronic pain management, particularly the physical and psychological therapy necessary as an aspect of optimal care. It is critical that the physician make the case that the patient is deteriorating and that "maintaining" the patient is in that patient's best interest. In the case of chronic pain management, utilizing other treatment interventions, such as physical therapy and psychotherapy, the ability to continue to function is neither negligible nor is it merely maintaining the status quo. The case must be made that these treatments are essential for the improvement of the patient, since the patient is deteriorating, physically and emotionally. It is imperative that physicians make the case directly to the company in a new letter and utilize as much objective data and clinical impression as possible. Unfortunately, as covered in Dr. Schatman's chapter in this book, the insurance carrier's emphases on cost containment and profit taking are inconsistent with the goal of the pain practitioner, who is obligated to consider relief of suffering as primary.

Obtaining Treatment Authorization: External or Independent Review

The majority of states have enacted legislation that provides for an independent appeal process. This process can be initiated by patients, their physicians, or their representatives, although the application must be made within a limited period of time after the initial appeal denial is received. It is essential that patients and their health care professionals understand the time frame, as failure to assiduously adhere to it will result in the loss of the opportunity for the appeal. This becomes somewhat complicated when there is a second level of appeal available to patients. External review time frames are generally triggered by the first appeal denial; filing and waiting for a decision on the second internal appeal will generally take longer than the time allotted for the submission of an external appeal and will result in the loss of that opportunity. Patients who wish to file a second internal appeal should file both appeal and request for an external review.

External reviews, like internal appeals, have provisions for the consideration of urgent care, mandating that decisions generally be made within 48 to 72 hours. The external reviewer or agency will start the clock after receiving all material. If new documentation is submitted, the insurance or managed care company will be given an opportunity to respond once the appeal has begun.

As with internal appeals, it is critical for patients and their health care professionals to provide additional information. This should include material similar to that cited above in the section on internal appeals. Once again, the assistance of an attorney can be of considerable value, although the mere presence of an attorney will not affect the process as it might in an appeal to the company.

Initiating a Court Action

If the appeals fail, then the patient can bring the case to court and request that the judge overturn the managed care denial and issue an injunction ordering the company to approve payment for the care. Generally, the patient must exhaust all administrative levels of internal review before a court will consider such a case. Patients do not have to obtain an external review; indeed, an external review denial will be almost impossible to overturn in court unless it can be demonstrated that the external review agent is engaged in gross negligence, which is an extremely difficult task.

If the patient is litigating, it is often the case that it must be proven that the company's decision was arbitrary and capricious. Although this is a high standard, it is by no means impossible. The patients must have available sufficient support from their health care professional. Having opinions of other experts is also very important. The task is the same as for an internal appeal, i.e., to demonstrate that the treatment is medically necessary and that the patient will be harmed if the care is not provided.

It is important to remember that managed care organizations are not obligated to provide the best medical care, only care that is "medically necessary." Countless patients have recognized in hindsight that if only they could have gone to a better physician or hospital, their medical condition would have been better. Even assuming that this is a correct assertion, managed care companies are only obligated to provide care that is "medically necessary" and not necessarily that which is provided by the best physician or hospital.

It should be remembered that litigating a case is typically an expensive and somewhat arduous process, even if brought to court by the quickest means. Patients are always in a better position when they attempt to win their case within the company's appeal process rather than in court.

A CAUTIONARY TALE FOR THE CHRONIC PAIN MANAGEMENT SPECIALIST

One impact of managed care has been to make pain management professionals cautious about having their requests for care approved. This might place the professional at risk, and the following case should be taken as cautionary.

In Bergman versus Eden Medical Center (15), a case that has had significant implications for all health care professionals involved in the management of pain, a California jury awarded $1.5 million against Dr. Wing Chin for inadequate pain treatment of the decedent, William Bergman. The suit, decided by a Jury in June 2001, had been filed by the advocacy group compassion in dying subsequent to the medical board of California failing to bring disciplinary action against the physician. The plaintiffs had alleged that the physician failed to manage an elderly cancer patient's pain and that his medical conduct violated the state's elder abuse statute. Notably, this was the first case of its kind brought pursuant to an elder abuse statute.

In the case, Mr. Bergman suffered from metastasized lung and bone cancer which made him unable to swallow. Accordingly, Mr. Bergman was prescribed intravenous Demerol, a narcotic, which was to be provided to him in 25 mg doses or 50 mg doses as needed while Mr. Bergman remained in the hospital. Hospital records indicated that his pain was rated between 7 and 10 on an assessment scale, with 10 representing "unimaginable pain." Accordingly, the nurses were considerably concerned about Mr. Bergman's pain levels.

The patient decided to die at home. When Mr. Bergman was discharged, Dr. Chin refused to prescribe stronger narcotics and only prescribed the relatively weak pain killer, hydrocodone, despite Mr. Bergman's pain being self-assessed as "10." After several days of intense pain, a second physician was consulted. This physician prescribed adequate doses of morphine, which immediately relived Mr. Bergman's pain.

The family sued both the medical center and the treating physician, claiming violation of the California Elder Abuse and Dependent Adult Civil Protection Act. The physician's defense contended that the physician prescribed the weaker medication because the physician feared that Mr. Bergman, who had previously experienced breathing problems when prescribed Demerol, would experience respiratory depression if the stronger medication were prescribed. The defense also argued that the physician had received no training in pain management during medical school or in continuing medical education courses. The family sought an order to require the doctor to receive pain management education.

COPING WITH THE SYSTEM

Patients and health care professionals can cope more effectively with the managed care system. For patients, this means obtaining their necessary care as well as reimbursement for care for which they have paid. For professionals, this means both assisting patients in obtaining treatment as well as making certain that the payment is forthcoming from the insurer or managed care organization. The following are suggestions for chronic pain practitioners to assist them in obtaining care for patients and in obtaining reimbursement for services.

General Precautions
1. Take notes!
2. Carefully notate all consideration regarding the use of opioid analgesics.
3. Carefully notate all considerations against the use of pain management medications.
4. In cases of concern, consult with a supervisor and note that consultation in the chart.
5. If concerned about a patient's understanding of the treatment or medical rationale, write the patient a letter.

When Dealing with Managed Care Companies
1. Get the name of every individual to whom spoken.
2. Get all approvals in writing. If an approval is verbal, tell the managed care agent that you will be sending a letter confirming the approval. Then send a confirmatory letter, stating the name of the patient, the treatment, the name of the managed care agent, and the content of the conversation.
3. Understand what constitute the usual and customary charges of the company.
4. If a patient is expected to pay for the balance after insurance, make certain that the patient agrees in writing.
5. Most states have prompt payment laws. Find out the number of days in your state in which the insurer has to pay for your care. If they do not pay in that time, send a letter indicating that they are beyond the prompt payment deadline.
6. Many states have hotlines, either in the Insurance Department, Health Department, or Attorney General's office to deal with complaints against insurance and managed care companies. Many of these hotlines attempt (quite successfully at times) to negotiate a solution to the problem. Utilize the hotlines.

7. If necessary, utilize the services of an attorney. Companies respond differently when an attorney is involved. However, before hiring an attorney, determine the cost effectiveness of doing so.

CONCLUSION

Managed care has presented the chronic pain professional with many challenges, many of which go against the traditional means of practicing. It is the task of responsible health care professionals to understand what they and their patients are up against, and then to do the best job to have the patient provided the care that is necessary. Understanding the system and how to manage it are essential to success.

REFERENCES

1. Pain Foundation Organization. Available at http://www.painfoundation.org/page.asp? file=Library/PainSurveys.htm (Accessed December 21, 2005).
2. Dilcher AL. Damned if they do, damned if they do not: the need for a comprehensive public policy to address the inadequate management of pain. Ann Health Law 2004; 13:81–144.
3. Ibid., p. 2.
4. National Pharmaceutical, Inc., Joint Commission on Accreditation of Health Care Organizations. Pain: current understanding of assessment, management, and treatment. Available at http://www.jcaho.org/news+room/health+care+issues/pain_ex_sum.pdf (Accessed December 15, 2005).
5. Carter C, Goldfarb NI, Hartmann CW, Roumm AR, Vallow SM, Durkin MS. Chronic pain management in managed care organizations: a national survey of medical directors. J Assoc Phys Ther 2003; 3:179–215.
6. American College of Physicians—American Society of Internal Medicine. Ambulatory care formularies and pharmacy benefit management by managed care organizations. Available at http://www.acponline.org/hpp/change_ai.htm (Accessed on December 15, 2005).
7. National Coalition on Health Care. Available at http://64.233.161.104/search?q=cache:U_xRYfphv3YJ:www.nchc.org/facts/cost.shtml+health+care+costs+gross+national+product&hl=en (Accessed on December 21, 2005).
8. Gallagher TH, St. Peter RF, Chesney M, Lo B. Patients' attitudes towards cost-control bonuses for managed care physicians. Health Aff 2001; 20:186–192.
9. Buckley JF, Prysby ND. State by State Guide to Managed Care Law, 2006. New York, NY: Aspen Publishers, 2005.
10. Trueman DL. Managed care liability today: current issues and trends. In: Gosfield AG, ed. Health Law Handbook, 2006 St. Paul, MN: West Group, 2006.
11. 540 U.S. 200, 124 S.Ct. 2488, 2004.
12. The Texas Health Care Liability Act (THCLA), Tex Civ Prac Rem Code Ann 2004; (supp pamphlet):§§ 88.001–88.003.
13. Trueman DL. The liability of medical directors for utilization review determinations. J Health Law 2002; 35:105–133; for a discussion of whether medical directors can be held liable for their conduct in the utilization review process. (The reader is once again referred to this author's article, managed care liability today (see note 13), as well his article).
14. Rand Institute for Civil Justice. Available at http://www.rand.org/pubs/research_briefs/RB9039/index1.html (Accessed December 21, 2005).
15. Cal. Super. Ct., No. H205732–1, June 13, 2001.

14 Ethical Issues in Testimony Regarding Chronic Pain Management

Barbara L. Kornblau

Departments of Occupational Therapy and Public Health, Nova Southeastern University, Fort Lauderdale, Florida, U.S.A.

INTRODUCTION

Bob Dell Monte is a 53-year-old man who works for the West Braska Bureau of Alcohol and Tobacco (BAT) as a sworn law enforcement officer. To satisfy campaign promises (and to allow this case study to fall under the Americans With Disabilities (1,2), the Governor of West Braska privatized BAT and several other state agencies shortly after coming into office in 2002.

In June 2004, while on his way to inspect cigarettes, a West Braska Power & Light bucket rear-ended his car. The air bag failed to deploy. Mr. Monte hit his head on the windshield, blacked out, and was taken to the hospital. He was diagnosed with a lumbar sacral sprain, arthritic changes in spine, "whiplash," a fractured hip, and a mild head injury. After successful hip surgery and several days as an inpatient at West Braska Memorial Hospital, Mr. Monte was discharged home.

Doctors gave Mr. Monte a "no work status" and referred him to physical therapy and occupational therapy for three months. At the end of three months, he was still complaining of low-back pain and was referred to an outpatient comprehensive pain program. Upon discharge from the pain program, he was referred to a work-hardening program, Wilma's Wonderful Work Hardening Clinic that he attended for six weeks. Mr. Monte's physician released him to light-duty work and he returned to BAT on March 18, 2005. Three months later, on June 18, 2005, he returned to work full duty, in spite of continuing complaints of pain.

Mr. Monte filed a workers' compensation claim because the workers' compensation carrier initially denied his claim incorrectly, believing his car excursion was not work related. It also argued that Mr. Monte was "exaggerating" his complaints of physical pain and psychological distress. The carrier denied payment for all psychological intervention.

In addition to the workers' compensation claim, Mr. Monte filed a personal injury negligence suit against the West Braska Power & Light Company for causing the accident and a defective product action against the car manufacturer for the failure of the air bag to deploy. These cases were eventually heard and concluded.

Meanwhile, Mr. Monte returned to work. After working almost one year in his regular, full-duty job, the Department assigned Mr. Monte to work on an underage drinking detail (sting operation) at a Memorial Day Rolling Stones Concert held at the city arena in Margaritaville, West Braska. This involved, among other things, walking the arena before, during, and after the concert while looking for underage drinkers. After standing and walking during the entire five-hour production, Mr. Monte complained to a coworker that his legs and low back were bothering him. The coworker informed the supervisor of Mr. Monte's complaint.

The supervisor prepared the following questionnaire for Mr. Monte's physician and sent him a form to fill out:

1. Does Mr. Monte still have pain from his original accident? Yes or No.
2. Is Mr. Monte at risk of reinjuring his back? Yes or No.
3. If Mr. Monte had to unload a truck full of beer by himself, over a six-hour period, would he be at risk of reinjuring his back? Yes or No.

The doctor answered, "Yes" to all the three questions and as a result, the Department demoted Mr. Monte. He was no longer a sworn law enforcement officer.

Mr. Monte did not believe he could perform the tasks required by the "new" position to which the Department demoted him, but he knew he could do the job that he was doing before he was demoted. Mr. Monte prepared to bring an action under the Americans with Disabilities Act (ADA) and State of West Braska's antidiscrimination law. His attorney contacted his treating physicians, occupational therapist and physical therapist, and psychologist about testifying on his behalf.

This scenario raises many issues for pain practitioners. While it might seem extreme at first blush, practitioners who work in chronic pain management know that many of the patients they encounter are involved in some sort of litigation or administrative claim. This raises a series of questions for the pain practitioner.

- What are the different roles that pain practitioners play when they present testimony?
- What is the pain practitioner's role in testifying in different types of cases?
- What are the pain practitioner's ethical obligations in presenting testimony?
- Is there a difference between one's ethical obligations as an expert witness versus a treating pain practitioner?
- What are the possible consequences of testimony on the pain practitioner and on the patient?

This chapter is not about malpractice or pain practitioners testifying about each other's skills or lack of skills. Rather, this chapter reviews the types of litigation or administrative claims in which chronic pain management practitioners might find themselves involved through their patient's involvement, and the ethical concerns and obligations this involvement brings. This chapter addresses:

- The roles pain management practitioners may play in litigation or administrative claims.
- The pain practitioner's ethical obligations in providing testimony related to chronic pain management and the possible consequences of the testimony.

The chapter also:

- Reviews the legal and ethical issues raised by testifying in different types of cases or claims based upon the same facts or occurrence.
- Compares and contrasts the goals and the content of testimony in cases involving a variety of types of claims and the ethical implications of the differing contexts each claim may present.

Finally, this chapter presents readers with a framework for looking at ethical dilemmas and ethical decision making within the context of providing testimony.

TYPES OF LITIGATION AND ADMINISTRATIVE CLAIMS

Mr. Monte's situation illustrates several kinds of actions in which pain practitioners may typically find themselves presenting testimony. This chapter focuses on the causes of actions in which Mr. Monte is a participant. These actions in which pain practitioners may find themselves serving as witnesses based upon their client's involvement include workers' compensation, negligence (which, in Mr. Monte's case, includes defective products or products liability claim and a person injury action), a Title I (Employment) ADA action, and finally, a social security claim.

WORKERS' COMPENSATION

On-the-job injuries, which lead to workers' compensation claims, are frequent claims for individuals in need of chronic pain management. Accidents resulting from defective products can leave the victim with chronic pain, and pain practitioners routinely see these patients in their practices. Since workers' compensation laws vary from state-to-state, some systems may allow for adversarial hearings (3) in which practitioners give depositions or testify live, while others may be more limiting in their approach, limiting attorneys fees and/or focusing on alternative dispute resolution.

Mr. Monte filed a workers' compensation claim because he sustained his injuries while on the job. Since the workers' compensations carrier asserted that the injury was not work related and that Mr. Monte did not sustain the magnitude of injuries he claimed, Mr. Monte had to pursue his claim for benefits by hiring an attorney. The treating pain practitioner may face a deposition and testimony in court to present the facts regarding the causal relationship between Mr. Monte's accident and his injuries and pain, the course of treatment, his cooperation or lack thereof, and whether or not Mr. Monte can return to work (RTW) with or without a reasonable accommodation (3,4) (Fig. 1).

Proof needed from:	
ATTORNEY/WITNESSES WORKING ON BEHALF OF **CARRIER/EMPLOYER**	ATTORNEY/WITNESSES WORKING ON BEHALF OF **CLAIMANT/PATIENT/EMPLOYEE**
1. Claimant *can* RTW (his/her job or any job)	1. Claimant *cannot* RTW (his/her job or any job)
2. Claimant does not want to work (not cooperating; deadbeat)	2. Claimant is unable to perform his/her job because of injury/pain
3. Claimant has no restrictions & limitations	3. Claimant has restrictions and limitations
4. What accommodations must be made to RTW *or* claimant needs no accommodations	4. Claimant needs RA or what you offered is not a RA or won't enable RTW
5. Claimant has no permanent impairment	5. Claimant has a permanent impairment

FIGURE 1 Proof needed for a workers' compensation claim. *Abbreviations*: RTW, return to work; RA, reasonable accommodations. *Source*: From Ref. 5.

Proof needed from:	
ATTORNEY/WITNESSES WORKING ON BEHALF OF **DEFENDANT**	ATTORNEY/WITNESSES WORKING ON BEHALF OF **PLAINTIFF/PATIENT**
1. Plaintiff *can* RTW (his job or any job)	1. Plaintiff *cannot* RTW (his job or any job)
2. Plaintiff does not want to work (not cooperating; deadbeat)	2. Plaintiff wants to RTW (suing to RTW)
3. Plaintiff is able to perform his job in spite of his injury/pain	3. Plaintiff has restrictions & limitations which do not allow RTW
4. Plaintiff can work with RA	4. There are no RA to enable RTW

FIGURE 2   Proof needed for a negligence action. *Abbreviations*: RTW, return to work; RA, reasonable accommodations. *Source*: From Ref. 5.

NEGLIGENCE ACTIONS

Mr. Monte also brought two other actions—one against Merrimotors, the manufacturer of the car, for failure of the air bag to deploy, and the other against the West Braska Power & Light Company, for hitting his car and causing his injuries. When a person has a workers' compensation claim concurrent with a negligence claim, the claims are often referred to as "third-party claims." The third-party claim against the car manufacturer is also called a "product liability" or "defective product" action. The car accident is usually referred to as a personal injury case. Both the claims fall under the category of negligence cases and the umbrella of tort cases in which someone is wronged by another.

In the negligence actions, Mr. Monte needed to prove four elements.

1. A duty existed between Mr. Monte and Merrimotors and West Braska Power & Light;
2. Merrimotors and West Braska Power & Light breached that duty;
3. The conduct of Merrimotors and West Braska Power & Light resulted in the injury to Mr. Monte; and
4. damages to Mr. Monte (6).

In this context, the attorney would want to use the pain practitioner's testimony to help prove the third and fourth elements—that Merrimotors and West Braska Power & Light's actions caused Mr. Monte's injuries and the nature and extent of Mr. Monte's injuries (Fig. 2).

AMERICANS WITH DISABILITIES ACT

After returning to work and finding himself demoted to a position beyond his functional capacities, Mr. Monte filed an action under the Americans with Disabilities Act. He believed that his employer discriminated against him by demoting him because he was able to do his job, in spite of his chronic pain. Mr. Monte's position was that he was in fact performing the essential functions of his job when the Department demoted him making him a qualified individual with a disability

(QIWD). As a QIWD, Mr. Monte believed that the Department should have allowed him to RTW. His position was that he did not even need any reasonable accommodations (RA) to perform the regular job he performed before he was demoted.

The attorney representing Mr. Monte needed to prove that the claimant was a QIWD. This meant meeting one of three definitions of disability, including

1. "a physical or mental impairment that substantially limits one or more major life activities," (7)
2. a record of having had such an impairment, (8) or
3. regarded as having a substantially limiting impairment (9).

It also meant proving that Mr. Monte was a QIWD. This meant that he was "an individual with a disability who satisfies the requisite skill, experience, education, and other job-related requirements of the employment position" he or she holds or desires, "and who, with or without reasonable accommodation, can perform the essential functions of the employment position that the individuals holds or desires" (10).

Mr. Monte's attorney would want pain practitioners to testify about Mr. Monte's impairments and his ability to perform his job, with or without RA. The pain practitioners would also provide testimony detailing the kind of RA needed to enable Mr. Monte's performance if he needed any.

For example, a job analysis indicated that Mr. Monte's position involved the following essential functions:

1. Inspecting cigarettes, including those in machines to determine the required tax stamp is present.
2. Seizing cigarettes found without the required tax stamps.
3. Inspecting alcoholic beverages to determine the required tax stamp was present.
4. Seizing alcohol found without the required tax stamps.
5. Monitoring bars and sales of alcohol to assure compliance with the drinking age laws.
6. Making arrests of those who did not comply with the alcohol and cigarette laws of West Braska.

The job analysis also showed that Mr. Monte was not required to unload or load trucks. Other people would be hired to do this kind of work should the need arise.

The pain practitioners involved in this case should have prepared themselves for testimony in which they compared the results of the job analysis with Mr. Monte's ability to perform the required job tasks in the environment in which he worked. The bottom line of this testimony: can Mr. Monte return to the position he held when Department demoted him? (Fig. 3).

SOCIAL SECURITY DISABILITY

Should Mr. Monte have found himself unable to return to his former job, and not have been able to perform the essential functions of his new job, he may have resorted to filing a claim for social security disability (12). Social security claims look at whether or not an individual with a disability can return to substantial gainful employment (SGE) in the open labor market (12). They consider factors

Proof needed from:	
ATTORNEY/WITNESSES WORKING ON BEHALF OF **CARRIER/EMPLOYER**	ATTORNEY/WITNESSES WORKING ON BEHALF OF **PLAINTIFF/PATIENT**
1. Plaintiff *cannot* RTW (his job or any job)	1. Plaintiff *can* RTW (his job or any job)
2. Plaintiff does not want to work (not cooperating; deadbeat)	2. Plaintiff wants to RTW (suing to RTW)
3. Plaintiff has restrictions & limitations which do not allow RTW (not a QIWD)	3. Plaintiff is able to perform his job in spite of his injury/pain (is a QIWD)
4. There are no RA to enable RTW or plaintiff not a QIWD ergo not entitled to RA	4. Plaintiff can work with RA

FIGURE 3 Proof needed for an Americans with Disabilities Act (Title I) (11) case. *Abbreviations*: RTW, return to work; RA, reasonable accommodations; QIWD, qualified individual with a disability. *Source*: From Ref. 5.

such as the specific diagnosis or type of disability, restrictions and limitations caused by the disability, age, education, and transferable skills.

Had Mr. Monte been unable to RTW, his attorney would have wanted the pain practitioner to testify regarding the nature and extent of Mr. Monte's impairments and how they interfered with his ability to perform SGE in the open labor market (Fig. 4).

Social security disability issues are covered in considerable detail in the chapter by Dr. Hefner in this textbook.

ETHICAL ISSUES RAISED BY DIFFERENT TYPES OF CLAIMS

Many issues come to the forefront when one considers the different types of claims in which Mr. Monte found himself involved, the ethical standards with which the

Proof needed from:	
ATTORNEY/WITNESSES WORKING ON BEHALF OF **SOCIAL SECURITY**	ATTORNEY/WITNESSES WORKING ON BEHALF OF **CLAIMANT/PATIENT**
1. Plaintiff *can* RTWs (his/her job or any job)	1. Plaintiff *cannot* RTW (cannot perform substantial gainful employment; (his job or any job)
2. Plaintiff is able to perform SGE in spite of his injury, pain, or impairment	2. Plaintiff has restrictions & limitations which do not allow Substantial Gainful Employment (SGE)

FIGURE 4 Proof needed for social security claims (12). *Abbreviation*: RTW, return to work. *Source*: From Ref. 5.

pain practitioner must comply, and the different requirements for proof in Mr. Monte's various claims.

As readers can see, the four cases illustrated required different kinds of proof that could potentially conflict with each other and lead to conflicting testimony. Attorneys on both sides of these disputes may have sought to use the pain practitioner's testimony as part of the evidence to support the elements of the claim that they desired to prove.

Suppose a pain practitioner testified on Mr. Monte's behalf in his workers' compensation case that he could not RTW because of pain and the resulting loss of function. The pain practitioner may have also testified in the negligence cases regarding permanent injuries sustained and the residual chronic pain Mr. Monte experienced as a result of the car accident and the failure of the air bag to deploy. Could the pain practitioner then testify at his ADA trial at another time that he could RTW and at the same time testify at a social security administrative hearing that Mr. Monte could not return to SGE? To answer these questions, one must look at the roles pain practitioners play as fact and expert witnesses and ethical obligations expected of pain practitioners.

THE ROLE OF THE PAIN PRACTITIONERS AS "WITNESS"

Pain practitioners have long played a role in providing testimony before courts and administrative hearing officers. In recent years, "witness" has become an integral role in many of the pain practitioner professions. For example, the preamble to the American Psychological Association's Ethical Principles of Psychologists and Code of Conduct discusses the various roles psychologists play including, among others, "researcher, supervisor, educator, diagnostician, therapist, . . . and expert witness" (13). The American Medical Association (AMA) takes the position that when testifying as an expert, physicians are engaged in the practice of medicine (14).

Of the 30 professional codes of ethics and policies of pain practitioners' professional societies and certification boards reviewed by the author, (14–33) of them specifically mention expert witness testimony and several mention the role of the treating practitioner as witness (31,33).

FACT WITNESS

A pain practitioner may testify as a fact witness or an expert witness depending upon the circumstance or his or her involvement. A fact witness is generally the treating pain practitioner. For example, the orthopedic surgeon who repaired Mr. Monte's hip and the professional staff members at the outpatient pain program who treated Mr. Monte would serve as fact witnesses if called to testify. Fact witnesses, as the name implies, may only testify as to actually facts. These may include for example, results of an Electromyogram test, a Minnesota Multiphasic Personality Inventory or range of motion assessment. Fact witnesses generally report objective findings from their assessment and treatment of the patient.

EXPERT WITNESSES

Courts permit expert witnesses the additional privilege and responsibility of offering their opinions during their testimony. In some cases, expert witnesses base their opinions upon their own assessment or an independent medical examination of the patient. In other situations, expert witnesses may base their opinions on a review of the pain practitioners' records and/or a review of another practitioner's deposition testimony. Generally, the opinion is given in response to a fact-heavy hypothetical question that includes an approximation of the facts at issue in the case. However, in order to function as an expert witness in court, one must meet two criteria. First, one must qualify as an expert, and second, one must provide the Court with testimony based upon tested theory.

To qualify as an expert, the Court will look at the pain practitioners' training, experience, publications, experience with the diagnosis at issue, and other factors that support the pain practitioner's "expertise" in his or her given field and with the given diagnosis. Based upon these factors, the Court will decide whether or not it will consider the witness as an expert.

The inquiry as to whether or not the expert may testify does not end with the qualifications of the proposed expert. The Court must examine the content of the proposed testimony—the proposed evidence—and determine whether or not it will assist the Court or fact finder in determining the facts of the case.

In *Daubert v. Merrell Dow Pharmaceuticals* (34), the United States Supreme Court sought to limit the potential for junk science or research conducted specifically for the purpose of litigation, a questionable ethical practice. The U.S. Supreme Court articulated four specific factors for judges to consider when deciding whether or not to admit scientific expert witness testimony under the Federal Rules of Evidence. *Fed. Rule Evid.* Rule 104(a) (35). See *Fed. Rule Evid.* Rule 702 (36).

1. Has the theory or technique been tested?
2. Has the theory or technique been subjected to peer review and publication in peer-reviewed literature?
3. In the case of a particular scientific (or pain management) technique, is there a known or potential rate of error, and standards controlling the technique's use?; quest; *and*
4. Is the underlying technique generally accepted in the scientific community? (34)

The Court applied *Daubert* in *Black v. Food Lion* (37), in which the plaintiff fell in a store and claimed her fall caused her fibromyalgia. A physician, board certified both in Pain Medicine and in Physical Medicine and Rehabilitation, testified that the fall "caused physical trauma to Black, which caused "hormonal changes" that caused Black's fibromyalgia" (37). The Court cited several articles from the literature in its opinion when it threw out the physician's testimony. As the Court so plainly stated, the doctor's testimony did "not bear the necessary indicia of intellectual rigor, whether measured by *Daubert* or the magistrate judge's reasoning" (37).

However, both the Court system and the pain practitioners confirm that the role of expert witness still lives post-*Daubert*. A study of judges and attorneys who practice in federal civil trials found that medical and mental health specialists were the category of expert witnesses most frequently presented to the Court (38). They accounted for 40% of the overall experts presented at trials. Medical professionals collectively accounted for one-third of all experts who testified (38). The most frequent issues addressed by the expert witnesses at trial were the nature and extent of the injury or damages, which occurred in 68% of the trials. The cause of the injury or damages was addressed by expert witnesses in 64% of the trials (38).

Another study, which surveyed medicolegal practice patterns among a multidisciplinary group of pain specialists, found that in the past year, 72% of them had engaged in some form of medicolegal practice, including providing expert witness testimony (39). Of these, 55% reported performing medicolegal work in their role as treating pain practitioners and 41% reported performing services in both capacities—as an expert for an insurance company or attorney, and as a treating pain practitioner (39). Functioning in both roles presents ethical issues for those providing testimony.

ETHICAL ISSUES IN PROVIDING TESTIMONY

Chronic pain management involves professionals from many different fields. Examination of codes of ethics and policies from the various professions show common themes. The nature of the relationship between patient and pain practitioner imposes certain duties and ethical obligations upon the practitioners. For example, treating practitioners or fact witnesses owe their first duty to their patients—nonmaleficence—to "do no harm" (40). Thus, one may find him/herself facing ethical distress if asked to testify as a fact witness, and the content of the pain practitioner's testimony might do the patient harm. For example, suppose Mr. Monte had spotty attendance at the outpatient pain program, or perhaps he was caught using recreational drugs during a toxicology screen. This testimony would probably harm the patient's reputation and/or his or her case, violating the code of ethics for the testifying pain practitioner.

Since a treating clinician who is a fact witness is obligated to the patient to do no harm, placing oneself in the dual role of treating clinician and expert witness can cause confusion. Who is the client? To whom is the "treating clinician," now "expert for the insurance carrier," obligated? What does one do when the changing role causes stress? The Ethics Charter from the American Academy of Pain Medicine asserts that in the role of witness, the physician should "provide testimony that is balanced, objective, and consistent with the best current standards of the medical profession regardless of whether the physician is testifying as a factual or expert witness for the plaintiff or defendant" (31).

ETHICAL OBLIGATION TO TELL THE TRUTH

Most codes of ethics and policies for the various pain professions that address expert witness testimony stress the need for veracity. Veracity is a basic principle for almost all codes of ethics for pain practitioners.

At first blush, the idea of violating a professional society's code of ethics may seem self-limiting, since professional societies can only enforce codes of ethics and policies against their own members. However, in reality, codes of ethics extend past the boundaries of membership. For example, The AMA Code of Ethics and its advisory opinions have been cited as authority in 181 published legal opinions between 1980 and 1999, including *Tarasoff v. Regents of University of California* (41). Further, licensing boards will take the lead from professional organizations and provide their own sanctions. One physician, licensed in North Carolina, discovered this when his untruthful testimony not only resulted in a six-month suspension from the American Association of Neurological Surgeons (AANS), but also resulted in the suspension of his license to practice medicine, which was later reversed in part (42). The physician had testified, in the absence of any supporting evidence, that another physician falsified records (42).

Another physician sanctioned by the AANS for lying in Court actually tried to sue the AANS for damages for injury to his professional reputation. In *Austin v. American Association of Neurological Surgeons*, (43) Dr. Austin was sanctioned for testifying that a patient's nerve damage was caused by a rushed operation, even though there was no evidence to support his assertion. The court found that neither article upon which he claimed to rely during his testimony actually supported his testimony. The Court stated that Dr. Austin "cannot obtain damages for any injury to his professional reputation...as a result of the "accurate" revelation of his having given irresponsible testimony under oath in a suit for medical malpractice" (43) (emphasis supplied).

Pain practitioners need to distinguish truth from consistency. This becomes difficult when they find themselves testifying in several different types of cases regarding the same accident or injury, such as in Mr. Monte's situations.

This inquiry looks at whether one's testimony is consistent considering context and other factors. Contradicting or recanting one's previous position puts witnesses in a tenuous ethical position (44). Unless specific factors have changed that allow the expert witness to change his or her testimony, he or she faces a serious ethical problem.

Several factors can change that will allow a witness to change his or her testimony. One factor is time. For example, as Mr. Monte's case demonstrated, a personal injury case, which stresses how impaired Mr. Monte remained within a few months of his recovery, is vastly different from an ADA case two years later, which stressed his ability to perform the essential functions of his job. At the time of the personal injury action, Mr. Monte was still on a no work status and recovering from a hip fracture and other limiting conditions. Two years later, those conditions had changed, and Mr. Monte has successfully returned to his job and performed according to expected standards. Thus, the passage of time and the old adage, "time heals all" allowed the witness to speak truthfully and ethically with a different message.

Context also gives expert witnesses justification to "change" their testimony. The U.S. Supreme Court addressed this issue in the case *Cleveland v. Policy Management Systems Corp.* (45) and allowed the plaintiff to argue two positions, which though at first blush looked different, were in fact consistent because of context. On one hand, Mrs. Cleveland argued in her claim for Social Security Disability Insurance that she was "disabled," and unable to do her previous work, and "unable to engage in SGE" (45). At the same time, she argued in her ADA case that she could perform the "essential functions of her previous job" with RA (45). The Court held that one could be "disabled" for social security purposes and not under the ADA because of the statutory context of the ADA, which provides for RA, the lack of which would render Mrs. Cleveland unable to work (45).

Technological changes may justify a change in testimony. For example, consider the fictitious case of Mary, a patient with regional complex pain syndrome. Mary was eventually able to return to the workplace because of the invention of a cosmic ray nerve enhancer, a brand new, fictitious, Star Trek-like invention that zaps cosmic rays through the nerves to stop pain reactions in the extremities. Despite previous testimony that Mary could not work, the technological changes ultimately enabled her to RTW.

Sometimes changes in case law might provide a basis for a change in testimony. For example, before the *Tarasoff* case, (41) government-employed psychiatrists treating chronic pain patients thought they had an absolute privilege to keep therapeutic communication confidential, and would not divulge that information even if a client expressed his or her intent to harm another individual. However, the Court's decision in *Tarasoff* changed the circumstances, and subsequently there has existed a legal obligation to disclose that information to prevent harm to the third person (41). Consequently, after *Tarasoff*, one's testimony might change based on the opinion rendered by the Court.

Pain practitioners must also look at the impact of RA on their testimony. Considering RA that one may make to the work, the worker, and the workplace, can the person with chronic pain now work? If the patient can work or function better with the reasonable accommodation in place, then the pain practitioner is not really changing his or her testimony.

ETHICAL OBLIGATION FOR TESTIMONY BASED UPON CURRENT SCIENTIFIC LITERATURE

According to the codes of ethics and policies for various pain-related professions, pain practitioners owe a duty to the court, the client, and society to testify based upon the most current scientific information available. Many of the codes of ethics (or supplemental policy statements) of the various pain practitioners' professional societies, which do address forensic issues or expert witness testimony, spell out this ethical obligation (15,16,20,24,26,28,31,32,46,47). For example, the Code of Ethics of the American Podiatric Medical Association (APMA) states in section ME5.21 that podiatrists should base their expert testimony on "recognized medical and scientific principles, theories, facts, and standard of care" (15). The International Association of Rehabilitation Professionals' Code of Ethics, Standards of Practice, and Competencies specifies in its Forensic Code that "Forensic Rehabilitation Experts/Consultants have an obligation to maintain current knowledge of scientific, professional, and legal developments. They are obligated to use that knowledge consistent with accepted clinical and scientific standards..." (26).

The "Expert Witness Affirmation," (48) adopted by several medical societies (48–50), and the "AMA Expert Witness Affirmation Statement" (14) both provide physicians with ethical principles to guide them through the expert witness process and request that physicians voluntarily sign the affirmation of these principles. The Expert Witness Affirmation stresses the obligation to provide testimony "that is complete, objective, (and) scientifically based..." (48).

While other professional societies' codes of ethics do not specifically mention expert witness testimony or specific standards for expert witnesses, they do imply the stated ethical obligation to use the current scientific information and professional literature in their practice (25,51–56). For example, the Occupational Therapy Code of Ethics states in Principle 4E that occupational therapists shall "(C)ritically examine available evidence so they perform their duties on the basis of current information" (53). The American Osteopathic Association's Code of Ethics in Section 5 states that a physician "shall practice in accordance with the body of systemized and scientific knowledge related to the healing arts. A physician shall maintain competence in such systemized and scientific knowledge..." (52) The American Psychological Association's Ethical Principles of Psychologists and Code of Conduct states in Ethical Standard 2.04 that "(P)sychologists' work is based upon established scientific and professional knowledge of the discipline" (13).

Taken as a whole, the various codes of ethics recognize that patients and clients are entitled to competent pain practitioners who, as fact or expert witnesses, keep current in their knowledge and practice. Therefore, the pain practitioner who testifies in Court should testify about, and form opinions based upon the most current scientific information available. Further, all pain practitioners should use current scientific knowledge in their clinical practice. Problems occur when clinicians and experts are not current in their knowledge of the literature and seem to rely on an "everybody does it" or "we have always done it that way" standard for clinical practice or expert testimony. Mr. Monte's case illustrated this principle.

Mr. Monte's workers' compensation carrier denied his claim for benefits because, among other things, it believed Mr. Monte was not exerting full effort in his treatment. There were allegations of "malingering" lodged against Mr. Monte by the outpatient pain program he attended. In his testimony, the director of the pain program, Dr. Hurts, stated that the program based its assessment of Mr. Monte's sincerity of effort on Waddell's signs (57). Dr. Hurts described Waddell's signs as the standard method for evaluating malingering and secondary gain in the chronic pain industry. Dr. Hurts articulated an "everybody does it standard," reporting "all pain clinics use this method which is accepted in the industry." On cross-examination, Dr. Hurts was asked if he could cite any current literature supporting his use of Waddell's signs. He merely repeated that everyone uses Waddell's signs and that it has been studied extensively in the literature.

Mr. Monte's expert witness, Dr. Smartz painted a different picture. He was current in his knowledge of the literature. Dr. Smartz explained that Waddell's signs were never intended for use to detect sincerity of effort, (57,58) but over time clinicians began to use them for that purpose.

Dr. Smartz presented two recent studies to the workers' compensation judge that cast serious doubt on the use of Waddell's signs for detection of malingering or nonorganic signs. Fishbain and colleagues conducted two evidence-based structured reviews of Waddell's signs (WS), (59,60) according to the Agency for Health Care Policy Research's (AHCPR) guidelines for such reviews (60). The first analysis reviewed 57 previous studies of WS using AHCPR's guidelines for strength and consistency of the data (59). Based upon their review, Fishbain and colleagues made the following seven conclusions:
WSs:

1. do not correlate with psychological distress;
2. do not discriminate organic from nonorganic problems;
3. may represent an organic phenomenon;
4. are associated with poorer treatment outcomes;
5. are associated with greater pain levels;
6. are not associated with secondary gain; and
7. studies, as a group, demonstrate some methodological problems (59).

Dr. Smartz explained Fishbain and colleagues second evidence-based structured review of WS, which focused on studies of the association between WSs and secondary gain and malingering. In this study, based on a review of 16 directly relevant studies, Fishbain and colleagues concluded that the preponderance of the evidence showed no association between Waddell's signs and secondary gain and malingering (60).

While these studies have their limitations and fall a level below meta-analyses, the level of evidence presented to the workers' compensation judge was certainly persuasive when compared to a practitioner who was not familiar with the latest research, could not cite any relevant literature and rested his/her laurels on the infamous "everybody does it" standard. Since Dr. Hurts was Mr. Monte's treating physician, he owed Mr. Monte the duty to do no harm. In addition to a failure to maintain current knowledge within pain management, Dr. Hurts made several additional ethical faux pas that had or could have had profound consequences on Mr. Monte's life.

Malingering is not a medical diagnosis, though mentioned in the DSM-IV (61). Labeling someone as a malingerer, based on tests that do not have definitive evidence of reliability and validity, is not ethical and may have caused the denial of Mr. Monte's workers' compensation benefits. This labeling may have also caused the need for Mr. Monte to bring this action in the first place. This hypothetical case illustrates the importance of pain practitioners' acknowledging that their opinions have serious consequences to their patients including, but not limited to loss of benefits, employment, and reputation.

ANALYZING POTENTIAL ETHICAL DILEMMAS IN TESTIMONY

Pain practitioners must comply with their ethical obligations within the context of testimony. When faced with potentially conflicting testimony or a case that causes the practitioner "ethical stress," the pain practitioner should step back and analyze his or her role. Fact witnesses or treating pain practitioners will probably find themselves subpoenaed or court mandated to testify. Potential expert witnesses on the other hand, have a choice in the matter.

Suppose for example, an attorney approaches a pain practitioner to testify as an expert witness for Mr. Monte. When the Federal Express box of records arrives, the cover letter indicates the expert for the employer is a highly respected colleague who wrote the textbook on work hardening. Immediately, the pain practitioner's the ethical stress meter rises. Without even reading Mr. Monte's enclosed records, the potential expert might question whether he or she holds the same level of expertise as the respected colleague and whether he or she could ever disagree with that colleague. How can pain practitioners address the rising ethical stress meter?

Figure 5 provides a framework for analyzing the potential ethical dilemmas in testimony that may make one's ethical stress meter rise.

1.	**Review the Facts:** What are the facts of the case?
2.	**Review the Relationship:** What is my role or relationship in this case?
3.	**Goals of Testimony:** What is/are the goal(s) of the testimony? Can I support that goal?
4.	**Competence:** Am I competent to testify in this area?
5.	**Objectivity:** Is my testimony objective? Is there evidence to back up my testimony?
6.	**Veracity:** Is my testimony truthful?
7.	**Consistency:** Is my testimony consistent considering context and other factors? Have factors changed to allow me to change my testimony? (Time, context, technology, case law, reasonable accommodations)
8.	**Consequences:** What are the consequences of my testimony?
9.	**Personal:** How do I feel about my testimony? How do my moral & ethical beliefs affect this situation?
10.	**Mentor:** Do I have a mentor with whom I can process the dilemma(s)?

FIGURE 5 Analyzing potential ethical dilemmas in testimony.

REVIEW THE FACTS

The first step is to review the facts of the situation. Reviewing the facts considers those involving the patient or subject of the litigation as well as the potentially uncomfortable situation in which pain practitioners may find themselves. Pain practitioners may find that writing down the facts of where they find themselves and why they feel a dilemma brewing provides a clearer picture. For example, Mr. Monte's case seemed very complicated with many different diagnosis, pain practitioners, and causes of action. By laying out all of the facts, the pain practitioner could have developed a better understanding of what this undertaking might entail, should he or she have decided to take the case on in an expert witness role.

REVIEW THE RELATIONSHIP

The next factor looks at the role of the pain practitioner and his or her relationship to the pain patient. Is the pain practitioner already a treating practitioner and a potential fact witness? Is the pain practitioner too close to the patient for objectivity? If so, pain practitioners will want to consider referring the case to another pain practitioner.

THE GOALS OF THE TESTIMONY

The next inquiry considers the goals of the testimony. What is the subject matter of the testimony? What does the lawyer need to prove to win his or her case? As a potential expert witness, can the pain practitioner ethically support that position? Will his or her testimony be truthful if he or she supports that position? If pain practitioners cannot ethically support the position required in their testimony, they should reject the case and refer it to another potential expert witness.

COMPETENCE

After considering the facts, one's relationship to the case, and the goals of the testimony, one must examine his or her competence. Chronic pain management is a broad field filled with many different kinds of practitioners and specialists. Expertise in one aspect of pain management does not mean one is in an expert in all. For example, Mr. Monte needed an expert to testify in his ADA case that he was able to work in spite of his chronic low-back pain. Obviously, a practitioner with expertise in shoulder pain and no expertise in job analysis was not the person most competent to testify on his behalf. A pain practitioner who lacked the expertise in chronic low-back pain would lack familiarity with the most current research and knowledge in this area and would benefit neither Mr. Monte nor the Court. Some codes of ethics recommend or require that in their role as expert witnesses, pain practitioners hold board certification or are currently or recently practicing (32,62). Pain practitioners who question their competence when asked about a particular area of testimony should take note: When in doubt, pain professionals should refer to another professional lest they put themselves in a position to show the Court their lack of expertise.

OBJECTIVITY

To comply with the *Daubert* standard, (34) potential expert witnesses need to consider whether their testimony would be objective. Can the expert witness testify objectively based upon the facts, medical records, and the complete dossier of the patient without omitting anything? How can one evaluate whether or not his or her testimony is objective? The American Society of Anesthesiologists offers guidelines for impartiality. It suggests in its Guidelines for Expert Witness Qualifications and Testimony (32) that "(t)he ultimate test for accuracy and impartiality is a willingness to prepare testimony that could be presented unchanged for use by either the plaintiff or defendant" (32).

Objectivity also implies that evidence exists to support the testimony. Potential expert witnesses need to look for evidence in the literature that supports their position. If there is no evidence-based research to support their position, the Court will not allow their testimony, and, once again, they will look quite foolish. Treating pain practitioners, as well as expert witness pain practitioners, should prepare reports that incorporate evidence to support the validity and reliability of their assessments and the effectiveness of their interventions. If there is no evidence to back up their testimony, pain practitioners should decline to take the case and refer it to another professional.

In Mr. Monte's case, ironically, the evidence that he could perform the essential functions of his job came from the fact that he was doing it at the time the department demoted him. However, if asked to testify on his behalf, pain practitioners would need to prepare themselves to support their particular assessment methods of Mr. Monte with peer-reviewed literature generally accepted by the pain management community.

VERACITY

The next consideration in analyzing ethical stress involves veracity. This principle asks pain practitioners whether their testimony is truthful. Prior to providing testimony, all witnesses, both fact and expert witnesses, take an oath or affirmation to tell the truth. Pain practitioners who cannot tell the truth should not commit to accepting a case as an expert witness. The consequences of perjury, including the possibility of state disciplinary action, (63) the possible loss of one's license to practice, (42) the loss of one's reputation, and possible prosecution for criminal perjury, (64) are not worth any possible benefit one could gain from providing expert witness testimony.

CONSISTENCY

All witnesses should consider the consistency dilemma. Pain practitioners should consider all of the facts of the situation. If asked to change their testimony, they need to analyze time, context, technology, relevant case law, and RA for the work, the worker, and the workplace. Potential expert witnesses need to examine the context in which they will testify and determine whether or not the change in context or differing contexts justifies taking a different position or approach. If it does not, then the expert witness risks losing his or her own reputation and credibility. Should pain practitioners find that they must change their testimony without any acceptable justification, he or she should refer the case to another expert.

CONSEQUENCES

When asked to testify in a case, potential experts should ask themselves, "what are the consequences of my testimony?" Those consequences can affect the person with chronic pain and his or her family, the employer, or the expert witness. After a thorough examination of the potential consequences, pain practitioners must decide whether or not they will take on a case in light of those consequences. For example, if asked to testify about something not supported by the literature, the potential expert can find his or her reputation negatively affected. Some of the consequences to those who experience chronic pain are outlined above. Should pain practitioners decide they do not like the consequence of their potential testimony, they should refer the case to another expert.

PERSONAL

Potential expert witnesses need to explore their own morals and beliefs with regard to the potential testimony they are contemplating. They should ask themselves two questions: "How do I feel about my testimony?" and "How do my moral and ethical beliefs affect this situation?" If, after exploring these questions, pain practitioners find their stress meters rising, they may want to refer the case to another expert.

MENTORS

Deciding whether or not to accept, an expert witness commitment can be a daunting undertaking. Pain practitioners who find themselves deciding whether or not to take a case may struggle long and hard to make a decision, and may have difficulty deciding whether they are doing the right thing. A mentor can provide invaluable assistance in decision making during this process, and pain practitioners may want to seek a mentor with whom they can establish a relationship, should these occasions arise.

CONCLUSION

Pain practitioners who find themselves involved in presenting professional testimony need to familiarize themselves with the ethical ramifications of their actions. They need to study their professional society's code of ethics and related policies. Preparing in advance and basing practice and testimony on the most current available evidence can help pain practitioners avoid ethical stresses. The system presented here is designed to help pain practitioners decide whether or not to take on the role of expert witness, and will hopefully assist with making role choices in the medicolegal arena.

REFERENCES

1. Americans With Disabilities Act, Title I Regulations. 29 C.F.R. §1630.1 et. seq. ; (1992).
2. If this hypothetical agency were a state agency, the ADA would not apply because state employees are no longer covered by the ADA under.
3. Florida Workers' Compensation Law Fl. Stat. § 440.01 et. seq. (2005).
4. Americans With Disabilities Act, 42, *See Alabama v. Garnett*, 531 US 356 (2001).
5. Kornblau BL. 1999.
6. Prosser WL. Law of Torts. 4th ed. St. Paul, MN: West Publishing Company, 1971.
7. 29 C.F.R. § 1630.2(g)(1).
8. 29 C.F.R. § 1630.2(g)(2).
9. 29 C.F.R.§ 1630.2(g)(3).

10. 29 C.F.R. § 1630.2(m).
11. 29 C.F.R. § 1630.1 et. seq.
12. 20 C.F.R. §404.1525 through §404.1575.
13. American Psychological Association. APA's ethical principles of psychologists and code of conduct. 2002; http://www.apa.org/ethics/code2002.html. Accessed February 20, 2006.
14. American Medical Association. American Medical Association Expert Witness Affirmation Statement. December 6, 2004; http://www.ama-assn.org/ama1/pub/upload/mm/465/bot8fin.doc. Accessed February 24, 2006.
15. American Podiatric Medical Association. APMA code of ethics. April 2005; http://www.apma.org/s_apma/bin.asp? TrackID=&SID=1&DID=8951&CID=171&VID=2&DOC=File. PDF. Accessed February 20, 2006.
16. American Academy of Otolaryngology-Head and Neck Surgery. Code of ethics. June 7, 2003; http://www.entlink.net/academy/policies/ethics.cfm. Accessed February 19, 2006.
17. American Academy of Ophthalmology. Code of ethics. http://www.aao.org/aao/member/ethics/code_ethics.cfm. Accessed February 18, 2006.
18. American College of Surgeons. (ST-8) Statement on the physician acting as an expert witness. March 2004; http://www.facs.org/fellows_info/statements/st-8.html. Accessed February 23, 2006.
19. American Academy of Physician Assistants. Guidelines for Ethical Conduct for the Physician Assistant Profession. June 2004; www.aapa.org/gandp/ethical-guidelines.pdf Accessed February 22, 2006.
20. American College of Emergency Physicians (ACEP). Expert witness guidelines for the specialty of emergency medicine. August 2000; http://www.acep.org/webportal/PracticeResources/PolicyStatements/ethics/emexpwitnessguidelines.htm. Accessed February 22, 2006.
21. American Dental Association. Principles of ethics and code of professional conduct. January 2005; www.ada.org/prof/prac/law/code/ada_code.pdf. Accessed February 22, 2006.
22. American Association of Neurological Surgeons. American association of neurological surgeons code of ethics. December, 2004; http://www.aans.org/about/aanscodeofethics_12_04.pdf. Accessed February 20, 2006.
23. American College of Obstetrics and Gynecology. Expert testimony. January 2004; www.acog.org/from_home/publications/ethics/ethics116.pdf. Accessed February 20, 2006.
24. Williams MA, Mackin GA, Beresford HR, et al. American academy of neurology qualifications and guidelines for the physician expert witness. Neurology 2006; 66:13–14..
25. American Chiropractic Association. Code of ethics. unknown; http://www.acatoday.com/about/ethics.shtml Accessed February 20, 2006.
26. International Association of Rehabilitation Professionals (IARP). IARP code of ethics, standards of practice, and competencies. March 2005; http://www.rehabpro.org/IARPCodesStandardsCompetencies.doc. Accessed February 22, 2006.
27. American Academy of Psychiatry and the Law. American Academy of Psychiatry and the Law Ethical Guidelines for the Practice of Forensic Psychiatry. November 19, 1996; American Academy of Psychiatry and the Law Ethical Guidelines for the Practice of Forensic Psychiatry. Accessed February 19, 2006.
28. American College of Occupational and Environmental Medicine (ACOEM). Ethical guidelines for occupational and environmental medicine expert witnesses. Unknown;http://www.acoem.org/position/statements.asp?CATA_ID=31. Accessed February 22, 2006.
29. American Academy of Physical Medicine and Rehabilitation. AAPM and R code of conduct. http://www.aapmr.org/academy/codea.htm. Accessed February 20, 2006.
30. American Society of Plastic Surgeons. Code of ethics. July 18, 2005; http://www.ama-assn.org/ama/pub/category/13354.html. Accessed February 22, 2006.
31. American Academy of Pain Medicine. Ethics charter from American Academy of Pain Medicine. Pain Med 2005; 6(3):203–212.
32. American Society of Anesthesiologists. Guidelines for Expert Witness Qualifications and Testimony. October 15, 2003; www.asahq.org/publications And Services/standards/07.pdf Accessed February 20, 2006.

33. American Academy of Orthopaedic Surgeons. Advisory statement orthopaedic medical testimony. April 2005; http://www.aaos.org/wordhtml/papers/advistmt/1006.htm. Accessed February 22, 2006.
34. *Daubert v. Merrell Dow Pharmaceuticals,* 509 U.S. 579 (1993).
35. *Fed. Rule Evid.* Rule 104(a).
36. *Fed. Rule Evid.* Rule 702.
37. *Black v. Food Lion,* 171 F.3d. 308 (5th Cir. 1999).
38. Kafka C, Johnson MT, Cecil JS, Miletich D. Judge and attorney experiences, practices, and concerns regarding expert testimony in federal civil trials. Psychol Pub Policy Law 2002; 8(3):309–332.
39. Kulich RJ, Driscoll S, Scrivoni SJ. A survey of medico-legal practice patterns among pain specialists. Pain Med 2004; 6(1):98–103.
40. Beauchamp TC, Childress JF. Principles of Biomedical Ethics. New York: Oxford University Press; 1994.
41. *Tarasoff v. Regents of University of California,* 17 Cal. 3d 425, 551 P.2d 334, 131 Cal. Rptr. 14; (Cal. 1976).
42. Cohen F. The expert medical witness in legal perspective. J Leg Med 2004; 25:185–209.
43. *Austin v. American Association of Neurological Surgeons,* 253 F.3d 967 (7th Cir. 2001).
44. Feder H. Ethical lapses by expert witnesses: dirty dozen. Expert Witness. 1999; 11(1):1.
45. *Cleveland v. Policy Management Systems Corp.,* 526 U.S. 795; (1999).
46. American Academy of Ophthalmology. Understanding Rule 16 of the Academy's Code of Ethics. http://www.aao.org/aao/member/ethics/articles.cfm. Accessed February 19, 2006.
47. Beresford HR, Williams MA, Sagsveen MG. The neurologist as expert witness. Neurology. 2006; 66:1.
48. American College of Surgeons. Expert Witness Affirmation. http://www.facs.org/education/ethics/index.html#ewa. Accessed February 23, 2006.
49. American Academy of Orthopaedic Surgeons. Expert witness affirmation statement. http://www6.aaos.org/expwit/statement.htm. Accessed February 22, 2006.
50. American Academy of Ophthalmology. Expert Witness Affirmation. November 17, 2006; http://www.aao.org/aao/member/ethics/articles.cfm. Accessed February 23, 2006.
51. American Pharmacists Association. Code of ethics for pharmacists. October 27, 1994; www.aphanet.org/pharmcare/ethics.html. Accessed February 20, 2006.
52. American Osteopathic Association. Code of ethics. http://www.do-online.osteotech.org/index.cfm?PageID=aoa_ethics. Accessed February 20, 2006.
53. American Occupational Therapy Association (AOTA). Occupational therapy code of ethics. http://www.aota.org/general/docs/ethicscode05.pdf. Accessed February 20, 2006.
54. American Academy of Pain Management. American academy of pain management code of ethics. 2002; www.aapainmanage.org/literature/Forms/CodeOfEthics.pdf. Accessed February 20, 2006.
55. National Association of Social Workers. Code of ethics of the national association of social workers. 1999; http://www.socialworkers.org/pubs/code/code.asp. Accessed February 20, 2006.
56. American College of Rheumatology. Code of ethics. unknown; http://www.rheumatology.org/about/codeofethics/II.asp?aud=mem. Accessed February 20, 2006.
57. Waddell G, McCulloch JA, Kummel E, Venner RM. Nonorganic physical signs in low-back pain. Spine. 1980; 5:117–125.
58. Kulich RJ, Driscoll J, Prescott JC, et al. The *Daubert* standard, a primer for pain specialists. Pain Med 2003; 4(1):75–80.
59. Fishbain D, Cole B, Cutler RB, et al. A structured evidence-based review on the meaning of nonorganic physical signs: Waddell signs. Pain Med 2003; 4(2):141–181.
60. Fishbain D, Cutler RB, Rosomoff HL, Rosomoff RS. Is these a relationship between nonorganic physical findings (Waddell signs) and secondary gain/malingering? Clin J Pain 2004; 20(6):399–408.
61. American Psychiatric Association. Diagnostic and statistical manual of mental disorders-fourth edition (DSM-IV). Washington D.C.: American Psychiatric Association, 1994.

62. American Academy of Orthopedic Surgeons. Standards of professionalism orthopaedic expert witness testimony. April 18, 2005; http://www.aaos.org/wordhtml/assoc/ewtestimony.pdf Accessed February 20, 2006.
63. Office of the Attorney General State of California. Opinion of the Bill Lockyer, Attorney General. http://www.calphys.org/assets/applets/ag_opinion_052004.pdf.
64. *Shumsky v. Chein*, 373 F.3d. 978 (9th Cir. 2004).

15 Ethical Issues in the Psychological Assessment of Chronic Pain Patients

C. David Tollison
Carolina Center for Advanced Management of Pain, Greenville, South Carolina, U.S.A.

Donald W. Hinnant
Carolina Center for Advanced Management of Pain, Asheville, North Carolina, U.S.A.

"Ethics is the study of those assumptions held by individuals, institutions, organizations, and professions that they believe will assist them in distinguishing between right and wrong and, ultimately, in making sound moral judgment" (1).

To consider qualities of an ethical person is different from considering the qualities of an ethical health professional involved in the assessment of patients in pain. While "knowing right from wrong," "doing the right thing," and "acting morally" are traits we might attribute to an ethical person, none of these qualities are adequate to describe our professional role. All miss an essential element: our professional role as health professionals assessing and treating chronic pain patients.

The assessment of pain—judged against the highest standards of clinical effectiveness and professional responsibility—is an interdisciplinary endeavor. Physicians, psychologists, nurses, physical therapists, occupational therapists, vocational therapists, and others contribute valuable expertise that, collectively, forms the clinical and scientific foundations of pain management. In the assessment and treatment of the chronic pain patient, we aspire to combine knowledge from various disciplines into a unified identification and appreciation of the multidimensional factors influencing chronic pain. Yet despite our adherence to an interdisciplinary clinical philosophy, each discipline ultimately remains responsible to a specific professional licensing board and, consequently, subject to explicit legal statutes.

In addition to discipline-specific practice and legal mandates, each health care discipline also has its own code of ethics. The reason for this stems from professional role. The relationship of psychologists to patients, for example, differs from the relationship that physicians, nurses, physical therapists, and other health professionals have with their patients. Because our role is central in determining the ethics of a profession, different health professionals have distinct codes of ethics, and being an ethical health professional differs from being an ethical person.

While numerous disciplines are involved in pain management each has its own codes of ethics and, to our knowledge, there does not exist a magnum opus of ethics specific to the discipline of pain management. While organizations such as the American Academy of Pain Management and the American Pain Society endorse generalized codes of professional ethics, each discipline in these organizations remains primarily responsible to its professional board or licensing authority. In contrast, the American Academy of Pain Medicine has developed a Code of Ethics specific to pain medicine (2). Membership in this organization, however, is restricted to physicians who continue to be held primarily responsible by state medical licensing boards.

Examination of ethical issues in the assessment of chronic pain patients must include the rules that govern our behavior as well as the process by which we apply those rules in our professional lives. Both ethical rules and decision-making processes deserve special attention, study, and adherence. This is a responsibility we have to our chosen profession of pain management. Moreover, as pain professionals, this is a critical responsibility that each of us has to our patients in pain.

In this chapter, we will discuss selected aspects of professional ethics in relationship to the psychological assessment of chronic pain patients. The American Psychological Association's (APA's) Ethical Principles of Psychologists and Code of Conduct (3) will be used as a reference. After five years, seven drafts, and a series of public comment periods, the current Ethical Principles of Psychologists and Code of Conduct (hereinafter referred to as the Ethics Code) became effective on June 1, 2002. It is noteworthy that lack of awareness or misunderstanding of an Ethical Standard is not itself a defense to a charge of unethical conduct. While selected aspects of the Ethics Code will be discussed in this chapter, psychologists are strongly encouraged to study the entire Ethics Code and be consistently guided by all appropriate professional standards.

APPLICABILITY OF THE ETHICS CODE

Application of the Ethics Code is restricted in the introduction to psychologists' activities that are part of their scientific, educational, or professional roles as psychologists. Furthermore, the introduction identifies application of the Ethics Code to areas "including but not limited to clinical, counseling, and school psychology practice; research, teaching, supervision of trainees, public service, policy development, social intervention, development of assessment instruments, conducting assessments, educational counseling, organizational consulting, forensic activities, program design and evaluation, and administration" (3).

Applicability of the Ethics Code is an increasingly frequent topic of discussion and growing debate among psychologists, particularly among psychologists working in health care settings such as hospitals or in private clinical practices with physician partners. The most frequently voiced question seems to be: how truly meaningful and equitable is the Ethics Code, given that it purports to govern fairly the behavior of psychologists within widely diverse practice specialties involved in markedly dissimilar professional activities? Simply stated, if specific Standards of the Ethics Code are applicable, for example, to a clinical pain psychologist, is it probable or even possible that the same Code is applicable to a school psychologist testing children or to psychology educators or administrators?

Opponents argue that the science and practice of psychology have grown beyond the "one size fits all" foundation of the current Ethics Code. Psychologists point to expanded professional opportunities beyond traditional academia and mental hospitals, particularly in multiple and innovative areas of health care delivery.

Proponents typically argue that we are all psychologists, first and foremost, and that the growing number of diverse professional opportunities for psychological practice remains secondary to our primary identification and responsibility as psychologists. Consequently, proponents generally agree with the APA that Ethics Code Standards are broadly written, in order to apply to psychologists in varied roles.

Although both opponents and proponents of the Ethics Code argue persuasively, there should be no mistake that application of the current Code remains firmly in force. Ethics Standards are, in fact, enforceable rules for governing the conduct of psychologists that are applied by APA and by other bodies that choose to adopt them (e.g., state licensing boards). Moreover, stated restriction of the Ethics Code only to "professional" activities of psychologists actually provides little in the way of defense against personal conduct violation. While the APA contends that this restriction is intended to distinguish professional activities from the personal and private lives of psychologists, which are not within the purview of the Ethics Code, any psychologist whose personal and private behavior results in conviction of a felony will quickly determine that the psychologist's behavior— although personal and private—also results in violation of the Ethics Code.

A less antagonistic yet equally ambiguous situation involving application of the Ethics Code and the stated differentiation between professional and personal behaviors occurs when a psychologist, as a private citizen, makes some comment or offers professional opinion regarding, for instance, an issue regarding pain or psychological functioning in which the psychologist has not been professionally involved. The potential and obvious threat is that an individual may consider such comment as professional psychological opinion. Statutes governing the behavior of physicians refer to this error because failure to establish a doctor–patient relationship and the intent of this mandate applies to psychologists as well.

Example

A psychologist was approached at a social function by an individual discussing about husband's recurrent headaches. The individual explained to the psychologist that the husband had undergone several medical tests and that, thus far, no etiology had been determined to explain the husband's subjective complaints. The psychologist suggested that pain complaints may be psychologically influenced, particularly in the absence of a nociceptive etiology, and recommended that the individual attempt to extinguish the husband's complaints through ignoring pain statements and reinforcing well behaviors. The husband was ultimately determined to have malignant tumor, required neurosurgical intervention, was left with residual hemiparesis, and a complaint was ultimately filed against the psychologist.

It was claimed that the psychologist was not working as a psychologist, nor did the psychologist have a professional relationship with the defendant or the defendant's wife. The psychologist maintained that the opinion and suggestion resulted from the psychologist's private, nonprofessional role and, therefore, the behavior was outside the scope of the Ethics Code.

While the psychologist may be technically correct, this behavior is highly questionable in terms of its impact on the defendant as well as the assertion that it had nothing to do with the psychologist's professional-related activities. It is strongly recommended that psychologists avoid personal behavior that would be questionably ethical were it part of their professional activities and expect to evade responsibility for their actions by claiming that it was done as part of their private, rather than professional lives.

ETHICS AND THE LAW

Historically, the general perception within the mental health community is that of major discrepancy between the actions and motivations of the legal system and the ethical principles and conduct code of psychologists. This perception may be acutely appreciated when a psychologist—as treating source for a patient involved in a personal injury or workers' compensation case—is afforded the opportunity to be legally deposed. However, a cursory survey of legal statutes and decisions suggests that similarities typically exceed potential conflicts. Unfortunately, discrepancies often are overly dramatized and occasionally serve to polarize the psychological and legal communities. However, implementation of the Health Insurance Portability and Accountability Act (HIPAA) and revisions in the 2002 Ethics Code further reduce the potential for legal–psychological conflict.

An area of periodic conflict in years past is the legal demand for discovery of a psychologist's records and raw test data. This demand occurs frequently in the assessment of pain patients due to the number of individuals suffering pain secondary to work-related or personal injury and, therefore, falling under workers' compensation statutes or actively involved in other forms of litigation.

The 2002 revised Ethics Code eliminates a prohibition in the earlier Code that prevents psychologists from releasing raw test data [e.g., P-3, Minnesota multiphasic personality inventory (MMPI), etc.] to individuals who are not qualified to use them. In fact, the current Code mandates release of test data to patients and their designees (e.g., attorneys) with written permission of the patient (3). While concerns of psychologists center on protection of confidentiality, the current Ethics Code waives the confidentiality privilege upon written agreement of the patient.

The Ethics Code also stipulates that, in the absence of a patient release of information, psychologists provide test data only as required by law or court order (3). Workers' compensation laws, for example, vary by state. In the state in which the authors practice, state law mandates release of information to all "parties with interest" in a workers' compensation legal case. Consequently, a subpoena for records, including raw test data, may be legally issued by the patients' attorneys as well as attorneys representing all defendants.

The current Ethics Code does permit psychologists to withhold test data to protect the patient from "substantial harm or misuse or misinterpretation of the data or the test" (3). However, it should be noted that HIPAA does not recognize the misuse or misinterpretation of data or psychological tests. Consequently, psychologists should exercise particular caution in such situations.

Unfortunately, interpretation of the standard permitting psychologists to withhold test data when release can potentially result in harm creates recurrent difficulty for the clinical pain psychologist treating patients involved in litigation. For example, it is generally accepted that pain patients often have MMPI profiles with elevations in scales 1 and 3 (4). For psychologists trained and experienced in pain, this test profile may be interpreted to reflect deterioration in coping skills and adaptive behaviors secondary to pain intensity, duration, and lifestyle. However, release of raw test data to a defendant's attorney who, in turn, releases the data with request for a second opinion to a clinical psychologist inexperienced in pain may result in a completely different test interpretation (e.g., conversion disorder, magnification, etc.), thereby resulting in harm to the patient as a result of "misinterpretation of the data or the test."

The Ethics Code does not require psychologists to break the law. Therefore, when confronted with an ethical dilemma the pain psychologist should first attempt to informally resolve the matter, for example, with appropriate consent or negotiating with all parties the release of test data to another psychologist trained and experienced in pain. Failing attempts to informally resolve the conflict, the psychologist may file a Motion for Protective Order, explaining in a formal manner the same issues previously discussed informally. Once the Motion has been filed, an evidentiary hearing will be convened by a judge to hear arguments on the merits of the two positions. If the Court orders the pain psychologist to release the record, the psychologist must do so. There is no ethical conflict in following a lawful Court Order.

BOUNDARIES AND MAINTENANCE OF COMPETENCE

Standard 2.01(a) of the Ethical Code mandates that psychologists provide services "with populations and in areas only within the boundaries of their competence, based on their education, training, supervised experience, consultation, study, or professional experience" (3). This Standard is considered particularly relevant for psychologists performing assessments and practicing with a population of chronic pain patients.

Most clinical psychologists were trained in traditional psychology graduate programs emphasizing the core curriculum required for APA program accreditation. With exception of hospital-based internship experiences selected by a percentage of doctoral-level students, most practicing psychologists completed clinical training with minimal experience with patients in pain. In fact, although clinical training does appear to be changing with development of behavioral medicine curriculums and with training in health psychology and psychopharmacology, most currently practicing clinical psychologists completed training with little experience in working as part of an interdisciplinary team with physicians, physical therapists, nurses, and other health professionals.

The psychological assessment and treatment of patients in pain is a challenging specialty within psychology. As such, competence in pain management requires specialized education, training, and supervised experience that are markedly beyond the core competencies of general clinical psychology. Simply stated, competence and experience in clinical psychology does not translate into competence in pain management. Consequently, it is of consistent ethical and clinical concern to the authors that a number of psychologists—without appropriate education and supervised training and experience—elect at various points within their professional careers to expand their clinical practice by assessing and treating patients in pain. It is worthy of reiteration that a doctoral degree in clinical psychology and years of experience in working with either children or adults with depression, neuropsychological disorders, anxiety, or other psychological disorders does not translate to competence in the assessment and treatment of patients in pain. To ignore this is to violate the Ethical Code.

The Ethical Code does, however, provide a mechanism for entering the practice of pain management. Standard 2.01(c) provides that "psychologists planning to provide services, teach, or conduct research involving populations, areas, techniques, or technologies new to them undertake relevant education, training, supervised experience, consultation, or study" (3).

In the practice of clinical pain psychology, it is insufficient to merely establish competence in the assessment and treatment of patients in pain. Standard 2.03 of the Ethical Code mandates that psychologists also undertake efforts to maintain competence. It should be noted that satisfying state licensing board requirements for continuing education in psychology does not satisfy the ethical requirement of maintaining competence in pain management. In addition to continuing education licensing requirements, the ethical pain psychologist—in order to maintain competence as a clinical pain psychologist—will participate in conferences and other continuing education offerings specific to the psychological assessment and treatment of pain. Such education should include knowledge of current scientific and professional information, current developments in psychological assessment instruments used with pain patients, normative data regarding the applications of psychological testing with pain patients, and guidelines governing a competent psychological pain assessment.

Example

An ethical complaint was filed against a psychologist who had conducted a psychological pain assessment of a patient presenting with a primary complaint of chronic benign pain. An investigation revealed that the psychologist, for over 20 years, had been in private practice with letterhead indicating competence in "psychological disorders of children and adults, including attention-deficit hyperactivity disorders, phobias, enuresis, depression, death and mourning, marital discord, sexual dysfunctions, anxiety disorder, and consultation to businesses and industries." The investigation further revealed that, approximately one year prior to the ethical complaint, a mailing had been distributed to physicians in the community announcing that the psychologist was accepting patients for assessment and treatment of pain. Other than attendance at a one day symposium on pain, the psychologist was determined to have no specialized education, training, or supervised experience in the assessment of pain. The psychologist was determined to be in violation of the Ethical Code.

INFORMED CONSENT

Ethical Code Standard 3.10 explains that psychologists may not conduct research or provide assessment, therapy, counseling, or consulting services in person or via electronic transmission or other forms of communication, without first obtaining the informed consent of the individual. Furthermore, the consent must use language that is reasonably understandable to that person. In addition, Standard 9.03 specifically addresses informed consent in psychological assessments and mandates the written consent of patients participating in psychological assessments, evaluations, or diagnostic services, except when testing is mandated by law or governmental regulations (3).

The issue of informed consent is particularly relevant to the practice of clinical pain psychology as a result of the nature of our professional practice. It is common for clinical pain psychologists to be requested to perform assessments by attorneys, long-term disability and workers' compensation insurance companies, workers' compensation commissions, personal injury courts, and administrative law agencies such as the Social Security Administration. Informed consent must include an explanation of the nature and purpose of the assessment, fees, involvement of third parties, and limits of confidentiality, as well as sufficient opportunity for the patient to ask questions and receive answers.

At the practical level, it is imperative that patients be informed that the pain psychologist has only limited control over release of the assessment document. The patient may provide informed consent for release of the assessment to a referring physician, for example, but the referring physician potentially may—without knowledge of the pain psychologist or patient—in turn release the assessment to another physician or insurance company. Furthermore, in cases involving litigation, the lack of confidentiality must be particularly emphasized to the patient.

A special issue of informed consent involves the use of language interpreters. The growing number of foreign natives with no or limited English proficiency positions this issue as an increasing challenge to all psychologists but, perhaps, even more so to the clinical pain psychologist. Pain is often the product of traumatic injury, and statistics indicate that more injuries occur in labor-intensive occupations (5). Given that many non–English-speaking individuals are obviously prohibited by language barriers from upper level vocations and, by necessity, gravitate as a group to labor-intensive work, we can expect to see an increasing number of non–English-speaking patients with complaints of pain and psychological symptoms.

Pain psychologists using the services of an interpreter must obtain informed consent from the patient to use that interpreter, ensure that confidentiality of test results and test security are maintained, and include in their recommendations, reports, and diagnostic or evaluative statements, including forensic testimony, discussion of any limitations on the data obtained. Failure to do so may be determined to be in violation of Standard 9.03(c) (3). In addition, the chapter authors elect to require the interpreter to sign a confidentiality statement prior to the clinical assessment. The confidentiality statement is intended to protect the patient from disclosure of information learned by the interpreter during the course of the psychological assessment. Copies of the endorsed confidentiality statement are distributed to the patient, interpreter, referring source, and maintained as part of the patient's record.

Example

A psychologist was charged with an ethical violation for failure to obtain a signed consent for psychological assessment by a patient referred by the court system for psychological assessment.

The psychologist defended that an attempt was made to obtain a signed consent, but that the patient refused to execute the document. The psychologist also explained that, upon refusal to sign the consent, both the nature and the purpose of the psychological assessment were verbally explained using language understandable by the patient, and the psychologist had provided the patient sufficient opportunity to ask any and all questions and was fully prepared to answer all questions before proceeding with the assessment. It was reported that the patient offered no questions, despite encouragement.

The psychologist was absolved of any ethical violation. Standard 9.03(b) cites that "psychologists inform persons with questionable capacity to consent or for whom testing is mandated by law or government regulations about the nature and purpose of the proposed assessment services, using language that is reasonably understandable to the person being assessed" (3).

THIRD-PARTY REQUESTS FOR PAIN ASSESSMENT

As previously discussed, it is the nature of the practice of pain psychology that requests will be made for clinical assessment by a variety of third parties. This referral situation requires special efforts on the part of the pain psychologist to clarify at the outset of the clinical service the nature of the relationship with all individuals involved (Ethics Code 3.07). This clarification includes the role of the psychologist (e.g., diagnostician, therapist, consultant, or expert witness), an identification of who is the client, the probable uses of the psychological services provided or the information obtained, and the fact that there may be limits to confidentiality (3). In regard to identifying who is the client, the chapter authors prefer to establish the referring source as the client. For example, when a pain patient is referred for psychological evaluation by an attorney representing the patient, financial arrangements are discussed with the attorney who is billed for professional services rendered. This policy helps in establishing the referring attorney as the client. Obviously, we then clarify to the patient that the patient's attorney is the client, explain the fees involved in the clinical assessment, and notify the patient that the attorney (client) will be billed for services rendered.

Ethics Code 4.02 deserves special consideration. It is imperative that limits regarding confidentiality be discussed with the pain patient (3). This situation is especially important when the patient presenting for psychological assessment is involved in litigation and, furthermore, also relates to our previous discussion of informed consent.

Consider the situation in which a defense attorney representing an employer and workers' compensation insurance company refers a pain patient for psychological assessment. Further consider that the clinical pain psychologist reaches a professional opinion that is not favorable to the defense attorney. There are some states that allow an unfavorable professional opinion rendered by an expert to be withheld from submission based on legal protections incorporated in attorney–client privilege. Conversely, there have been legal rulings in other states that once the defense raises a psychiatric issue or a mental health defense, the defendant has essentially waived attorney–client privilege and results of the clinical assessment must be made available to all parties (6). What could conceivably happen under these circumstances is that a psychologist, originally retained by the defense, may render a clinical opinion unfavorable to the defense and, then, could be subsequently subpoenaed and compelled to testify as a witness for the plaintiff. Clearly, this scenario and similar others seriously threaten confidentiality. Consequently, pain psychologists should be knowledgeable of applicable law in the state or Federal jurisdiction in which the psychologist practices. Once this legal knowledge is obtained, the pain psychologist can then incorporate it into both a verbal explanation to the patient and a written informed consent document.

Example

"You have been referred to me by your attorney for psychological assessment. You should understand that you are not my patient; your attorney is my client. I will be charging your attorney for my services today and your attorney will be paying. However, you should discuss finances with your attorney because she may, in turn, later bill you for the cost of this assessment as part of her expenses in developing your case. That is between you and your attorney. My role today is to perform a psychological evaluation and it is likely that your attorney may submit my report into evidence as part of your workers' compensation case. And since you are not my patient and my role is restricted to assessment, and since you are involved in a legal matter, you do not have confidentiality protection. Therefore, anything you say to me as well as my clinical opinions may be incorporated into my report. Furthermore, my report may be reviewed by attorneys representing the other side, judges, insurance company personnel, and others. In addition, portions or even the entire report may be discussed at your hearing or trial and anyone in attendance or later reading the trial transcript may have access to information on you contained in my report. It is also possible that I could be subpoenaed to appear in court to answer questions from your lawyer, lawyers for the other side, or the judge regarding my assessment of you today. Certainly it is your choice whether you wish to proceed with this assessment today but if you elect to continue, you should do so with full knowledge of all I have said. I am going to give you an informed consent form that details what I have said to you. You should read the document carefully. If you are in agreement and wish to proceed with the assessment, you must sign in the place designated. Now, please ask any questions you may have and do not sign the document until all questions have been answered to your full satisfaction."

An additional threat to ethical pain practice involves a pain psychologist employed by a third party. Both of the authors of this chapter have worked, in years past, providing pain assessment and treatment under employment contracts with hospitals. Although a common relationship in health care, the pain psychologist must be sensitive to the possibility of conflict between the Ethics Code and organizational demands. Ethics Code 1.01 mandates that if psychologists learn of misuse or misrepresentation of their work, they must take reasonable steps to correct or minimize the misuse or misrepresentation (3). Furthermore, Ethics Code 1.03 states that if the demands of an organization with which psychologists are affiliated or for whom they are working conflict with the Ethics Code, psychologists must clarify the nature of the conflict, make known their commitment to the Ethics Code, and to the extent feasible, resolve the conflict in a way that permits adherence to the Ethics Code (3).

Example

A clinical pain psychologist employed by a hospital pain service regularly received consultation requests for psychological assessment of hospitalized patients in pain. Consultation requests were routinely generated by attending physicians as well as hospital personnel including nurses, physical therapists, and others.

The pain psychologist ultimately learned that the hospital had incorporated a policy designed to relocate patients from both orthopedic and neurosciences units to a newly developed, less labor-intensive, and less expensive "step down" unit of the hospital, based on projected duration of required hospitalization. The psychologist also determined that a primary factor in the formula for identifying patients for "step down" relocation was psychological issues associated with primary complaints of pain. Upon questioning, the psychologist learned that information contained in the psychological reports was routinely used by hospital personnel— without permission or knowledge of the psychologist or patient—as the primary justification for relocating patients to the "step down" unit designed to save the hospital considerable money.

The pain psychologist was of the opinion that the actions of the employer represented a misuse of the psychologist's psychological work (Ethics Code 1.01) as well as a conflict between the psychologist's adherence to professional ethics and organizational demands (Ethics Code 1.03). The psychologist clarified the nature of the conflict and made known the commitment to the Ethics Code. Subsequently, the pain psychologist participated in a committee of hospital staff that developed bio-psychosocial criteria for identifying "step down" patients, with results of psychological assessment being only one of numerous factors considered in the decision.

ADEQUACY AND USE OF PAIN ASSESSMENT

The clinical value of thorough and competent psychological assessment of the patient in pain cannot be overly stated. Furthermore, assessment of patients must also be conducted with ethical considerations firmly in mind.

Ethics Standard 9.01(a) notes that psychologists base opinions contained in their recommendations, reports, and diagnostic or evaluative statements, including forensic testimony, on information and techniques sufficient to substantiate their findings (3). Obviously, this standard shares equal importance with requirements of competent clinical practice. Furthermore, Standard 9.01(b) discusses the importance of providing clinical assessment only after the psychologist has conducted an examination of the patient sufficient to support psychological statements or conclusions (3).

These two standards (9.01a and 9.01b) form the basis of psychological assessment: personal examination of the patient in pain and psychological diagnosis and treatment recommendations based on scientific research and clinical expertise. In addition, these two standards relate to our previous discussion of boundaries and maintenance of competence. It is difficult to imagine that a traditional clinical psychologist could continue to remain competent in the specialty of pain management while engaging in a general practice of psychology.

Example

A pain patient in psychological treatment was referred by the workers' compensation insurance company to another psychologist for consultative second opinion. The consulting psychologist failed to review treatment records and results of a P-3 (i.e., Pain Patient Profile) (7) psychological test, claiming that this information was not provided and further explaining that the treatment and psychological test data would not have been reviewed even if provided because it would have "biased" the psychologist's conclusions. The consulting psychologist did, however, review a copy of the initial psychological assessment and results of MMPI testing conducted as part of the initial assessment. Following a clinical interview, the consulting psychologist concluded that the patient was malingering.

This example clearly illustrates an inadequate basis for a conclusion of this magnitude, given the case involved pain and no psychological pain assessment was conducted. Conclusions reached by the consulting psychologist appear largely subjective and without scientific substantiation.

Because psychological evaluations including assessments of chronic pain patients, typically involve psychological testing, it is hardly surprising that professional ethics also address this aspect of our clinical practice. Standard 9.02 addresses several professional responsibilities related to psychological assessment. Ethics Code 9.02(a) states that "psychologists administer, adapt, score, interpret, or use assessment techniques, interviews, tests, or instruments in a manner and for purposes that are appropriate in light of the research on or evidence of the usefulness and proper application of the techniques" (3). We previously discussed that clinical interpretations of the MMPI, for example, will vary depending on patients' individual symptoms and situations. Consequently, MMPI interpretations in a population of pain patients should differ from interpretation of similar test profiles of patients from an outpatient mental health center or university counseling center (7). To adopt a universal "cookie cutter" psychological test interpretation philosophy that does not recognize interpretation based on research and clinical evidence is in violation of the Ethics Code.

The Ethics Code also mandates that psychologists use assessment instruments whose validity and reliability have been established for use with members of the population tested (3). This standard is particularly relevant for clinical pain psychologists, given the proliferation of psychological tests advertised for use in the assessment of pain patients. In fact, several analgesic pharmaceutical firms distribute without charge various surveys and inventories purported to assess psychological factors involved in pain and, to the best of our knowledge, these instruments have little if any studies of reliability and validity with pain populations.

While there are several very excellent psychological test instruments for use with pain patients, the authors of this chapter practice in a large nine-person pain practice that routinely uses the P-3 (i.e., Pain Patient Profile) (7) as part of initial patient assessments and for objective measurement of progress throughout treatment. Admittedly, the first author of this chapter is also the author of the P-3. Regardless, our partners share both clinical and ethical comfort in the knowledge of P-3 validity and reliability based on a national population of patients in pain.

Standard 9.08 provides an excellent illustration of how we use our background, training, and experience in psychology to close the gap between an ethical standard and clinical practice (3). Standard 9.08 consists of two clauses, both emphasizing usefulness of an assessment instrument as the determining criterion for selection (3). While this standard is sometimes mistakenly interpreted to mean that anything other than a test's current edition is obsolete—a rigid interpretation that leaves no room for professional judgment—the standard actually directs psychologists to determine what instrument is most appropriate for a given purpose. To make this determination in pain assessments, psychologists use their knowledge of a test's application, knowledge from psychological and pain training, and experience as a pain psychologist to adhere to Standard 9.08 and decide which test or version to use.

Example

A pain psychologist, in replying to an insurance company's letter of denial of charges submitted for psychological testing, described the MMPI as "a psychological magnetic resonance imaging" and further opined that the test "removes any controversy over truth versus magnification and helps to identify hidden and unconscious information that could have a significant impact on functioning."

Unfortunately, these statements exceed the bounds of any available research and, therefore, represent a violation of the Ethics Code.

ADVERTISING AND OTHER PUBLIC STATEMENTS

Section 5 of the Ethics Code deals with advertising and public statements. Public statements are defined in Code 5.01 as "paid or unpaid advertising, product endorsements, grant applications, licensing applications, other credentialing applications, brochures, printed matter, directory listings, personal resumes or curriculum vitae, or comments for use in media such as print or electronic transmission, statements in legal proceedings, lectures and public oral presentations, and published materials"

(3). Psychologists do not knowingly make public statements that are false, deceptive, or fraudulent concerning their research, practice, or other work activities or those of persons or organizations with which they are affiliated. Furthermore, psychologists are barred from making inaccurate statements regarding their training, experience, or competence, academic degrees, credentials, institutional or association affiliations, professional services, and publications and research findings. And finally, psychologists claim degrees as credentials for their health services only if those degrees were earned from a regionally accredited institution or were the basis for psychology licensure by the state in which they practice.

The reader is reminded that psychological assessments of pain patients often are conducted within an interdisciplinary clinical setting and that every health care discipline has its own unique ethical standards. Consequently, care must be taken that the pain psychologist, as member of a multidisciplinary group, is not "grouped" into clinic statements or clinic advertising that satisfies the ethical standards of other health professionals but violates the ethical standards of psychologists. For example, a physician and senior partner of an interdisciplinary private pain practice agreed to provide a testimonial recommending the manufacturer of a particular spinal cord stimulation system. The testimonial was part of a health care magazine advertisement paid for by the stimulator manufacturer. The printed testimonial identified the name and geographical location of the pain clinic and included the statement "My partners and I use the Brand X stimulator and we strongly recommend it as the most clinically useful and effective unit available." Unfortunately, three of the 12 clinic partners were pain psychologists who had no prior knowledge of the endorsement and who, obviously, did not implant spinal cord stimulators and who had no training, experience, or license to surgically implant stimulators. However, these psychologists—at least by reference—found themselves included in a printed testimonial advertisement that likely is ethically acceptable for physicians but, by nature of content, would be considered deceptive by psychologists' standards.

Related to the above illustration is the ethical mandate for psychologists to take reasonable steps to correct any mis-statement or misrepresentation made by others of psychologists' credentials, training, and expertise (3). The first author, having performed a psychological assessment on a patient, was subpoenaed to court in a case involving personal injury and residual pain. The patient's attorney, apparently in an effort to bolster the case and maximize clinical opinion contained in the report to jury members, read from the author's curriculum vitae, dramatically pausing upon reading of every vitae entry and asking the author "Is that correct?" The attorney then turned to the jury and offered the following summary: "Ladies and gentlemen, this doctor has practiced pain management since the nineteen-seventies, has written numerous books on diagnosing pain problems, is universally recognized as a grandfather in pain treatment, and probably knows more about pain than most anybody in the country!" Obviously, in an attempt to strengthen the case, the attorney falsely and deceptively characterized the author in a grossly magnified and totally unsupported manner. Consequently, at first opportunity, the first author attempted in a respectful manner to avoid ethical violation by stating, "If I may, it is my ethical responsibility to provide a different and, I believe, more accurate representation of myself as a clinical pain psychologist. While the flattering remarks of counsel are recognized, I hope that the record will reflect that it is improbable—highly improbable—that I know more about pain than most anybody in the country. In fact, there are many, many pain psychologists who are universally recognized as highly qualified, experienced, and in whom I have the utmost confidence and respect. And as far as counsel's characterization of me as a pain grandfather, I doubt that anyone in this courtroom takes professional credit for merely growing older."

The current popularity of psychological-based help and advice is evidenced in television programming (e.g., Dr. Phil, Dr. Joyce Brothers, Dr. Dyer, etc.), psychological health columns in newspapers, radio programming, and Internet offerings. Likewise, the growing interest in pain affords increasing opportunities for pain psychologists to participate in media presentations.

Be cautioned that Ethics Code 5.04 addresses media presentations and warns that when psychologists provide public advice or comment via print, Internet, or other electronic transmission, they take precautions to ensure that statements are based on their professional knowledge, training, or experience in accordance with appropriate psychological literature and practice (3). Furthermore, it is imperative that psychologists participating in media presentations do not imply or indicate that a professional relationship has been established with the recipient.

Example

A pain psychologist who functioned as the managing partner of a five-person clinical pain practice developed and distributed to members of the medical community, area workers' compensation and personal injury attorneys, and selected insurance companies a letter advertising clinical services in pain assessment and psychological treatment. The letter identified each professional with the title "Doctor" preceding the person's name and further characterized the group as "Caring and experienced Doctors specializing in the psychological aspects of pain." Furthermore, the letter included a glowing testimonial from a pain patient. A charge of ethical violation was filed.

Upon investigation, it was determined that two of the five professionals held doctoral degrees from correspondence institutions with no regional accreditation. Neither of these individuals was licensed to practice psychology. Furthermore, one of the three licensed psychologists had no training or experience in pain and, in fact, had completed educational training and licensing requirements—with primary education and internship training in child psychology—less than two months prior to distribution of the letter. Finally, it was determined that the testimonial advertisement was solicited from a patient currently involved in treatment. Obviously, this solicitation establishes a strong potential for vulnerability to undue influence.

RELATIONSHIP TO OTHER PROFESSIONALS

Pain psychology—perhaps more than any other psychological specialty—offers opportunities for regular interaction and cooperation with health professionals representing a variety of clinical and academic disciplines. In fact, as previously discussed, interdisciplinary practice is considered by most authorities as the pinnacle of pain management effectiveness and professionalism. Many pain psychologists clinically practice on a daily basis with physicians of various specialties, nurses, physical therapists, vocational specialists, and others. Although each professional functions in accordance with core discipline training—with the pain psychologist typically contributing expertise in assessment, psychotropic medication recommendations, and psychological treatment—members primarily function as a "pain team," sharing information and collectively addressing the physical, psychological, and psychosocial needs of the patient in pain.

Ethics Code 3.09 encourages cooperation with other professionals by stating that, when indicated and professionally appropriate, psychologists cooperate with other professionals in order to effectively and appropriately serve their patients (3). However, a word of caution is warranted. Ethics Code 4.05 mandates that psychologists may disclose confidential information only with appropriate consent of the patient (unless prohibited by law) (3). Consequently, pain psychologists interacting with other professionals—either one-to-one or as part of an interdisciplinary pain team—must obtain appropriate consent before confidential information is shared.

Example

A pain psychologist, obtaining a vocational history as part of a psychological pain assessment, was informed by the patient of previous work experience as an exotic dancer, several years prior, at an area nightclub. Subsequent to the work experience, the patient had graduated from college and held several highly responsible positions in both education and business. The psychologist, participating in an informal staff discussion of the office Christmas party, suggested, "Maybe we could get (patient name). We're searching for entertainment and she used to be a stripper."

In addition to violating perhaps every imaginable yardstick of appropriateness, the psychologist's disclosure also violated the professional Ethics Code. The psychologist, in an inappropriate and failed attempt at humor, disclosed information that was not indicated and appropriate, had no bearing on the clinical condition or treatment of the psychologist's condition, and was released without consent of the patient.

A special situation involving relationships with other health professionals often challenges pain psychologists who are requested by patients or third parties to perform psychological assessments or second opinions on patients currently receiving psychological services provided by other professionals. Ethics Code 10.04 warns the psychologist to proceed with caution and sensitivity to the relevant issues and carefully consider the patient's welfare. The psychologist should discuss these issues with the patient and also should consult with the other service provider prior to the assessment in order to minimize potential confusion and conflict (3).

RESOLUTION OF ETHICAL ISSUES

The Ethics Code is intended to provide guidance for psychologists and standards of professional conduct (3). However, despite the best intentions and efforts of pain psychologists to strictly adhere to the Ethics Code, both questionable and obvious violations do occur. It is incumbent upon the pain psychologist with knowledge of either questionable or obvious violation of personal professional behavior to take appropriate action to resolve ethical issues. When psychologists believe that there may have been an ethical violation by another psychologist, they attempt to resolve the issue by bringing it to the attention of that professional. However, if an ethical violation has substantially harmed or is likely to harm a patient and is not resolved through notification of the offending professional, psychologists take further action appropriate to the situation. Such action might include referral to state or national committees on professional ethics, to state licensing boards, or to the appropriate institutional authorities. However, this mandate does not apply when such reporting would violate the confidentiality of patients.

Given the potential legal and professional repercussions involved in reporting a colleague to authorities, it is recommended that psychologists proceed in this endeavor with particular caution and seek consultation from other psychologists. Ethics Code 1.07 attempts to discourage improper ethical complaints against psychologists by placing a burden of responsibility on the reporting psychologist. A psychologist reporting another psychologist must accept professional responsibility for reckless disregard for or willful ignorance of facts that would disprove the allegation (3). Consequently, the potential exists for a backlash or rebound effect and a psychologist who reports another psychologist for ethics violation may unexpectedly find to subsequently become the target of ethics charges.

Example

A clinical pain psychologist employed by a medical university was reported to the state licensing board for a possible ethical violation by an associate faculty psychologist who did not treat pain. The state licensing board launched an investigation and the pain psychologist, after almost one year, was absolved of any violation. Several months later, the pain psychologist applied for academic promotion and the application was ultimately rejected. The psychologist who had filed ethical charges also served on the promotions committee that rejected the pain psychologist's application.

The pain psychologist maintained that the reporting psychologist did not attempt to notify the pain psychologist of ethical concerns, did not attempt an informal resolution of ethical concerns, and disregarded information that would have disproved the allegation. Furthermore, under Freedom of Information, the pain psychologist obtained information on the promotion committee's deliberations and determined that the reporting psychologist had voiced strong objections to promoting the pain psychologist based, in part, on possible ethical violation and prior charges of the same.

The pain psychologist considered reporting violations of Ethics Codes 1.04 and 1.08 but elected instead to terminate employment from the university.

SUMMARY

The practice of clinical pain psychology is a unique privilege afforded to those professionals who prepare themselves with specialized education, training, and experience above and beyond our education and training as psychologists. In order to warrant and continue this privilege, each of us share responsibilities to uphold the integrity of our profession and protect the patients we treat. In other words, first as psychologists and second as pain psychologists performing assessments of pain patients with particular needs and vulnerabilities, we must embrace and be held accountable to the highest level of professional conduct.

Adherence to ethical psychological assessment of chronic pain patients is first and foremost a matter of professional commitment. The APA's Ethical Principles of Psychologists and Code of Conduct serves as a behavioral guide that should be studied and periodically reviewed. When questions arise, consultation with colleagues or state psychological association Ethics Committee members should be undertaken. Lack of awareness or misunderstanding of an Ethics Standard is neither an excuse nor a valid defense against unethical professional behavior.

Beyond commitment to the Ethics Code as a voluntary guide to clinical pain practice, the Ethics Code also is a governance directive of professional behavior with severe enforceable penalties imposed for violation. The APA may impose sanctions on its members for violations of the standards of the Ethics Code and may notify other individuals, organizations, and agencies of its action. Furthermore, ethical violations may also lead to sanctions against psychologists whether or not they are members of APA through actions of state psychological associations, other professional groups, state psychological licensing boards, other state and federal agencies, and payers for health services. The Ethics Code is written to allow professional judgment on the part of psychologists. It is strongly recommended that pain psychologists utilize reasonable and appropriate judgment as defined by the prevailing professional judgment of pain psychologists engaged in similar activities and in similar circumstances, given knowledge that the pain psychologist had or should have had at the time. Once again, regular consultation and discussion with pain psychologist colleagues is recommended.

In the process of making decisions regarding professional behavior, psychologists must consider the Ethics Code in addition to applicable laws and psychology board regulations. In applying the Ethics Code to their professional work, psychologists may consider other materials and guidelines that have been adopted or endorsed by scientific and professional psychological organizations. However, pain psychologists should use caution in interpreting this flexibility to include materials and guidelines endorsed by pain societies (e.g., American Pain Society, International Pain Society, American Academy of Pain Management, etc.) because such organizations are multidisciplinary in membership and, therefore, materials and guidelines may not be consistent with psychological agencies and licensing boards. If the Ethics Code establishes a higher standard than is required by pain society or law, pain psychologists must meet the higher ethical standard.

REFERENCES

1. Bersoff DN, Koeppl PM. The relationship between ethical codes and moral principles. Ethics Behav 1993; 3:345–357.
2. American Psychological Association. Ethical principles of psychologists and code of conduct. Washington, D.C., 2002; www.apa.org/ethics/code2002.
3. American Academy of Pain Medicine. Ethics charter. Chicago, Illinois, 2003.
4. Hinnant DW. Psychological evaluation and assessment of pain. In: Tollison CD, Satterthwaite JR, Tollison JW, eds. Practical Pain Management. Philadelphia: Lippincott Williams & Wilkins, 2002.
5. Shook L. Pain in workers' compensation and personal injury law. In: Tollison CD, Satterthwaite JR, Tollison JW, eds. Practical Pain Management. Philadelphia: Lippincott Williams & Wilkins, 2002.
6. Shapiro D. Ethical issues in forensic practice. In: Van Dorsten B, ed. Forensic Psychology. New York: Kluwer Academic, 2002.
7. Tollison CD. Recent advances in psychometric assessment. In: Tollison CD, Satterthwaite JR, eds. Sympathetic Pain Syndromes: Reflex Sympathetic Dystrophy and Causalgia. Baltimore: Williams & Wilkins, 1996.

16 Ethical Issues in the Medical Assessment and Subsequent Treatment of Chronic Pain

Nelson Hendler

Mensana Clinic, Stevenson, Johns Hopkins University School of Medicine, and School of Dental Surgery, University of Maryland, Baltimore, Maryland, U.S.A.

INTRODUCTION

Pain is a totally subjective experience influenced by many factors. Therefore, the evaluation of a chronic pain patient requires a multidisciplinary approach, with the understanding that one factor may produce different responses in different individuals. These factors include the perception of pain, the resulting disability from the pain, the use of medication, the presence or absence of litigation, the pre-existing psychopathology of the patient, the resultant psychiatric problems produced by chronic pain, the skill of the physician involved in the care of the patient, family issues, financial issues, and social issues. All these factors are associated with ethical quandaries, with the ability of the physician to practice chronic pain management often limited by forces beyond the physician's control. The purpose of this chapter is to look at the importance of accurately diagnosing and confirming the diagnosis of the chronic pain patient, looking at some of the evidence supporting the importance of doing so—not just for the patient and the physician, but for the insurance industry as well. While a discussion of all of the existing impediments to the provision of the highest quality of chronic pain management is beyond the scope of this chapter, some of the crucial impediments with which the practitioner is faced are examined.

DIAGNOSIS: THE CORNERSTONE OF HIGH-QUALITY CHRONIC PAIN MANAGEMENT

The importance of an accurate diagnosis cannot be emphasized enough. A proper diagnosis allows a physician to a roadmap for all of the diagnostic tests for a patient, selection of appropriate care, and also provides a prognosis. An improper diagnosis can lead to delays in treatment, inappropriate treatment, no treatment, and a patient who never gets well. A proper diagnosis benefits the patient, and in the long run the insurance carrier, who does not have to pay for inappropriate testing or valueless treatments. It helps attorneys, whether they are plaintiff or defense attorneys, because the prognosis and definitive treatment are subsumed under a proper diagnosis. It could be quite devastating to a plaintiff attorney to bring suit, only to discover that the client was not properly diagnosed. On the other hand, a defense attorney has to be able to advise the client of the potential liability, and a proper diagnosis could actually limit the liability, and provide cost containment. In either case, a proper diagnosis creates a win-win-win situation for all parties involved, especially for the patient.

Hendler and colleagues have addressed issues of overlooked or missed diagnoses for a variety of conditions. In an article reporting on 60 cases referred to a multidisciplinary diagnostic and treatment center for chronic pain, Hendler et al. found that 66.7% of the patients had diagnoses overlooked, i.e., not mentioned by the referring physician (1). Additionally, the diagnoses that they had received prior to admission to the clinic were incorrect, and were often simply descriptions, such as "low-back pain." Patients were referred with diagnoses of cervical or lumbar strain (25%), chronic pain of unknown etiology (31.6%), degenerative disc disease (16.6%), and psychogenic pain (10%), as well as a host of other diagnoses. None of these diagnoses was substantiated after a diagnostic evaluation at the clinic where the study was conducted. The most frequently overlooked diagnoses were myofascial disease (60%), facet disease (36.6%), peripheral nerve entrapment (31.6%), radiculopathy (36.6%), and thoracic outlet syndrome (13.3%).

In a subsequent study of 120 patients, Hendler and coworkers found that 40% of patients were referred without proper diagnoses (2). Patients were referred with the "diagnosis" of chronic pain, unknown etiology (20%), cervical or lumbar strain (10.8%), psychogenic pain (9.1%), and reflex sympathetic dystrophy (RSD) (5%). Of the 120 patients evaluated, 37 of 120 were discharged with a diagnosis, confirmed by objective testing, of herniated disc (30.8%), radiculopathy (45.8%), thoracic outlet syndrome (31.6%), facet disease (33.3%), nerve entrapment (25%), temporomandibular joint syndrome (23.3%), and a host of other diagnoses.

When one examines a specific disease, such as RSD, or, as it is now called, complex regional pain syndrome type I (CRPS I), the numbers become even more disturbing. Hendler reported that 27 of the 38 patients (71%) referred to Mensana Clinic with the diagnosis of RSD or CRPS I were initially diagnosed inaccurately, and many of them never had received the appropriate diagnostic studies to confirm this diagnosis (3). A full 100% of the patients referred were never tested for allodynia, never underwent peripheral nerve blocks or phentolamine testing, 31 of the 38 (81.5%) never had received a bone scan, and 16 of the 38 (42%) never had received sympathetic blocks. These are all essential tests for establishing a diagnosis and differential diagnosis of CRPS I. After evaluation, these patients were provided with a variety of other diagnoses to explain their symptoms, confirmed by objective testing. The most commonly overlooked diagnosis was nerve entrapment found in 37 of the 38 patients (96%), followed by thoracic outlet syndrome in 16 of the 38 patients (42%).

Patients who have survived lightning strikes or severe electrical shock are misdiagnosed at a rate of 93 and 98.2%, respectively (4). Finally, the "disease d'jure" of "fibromyalgia" is inappropriately assigned to patients. In a review of 45 patients, Hendler and colleagues found that 98% of the patients referred with this diagnosis did not meet the diagnostic criteria for this disorder, established by the American Academy of Rheumatology (5).

These studies reflect a cross-section of medical care across the United States, since 75% of referrals to the clinic at which they were conducted were from 44 states (and eight foreign countries). Therefore, the problems with misdiagnosis are neither local nor regional, but national. However, the large percentage of missed diagnoses found in these reported special cases of medicine begs the questions: If the majority of cases of chronic pain, complex regional pain syndrome, electric shock, and lightning survivors are misdiagnosed, is the standard of care really substandard medicine? To what do we ascribe the failure to diagnosis?

Achieving an accurate diagnosis is based on obtaining an accurate history before ordering any tests. This history involves information regarding the onset of the injury, the location of the injury, what make the pain better and worse, the results of past tests, the genetic predisposition to an illness, past illnesses that may have contributed to the current problem, response to medication, the use of various braces and casts, psychological impact either contributing to prolonging an injury or resulting from the injury, and sociological issues, such as litigation, workers compensation, and family dynamics. As one can see, an accurate history is accomplished only by listening to a patient for a long period of time.

This process is complicated by the type of patient being evaluated. Hendler and colleagues reported that the average IQ of patients involved in litigation was 93, while the average IQ of patients in the general population is 100 (2). As the result of this disparity in intellectual capabilities, obtaining an accurate history from a workers compensation patient is often compromised by lack of adequate vocabulary, a 6% illiteracy rate, lack of knowledge of names of body parts, deficits in comprehension, slow mentation, and memory issues. It is not uncommon to ask patients if they are experiencing pain in their shins, only to have them say, "I don't think so, Doctor, it is just in my leg." However, if the physician asks these patients to point to the area of the body where they have pain, they will point to their shins.

Herein lays the ethical dilemma. The necessity for accurate history taking is at the core of accurate diagnosis. However, in an intellectually challenged population, a one-hour evaluation is simply not enough time to establish diagnoses. The history taking process needs to progress over time, very often taking five or more sessions. Even after multiple diagnostic interviews, the patient might say, "you know Doctor, I forgot to tell you that my pain gets worse when I have a bowel movement or I cough and sneeze or when I lean forward." However, in most medical settings, the amount of time spent with a patient is limited by financial constraints, and the need to see a certain number of patients per day. In this environment, the conflict between patient benefit and financial gain poses a substantial ethical dilemma for the treating physician.

Having stated the above, once the clinical diagnoses are established, proper laboratory testing should be ordered. Tests are confirmatory, not diagnostic, and fall into two broad categories: anatomical and physiological tests. This distinction is not artificial, because these two types of tests measure two completely different bodies of information. As an example, pain is a physiological phenomenon that tells the body something is wrong. Pain occurs as the result of tissue damage, which then sends chemical messages to the nerves that carry the message of pain (6). Because pain is a biochemical reaction causing irritation of sensory nerve fibers, it is, by definition physiological, not anatomical. A broken arm is anatomical, but as the result of a break, injury to the pain fibers occurs, producing a physiological correlate to an anatomical event. Therefore, a physician can take a picture of the broken arm, and assume that there is pain associated with this event. However, this is not necessarily true of a disc in the neck or back. Discs have pain fibers in them, and these fibers can be damaged without any anatomical deformity. Therefore, a damaged disc that does not anatomically protrude will not be evident on magnetic resonance imaging (MRI), computer tomography (CT), or myelogram, and conversely, a frankly herniated disc does not have to be painful. The only way to truly measure the integrity of the disc is by using a provocative discogram, in which the physiological response to an injection into the disc while the patient is awake determines whether that disc is causing pain (7). Other examples of physiological tests are bone scans, flexion-extension X rays, positron emission tomography scans of the brain, single photon emission computed tomography scans of the brain, electroencephalograms, and electromyography/nerve conduction velocity tests, to name a few. However, each of these tests has its own limitations.

Once a diagnosis is properly established, appropriate treatment can be employed. This may be in the form of medication, to control the pain and help a patient function effectively, group therapy (8), or individual therapy to help the patient address the psychological issues caused by chronic pain, and to reduce the risk of suicide, which occurs at two to three times higher rate in chronic pain patients, than the general population (9). Each of these issues should be addressed as an ethical consideration, and is done so in other chapters of this book.

PHARMACOLOGIC TREATMENT OF CHRONIC PAIN: INFREQUENTLY DISCUSSED LEGAL AND ETHICAL CONTROVERSIES

The medical assessment of a chronic pain patient proceeds after working diagnoses are established. The medical diagnostic studies may not be revealing, and in the absence of clear-cut medical diagnoses or surgically correctable lesions, the clinician is left with symptomatic treatment for the patient. Usually, this takes the form of medication. The use of opioids is well addressed in other chapters in this book, so these issues will not be discussed here. However, the use of a plethora of other types of medications needs to be addressed.

These medications will be prescribed for the clinical problems that are common to all chronic pain patients:

1. Pain
2. Depression
3. Anxiety
4. Sleep disturbance

While these symptoms may seem quite obvious, they are, nonetheless, their identification is an essential part of the ethical assessment of chronic pain patients.

The various types of pain that a patient experiences can be divided into broad categories by the type of tissue damage presumed to produce the pain. Neuropathic pain, i.e., pain produced by damage to nerves, has a different set of clinical features than bone pain. The former seems to respond better to anticonvulsant treatment than the latter, and the latter seems to be notoriously resistant to pain relief from a variety of categories of medication. Therefore, once diagnoses are established, categorizing the various etiologies of pain is actually a practical step in the assessment of the patients, because it may predict the efficacy of various pharmacological agents.

In addition to opioids, other broad categories of medication for chronic pain patients that address the four broad clinical manifestations of pain include anti-inflammatory drugs, anti-convulsants, anti-depressants, muscles relaxers, anti-anxiety drugs, and hypnotics (10). Very often, the medications may have multiple effects, and of course, side effects. Therefore, while certain medication should theoretically work in certain ways, in practice this is often not the case. Additionally, it is not uncommon for a medication to be ineffective at a low dose, and as a physician increases the dose, the medication becomes more effective. However, side effects also may become more evident, and thereby preclude its use.

In addition to issues of side effects, there is also the concept of "off-label use." "Off-label use" is defined as prescribing a medication for a reason that is not approved by the Food and Drug Administration (FDA). Obviously, this places the burden of an untoward response to the medication squarely on the shoulders of the physician. If an adverse side effect or even a lethal event occurs, the pharmaceutical company which produces the medication can point to the volumes of research contained in the greatest legal disclaimer of all, the physicians desk reference, and say, "We told you, the doctor, of all the potential side effects of this medication, and we never said that you could use it for the purpose you did." Again, the physician is presented with an ethical (and potentially legal) dilemma.

The medical literature is replete with articles describing the off-label use of medication. A classic example of this is the combination of Inderal and Elavil for the control of migraine headaches. For a number of years, these medications were not approved for the control of migraines. Likewise, calcium channel-blocking agents are also used in the control of migraines. However, an effort to provide the highest level of medical care can easily result in a physician taking a legal risk. Unfortunately, the physician has no defense if there are adverse responses to the medication. Even using the Daubert criteria for medical evidence as outlined by the Supreme Court, which allows a doctor to form an opinion based on "accepted medical information, published in peer-reviewed articles in the medical literature," the physician is still at risk.

Because the assessment of responses to medication is, by definition, trial and error, and the response to a medication provides additional diagnostic information to the physician, the use of medication, and the patient's response to various categories of medication, is an essential component of diagnosis and treatment of chronic pain patients.

If the "off-label" use of medication does not present enough of an ethical dilemma for the physician, the cost of medication and refusal of insurance companies to cover payment for certain medications is another major consideration. There are many organizations advocating the recycling of prescribed medications. Such organizations contend that if medications do not work for a particular patient for whom the medication was prescribed, rather than discarding the expensive prescription, the unused portion of the medication should be recycled and given to a patient who cannot afford the same medication (11). An editorial in the New York Times (11), focused on the efforts of M.I.T. faculty member Dr. Moshe Alamaro to combat the wasteful practices dictated by the FDA, which prohibits the redistribution of prescription drugs. Fortunately, individual states can override the federal mandates. In fact, in California, four medical students from Stanford were recently able to persuade Governor Arnold Schwarzenegger to sign into law a bill that permits pharmacies to dispense previously sold medication to patients with low income or severe disabilities, provided the prescriptions are unexpired and unopened (12). It is estimated that California discards over $100,000,000 worth of unused medication each year. Other states have experienced similar waste. California joins nine other states that have enacted comparable laws.

Yet another medication-related ethical dilemma often arises in a pain physician's office. It is not unusual for patients to bring unused portions of their medications back to a physician, stating "Doctor, I just spent $60 on this prescription, and the medication doesn't work for me. Maybe you can give this to someone who can't afford it." The physician is not a pharmacy, and the medication has been opened, but the physician knows there are other patients who cannot afford the proffered medication that could benefit from it.

In the state of Maryland, a physician is required to have a dispensing license in order to distribute medication. This is a little known fact, and in a recent private poll, only one physician in 20 (5%) knew about a dispensing license, and this physician's awareness may have been related to the fact that the physician's father happened to be a pharmacist. Therefore, in Maryland, if a physician tries to help the medically indigent patients by redispensing non-narcotic, non-controlled substances, the physician is in technical violation of the law.

Again, this presents an ethical dilemma for the physician. Faced with an indigent patient, or a patient for whom an insurance company has denied a medication due to the "off-label use" of the pharmaceutical, how does a doctor help the patient? Does the physician merely shrug the shoulders and say, "Tough luck. You can't have the medication I think you need?" Or does the physician stay true to the Hippocratic Oath? Is relieving a patient's suffering more important or less important than the law? Faced with the following situation, what should an ethical physician do?

In Maryland, a 76-year-old African-American woman suffering from shoulder pain was covered only by workers compensation insurance for her shoulder pain, and Medicare for the rest of her medical coverage. At an office visit, her blood pressure was 210/140. Workers Compensation would not cover any medication not related to her shoulder pain, and rejected the notion that chronic pain produced elevated blood pressure. The patient did not have coverage for medication through Medicare. The physician realized that this patient was at risk for a stroke. In an effort to lower her blood pressure, the physician gave the patient Clonidine 1 mg qid and Furosimide 40 mg qam that belonged to two other patients. The physician did not have a dispensing license. In Maryland, this physician had now violated the law. Should the state Board of Physicians have suspended the physician's license? This really is not as black and white as it seems.

There is a concept in the law referred to as "principles of justification." In section 503 of the model penal code, and again in section 3.02, there is a general concept of justification. The general rule states:

"(a) general rule—conduct which the actor believes it to be necessary to avoid harm or evil to himself or to another is justifiable if:

(1) The harm or evil sought to be avoided by such conduct is
...greater than that sought to be prevented by the law
...defining the offense charged."

This concept is called "de minimus" in the law, and once again presents an ethical dilemma for the treating physician. In an effort to protect and/or treat the patients, does the physician act in the patient's best interest, even if it violates the law? This is a question that each doctor has to answer for him or herself on a case-by-case basis. The goal of any treating physician should be to provide the best medical care possible for the physician's patients. However, legal implications need to be considered along with issues of ethical practice.

IMPEDIMENTS TO ACCURATE DIAGNOSIS LEADING TO APPROPRIATE TREATMENT

The best measure of the efficacy of treatment is published outcomes studies that document the effectiveness of the diagnostic and treatment process. Most insurance companies report that claimants out of work for two years or more for workers compensation injuries have less than a 1% chance of returning to work. At Mensana Clinic, the return to work statistics for patients out of work for two years or more is 19.5% for workers compensation and 62.5% for auto accident cases (13). The difference between the two groups has been attributed to the type of litigation (14).

As demonstrated, proper diagnosis can lead to good treatment outcomes. Good treatment outcomes can, in turn, lead to cost containment and cost savings. One example of this principle is based on case studies. Six patients, originally diagnosed with RSD were reviewed, and four of the six were found to have only nerve entrapments, while the other two had RSD and other pathology, including thoracic outlet syndrome, herniated discs, and nerve entrapment. To explore cost savings with proper diagnosis, the total costs of (i) prior treatment was added to, (ii) the cost of subsequent treatment, and (iii) the cost of disability or workers compensation payments from the date of the injury to the date of the return to work following treatment. This figure was compared to projected life time treatment, since there was an absence of proper diagnosis, represented by (i) total costs of prior treatment, (ii) the projected cost of treatment per year based on past treatment multiplied by the expected age at death of the patient, and (iii) the cost of disability or workers compensation payments from the date of the injury to the date of the death of the patient. When the figures were calculated for the six patients, the potential cost savings per patient ranged from $90,000 to $2,500,000.

What causes the failure to diagnose accurately? Briefly stated, there has been a significant change in the way medicine is practiced over the last 30 years. The advent of Health Maintenance Organizations (HMOs), cost containment by health insurance carriers, government incursions into regulation of fees and control of the medical delivery system, the Stark amendment, mail-in prescription medications, and other such innovations have impacted the manner in which physicians practice medicine.

The entire premise of capitated health care reimbursement flies in the face of the Hippocratic Oath, and make it the "hypocritic oath." Under the HMO system, a set fee per month per patient for all patients in the physician's practice is paid, regardless of whether the patients see the doctor or not. However, in exchange for this fee, the physician must pay for all laboratory studies and consults from the fee. Obviously, this was designed as a cost-containment measure, but it actually results in reticence on the part of a physician to order laboratory studies and to refer the patient for appropriate consults. Moreover, in settings in which the medical practice is under the control of a "practice management" group, the physician is told about a quota for the minimum number of patients that must be seen in a day, and is chastised or fined for spending too much time with a patient or not meeting the quota. This creates a situation in which the amount of time that a physician spends with a patient is reduced to ten or even five minutes.

Even in a non-HMO setting, the physician encounters enormous barriers to providing good health care. Frequently, requests for laboratory studies or medications are denied by the insurance carrier. Worker compensation situations are even worse. In a small study of six patients insured by a state insurance fund, Hendler reported average delays of seven months from the time of request for a laboratory test until the time of approval. The latency between a request for a consultation with a surgeon and the time of approval averaged nine months, and from the time the surgeon indicated that the patient needed surgery until the time of approval for the surgery, the delay was 16 months (Hendler, Unpublished data).

In these types of treatment climates, the physician is at greater risk of missing a diagnosis. This can create fertile ground for increased malpractice suits, bringing to question whether the culprits are the attorneys, the physicians themselves, the insurance carriers, or the health care system. By working together to help achieve accurate diagnosis, all parties involved can benefit. Of greatest importance, the patient gains enormously from accurate diagnosis, which leads to proper treatment. When distilled to its finest essence, that is, what medicine should be.

In the formula of chronic pain patient assessment, the insurance company is unfortunately the "tail that wags the dog." The insurance industry has been plagued by an increased number of claims in recent years, especially in the area of workers compensation and long-term disability. Recent statistics show that the number of cases of carpel tunnel syndrome rose by 467% within one year, while claims for low-back and disc injury have climbed 215% (15). Liberty Mutual published data in 1986, indicating that while the median cost of a workers compensation case was $391.00, the average cost of a case was $6,900.00. They attributed 95% of the expense to 25% of the cases (16). Most of these claims related to low-back, neck, and limb pain. However, by 2001, the average cost of all types of workers compensation cases in New York state was $11,583, and the costs of permanent partial disability claims ranged from $25,000 to $115,000, depending on the state in which the claim was filed (17).

Due to these increased expenses, the need to differentiate valid claims from false claims is essential, so that resources can be allocated to the people who deserve the support, and denied to people who are abusing the system. There are several approaches to determine disability. Many methods have been employed to validate the complaint of pain. Researchers have attempted to measure pain, without great success (18). Merskey and colleagues have reported that cultural differences alter the expression of pain (19). Moreover, pain reduction does not correlate with return to work results (13,14). Therefore, trying to quantify pain is a formidable task, without any tangible benefits to the insurance industry. Currently, the insurance industry relies on independent medical evaluations and surveillance to evaluate the validity of claims. However, California State Auditor Elaine Howle has suggested that the $30,000,000 annual assessment to combat fraud may be wasted, and that carriers cannot measure the effectiveness of their effort. They are relying on anecdotal testimony from stakeholders in the Workers Compensation Community, unscientific estimates, and description of local cases involving fraud. The fraud division publishes statistics regarding the number of investigations, arrests, convictions, and restitution, but cannot provide objective evidence that antifraud efforts are cost effective (20). Moreover, many of the independent medical examinations do not meet the Daubert criteria for admissible medical testimony in Federal Court, because they do not rely on evidence-based medicine to render their opinions (21). No reports exist in the literature to evaluate the accuracy of independent medical examinations, but Hendler and colleagues reported that 40% to 67% of patients involved in litigation are misdiagnosed by their own treating Doctors that results in inaccurate "negative" reports (1,2). Ambiguous assessment strategies and variations in examination in the determination of disability involving the presence of pain have also led to increased litigation (22,23). Psychological tests, such as the Minnesota multiphasic personality inventory, do not correlate with the presence or absence of organic pathology (24–26). Again, this results in inaccurate "negative" reports. However, in a study of subjects reporting no back pain, abnormalities such as bulging or displaced discs were found on lumbar MRI in 27 of the 91 participants, for a false-positive rate of 30% (27). Thus, there occur both false-positive findings that create inaccuracies in the assessment of the validity of pain and false-negative findings due to inaccurate diagnosis.

When an effective case management tool is implemented, an insurance adjustor can better allocate resources, and thereby avoid authorizing unnecessary and expensive medical testing. This concept is exemplified by the development of the Ottawa Ankle Rules and the Ottawa Knee Rules for use in Canadian emergency rooms, which was found to decrease ankle radiography referrals up to 26%, with cost savings of up to $50,000,000 per year (28–30).

The Mensana Clinic Pain Validity Test had been developed 17 years prior to the Ottawa Ankle and Knee Rules, and embodied the same principles, i.e., using a verbal report and correlating the verbalization with the presence or absence of organic pathology (31). However, the Mensana Clinic Pain Validity Test was designed to correlate with the presence or absence of objectively quantified physical abnormalities in patients with chronic back, neck, and limb pain (24–26,31). This test divides claimants into three broad categories, listed below, which accurately predict the presence or absence of organic pathology.

Objective Pain Patients

These patients have a good premorbid adjustment, no frank psychiatric problems, and objective bases to their complaint of pain, and go through four states of adaptation to pain similar to Kubler–Ross' stages of acceptance of death in response to their pain (32–37). The most prevalent of these four stages is that of depression, seen in 77% of patients with chronic pain (13). However, it is important to note that 89% of these depressed patients were never depressed prior to the onset of their pain (13). The Mensana Clinic Pain Validity Test was able to predict the presence of organic pathology in objective pain patients in 85% to 91% of cases (24–26).

Exaggerating Pain Patients

These patients have poor premorbid adjustments, have a minor origin to their pain, and do not become depressed as a result of their pain. Additionally, they may be experiencing issues of secondary gain (33,34). The Mensana Clinic Pain Validity Test was able to predict minimal or the absence of organic pathology in exaggerating pain patients 85% to 100% of the time (24–26).

Mixed Objective/Exaggerating Pain Patients

These patients have objective organic pathology, but also poor premorbid adjustments (33,34). In the mixed objective/exaggerating pain patients, the Mensana Clinic Pain Validity Test was able to predict the presence of organic pathology in 45% of cases, and the absence of pathology in 55%, which was no better than chance alone (24–26).

Research by Hendler and colleagues on patients at the Johns Hopkins Hospital Chronic Pain Treatment Center has indicated that these hospital-treated patients represent a population of the most difficult to diagnose and treat, and that many had histories of drug or psychiatric problems (31,33,37). These patients were not typically involved in litigation. Only 62% of this patient population consisted of objective pain patients (31). On the other hand, 17% of this nonlitigant chronic pain patient group was deemed to be exaggerating their symptoms (31). However, in a population of patients involved in either workers compensation or auto accident litigation, 13% were determined to be exaggerating the severity of their pain (24–26). In an effort to test the efficacy of the Mensana Clinic Pain Validity Test for detecting valid claims on a long-term disability insurance population as opposed to a hospital population, the following study was undertaken.

In research published by Hendler on the website of the National Council on Compensation Insurance, The Mensana Clinic Pain Validity Test was mailed to 63 long-term disability claimants selected by a major insurance carrier. These cases had chronic neck, back, or limb pain, and had been out of work for at least six months. Fifty-five claimants returned the test, and based on their scores, they were assigned either to the objective, exaggerating, or mixed objective-exaggerating pain patient category. This assignment allowed a prediction to be made regarding the presence or absence of organic pathology. After the prediction was recorded, the charts were reviewed by insurance company nurses to determine the presence or absence of organic pathology documented in the chart, as well as the severity of the pathology. The presence or absence of moderate or severe pathology was recorded, and compared to the predictions, based on the score of the Mensana Clinic Pain Validity Test.

The cost of evaluating the validity of the claimants' impairment and disability was also examined. Expenses were divided into three broad categories.

1. Those in which costs for independent medical evaluations, surveillance, unannounced home visits for activity checks, and chart reviews were incurred by the long-term disability carrier were recorded. For the purpose of this study, these were defined as efforts to assess the validity of the claim.
2. Costs of functional capacity evaluations, vocational rehabilitation evaluations, job analyses, developmental assessments, and Equifax, Gennix, and Allsup evaluations were not considered, because these were considered administrative or rehabilitative efforts that would have been incurred in any case. Excluding these expenses biased the results against the findings of this research, i.e., had these expenses been included, the cost savings would have been greater.
3. Any independent medical examinations or surveillance paid for by another insurance carrier (usually the workers compensation carrier) were not included in the cost of the case. Cost of medical care was not reported. Additionally, even though the independent medical evaluations, surveillance, unannounced home visits for activity checks, and chart reviews may have been performed at the request of the disability carrier, if no cost was recorded in the chart, no dollar value was assigned to the case. Again, had this been done, the cost savings would have been greater.

In this analysis, the actual cost of case management was grossly underestimated, which biased results against the claim that the Mensana Clinic Pain Validity Test could save insurance carriers money. Also, by not including an expense, unless it was incurred only to determine the validity of the claim, results were biased against the claim of cost savings. Twelve cases were found that met the following three criteria: (i) actual expenses were recorded in the chart, (ii) the expenses were only for independent medical evaluations, surveillance, unannounced home visits for activity checks, and chart reviews, and (iii) the long-term disability carrier, not some other insurance carrier, paid for the items listed in (2). Fifty-five questionnaires were returned and scored. In 47 of the 55 cases, the charts contained medical records that were sufficiently complete to determine the severity of medical problems, substantiated by documentation. Thirty-nine cases were found to be objective back pain cases, using the rating scale from the Mensana Clinic Pain Validity Test. This represented 83% of all claimants with complete charts. One hundred percent of these objective back, neck, or limb pain cases were found to have a moderate or severe abnormality on at least one objective laboratory study, confirming organic pathology. Seventeen percent were interpreted as mixed objective/exaggerating claimants. One case had no objective findings, two claimants were presumed to have moderately abnormal findings from the descriptions of medical tests in the chart, and the remaining five patients had moderate or severe objective organic pathology. The Mensana Clinic Pain Validity Test accurately predicted organic pathology in 87% of the mixed objective/exaggerating claimants. None of the cases reviewed yielded any exaggerating patients. Therefore, the Mensana Clinic Pain Validity Test was 97% accurate in predicting the presence of moderate or severe organic pathology.

Using the Fisher's exact test (38,39), the ability of the Mensana Clinic Pain Validity Test to accurately predict the presence or absence of organic pathology in a long-term disability claimant population was calculated. The results yielded a χ^2 score of 4.8 using the Fisher's exact test, which was statistically significant at the $p < 0.05$ level. This finding suggests that the Mensana Clinic measure is an accurate predictive test.

Chi square analysis of the chronic pain patient population at the Johns Hopkins Hospital versus the long-term disability claimant population was also calculated. The χ^2 score was 9.7, which is significant at the $p < 0.01$ level, indicating the presence of a statistically significant difference in the two populations.

Twelve cases were found in the hospital patient population in which the long-term disability carrier paid for evaluations to assess the validity of the claim (independent medical evaluations, surveillance, unannounced home visits for activity checks, and chart reviews). These 12 cases cost the long-term disability carrier $21,048.00, or an average of $1754.00 per case. The insurance carrier had made some effort to analyze the presence or absence of organic pathology in 12 other cases, using independent medical evaluations, surveillance, unannounced home visits for activities checks, and chart reviews. However, no financial figures were available for these cases, or the evaluation was paid for by a carrier other than the long-term disability carrier. Accordingly, these 12 cases were not included in the analysis.

If the long-term disability carrier had used the Mensana Clinic Pain Validity Test, which costs only $200.00 per use, the total cost for validating the complaint of pain, for the first 12 cases, would have been only $2400.00. Therefore, if the long-term disability carrier had used this measure, it would have used a test that was 97% accurate for validating the complaint of pain, and saved them $1554.00 per case.

The composition of the chronic pain patient population at Johns Hopkins Hospital was significantly different from the population of patients who filed for long-term disability (Table 2).Only 62% of the patients at Johns Hopkins Hospital were identified as objective pain patients, compared to 83% found in this study on long-term disability patients. This discrepancy may be due to differences in the types of patients in the studies. The patient who is difficult to manage or diagnose would be more likely to be referred to a tertiary treatment center, such as Johns Hopkins Hospital. This is in distinction to a long-term disability claimant, who may have obvious organic pathology, and is less of a management problem. In the absence of demographic data from the two populations, one can hypothesize that the Johns Hopkins Hospital patients had more severe depression and drug problems associated with their pain, as well as more pathological premorbid personalities (33–35,37). This would also account for the higher number of exaggerating patients seen at Johns Hopkins Hospital (17%), compared to the long-term disability group (none). The absence of exaggerating pain patients in the long-term disability patient population could also be attributed to the refined assessment skills of the long-term disability carrier and the nurses and adjusters assigned to manage the cases.

Assessing organic pathology manifesting as pain is a more reliable approach, as opposed to trying to assess pain by subjective comparisons of pain construct indices, as the Glasgow Pain Test does for determining disability (40). There is less error due to interpretation, but even evaluating physical problems is subject to error if the right tests are not employed.

There are no published data to document the efficacy or accuracy of independent medical evaluations, surveillance, unannounced home visits, or chart reviews for determining the validity of a claimant's illness. In fact, there is data indicating that the use of these techniques is not cost effective (20). The independent medical evaluation can be used in litigation against a claimant, but a report that is favorable to the insurance company helps only the legal, but not the medical aspects of a case. If a patient is misdiagnosed and improperly treated, the patient will not return to work, even if the independent medical examination fails to identify any organic findings, thus contributing to the $55 billion a year loss in work days due to pain (41,42). One example of this disturbing trend can be found in the workers compensation literature. Liberty Mutual reported that if an injured worker is out of work for two years or more, the return to work rate is less than 1% (43). In an independent study, the return to work rate for workers compensation claimants, out of work for an average of 4.9 years, was 19.5%, while the return to work rate for patients injured in auto accidents was 62.5% (13). The only difference between the workers compensation and auto accident group to account for the discrepancy in return to work rates was the type of litigation in which patients were involved (14).

The difference between the return to work rates in the Liberty Mutual study and the independent study is more interesting, and has great financial implications for insurance carriers. The cost of accurately diagnosing and treating a patient in order to close a case versus the cost of keeping a case open for a certain number of years, discounted to present value, must be done on a case by case basis. In fact, outcome data indicate that the population of workers compensation low-back-injured patients participating in pain treatment programs consumed fewer analgesics, required fewer hospitalizations for additional diagnostic testing and/or treatment, and were more likely to return to work than a comparison group of patients denied comparable treatment (44). In other studies, the referral to surgery rate for chronic pain patients involved in litigation was 50% to 55% (1,2), while the misdiagnosis rate by the referring physician ranged from 40% to 67% (1,2).

Even if one assumes that the accuracy of "validating" techniques, such as independent medical evaluations (45), the patient's subjective perspective (46–48), surveillance, objective physical measurements (49,50), unannounced home visits, or chart reviews, are equal to that of the Mensana Clinic Pain Validity Test, the cost of even just one of these "validating" techniques is far higher than $200.00 for the Mensana Clinic measure. Moreover, the Mensana Clinic Pain Validity Test is available on the Internet (51), takes 5 to 15 minutes for the claimant to complete, and only three seconds are required to email back an interpretation of the test to the clinician or insurance carrier. This is in contrast to the new Multiperspective multidimensional pain assessment protocol (MMPAP), which is a lengthy instrument that requires more than two hours to complete (46,47). The developers of the MMPAP admit that it is not appropriate in situations in which a "quick" screening tool is required (46,47). The validity of the MMPAP is based upon a patient's subjective self-report and a physical examination by two physicians. This test is ultimately far more costly than the Mensana Clinic Pain Validity Test, which allows insurance companies to allocate their resources more appropriately.

While no screening test is perfect, the Mensana Clinic Pain Validity Test offers long-term disability, Workers Compensation, and automobile insurance carriers an inexpensive and accurate alternative to current methods of assessing the validity of claims.

Other considerations in evaluating chronic pain patients in a way that increases the likelihood of appropriate treatment are the role of the physician and the insurance company, the use of medication, and the legal system.

The physician can function as a treating doctor, or as an agent of the insurance carrier. One group of authors pejoratively labeled physicians who try to fully investigate their patients' complaints as "rule out," physicians, and claimed that a thorough investigation of what they believe are "benign and self-limited symptoms" may lead to the development of a "chronic disability syndrome" (52). The fact that none of the authors of this study are physicians resulted in the issue of possible misdiagnosis not being addressed, rendering their assumptions as presumptive. This study fails to address the hundreds of thousands of cases of "low-back pain," which is a nondiagnosis, and "lumbar or cervical strain" that, by definition, are self-limiting conditions that should not last more than three weeks, as representing the result of faulty diagnosis. Sprains are defined as stretching ligaments that hold joints together (53). Strains are defined as overextension of a muscle, which moves bone, with separation of muscle fibers (52). Sprains cause an average of 7.5 days of restricted activity, two days of bed disability, and 2.5 days of work loss (54). Nowhere in the article by Dersh et al. (52) is this concept advanced. To the contrary, the authors ascribe assigning a diagnosis to patients as being financially motivated, "when health care practitioners intentionally use diagnoses that qualify patients (and therefore, doctors) for insurance reimbursement, even when they do not believe the diagnoses are accurate" (52). As an example, the authors site the use of the diagnoses of "degenerative disc disease" and "spondylosis" as "medicalizing a normal phenomenon" (52), because this is likely to lead to payment for treatment. They ascribe malfeasant motivation to one of the most common errors in medical practice, i.e., relying on radiological studies instead of physiological studies for diagnosing pain, which is a physiological event. Moreover, these authors totally ignored the failure of radiological studies, such as MRIs, to properly diagnose disc pathology. One group of investigators (27) reported that when MRIs were given to 98 patients with no back pain, 27 were found to have protruding disc (a 28% false-positive rate). On the other hand, when MRIs with positive Modic signs (vertebral end-plate changes) were reviewed, 21 of 23 patients had positive provocative discograms. However, when 90 patients with positive provocative discograms were reviewed, only 23% had Modic changes, and 77% displayed no changes on the MRI (55). Therefore, MRIs have a 77% false-negative rate for detecting damaged discs in the back. In summary, using an anatomical test, such as an MRI, to detect the presence of pain in a person with a damaged disc may lead to faulty conclusions, with a 28% false-positive rate, and a 77% false-negative rate.

This error rate can be explained by understanding the neuroanatomy of a disc. A disc is like a jelly donut. Pain fibers are found in the rear one-third of the disc (56). A herniation involves the protrusion of the "jelly" from the disc. This herniation can easily be detected by MRI, CT, or myelogram. However, pain fibers can be irritated without any anatomical distortion of the disc, potentially resulting in the MRI, CT, and myelogram (which are merely anatomical tests), yielding negative results (56). Pain from internal disc disruption cannot be distinguished from that due to a herniated disc pushing on a nerve root with pain in a radicular distribution (56). However, because the ability to detect this physiological problem of pain fiber irritation is below the level of detection of an anatomical test, such as an MRI, CT, or myelogram, then a physician needs to use a physiological test to detect the pain fiber irritation. The appropriate test in this situation is a provocative discogram (57). This is a physiological test, not an anatomical test. Saline is injected into the donut portion of the disc. This injection distends the pain fibers in the rear one-third of the disc. If this injection reproduces the pain, the test is considered positive. In such cases, a local anesthetic is injected into the damaged disc to temporarily block the pain the patient normally feels. If this is effective, the patient has had a positive provocative discogram, and the damaged disc has been identified using a physiological test, even if all the anatomical tests (X ray, MRI, CT, and myelogram) are normal.

CONCLUSIONS

In summary, there are multiple issues at play in the evaluation and treatment of a chronic pain patient. What is ethical does not always necessarily correlate well with what is legal, which can be noted in the section of this chapter on dilemmas associated with providing medications to patients in need. The ethics of a physician who panders to an insurance carrier must be compared to the ethics of a physician who panders to personal injury attorneys. The ethics of insurance companies denying payments for claims they know they will eventually have to pay must be weighed against the ethics of a claimant who exaggerates the claim in order to receive compensation. The ethics of health care providers who knowingly provide countless sessions of ineffective treatment to chronic pain patients must be compared to the independent medical examiner who never finds anything wrong with a patient. These are all errors of commission. These require conscious, if not unethical, choices, and there will always be cheats and liars. However, what is more troublesome are the errors of omission, in which lack of medical education, lack of legal knowledge, or failure to fully understand a problem results in poor care for a patient. The ethical issues in these situations are more difficult to define, for they require that a person has insight into his or her own failings, and makes an effort to correct them. Therefore, the Diagenean* task of wandering the streets with a lantern looking for an honest man, becomes daunting.

      Diogenes was a Cynic philosopher of Sinope. His father, Icesias, a banker, was convicted of debasing the public coin, and was obliged to leave the country; or, according to another account, his father and himself were charged with this offense, and the former was thrown into prison, while the son escaped and went to Athens. Here he attached himself, as a disciple, to Antisthenes, who was at the head of the Cynics. Antisthenes at first refused to admit him into his house and even struck him with a stick. Diogenes calmly bore the rebuke and said, "Strike me, Antisthenes, but you will never find a stick sufficiently hard to remove me from your presence, while you speak anything worth hearing." The philosopher was so much pleased with this reply that he at once admitted him among his scholars. Diogenes fully adopted the principles and character of his master. Renouncing every other object of ambition, he distinguished himself by his contempt of riches and honors and by his invectives against luxury. He wore a coarse cloak, carried a wallet and a staff, made the porticoes and other public places his habitation, and depended upon casual contributions for his daily bread. He asked a friend to procure him a cell to live in; when there was a delay, he took up abode in a pithos, or large tub, in the Metroum. It is probable, however, that this was only a temporary expression of indignation and contempt, and that he did not make it the settled place of his residence. This famous "tub" is indeed celebrated by Juvenal; it is also ridiculed by Lucian and mentioned by Seneca. But no notice is taken of this by other ancient writers who have mentioned this philosopher.

Another unconfirmed tale talks of Diogenes, after a heated discussion of ethics of the Athenian politicians, walking the streets of Athens, with a lantern late in the evening. When asked by a passer-by why he was wandering as such a late hour, Diogenes the Cynic replied, "Why, I am looking for an honest man." Whether or not this story, reported by Lucian, is truthful itself, or the product of the imagination of the chroniclers of Diogenes remains in doubt, but certainly portrays the contempt and cynicism that Diogenes felt for many of his fellow men.

It cannot be doubted, however, that Diogenes practiced self-control and a most rigid abstinence—exposing himself to the utmost extremes of heat and cold and living upon the simplest diet, casually supplied by the hand of charity. In his old age, sailing to Aegina, he was taken by pirates and carried to Crete, where he was exposed to sale in the public market. When the auctioneer asked him what he could do, he said, "I can govern men; therefore sell me to one who wants a master." Xeniades, a wealthy Corinthian, happening at that instant to pass by, was struck with the singularity of his reply and purchased him. On their arrival at Corinth, Xeniades gave him his freedom and committed to him the education of his children and the direction of his domestic concerns. Diogenes executed this trust with so much judgment and fidelity that Xeniades used to say that the gods had sent a good genius to his house.

During his residence at Corinth, an interview between him and Alexander is said to have taken place. Plutarch relates that Alexander, when at Corinth, receiving the congratulations of all ranks on being appointed to command the army of the Greeks against the Persians, missed Diogenes among the number, with whose character he was acquainted. Curious to see the one who exhibited such haughty independence of spirit, Alexander went in search of him and found him sitting in his tub in the sun. "I am Alexander the Great," said the monarch. "And I am Diogenes the Cynic," replied the philosopher. Alexander then requested that he would inform him what service he could render him. "Stand from between me and the sun," said the Cynic. Alexander, struck with the reply, said to his friends, who were ridiculing the whimsical singularity of the philosopher, "If I were not Alexander, I should wish to be Diogenes." This story is too good to be omitted, but there are several circumstances, which in some degree diminish its credibility. It supposes Diogenes to have lived in his tub at Corinth, whereas it is certain that he lived there in the house of Xeniades, and that, if he had ever dwelt in a tub, he left it behind him at Athens. Alexander, moreover, was at this time scarcely 20 years old, and could not call himself Alexander the Great, for he did not receive this title till his Persian and Indian expedition, after which he never returned to Greece; yet the whole transaction represents him as elated with the pride of conquest. Diogenes probably was visited by Alexander, when the latter held the general assembly of the Greeks at Corinth, and was received by him with rudeness and incivility, which may have given rise to the whole story. The philosopher at this time would have been about 70 years of age.

Various accounts are given concerning the manner and time of his death. It seems most probable that he died at Corinth, of mere decay, in the 19th year of his age and in the 114th Olympiad. A column of Parian marble, terminating in the figure of a dog, was raised over his tomb. His fellow-townsmen of Sinope also erected brazen statues in memory of the philosopher. Diogenes left behind him no system of philosophy. After the example of his school, he was more attentive to practical than to theoretical wisdom. The author of this article is anonymous. The IEP is actively seeing an author who will write a replacement article (58). The internet Encyclopedia of Philosphy.

REFERENCES

1. Hendler N, Kozikowski J. Overlooked physical diagnoses in chronic pain patients involved in litigation. Psychosom 1993; 34:494–501.
2. Hendler N, Bergson C, Morrison C. Overlooked physical diagnoses in chronic pain patients involved in litigation II. Psychosom 1996; 37:398–405.
3. Hendler N. Differential diagnosis of complex regional pain syndrome type I (RSD). Pan Arab J Neurosurg 2002; 6:1–9.
4. Hendler N. Overlooked diagnoses in chronic pain: analysis of survivors of electric shock and lightning strike. J Occup Environ Med 2005; 47:796–805.
5. Hendler, Romano. 2006. Article submitted.
6. Hendler. Pain. World Book Encyclopedia. 2004.
7. Hendler N. Chronic pain: which test is best? J Workers Comp 1996; 6:24–31.
8. Hendler N, Vierstein M, Shallenberger, et al. Group therapy with chronic pain patients. Psychosom 1981; 22:334–340.
9. Fishbain D, Goldberg M, Rosomoff, et al. Completed suicide in chronic pain patients. Clin J Pain 1991; 7:29–36.
10. Hendler N. Pharmacological management of Pain. In: Prithviraj P, Mosby MD, eds. Practical Management of Pain, 3rd, eds. St. Louis: Mosby, 2000:145–155.
11. Strom S. Old pills finding new medicine cabinets. The New York Times, May 18, 2005.
12. Spector R. Students plan for unused prescription drugs wins approval from the Governor. Stanford Report, Oct 19, 2005.
13. Hendler N. Validating and Treating the Complaint of Chronic Pain: the Mensana Clinic Approach. In: Black D, ed. Clin Neurosurg 1989; 35:385–397.
14. Talo S, Hendler N, Brodie J. Effects of active and completed litigation on treatment results: workers' compensation patients compared with other litigation patients. J Occup Med 1989; 31:265–269.
15. Minor AF, ed. Health Insurance Institute of America. Washington, DC: Book of Health Insurance Data,1998:234–235.
16. Deyo C, Cherkin R, Conrad S, Violinn F. Annu Rev Public Health 1988; 12:141–158.
17. The Public Policy Institute of New York State, Inc. Table 38. From National Council on Compensation Insurance, http://www.ppinys.org/report/jtf/Table%2038.htm.
18. Beecher HK. Quantification of the subjective pain experience. Proceedings of the Annual Meeting of the American Psychopathological Association. Vol. 52, 1965:111–128.
19. Merskey H, Spear FG. Pain: Psychological and Psychiatric Aspects, London, Balliere: Tindall & Cassell, 1967.
20. Howle E. Workers' Comp Report 2004; 15:206.
21. Daubert v. Merrell Dow Pharmaceuticals (92–102). 509 U.S. 579. Supreme Court of the United States, 1993, http://supct.law.cornell.edu/supct/html/92–102.ZS.html.
22. Moothart v. Bowen. Individual suit. 934 F2d. 114, 7th cir, 1994.
23. Dixon v. Sullivan. Class action suit. No. 83. CIV 7001, (WCC) 1992, SDNY.

24. Hendler N, Mollet A, Viernstein M, et al. A Comparison between the MMPI and the "Hendler Pain Validity Test" for validating the complaint of chronic back pain in men. J Neurology Ortho Med Surg 1985; 6:333–337.
25. Hendler N, Mollett A, Viernstein M, et al. A comparison between the MMPI and the "Hendler Pain Validity Test" for validating the complaint of chronic back pain in women. Pain 1985; 23:243–251.
26. Hendler N, Mollett A, Levin S. A comparison between the Minnesota Multiphasic Personality Inventory and the "Mensana Clinic Pain Validity Test" for validating the complaint of chronic back pain. J Occup Med 1988; 30:98–102.
27. Jensen MC, Brandt-Zawadski MN, Obuchowski N, et al. Magnetic resonance imaging of the lumbar spine in people without back pain. N Eng J Med 1994; 331:69–73.
28. Ravaud P. Use of ottowa ankle rules reduces number of radiology requests. JAMA 1997; 277:1935–1939.
29. Stiell IG, Greenberg GH, McKnight RD, et al. Decision rules for the use of radiography in acute ankle injuries: refinement and prospective validation. JAMA 1993; 269:1127–1132.
30. Stiell IG, Greenberg GH, Wells GA, et al. Prospective validation of a decision rule for the use of radiographs in acute knee injuries. JAMA 1996; 275:611–615.
31. Hendler NH, Viernstein M, Gucer P, et al. A preoperative screening test for chronic back pain patients. Psychosom 197; 20:801–808.
32. Kubler-Ross E. On Death and Dying. New York: Macmillan Co., 1969.
33. Hendler N. Depression caused by chronic pain. J Clin Psych 1984; 45:30–36.
34. Hendler N. Diagnosis and Non-Surgical Management of Chronic Pain. New York: Raven Press, 1981.
35. Hendler N. The four stages of pain. In: Hendler N, Long D, Wise T, eds. Diagnosis and Treatment of Chronic Pain. Chapter 1. Littleton, Massachusetts: John Wright/PSG, 1982:1–8.
36. Hendler N, Derogatis L, Avella J, et al. EMG biofeedback in patients with chronic pain. Diseases of the Nervous Syst 1977; 38:505–508.
37. Hendler N, Cimini C, Ma T, et al. A comparison of cognitive impairment due to benzo-diazepines and to narcotics. Amer J Psych 1980: 137:828–830.
38. Dawson-Saunders B, Trapp R. Basic and Clinical Biostatistics. Norwalk, Connecticut: Appleton and Lange, 1990:148.
39. Dawson-Saunders B, Trapp R. Basic and Clinical Biostatistics. Norwalk, Connecticut: Appleton and Lange, 1990:150–151.
40. Thomas RJ, McEwen J, Ashbury AJ. The glasgow pain questionnaire: a new generic measure of pain; development and testing. Int J Epidemiol 1996; 25:1060–1067.
41. American Medical Association. Guidelines to the Evaluation of Permanent Impairment. 4th ed. Chicago: American Medical Association, 1993.
42. Mendelson C. Psychological factors and the management of physical illness: a contribution to the cost-containment of medical care. Aust N Engl J Psych 1984: 18:211–216.
43. Snook S, Jensen RC. Pope M, Frymoyer J, Anderson G, eds. Cost in Occupational Low Back Pain. New York: Praeger Publishers, 1984:115–121.
44. Tollison CD, Kriegel MD, Saterthwaite JR, et al. Pain clinic: comprehensive pain center treatment of low back workers' compensation injuries. An industrial medicine clinical outcome follow-up comparison. Orthop Rev 1989; 18:1157–1162.
45. Hurri H. The Swedish back school in chronic low back pain II. Scand J Rehabil Med 1989; 21:41–44.
46. Richards JS, Nepomuceno C, Riles M, et al. Assessing pain behavior: the UAB pain behavior scale. Pain 1982; 14:33–38.
47. Tiernan BH, Lewandowski MJ. The behavioral assessment of pain questionnaire: the development and validation of a comprehensive self-report instrument. Am J Pain Med 1992; 2:181–191.
48. Waddell G, McCulloch JS, Kummel E, et al. Nonorganic physical signs in low back pain. Spine 1980; 5:117–125.
49. Hall KM, Hamilton BB, Gordon WA, et al. Characteristics and comparisons of functional assessment indices: disability rating scale, functional independence measure, and functional assessment measure. J Head Trauma Rehabil 1993; 8:60–74.

50. Rucker KS, Metzler HM, Kregel J. Standardization of chronic pain assessment: a multi-perspective approach. Clin J Pain 1996; 12:94–110.
51. www.mensanadiagnostics.com.
52. Dersh J, Gatchel R, Kishino N. The role of tertiary gain in pain disability. Pract Pain Manage 2005; 5:13–28.
53. Bonica JJ, Teitz RM. The Management of Pain. 1990:375.
54. DHHS # PHS 87–1592, 1987.
55. Braithwaite I, White J, Saifuddin A, et al. Vertebral end-plate (Modic) changes on lumbar spine MRI: correlation with pain reproduction at lumbar discography. Eur Spine J 1998; 7:363–368.
56. Bogduk N, McGuirk A. Pain Research and Clinical Management Vol. 13. Amsterdam: Elsevier, 2002:121.
57. Bogduk N, Aprill C, Derby R. Discography. In: White AH, ed. Spine Care. Diagnosis and Conservative Treatment, St. Louis: Mosby, 1995:219–238.
58. http://www.iep.utm.edu/d/diagsino.htm

Clinical Practice Guidelines: Practical and Ethical Issues in Their Development and Implementation

Alexandra Campbell

Pain Program Accreditation/Outcomes Measurement, American Academy of Pain Management, Sonora, California, U.S.A.

INTRODUCTION

The field of guideline development has exploded in the United States, Canada, and the United Kingdom since the early 1990s. In the United States, the Agency for Health Care Policy and Research was tasked with creating medical practice guidelines. The current name of this federal group is the Agency for Health care Research and Quality (AHRQ). A search of the National Guideline Clearinghouse (NGC) database in November 2005 resulted in a list of at least 67 guidelines pertaining to acute and chronic pain conditions as opposed to three in 1994 (1), a greater than 400% increase in the number of pain guidelines in approximately a decade.

The NGC uses the definition of guidelines promulgated by the Institute of Medicine: clinical practice guidelines (CPGs) are systematically developed statements to assist practitioner and patient decisions about appropriate health care for specific clinical circumstances (2). According to the Institute of Medicine (IOM), good practice guidelines:

- are valid and result in appropriate health care outcomes,
- are reliable and reproducible,
- are clinically applicable,
- allow for clinical flexibility,
- are clear,
- are developed according to a multidisciplinary process,
- have scheduled review and revisions,
- include documentation of the process (participants, evidence, and assumptions).

The purpose of this chapter is to give the reader an overview of some of the important practical and ethical issues pertaining to the development and implementation of CPGs in general, and those that relate to chronic nonmalignant pain treatment in particular.

The very definition of CPGs contains the seeds of controversy within it, and some of the practical and ethical issues surrounding this field will become clear as we unravel the meanings contained in the definition put forth by the Institute of Medicine.

First, what is meant by "systematically developed?" We shall see that at least several methods of guideline development exist and that there is not always agreement as to what constitute legitimate guidelines. Second, what is meant by "statements?" What types of statements make up the best guidelines: those that are very specific and prescriptive or those that are more general and broad-based; those that are lengthy or those that are brief? Third, CPGs are intended to "assist" practitioners. This begs the question of what other participants in the health care delivery system might be interested in guidelines and their uses. We shall see that practitioners are definitely not the only health care personnel with a stake in using CPGs to guide health care decisions and that guidelines can become double-edged swords in the hands of payers and the legal system. Bias and conflict of interest might affect the development of guidelines. What safeguards are in place to protect the public in this arena? What type of role should patients play in the development and use of CPGs? Are guidelines going to be perceived as legitimate and trustworthy if they do not take into account patient preferences and opinions? Fourth, what is "appropriate health care?" If guidelines are only prescriptive of traditional, allopathic methods, how do the practitioner and patient make decisions about complementary methods that might be helpful but that might not have yet accumulated the evidence base to formulate guidelines for their use? Finally, how can CPGs best be implemented in "specific clinical circumstances?" Just as the average height of a sample of a population may not describe any one individual's height within the sample, how does the practitioner sift through all of the information about the patient at hand in an attempt to use practice guidelines to make individual treatment decisions? These are some of the general issues that we will attempt to explore and clarify before we turn our attention to some of the specific ethical questions surrounding the use of CPGs for chronic, nonmalignant pain.

EVOLUTION OF GUIDELINE DEVELOPMENT METHODOLOGY

In 1992, evidence-based medicine (EBM) proponents declared that a new paradigm for health care whose practice is based on scientific data from applied clinical health care research would result in better patient care than that based on the traditional approach of understanding basic physiological disease mechanisms coupled with clinical expertise (3). The concept of EBM stirred controversy and raised expectations for improving the quality of health care by reducing variability in practice and controlling costs (4). The development and implementation of practice guidelines was one method of attempting to reach these goals.

Guidelines should address areas where there is large variation in practice, contain new evidence that will have an impact on practice or have a major impact on outcomes or costs (5). In order for guidelines to be useful, Jackson and Feder (6) stated that CPGs need to (i) address only key health care decisions or else they will be too unwieldy for practical decisions, (ii) be based on valid scientific evidence, and (iii) be presented in a concise, accessible format for quick interpretation and use.

In the traditional health care paradigm, panels of experts convened by medical specialty societies produce practice guidelines based on collective expert opinion, often with no explicit consideration of the quality of evidence used to make the recommendations. In the new paradigm, guidelines are developed using formal methods that evaluate the quality of the evidence when summarizing the clinical research literature. The latter are generally more time-consuming and expensive to create than the former (7), but theoretically should be of higher quality.

A guideline development group, ideally composed of six to 15 members (8), refines the clinical question of interest and identifies and collects all of the relevant medical research evidence. Evidence-based guidelines rely heavily on the systematic review and, if available, meta-analyses of studies involving the relevant clinical area. The Cochrane Collaboration is an online repository of systematic reviews and is often used in conjunction with a computer search of Medline (and other medical databases) to locate all research relevant to a specific clinical question. Questions about efficacy are addressed by summarizing the results of randomized-controlled trials, while concerns about the effectiveness of a treatment in actual practice are often best answered by examining studies that have employed a prospective cohort design. The group then sorts the identified studies for relevance to the clinical question and summarizes results regarding benefits, harms, and costs of an intervention.

Ranking the Strength of Evidence

Effectiveness studies can be ranked according to the strength of the evidence therein. Classification schemes that rank studies by experimental design type ensure that studies that attempt to limit sources of bias will receive the most weight in the guideline development process (9). Evidence based on meta-analyses of randomized controlled trials receives the highest rankings while evidence based on expert opinion or respected authorities should receive the least weight in developing a guideline. Regardless of the process used to weigh opinions about the evidence gathered, transparency and explicitness about the process is critical and must be reported in the guideline itself. Recommendations are derived as the group (i) weighs the evidence for efficacy and effectiveness, (ii) considers the applicability (generalizability) of the evidence for a specific population, and (iii) considers factors including costs, resources, and the nature of the relevant health care delivery system (8). The beliefs and values of the panel members also contribute to the recommendations that are made, although these are often not made explicit.

Evaluating Guideline Quality

Grading recommendations in a guideline provide users with information about the confidence with which specific recommendations may result in a desirable health outcome. Group consensus or voting is used to grade the recommendations in accordance with the type of evidence evaluated, often in an A (strongest recommendation) to D (weakest recommendation) format (8).

There are many systems for classifying evidence and grading recommendations, and these systems give different weights to consensus and evidence. The AGREE instrument (10) and the GRADE approach (11) are two of these. Some authors (12) argue that the variability in grading systems defeats the purpose of EBM, which is in part to reduce inconsistencies and standardize practices. Ironically, in spite of the existence of methods for evaluating the quality of guidelines, many CPGs do not adhere to any accepted standards of identifying, evaluating, and synthesizing the scientific evidence (13).

In 2002, the AHRQ issued a report that identified at least 40 systems for rating quality of a body of evidence (14). The Agency reported that evaluation of the key elements of quality (or validity), quantity, and consistency of evidence should be present in any evidence ranking system. However, of the 40 systems examined by the AHRQ, only seven addressed all three of these criteria. In 2004, Ebell et al. (15) published the strength of recommendation taxonomy grading scale that addresses all three of the criteria. This system consists of a simple three-level grading scale. A recommendation with the rating of "A" indicates that the evidence base is consistent and is comprised of high-quality studies that contain patient-oriented outcomes measures. A rating of "B" is given when evidence is of inconsistent or limited quality. A rating of "C" is given to any recommendation based on consensus, opinion, or "usual practice," or is limited to disease-oriented outcome measures.

The following are the current criteria for the inclusion of CPGs in the NGC: (i) CPG contains systematically developed statements including recommendations, strategies, or information to assist practitioners and patients in making appropriate health care decisions in specific clinical circumstances, (ii) The guideline must have been produced by a medical specialty association, professional society, public or private organization, government agency, or health care organization or plan, (iii) Evidence that a systematic literature review from peer-reviewed journals was used in the development of the guideline can be produced along with documentation detailing specific gaps in the scientific evidence for some recommendations contained in the guideline, and (iv) The full text is available upon request in electronic or print format free or for a fee in English. The guideline is current and has been reviewed in the past five years with revisions made as evidence warrants (16). The NGC is a valuable resource for the busy clinician. One can sign up for weekly email alerts that let the practitioner know whenever a new guideline has been added to the NGC database, as well when a guideline has been updated or removed from the system.

Standardization of Guideline Development

The Conference on Guideline Standardization was created in 2002 to develop a set of standards for describing guidelines that would promote improved guideline quality and to facilitate their implementation (17). Conference participants created an 18-point checklist describing important guideline characteristics including defining the target population, stating the methods used to collect evidence, and naming the developer and funding source for the particular guideline. It is hoped that this system of reporting details surrounding a guideline's development will aid in its being understood by the end user by reducing the variability in the style and quality of guidelines.

GUIDELINE LEGITIMACY

Shekelle et al. (8) recommended that a guideline development group be representative of all stakeholders in a given medical area. Multidisciplinary involvement is critical to prevent bias since one specialty group might be "systematically biased in favor of performing procedures in which it has a vested interest" (8). Haycox et al. (18) recognized that medical specialty societies, pharmaceutical companies, insurance companies, governmental agencies, and patient advocacy groups all have a stake in the development of treatment guidelines. Transparency in the guideline development process is imperative so that the influences of special interest groups can be evaluated.

Guidelines need external review to establish validity and utility. Many guidelines have an "expiration date" by which time they should be updated (19). However, merely using a calendar-based system to update guidelines may lead to inappropriate use of resources necessary to accomplish the review. If a field is evolving slowly, an arbitrarily scheduled update may yield no new recommendations. In a quickly evolving field, an update might become necessary well before the scheduled review date. Shekelle et al. (19) propose a systematic model for the review of guidelines by multidisciplinary groups with expertise in the relevant clinical domains. A decision tree is used by the panel to come to a reasonable consensus about whether a revision is called for or whether the guideline can remain in use as published.

Physician Opinions About Guidelines

From the outset of the evidenced-based health care movement, some physicians have been leery of embracing the principles and methods inherent in this approach to taking care of their patients. Concerns about "cookbook" health care, legal precedents, constraining local practice flexibility and the preemption of resources are valid concerns that have been raised (19)????18??. The greatest danger posed with the speedy implementation of even high-quality guidelines is that they may lead to the widespread adoption of practices that have not had a chance to be evaluated in the long-term and that might not at all be cost effective. A review of qualitative studies and physician surveys identified the following internal barriers to physician adherence to CPGs: lack of awareness, lack of familiarity, lack of agreement with the guideline recommendations, lack of self-efficacy, and lack of outcome expectancy and practice inertia (20). External barriers can also impede guideline implementation, including those related to the guidelines themselves (e.g., difficulty of use and inconvenience) and to the local practice environment (e.g., lack of resources, need for new technology, insufficient staffing, and lack of reimbursement).

Input from the "Persons Served"

Haycox et al. (18) also note that the perspective of the patient must be addressed in the development of guidelines to ensure their ultimate acceptability and implementation. Because the ultimate goal of "patient-centered care" (21) is to help the patient to make informed health care decisions, patient preferences must at least be considered when guidelines are in the development stage. Methods of eliciting patient preferences need to be evaluated (22). Patients may be resistant to accepting recommendations based on guidelines that do not agree with their personal preferences for health care, and many physicians are reluctant to use guidelines if they perceive that patients will not accept the recommendations (19).

Bias and Conflict of Interest in the Development of Clinical Practice Guidelines

Because medical practice guidelines can play an important role in determining, which patients are seen as eligible for certain treatments, it is imperative that guideline development be transparent regarding potential conflicts of interest among their authors. Unfortunately, the reporting of potential conflicts of interest in clinical guidelines has been scant. Papanikolaou et al. (23) reported that in 1999 only 3.7% of guidelines published that year ($n = 40$) disclosed any potential conflicts of interest among the authors publishing in six major clinical journals. It is well established that a significant proportion of authors of articles in biomedical journals serves on scientific advisory boards of biotechnology firms, are shareholders in such companies, or are listed as inventors on patents (24). Because conflicts of interests can potentially harm the credibility and acceptance of guidelines, it is important that the process of disclosing potential conflicts be standardized and become as transparent as possible.

Use of Clinical Practice Guidelines for Health Care Rationing

Deontological or duty-based ethics demand that health care providers act in the best interest of each individual patient, while utilitarian or outcome-based ethics attempt to maximize the greatest good for the largest number of people in a society (25). While medical practitioners may be able to act based on deontological principles, administrators and payers may be obliged to apply utilitarian standards. Problems arise between these two approaches to making health care decisions when resources are limited. Practice guidelines may be useful in assisting a practitioner to make difficult decisions, but when psychosocial criteria are used to determine treatment eligibility ethical dilemmas may arise. For example, psychosocial criteria including (i) behavioral and psychological make-up, (ii) availability of family or other support systems, (iii) financial resources, (iv) occupational and social roles, (v) environmental factors, and (vi) a mixture of factors including age, disability, and lifestyle were found to influence the selection of patients for cardiac procedures in Canada (26). Similar types of screening criteria are used to determine pain patients' acceptance for invasive procedures. For example, Janata (27) listed major depression, untreated addiction, lack of social support, and unresolved compensation issues as reasons to consider denial for invasive treatment, in spite of recent evidence that patients who have pending compensation litigation may make more progress in pain management programs than patients who do not (28). The issue of guideline legitimacy becomes very important when the guidelines are used to withhold potentially beneficial treatment from patients.

DISSEMINATION AND IMPLEMENTATION OF CLINICAL PRACTICE GUIDELINES

Feder et al. (29) noted that the existence of a high-quality CPG does not guarantee its successful implementation in the clinical setting. Passive dissemination through publication in journals or on the Internet rarely leads to substantive change in practitioner behavior. Obstacles to implementation can exist at the organizational, peer group, and individual levels.

Paper-Based Guidelines

The most commonly used guideline format has been paper based. Whether published on the Internet or not, these are static documents that must be periodically reviewed, evaluated, and updated. Paper-based guidelines are still used because a computing infrastructure that would support the use of computer-based guidelines is not available in many health care environments. In addition, the use of computer-based guidelines requires a more technical (i.e., expensive) approach, in terms of their development and implementation (30).

Finding a Common Platform for Computer Guideline Language: Contributions of Medical Informatics

The medical informatics community is attempting to use computer technology to create ways to communicate narrative, population-based guidelines using modular, patient-specific decision support systems at the point of care (31). Rule-based approaches are used to encode clinical rules as medical logic modules (MLMs).

Augmented decision tables (ADTs) add information about probability and utility. The drawback of the rule-based approach is that MLMs and ADTs are not adequate to model a multistep guideline that must be carried out over time. These methods, used in the early 1990s, have begun to be supplanted by a task-based paradigm or task-network model (TNM) in order to support multistep guidelines. The TNM can model alternative pathways and sequences of tasks and supports visual representation of pathways and the tasks within them.

There are at least six TNM guideline representation languages: Arden Syntax, Asbru, EON, The Guideline Interchange Format, GUIDE, PRODIGY, and PROforma. Peleg et al. (31) conclude that it may be possible to reach a certain degree of standardization in (i) structural format, (ii) expression language, and (iii) patient information models. The goal of using a common medical concept model may be out of reach currently, but is something to aim for in the future. The languages differ in their scopes, decision models, and the ways that clinical goals are represented. These authors hope that the computer-interpretable guideline development community will come to a consensus and standardize as many elements as possible while maintaining the freedom to investigate the unique aspects of each representation language.

When a guideline is embedded in a computer-based electronic medical record (EMR), rules are triggered by patient data that have been put into the system (4). These most sophisticated forms of guideline-based patient-specific reminders have been shown to be among the most effective because they are integrated into the clinician's normal workflow and can aid decision making in real time (32). Even the best, most effective guideline implementation methods are perceived differently by different medical professionals. Lyons et al. (33) reported that administrators are often convinced of the value of computer-based guideline implementation methods, while physicians and nurses may remain skeptical of their value.

Local Adaptation

All guidelines require adaptation for use within local health care settings. Recommendations may need to be reformatted and written in terms that can create measurable criteria and targets for quality improvement (QI) projects (29).

Methods of Encouraging Guideline Implementation

Continuing Education

In order to move practitioners from mere awareness of the existence of new CPGs to agreement with the guidelines and on to their adoption in the treatment of individual patients, continuing education that takes into account principles of adult learning will be helpful (34). Practitioner resistance may be overcome through CE methods that go beyond didactic lectures that take place at nonpractice locations. New methods that may facilitate the adoption of quality guidelines include interactive workshops, small group sessions, and peer review at practice locations. Matching learning styles with educational methods and directly addressing practitioners' needs and perceived barriers to the implementation of guidelines in programs that are brief and authoritative may lead to a greater magnitude of change in provider behavior (35).

Incentives for Clinicians Implementing Guidelines

"Pay for performance" is the new jargon used to describe efforts of payers to reward clinicians for (hopefully) improving the quality of health care while at the same reducing costs. Guidelines provide clear goals that can be used to evaluate provider behavior. One method of using monetary incentives to reward provider adherence to CPGs involves tracking provider compliance with a specific guideline-based health care action deemed, at the organizational level, to be important for improving the quality and/or cost effectiveness of care. For a given time period, providers who have complied with a specific recommendation (e.g., ordered a specific test as a result of a clinical reminder that came up in a computerized decision support system, or refrained from ordering a test) become eligible for a random drawing for a modest monetary bonus above their base salary or pay rate. Other providers who complied with the guideline are also eligible for the drawing. Monetary bonuses for compliance that are modest and frequently awarded show promise in changing provider behavior in ways that are desired by the health care organization (36). A full discussion of the ethical issues surrounding "pay for performance" is beyond the scope of this chapter, but the issues need to be addressed by the health care industry.

Legal Threats and Regulatory Mandate

Hurwitz (37) noted that Plato had an opinion as long ago as the forth century BC about the inferiority of guidelines over medical treatment delivery based on the practical expertise and knowledge base of the individual clinician. All guidelines presuppose an average patient and do not adequately enable the clinician to make decisions about the particular patient before that patient. Once expertise is thought to reside in the guidelines and their developers, it is effectively removed from the clinician and hamstrings the clinician's ability to rely on professional judgment on a case-by-case basis, taking into account all of the nuances and complexities of the actual situation. A common complaint about the increasing reliance of the health care industry on CPGs is that they may cause harm to clinicians when used in malpractice cases to prove that the care delivered to a plaintiff was inadequate or harmful. The overly prescriptive language of some guidelines and the use of arbitrary numbers (e.g., months of treatment and intervals between tests) along with simplistic algorithms for appropriate medical action might be used as evidence against a clinician who used a thorough yet complex process of clinical judgment to make treatment decisions that seemed to be best for the particular patient (38).

In the area of treatment of acute pain and pain surrounding terminal illness such as cancer, plaintiffs are able to point at increasingly well-established standards of care and CPGs published by government agencies and medical societies (39). Failure to properly assess, treat, and manage pain is considered professional negligence (40). The situation is less clear regarding the treatment of chronic pain, especially that of benign origin.

GUIDELINE EVALUATION IN THE FIELD

Pilote and Tager (41) noted that despite the publication of numerous practice guidelines of various types, clinical outcomes research to evaluate them had been scant. They noted that efficacy studies that were conducted in select groups of patients under highly controlled conditions were often used to create guidelines that then needed to be applied in the "real world." Effectiveness studies are then used to evaluate the guidelines. These authors proposed a methodological framework based on the model of chronic disease epidemiology, whereby effectiveness studies carried out in less controlled, real clinical situations also be used to inform the development of guidelines. Although CPGs are numerous, randomized controlled studies to evaluate their effectiveness have been rare and not always supportive.

The Final Link in the Quality Medical Care Chain: From Guideline to Quality Improvement (Outcomes Research)

How are guidelines translated into care of individual patients? How is care based on a particular guideline evaluated in a specific setting? While the EBM movement is having its impact on clinical research methodology and the practice of medicine, the field of QI has continued, for the most part, to be based on personal intuitions and anecdotal reports within organizations (42). Early in the EBM movement, it was thought that if clinicians developed systematic and critical reading habits for evaluating the clinical research, they would naturally put new evidence into practice. Unfortunately, clinicians simply do not have the time to review and analyze all of the relevant literature in any given clinical area. Hence, the appearance of systematic reviews and, ultimately, CPGs. However, relying on the passive diffusion of information in reviews and guidelines has not lead to the successful adoption of recommendations given in many published guidelines (42). Barriers such as clinician disagreement with guidelines, resistance to perceived violations of physician autonomy, and logistic and financial concerns are common.

The field of QI has historically consisted of an incremental approach, attempting to take the fruits of EBM, for example, CPGs, and applying them in specific clinical situations. Shojania and Grimshaw (42) complain that QI is usually a haphazard endeavor that usually does not conform to even the basic principles of scientific investigation (e.g., quantifying and tracking preintervention values for relevant clinical outcomes, reporting variability of data collected, reporting numbers of subjects used, blinding, and randomization). Redesigning whole systems of care represents a faster way to create change in health care delivery, but is very expensive and does not always lead to better and more cost-effective care, in spite of substantial investments. Shojania and Grimshaw (42) propose that QI efforts be based on rigorous experimental design principles, that time-series analysis is used to control for background variation in outcomes measures, and that controlled before–after designs are used when time series is not feasible. They strongly recommend performing pilot studies before embarking on a potentially useless QI intervention. In their review of the field, these authors found that using multifaceted change strategies and targeting provider behavior in QI studies may lead to the best outcomes in attempts to implement CPGs. With more attention paid to ascertaining why a particular QI intervention works and to understanding the factors that are obstacles to successful change, modest success will be made in establishing evidence-based care in real-world clinical settings.

GUIDELINES AND THE USE OF COMPLEMENTARY/ALTERNATIVE MEDICINE FOR PAIN

Complementary/alternative treatment approaches are becoming more and more popular among patients and some allopathic practitioners, especially in the area of managing chronic illness, including pain. A report issued by the Institute of Medicine on Complementary and Alternative Medicine (CAM) in 2005 (43) recommends that national professional organizations for CAM disciplines develop practice guidelines in order to overcome inappropriate practice variations that are defended by some practitioners as necessary for "individualized" treatment. The report points out that traditional medical providers also tailor therapies for individual patients and are able to do this within the reasonable constraints of practice guidelines based on evidence.

The question of guideline creation for CAM interventions cannot realistically begin to be addressed until there is a sufficient evidence base for complementary treatments (e.g., acupuncture, massage therapy, therapeutic touch, etc.). In the area of acupuncture, for example, enough high-quality randomized controlled trials have accumulated for the National Institutes of Health (NIH) to publish a consensus statement concluding that acupuncture is effective for the prevention and control of nausea related to chemotherapy (44). Other recent high-quality systematic reviews have concluded that acupuncture may also be helpful in treating recurrent headache and dental pain (45).

Self-regulation strategies for promoting relaxation (self-hypnosis/guided imagery/muscle relaxation) have become established as an "empirically supported therapy" (46) for recurrent pediatric migraine, although psychologist practitioners of "behavioral medicine" may not agree that this type of therapeutic approach belongs in the "alternative" medicine category. The IOM committee acknowledged that one of the major difficulties surrounding progress in the area of CAM research and policy development is the definition of the term.

The Committee report stated, "the same principles and standards of evidence of treatment effectiveness (should) apply to all treatment, whether currently labeled as conventional medicine or CAM." The report affirmed that the RCT is the "gold standard" for building an evidence base for CAM treatment efficacy but suggested several other approaches for establishing treatment effectiveness. The committee also attempted to set guidelines for funding CAM research based on several criteria including biological plausibility and the existence of at least some evidence of an intervention's effectiveness. Unfortunately, many lower-quality studies continue to be published that may exaggerate various CAM treatment effects.

ISSUES SPECIFICALLY RELATED TO THE CPGs FOR CHRONIC NONMALIGNANT PAIN DISORDERS

As noted at the beginning of this chapter, there are many CPGs for the treatment of chronic benign pain. Some of them are multidisciplinary in nature, while others are specific to distinct treatment modalities. The general practical and ethical concerns discussed above are relevant to the development of all CPGs, including those addressing the treatment of chronic pain. In 2000, the American Pain Society published the results of a survey of practitioners who attempted to identify the most important ethical dilemmas encountered in the practice of pain management (47). Several of these and a number of others pertain to areas for which guidelines have been written. In this chapter, I will focus on the following guideline areas that have associated ethical problems: (i) the long-term use of opioids for chronic nonmalignant pain, (ii) the appropriate use of invasive medical procedures in pain treatment, (iii) multidisciplinary chronic pain management guidelines and payer resistance.

The Long-Term Use of Opioids for Chronic Pain of Nonmalignant Origin: The Pain and Policy Studies Group vs. DEA Debacle and Current Guidelines

The headlines grab the attention. A famous radio talk show host is accused of doctor-shopping for pain medication and of acquiring opiates on the black market. Books are published sensationalizing the abuse of certain long-acting opioid preparations in poor rural communities. Physicians are afraid to prescribe opioids to their chronic pain patients for fear of being targeted and raided by the Drug Enforcement Administration. Patients' families are afraid that their loved ones will be turned into drug addicts by their doctors. Patients are reluctant to take their medications as prescribed for the same misguided reason and so suffer needlessly. Who can make sense out of and bring some order to this madness?

In August of 2004, a joint publication by the Drug Enforcement Agency (DEA), Last Acts Partnership, and the Pain and Policy Studies Group in the form of "frequently asked questions and answers" was posted to the Internet (48). This publication included a specific disclaimer that it was not to be seen as a CPG and yet it was comprised of fairly specific recommendations for the use of opioid medication in treating pain of different sorts. The main thrust of the "frequently asked questions (FAQ)" was to balance access to necessary opioid medication for the chronic pain patient with the need of society as whole to be protected against criminal drug abuse and/or diversion of prescription medication to the black market. However, almost as soon as the "FAQ" was posted (two months later), it was pulled from the DEA website and from the P&PSG website soon after that. It appears that the DEA felt that some of the comments included in the "FAQ" were inappropriate and perhaps were not helpful to the "war on drugs." The DEA claimed that in spite of the administration's own input into the "FAQ" document, it contained "misstatements of law and statements that could create confusion . . . and created misleading perceptions about physicians' obligations to remain within the bounds of accepted medical practice" (49). In response, Joranson and colleagues (50) pleaded with the DEA to "maintain balance." They reiterated that it is ethically imperative that prescribers avoid contributing to drug abuse and diversion, but that it is equally imperative that law enforcement efforts to control diversion "never interfere in clinical pain management." They concluded that the DEA's withdrawal of the document stood to undermine years of effort spent in educating clinicians about optimal pain treatment and ways to effectively manage potential legal risks associated with prescribing controlled substances. An Interim Policy Statement issued by the DEA in November of 2004 (51) only served to confuse physicians further and created a climate of fear regarding prescribing controlled substances. In a November 2004 letter to the DEA Office of Diversion Control (52), Joranson asked federal authorities to reopen the dialog, especially regarding the issue of a physician writing more than one prescription at a time (some to be filled at specific later dates) for the convenience of the pain patient and furtherance of the medical treatment plan. Consequently, in January of 2005, the DEA solicited comments on the subject of dispensing controlled substances for pain treatment and reported the feedback in August 2005 (53). The DEA has stated that it plans to issue another document in the Federal Register that will clarify its position on the legal principles pertaining to the dispensing of controlled substances for pain treatment. The pain community is still waiting for this document.

This debacle underscores some of the ethical issues that are prominent with respect to the use of opioid medication in the treatment of chronic nonmalignant pain. While great strides have been made, for the most part, in establishing accepted guidelines for the treatment of pain associated with cancer or at the end of life (54–56), the attention of the guideline development community has finally turned to creating guidelines for use of opioids with chronic noncancer pain patients.

The prominent ethical issues involve maintaining access to opioids for those patients who need them, clarification of concepts surrounding "addiction," and providing safeguards for physicians who want to help their patients in pain. In 1997, the American Academy of Pain Medicine and the American Pain Society published a brief nonevidence—based consensus statement supporting the appropriate use of opioids for the treatment of chronic noncancer pain (57). In 2003, the Veteran's Administration/Department of Defense published evidence-based guidelines for the use of opioid therapy for chronic pain (58). These guidelines were arrived at by the consensus of experts based on a systematic review of the relevant literature. Strength of evidence rules and method of grading of recommendations were clearly described in the report. For the patient who has not achieved a substantial reduction in pain using other treatment methods, the panel found that a trial of opiates could be warranted. An opioid trial should take place after a comprehensive assessment has been performed with due consideration of the potential legal and medical contraindications to this approach. The guideline did not rule out the prescribing of opiates for pain in patients with a history of substance use problems, but recommended that any substance abuse problems could be treated concurrently by an addiction specialist. Complicated patients should be referred to a multidisciplinary pain program for treatment. Patient education and family involvement in understanding the risks and benefits of an opioid trial, including the discussion and use of a signed opioid treatment agreement, were recommended. Use of a specific treatment plan that usually includes the coordination of the use of opiates with other nonpharmacological treatment modalities is important. A very carefully titrated opioid trial with detailed written documentation was recommended using a long-acting preparation on a time-contingent dosing schedule. Thorough documentation of prescriptions to be filled within seven days of issuance is required in the VA setting. Ongoing assessment of the effectiveness of the opioid trial with attention to pain reduction and functional improvement is imperative for success. The guideline recommended that opioid therapy be discontinued by tapering should the evidence that harm outweighs benefit become apparent or should the patient wish to stop the treatment. Descriptions of the development of compulsive/addictive behaviors were given with the recommendation to refer the patient to an addiction specialist if necessary. Detailed instructions for tapering medication and an emphasis on maintaining the practitioner–patient relationship (i.e., the importance of nonabandonment of the patient) were provided. These guidelines appear to be the most detailed and clear publication in the field. While they were written specifically for the population of veterans, the common sense they contain make them necessary reading for any practitioner looking for guidance in prescribing opioids for their chronic nonmalignant pain patients.

Conflict of Interest in the Development of Guidelines for the Use of Invasive Techniques to Relieve Chronic Pain

In July 2002, Sanders published an opinion piece in the American Pain Society Bulletin (59) that questioned the "almost knee-jerk" use of lumbar epidural steroid injections and sympathetic nerve blocks for acute and chronic low back pain patients. Sanders noted that the use of these invasive techniques generate upwards of $203 million dollars per year in income for the anesthesiologists who perform them. Sanders objected that the evidence base was lacking and that there was only very limited empirical support for the techniques. According to Sanders, the most well-designed study at that time failed to show any substantial benefit of epidural steroids over saline injections at three months follow-up. The rate of patients in both groups who ended up having surgery after a year was almost identical.

In spite of the paucity of high-quality data demonstrating the efficacy of epidural steroid injections, the American Society of Anesthesiologists (ASA) published guidelines in 1997 (60), which have not yet been updated, that recommend the use of this treatment approach. Specifically the guidelines state: "The panel of consultants supports the importance of locally injected corticosteroids in improving analgesia and enhancing patient functioning and quality of life."

In defense of the ASA guidelines, the panel did state that the decision to use steroid injections must be made within "the context of the patient's overall treatment plan," but this may represent an instance of the difficulty faced by specialty societies in attempting to produce unbiased guidelines. An analogy may help in understanding this ethical dilemma: if one asked a carpenter to come up with a guideline for the building of a tool shed, could one really expect the guideline not to recommend the use of wood and nails, as opposed to, say, prefabricated metal and screws? While the vested interests of specialty groups may bias the guidelines they publish, one should be cautious in assuming any bad faith on the part of the groups. This problem of bias could certainly be addressed through the establishment of multidisciplinary guideline panels to ensure that the best evidence for all of the possible chronic pain treatment modalities is gathered in one resource.

Indeed, the recently published guideline entitled "Assessment and Management of Chronic Pain" by the Institute for Clinical Systems Improvement (ICSI) in 2005 (61) was developed by a multidisciplinary panel including representatives of the fields of Physical Medicine and Rehabilitation, Psychology, Occupational Medicine, Neurology, Nursing, Pharmacy, and Anesthesiology. This group proposed a two-tiered treatment approach that recommends a comprehensive bio-psychosocial initial evaluation and the involvement of a multidisciplinary team. Level I treatments (which include psychosocial management, pharmacotherapy, and fluoroscopically guided epidural steroid injections) are more conservative, while Level II treatment modalities (including surgery, ablative neurosurgery, and stimulation device implantation) may be necessary for the more complex patients who have clearly failed to benefit from conservative approaches.

The guideline states that invasive treatments for mechanical/compressive pain (e.g., low back pain) including epidural steroids, have limited scientific evidence of efficacy, as does surgery for chronic low back pain. The authors of the guideline noted that the evidence for these approaches to treating back pain come mainly from nonrandomized studies and consensus statements (Classes C and R in their strength of evidence rating system).

Clearly, guidelines that come out of multidisciplinary panels will most likely be more cautious in their recommendations. Sanders (62) recommends that guidelines be clear about the types of chronic pain patients to whom they apply, rely only upon the best evidence (with prospective, randomized, controlled trials as the minimum standard), minimize reliance on expert consensus for making recommendations, minimize bias and conflict of interest by requiring multidisciplinary involvement and full public disclosure of the development process, and establish federal funding sources for guidelines (rather than relying on the financial support of specialty medical groups).

Multidisciplinary Pain Management Guidelines: Conflicts Between the Evidence Base and Payer Willingness to Reimburse

As discussed above, the ICSI guidelines for the treatment of nonmalignant chronic pain recommend the involvement of a multidisciplinary team in the assessment and treatment of chronic pain patients (61). After a thorough bio-psychosocial assessment and the attempted determination of the biological mechanisms of pain, Level I treatment recommendations include functional rehabilitation and psychosocial management in a personal "plan of care" that the patient is heavily involved in creating. The use of pharmacological therapy (especially nonopioid analgesics, antidepressants, short-term muscle relaxants, and anticonvulsants) and nonpharmacological techniques (e.g., cognitive behavioral therapy, exercise, and relaxation) should be considered among the first line of treatment approaches. In order to consider implementing Level II interventions (e.g., surgery and spinal cord stimulation), the team must conclude that a sufficient trial using conservative approaches has been effectively implemented with limited benefit. This guideline's emphasis on the importance of multidisciplinary, or better yet, interdisciplinary assessment and treatment planning and implementation confirms the work of Turk and Burwinkle (63), who has published extensively on the benefits of interdisciplinary pain rehabilitation approaches. Turk maintains that reliable data not only confirm that interdisciplinary programs are clinically effective (in terms of pain reduction, decreased opioid intake, decreased health care utilization, increased activity, and return to work rates along with closure of disability claims) but are also cost effective. Turk noted that despite these facts, the insurance industry has been unfairly biased in its denials for payment for these seemingly "expensive" programs when, in fact, these are more cost effective than unitary treatment approaches over the long run. Short-term, quick-fix thinking may predominate among third-party payers who at times seem more willing to reimburse for expensive yet circumscribed treatment approaches. There may be an unfair negative bias against interdisciplinary pain treatment programs due to anecdotal stories about some failures of longer-term pain management programs. The insurance industry must be made to understand that the evidence supports the effectiveness of the interdisciplinary treatment model for difficult chronic pain problems and to take a long range and broader social view with respect to cost effectiveness. Perhaps, the new guidelines published by the ICSI will help open their eyes to the truth.

CONCLUSIONS: THE FUTURE OF CLINICAL PRACTICE GUIDELINES

The explosion of the guideline industry, while leading to modest improvements in health care quality, has created inherent problems as well. There is a veritable "guideline industry" now that has frankly overwhelmed physicians (64). The danger in this is that clinicians may give up and ignore relevant guidelines for their areas of practice. They do this at their own, and possibly their patients', peril. Guidelines are not always based on the best available evidence, are not always developed systematically, and may represent the values of specific groups or vested business interests (64). Clinicians have a duty to make themselves knowledgeable about the guideline creation process so that they can effectively ignore the worst CPGs and spend their limited time absorbing the information in the best CPGs. The use of computerized EMR systems, which build in CPG information, may help in this area. However, this will require adding an entirely new layer of information technology workers to input guideline information into systems and keep them current. It should be incumbent upon all practitioners to make use of the Internet and the NGC to maintain up-to-date knowledge on relevant guideline publication and revisions.

The translation of evidence into guidelines that will have the intended practical benefits of improving health care quality and/or reducing cost has proven to be quite difficult to accomplish in the real world. Heterogeneous populations and individual variation make the application of guidelines a less than precise science. There will always be a place for expert clinical judgment, with sensitivity to the needs and desires of the individual patient. The application of CPGs, whether for chronic pain or any medical condition, may always be more of an art than a science.

REFERENCES

1. Cahn MA. Practice guidelines: a piece of the quality puzzle. Bull Med Libr Assoc 1994; 82(3):312–314.
2. Institute of Medicine. In: MJ Field, KN Lohr, eds. Clinical Practice Guidelines: Directions for a New Program. Washington, D.C.: National Academy Press, 1990.
3. Haynes RB. What kind of evidence is it that evidence-based medicine advocates want health care providers and consumers to pay attention to? BMC Health Serv Res 2002; 2(3) (published online before print March 6, 2002).
4. Zielstorff RD. Online practice guidelines: issues, obstacles and future prospects. J Am Med Inform Assoc 1998; 5(3):227–236.
5. Norheim OF. Health care rationing: are additional criteria needed for assessing evidence based clinical practice guidelines? BMJ 1999; 319(7222):1426–1429.
6. Jackson R, Feder G. Guidelines for clinical guidelines: a simple, pragmatic strategy for guideline development. BMJ 1998; 317(7156):427–428.
7. Cruse H, Winiarek M, Marshburn J, Clark O, Djulbegovic B. Quality and methods of developing practice guidelines. BMC Health Serv Res [serial online] 2002; 2(1).
8. Shekelle PG, Woolf SH, Eccles M, Grimshaw J. Clinical guidelines: developing guidelines. BMJ 1999; 318:593–596.
9. Golditz GA, Miller JN, Mosteller F. How study design affects outcomes in comparisons of therapy I: medical. Stat Med 1989; 8:441–454.
10. MacDermid JC, Brooks D, Solway S, Switzer-McIntyre S, Brosseau L, Graham ID. Reliability and validity of the AGREE instrument used by physical therapists in assessment of clinical practice guidelines. BMC Health Serv Res [serial online] 2005; 5(18) (Accessed November 2005).
11. Atkins D, Briss PA, Eccles M, et al. Systems for grading the quality of evidence and the strength of recommendations II: pilot study of a new system. BMC Health Serv Res [serial online] 2005; 5(25).
12. Upshur R. Are all evidence-based practices alike? Problems in the ranking of evidence. CMAJ 2003; 169(7):672–673.
13. Shaneyfelt TM, Mayo-Smith MF, Rothwangl J. Are guidelines following guidelines? The methodological quality of clinical practice guidelines in the peer-reviewed medical literature. JAMA 1999; 26(28):1950–1951.
14. Systems to rate the strength of scientific evidence. Summary, evidence report/technology assessment: number 47. AHRQ pub. No. 02-E015, March 2002. Agency for

Health care Research and Quality. Rockville, MD. Available at www.ahrq.gov/clinic/epcsums/strengthsum.htm (Accessed on November 15, 2005).

15. Ebell MH, Siwek J, Weiss BD, Woolf SH, et al. Strength of recommendation taxonomy (SORT): a patient-centered approach to grading evidence in the medical literature. J Fam Pract 2004; 53(2):111–120.

16. National Guideline Clearinghouse. Inclusion criteria. Available at http://www.guideline.gov/about/inclusion.aspx (Accessed December 15, 2005).

17. Schiffman RN, Shekelle P, Overhage JM, et al. Standardized reporting of clinical practice guidelines: a proposal from the conference on guideline standardization. Ann Intern Med 2003; 139:493–498.

18. Haycox A, Bagust A, Walley T. Clinical guidelines-the hidden costs. BMJ 1999; 318:391–393.

19. Shekelle P, Eccles M, Grimshaw J, Woolf S. When should clinical guidelines be updated? BMJ 2001; 323:155–157.

20. Cabana MD, Rand CS, Powe NR, et al. Why do not physicians follow clinical practice guidelines? A framework for improvement. JAMA 1999; 282(15):1458–1465.

21. Insuring America's Health: Principles and recommendations. Committee on the Consequences of Uninsurance, Board of Health Care Services. Institute of Medicine of the National Academies. Washington, D.C.: National Academies Press, 2004. Available at http://fermat.nap.edu/books/0309091055/html/R1.html.

22. Walker RD, Howard MO, Lambert MD, Suchinsky R. Medical practice guidelines. West J Med 1994; 161:39–44.

23. Papanikolaou GN, Baltogianni MS, Contopoulos-Ioannidis DG, Haidich AB, Giannakakis IA, Ioannidis JP. Reporting of conflicts of interest in guidelines of preventive and therapeutic interventions. BMC Med Res Methodol [serial online] 2001; 1(3) (Accessed November, 2005).

24. Krimsky S, Rothenberg LS, Stott P, Kyle G. Scientific journals and their author's financial interests: a pilot study. Psychother Psychosom 1998; 67:194–201.

25. Dossetor JB. Psychosocial patient selection criteria in clinical practice guidelines: an ethical basis for rationing? CMAJ 2001; 164(5):642–643.

26. Giacomini MK, Cook DJ, Streiner DL, Anand SS. Guidelines as rationing tools: a qualitative analysis of psychosocial patient selection criteria for cardiac procedures. CMAJ 2001; 164(5):634–640.

27. Janata JW. Psychological evaluation for interventional therapy. Presented at the American Academy of Pain Management. 16th Annual Clinical Meeting: Clinicians United to Manage Pain, San Diego, CA, 2004.

28. Lynch P. Litigation does not affect physical recovery-new research. Accessed online: http://www.irishmedicalnews.ie/articles.asp?Category=news&ArticleID=15102. December 20, 2005.

29. Feder G, Eccles M, Grol R, Griffiths C, Grimshaw J. Clinical guidelines: using clinical guidelines. BMJ 1999; 318:728–730.

30. Owens DK. Use of medical informatics to implement and develop clinical practice guidelines. West J Med 1998; 168:166–175.

31. Peleg M, Samson T, Bury J, et al. Comparing computer-interpretable guideline models: a case-study approach. J Am Med Inform Assoc 2003; 10:52–68.

32. Johnston ME, Langton KB, Haynes RB, Mathieu A. Effects of computer-based clinical decision support systems on clinician performance and patient outcome. Ann Intern Med 1994; 120:135–142.

33. Lyons SS, Tripp-Reimer T, Sorofman BA, et al. VA QUERI informatics paper: information technology for clinical guideline implementation: perceptions of multidisciplinary stakeholders. J Am Med Inform Assoc 2005; 12(1):64–71.

34. Davis D. Clinical practice guidelines and the translation of knowledge: the science of continuing medical education. JMAC 2000; 163(10):1278–1279.

35. Stross JK. Guidelines have their limits. Ann Int Med 1999; 131(4):304–306.

36. Marder B. Providing quality incentives for your medical staff? Patient Saf Qual Mon [e-newsletter] 2006; 5(1).

37. Hurwitz B. Clinical guidelines: legal and political considerations of clinical practice guidelines. BMJ 1999; 318:661–664.

38. Woolf SH, Grof L, Hutchinson A, Eccles M, Grimshaw J. Clinical guidelines: potential benefits, limitations, and harms of clinical guidelines. BMJ 1999; 318:527–530.
39. Gordon DB, Dahl JL, Miaskowski C, et al. American Pain Society recommendations for improving the quality of acute and cancer pain management. Arch Intern Med 2005; 165:1574–1580.
40. Furrow BR. Failure to treat pain: no more excuses. Trial [serial online] 2002; 38(10).
41. Pilote L, Tager I. Outcomes research in the development and evaluation of practice guidelines. BMC Health Serv Res [serial online] 2002; 2(7).
42. Shojania KG, Grimshaw JM. Evidence-based quality improvement: the state of the science. Health Aff 2005; 24(1):138–150.
43. Institute of Medicine. Complementary and Alternative Medicine in the United States. Washington, D.C.: The National Academies Press, 2005.
44. National Institutes of Health. Acupuncture. NIH Consensus Conference. JAMA 1998; 280(17):1518–1524.
45. Linde K, Vickers A, Hondras M, et al. Systematic reviews of complementary therapies-an annotated bibliography. Part I: acupuncture. BMC Complement Altern Med [serial online] 2001; 1(3).
46. Tsao JCI, Zeltzer LK. Complementary and alternative medicine approaches for pediatric pain: a review of the state-of-the-science. eCAM Adv Access Publ [serial online] 2005; 2(2):149–159.
47. Dubois MY. Ethics in pain management: a progress report. Am Pain Soc Bull [serial online] 2000; 10(1).
48. U.S. Drug Enforcement Administration, the Last Acts Partnership and the University of Wisconsin Pain and Policy Studies Group. Prescription pain medications: frequently asked questions and answers for health care professionals, and law enforcement personnel, 2004.
49. Walker letter to Joranson. October 4, 2004. Available at http://www.medsch.wisc.edu/painpolicy/DEA/Mr.%20David%20Joranson.PDF (Accessed December 15, 2005).
50. Joranson, Portnoy, Passik letter to Tandy. October 26, 2004. Available at http://www.medsch.wisc.edu/painpolicy/DEA/letter%20to%20DEA.pdf (Accessed December 15, 2005).
51. Drug Enforcement Agency Interim Policy Statement. Dispensing of controlled substances for the treatment of pain. November 16, 2004. Docket No. DEA-258S. Available at http://a257.g.akamaitech.net/7/257/2422/06jun20041800/edocket.access.gpo.gov/2004/pdf/04-25469.pdf (Accessed December 15, 2005).
52. Joranson letter to Leonhart. November 24, 2004. Available at http://www.medsch.wisc.edu/painpolicy/DEA/IPSresponse.pdf (Accessed December 15, 2005).
53. Department of Justice Drug Enforcement Administration. Clarification of existing requirements under the Controlled Substances Act for prescribing Schedule II controlled substances. August 26, 2005. Docket No. DEA-271N. http://www.medsch.wisc.edu/painpolicy/DEA/FR8.26.05.pdf.
54. American Pain Society Quality of Care Task Force. American Pain Society recommendations for improving the quality of acute and cancer pain management. Arch Intern Med 2005; 165:1574–1580.
55. National Consensus Project for Quality Palliative Care. Clinical Pract Guidel Qual Palliat Care 2004; 1–22.
56. APS Task Force on Pain, Symptoms and End of Life Care. Treatment of pain at the end of life: a position statement from the American Pain Society. Am Pain Soc Bull 1997; 7(1):11.
57. American Academy of Pain Medicine and the American Pain Society. The use of opioids for the treatment of chronic pain. Am Acad Pain Med Am Pain Soc 1997.
58. Veterans Health Administration, Department of Defense. VA/DoD clinical practice guideline for the management of opioid therapy for chronic pain. Washington, D.C.: Veterans Health Administration, Department of Defense, 2003.
59. Sanders S. Nerve block therapy for low back pain: show me the money and the science. Am Pain Soc Bull [serial online] 2002; 12(4).
60. American Society of Anesthesiologists. Practice guidelines for chronic pain management. Anesthesiology 1997; 87:995–1004.

61. Institute for Clinical Systems Improvement (ICSI). Assessment and Management of Chronic Pain. Bloomington (MN): Institute for Clinical Systems Improvement (ICSI), 2005.
62. Sanders S. Integrating practice guidelines for chronic pain: from the Tower of Babel to the Rosetta Stone. Am Pain Soc Bull [serial online] 2000; 10(6).
63. Turk DC, Burwinkle TM. Treatment of chronic pain sufferers-An antidote to mural dyslexia. Pain Pract 2004; 14(3):20–25.
64. Grol R. Improving the quality of medical care: building bridges among professional pride, payer profit, and patient satisfaction. JAMA 2001; 284:2578–2585.

18 Ethical Issues in Chronic Pain Research

Robert J. Gatchel

Department of Psychology, College of Science, The University of Texas at Arlington, Arlington, Texas, U.S.A.

Perry N. Fuchs

Department of Psychology and Biology, The University of Texas at Arlington, Arlington, Texas, U.S.A.

Colin Allen

Department of History and Philosophy of Science, Indiana University, Bloomington, Indiana, U.S.A.

"Researchers are responsible for the ethical conduct of research conducted by them and by others under their supervision or control."

Tangney, 2000

INTRODUCTION

As the above quote clearly highlights, it is the responsibility of researchers and research supervisors to be certain that their research staff and students assistants are very familiar with all of the ethical principles and current standards relevant to the research they are conducting. Indeed, they must take an active role in being certain that their research staff and students complete appropriate training in these ethical principles and standards, and how they apply them to the research context in which they are working. This is especially important in areas in which there may be physical harm such as chronic pain research.

During the past decade, there has been a great increase in research of chronic pain, with breakthroughs in better understanding its etiology, assessment, and treatment (1,2). Obviously, much of this research was conducted using humans and animals as subjects. As a consequence, there were a number of ethical issues that investigators have to be cognizant of when conducting their studies. In this chapter, we will discuss such ethical issues in three major areas: (i) laboratory research with human subjects; (ii) laboratory research with animals; and (iii) translating these laboratory research findings to "real world" applications in the clinical treatment arena.

LABORATORY RESEARCH WITH HUMAN SUBJECTS

There has been a long history in psychology of using experimentally induced pain (such as the administration of electric shock) as both independent and dependent variables (3). For example, the presence/absence of electric shock (an independent variable) has been used to evaluate the effects of pain on learning and other behaviors. Also, the effects of perceived control on pain threshold/tolerance, using electric shock or other painful stimuli as the dependent variable, have also been investigated. As a result of a plethora of such research studies that were not designed to evaluate pain per se, a great deal of adjunctive information was nevertheless gathered about what biopsychosocial factors affect pain and, vice versa, how pain affects various biopsychosocial factors. For example, a number of important findings concerning pain were revealed, such as gender and ethnic differences in pain threshold/tolerance as well as emotional reactivity to pain; placebo effects on pain reactivity; relationships among pain, anxiety and depression; effects of perceived control and predictability on psychophysiological responses to pain; and how pain affects the hypothalamic–pituitary–adrenal axis (3), to name a few areas.

In the "early days" of such psychological research (i.e., the 1960s and 1970s), subject safety and ethical issues were not carefully monitored or controlled by Institutional Review Boards (IRBs). In fact, as Vanderpool (4) noted in his review of the history of research ethics and guidelines, biomedical researchers in the United States resisted ethical and regulatory oversight of their investigations between 1946 and 1966. It was not until a hallmark article by Beecher (5), published in the New England Journal of Medicine, which included an "expose" of 22 examples of unethical research conducted between 1948 and 1965, and in which the health and life of the research subjects involved was investigated, did the federal government become involved in research ethics. More responsibility to carefully monitor research was demanded of IRBs. However, as more awareness developed concerning the improper use and deception of research subjects, pressure was brought to bear by federal and state agencies to protect the safety and rights of such subjects. As a result, there developed the demand for all federally funded research supported by agencies such as the National Institutes of Health and the National Science Foundation, to be carefully reviewed for subject safety by IRBs. Moreover, professional organizations such as the American Psychological Association (APA) developed ethical guidelines for research, directly addressing issues such as informed consent to research and deception in research. For example, in terms of informed consent to research, the APA Ethics Code (8.02) specifically states the following:

1. When obtaining informed consent as required in Standard 3.10, Informed Consent, psychologists inform participants about (1) the purpose of the research, expected duration, and procedures; (2) their right to decline to participate and to withdraw from the research once participation has begun; (3) the foreseeable consequences of declining or withdrawing; (4) reasonably foreseeable factors that may be expected to influence their willingness to participate such as potential risks, discomfort, or adverse effects; (5) any prospective research benefits; (6) limits of confidentiality; (7) incentives for participation; and (8) whom to contact for questions about the research and research participants' rights. They provide opportunity for the prospective participants to ask questions and receive answers.

2. Psychologists conducting intervention research involving the use of experimental treatments clarify to participants at the outset of the research (1) the experimental nature of the treatment; (2) the services that will or will not be available to the control group(s) if appropriate; (3) the means by which assignment to treatment and control groups will be made; (4) available treatment alternatives if an individual does not wish to participate in the research or wishes to withdraw once a study has begun; and (5) compensation for or monetary costs of participating including, if appropriate, whether reimbursement from the participant or a third-party payer will be sought [Standard 8.02a, Informed Consent to Research (6)].

In terms of deception in research, the APA Ethics Code (8.07) explicitly states the following:

1. Psychologists do not conduct a study involving deception unless they have determined that the use of deceptive techniques is justified by the study's significant prospective scientific, educational, or applied value and that effective nondeceptive alternative procedures are not feasible.
2. Psychologists do not deceive prospective participants about research that is reasonably expected to cause physical pain or severe emotional distress.
3. Psychologists explain any deception that is an integral feature of the design and conduct of an experiment to participants as early as is feasible, preferably at the conclusion of their participation, but no later than at the conclusion of the data collection, and permit participants to withdraw their data (7).

As a result of these ethical guidelines, it is now more difficult to conduct research when pain is experimentally induced. Some have claimed that this has "handcuffed" them from conducting needed research on pain in humans, based upon promising findings from animal research studies. Others argue that such "handcuffs" are needed for subject protection.

LABORATORY RESEARCH WITH ANIMALS

Ethical concerns about laboratory research with animals are based on the assumption that animals perceive and experience noxious information. Both philosophers and scientists have, until now, tended to focus only on the most basic responses to painful stimuli such as withdrawal and nursing behaviors as well as the mechanisms supporting these responses. This has fostered some rather simplistic views about the functions of pain sensations (8,9) that have, in turn, supported a polarized debate. On the one side are those who point to withdrawal and nursing behaviors in nonhuman animals as evidence that their pain systems are essentially no different from the human pain system. On the other side are those who point out that these responses can be implemented with mechanisms that provide little confidence for the attribution of conscious experiences. If one limits oneself to these kinds of behaviors, it is indeed hard to think of empirical studies that would depolarize this debate. Philosophers, in particular, have an unfortunate tendency to think that if they cannot imagine any relevant experiments to address a particular question, then none can exist. It is our belief that ethical concerns on laboratory research with animals are important, and that pain is present in nonhuman species. There is much potential for investigating functional aspects of the experience of pain, providing, we hope, a fertile middle ground in which sophisticated comparisons of different species can grow, as can continual development for guidelines concerning laboratory research with animals.

The Committee for Research and Ethical Issues of the International Association for the Study of Pain (IASP) has published ethical guidelines for research involving the use of conscious animals in experimental pain studies (10). The following are the guidelines that investigators should consider when performing such studies. These guidelines attempt to address factors related to the importance of performing research as well as the severity and duration of the pain stimulus.

1. It is essential that the intended experiments on pain in conscious animals be reviewed beforehand by scientists and laypersons. The potential benefit of

such experiments to our understanding of pain mechanisms and pain therapy needs to be shown. The investigator should be aware of the ethical need for a continuing justification of such studies.

2. If possible, the investigator should try the pain stimulus on himself or herself; this principle applies for most noninvasive stimuli causing acute pain.
3. To make possible the evaluation of the levels of pain, the investigator should give a careful assessment of the animal's deviation from normal behavior. To this end, physiological and behavioral parameters should be measured. The outcome of this assessment should be included in the manuscript.
4. In studies of acute or chronic pain in animals, measures should be taken to provide a reasonable assurance that the animal is exposed to the minimal pain necessary for the purposes of the experiment.
5. An animal presumably experiencing chronic pain should be treated for relief of pain, or should be allowed to self-administer analgesic agents or procedures, as long as this will not interfere with the aim of the investigation.
6. Studies of pain in animals paralyzed with a neuromuscular blocking agent should not be performed without a general anesthetic or an appropriate surgical procedure that eliminates sensory awareness.
7. The duration of the experiment must be as short as possible, and the number of animals involved kept to a minimum (10).

In addition to the outlined IASP guidelines, additional guidelines for the care and use of animals have been developed by the APA and various local, state, and federal agencies (10–16). The importance of such consideration is that if investigators do not accept that nonhuman species possess the capability of painful experiences, then laboratory research involving animals is inherently limited in its application to human pain.

Conscious Pain Experiences

The extent to which animals (e.g., rats) provide a model of conscious pain experiences remains a matter of uncertainty among most pain researchers and controversy among others. It is relatively well known that nociception, the basic capacity for sensing noxious stimuli, is widespread in the animal kingdom. Even relatively primitive animals such as leeches and sea slugs possess functionally specialized mechanisms for sensing noxious stimuli (17). Vertebrate spinal cords play a sophisticated role in processing and modulating nociceptive signals, providing direct control of some motor responses to noxious stimuli and a basic capacity for Pavlovian and instrumental conditioning (18,19). Higher brain systems provide additional layers of association, top-down control, and cognition. In humans, at least, these higher brain systems also give rise to the conscious experiences that are characteristic of pain.

"Analogical" arguments are widely exploited in the animal welfare literature (8). Anatomical similarities, including the presence of nociceptors connected to a central nervous system, physiological similarities including the existence of endogenous opioids, and behavioral similarities such as withdrawal, vocalization, and "nursing" responses to injury, have all been cited to support the view that many nonhuman animals suffer from pain and thus deserve moral consideration and legal protection. Some of the authors working in this area acknowledge that there is room for doubt about the force of the argument by analogy, but they apply the precautionary principle that it is better to err on the side of too much protection rather than too little (9,20). Other authors, however, place considerably more weight on the analogy argument, considering it to be firmly established scientifically that there are no significant differences between humans and many other animals in the capacity to feel pain. This conclusion is often bolstered by appeal to evolutionary continuity between the species (21,22).

The standard analogy arguments that have been advanced by many philosophers are not sufficient to overcome arguments that conscious experiences of any sort are beyond the reach of empirical investigation, and that there exists significant disanalogies between humans and other animals, which make it unlikely that the experiences of nonhuman animals are anything like the conscious experiences of humans. This is because the providers of these lists of similarities generally do not provide any theoretical reasons for connecting them to attributions of conscious pain. Specialized nociceptors are found in such relatively primitive organisms as sea slugs and leeches and, as such, do not provide strong grounds for attributing conscious pain to these organisms. Opioid systems are also widespread among animals. Many withdrawal responses, and even some forms of learning about noxious stimuli, can be accomplished by spinal cords without mediation by higher brain systems (19). If items on the list do not individually entail conscious experience of pain, it is not clear why satisfying multiple criteria should add up to conscious experience. Analogy arguments are vulnerable because, for all the similarities between humans and other nonhuman animals, there are dissimilarities that can be used to deny the inference to conscious pain in nonhumans (23). While human brains may be similar to animal brains at the level of gross anatomy and physiology, more fine-grained analysis reveals numerous differences. It is also open to critics to point out the many ways in which human behavior is not identical to the behavior of other animal species. Consequently, without an adequate framework for understanding the connection between the observed similarities and conscious pain, analogy arguments remain essentially weak.

A "functional" understanding of pain in the context of learning would provide a framework for assessing comparisons of anatomy, physiology, and behavior (8). Recent work on the sensory and emotional aspects of pain experiences in rats provides a context in which the functional roles of different components of the phenomenology of pain could be investigated with respect to anatomy (particularly the role of the anterior cingulate cortex), physiology (the effect of opioid substances), and behavior (avoidance of aversive contexts) (24–28). While the development of such a framework may not ultimately convince all skeptics, it may help to preempt skeptical and antiskeptical arguments that are based on overly simplistic ideas about the functions of pain. The aim is to chart a middle course between the excessively skeptical view that animal pain cannot be studied empirically and the overly credulous view that scientific investigation has already revealed that other animals (other mammals, at least) feel pain much as we do. The intent is not to show that rats experience pain consciously, but rather to suggest that an empirical research program based on a functional understanding of pain allows sophisticated comparisons to be drawn between the pain experiences of humans and those of other animals. The move from simple behavioral measures (stimulus-response) to more sophisticated operant behavioral techniques suggests additional methods for investigating the roles that different dimensions of painful experiences might play in higher order forms of learning. For example, is long-term conditioning differentially affected by blocking the sensory and affective components of pain processing? Does treatment with morphine affect the ability of rats to learn about noxious stimuli? Would treated rats fail to learn associations between contextual cues and noxious stimuli, or is sensory awareness sufficient? Would the effect vary for different types of pain conditions (i.e., is sensory awareness sufficient for acute conditions but not chronic conditions?). Additionally, if given the choice, would rats learn to self-administer sensory and affective pain relief differentially?

A second topic of interest is motivational drives. Do animals experiencing food deprivation and pain simultaneously choose to eat, or does the pain drive supersede the hunger drive? Is their choice differentially affected by blocking sensory and affective components of pain processing? Furthermore, is the loss of pain affect associated with loss of affect in other behaviors (i.e., mating, predator/prey, and maternal behaviors)? Do losses of pain affect versus sensory pain experience differentially modify these behaviors? The ability to investigate such questions at a functional level of analysis opens the door to much more detailed analyses of the importance of these different aspects of painful experiences. It is also worth noting that the utility of these measures depends to a large degree on animals exercising choices in conditions in which they are not in so much pain as to be rendered immobile or dysfunctional. While the deliberate infliction of pain on another organism is always a matter of ethical and moral concern, the experiments we propose generally involve a degree of pain that would be consistent with good overall welfare. Furthermore, while informed consent is unattainable with nonhuman subjects and causes the animals' insertion into the experimental situation not to be regarded as voluntary, the use of operant conditioning techniques comes closer than other methods to giving the animal subjects voluntary control over their exposure to noxious stimuli within the experimental situation.

Recent Advances in Animal Pain Studies
Recent advances in animal pain studies are beginning to make it possible to describe more precisely the roles played by different aspects of painful experiences. An understanding of how the unpleasantness of pain connects to the complex cognitive capacities of organisms would provide an explanatory framework that would allow behavioral evidence from a variety of species to be assessed. Of course, it is open to the more ideological skeptic to maintain that none of this tells us anything about the conscious nature of animal experiences, because all the anatomical, physiological, and behavioral evidence in the world is compatible with the complete absence of conscious experience. But this view applies just as much to the ability to investigate human experiences of pain as it does to nonhuman animals and, as such, provides no special barrier to our understanding of animal pain. Another kind of skeptic believes that outstanding differences in higher cognitive abilities such as language processing or theory of mind abilities are the crucial elements for understanding the nature of conscious experience. They may be correct, but no empirical method has been provided for testing the hypothesis that consciousness serves those functions. In contrast, novel behavioral techniques now make it possible to test an alternative class of hypotheses linking the phenomenology of painful experiences to specific motivational and learning functions. By manipulating dimensions of the painful experience, we stand to gain a more

detailed view of the complex relationship between behavior, mechanism, and experience, which, in turn, strengthens the basis for analogical comparisons of animals and humans. Ultimately, we can relate this information to address ethical issues in animal pain research.

TRANSLATING LABORATORY RESEARCH TO THE CLINICAL TREATMENT ARENA

Traditionally, the "gold standard" assumed to provide the best evidence for the efficacy of a new treatment technique is the randomized controlled trial (RCT). In such a trial, subjects are randomly assigned to either an active treatment group (e.g., a new medication assumed to alleviate pain) or a control treatment group in which the attention and time spent by subjects with a clinician is the same as in the active treatment group. Subjects in a control treatment group are given a similar "medication" (in this case, an inactive placebo pill which looks like the active medication pill). Subjects in this latter group assume that they are actually being given the new active medication. Such RCTs can similarly be conducted comparing other active treatment techniques for reducing pain, such as cognitive-behavioral therapy, to inactive or placebo treatments such as nondirective psychotherapy in which the time spent in treatment is equal between groups. Many scientific journals will not accept treatment-outcome studies of new pain management techniques, even if they are based upon solid evidence from laboratory studies, unless they are RCTs.

Unfortunately, today there are some major ethical considerations that often prevent the use of an RCT methodology in many clinical trials, especially in the United States (29). Indeed, in an early review of this issue, O'Leary and Borkovec (30) pointed out that, when considering attention placebo-control groups, their use in many research projects may be "theoretically, methodologically, practically, and ethically unsound" (p. 823 Ref. 30). They stated that the theoretical and methodological problems in developing placebo groups include difficulties developing a truly "inert" treatment; the likelihood of a therapist not being able to accept or have any confidence in implementing a placebo condition for more than one or two sessions; and the probability that patients would drop out of a placebo group over time. Ethical considerations include the fact that placebos are inherently deceptive, and they deter the patient from seeking active treatment during the course of the experimental evaluation; when patients discover that they were given a placebo, they may feel angered that time was wasted at their expense, and, finally, subjects given a placebo will not improve and some may deteriorate, resulting in potential harm to the subject. This would seriously violate the ethical concern of the right to treatment. Moreover, Freedman (31) and Levine (32) have cogently reviewed significant bioethical concerns associated with placebo-control groups. In addition, the World Medical Association's Declaration of Helsinki does not recommend the use of a placebo or no treatment control group, except in studies in which no proven prophylactic, diagnostic, or therapeutic methods exist (33). Fortunately, though, there are good alternatives to RCTs that can be used to demonstrate treatment efficacy (34). Concato et al. (35) have appropriately noted that the popular belief that only RCTs will unequivocally produce trustworthy results, and that all observational studies may be misleading, is not accurate. Concato and associates highlight the fact that the results of a well-designed observational study (with either a cohort or a case–control design) do not systematically overestimate the magnitude of the effects of treatments, relative to those in RCTs on the same topic. Even though an RCT can be viewed as a important benchmark to use in considering the validity of treatment-outcome results, many RCTs vary greatly in the degree of internal and external validity that make them less than "perfect" in nature. Fortunately, there are a host of other experimental designs that may be appropriately employed to yield important scientific data to help in delineating cause–effect relationships (e.g., quasiexperimental designs). Some may actually have greater internal or external validity than certain RCTs. Moreover, Heinsman and Shadish (36) have pointed out that a well-designed nonrandomized study can often yield a reasonable comparable effect size when compared with randomized designs. Thus, one should not be misled into accepting the argument that an RCT is the only research methodology available to produce scientifically acceptable treatment-outcome results. We must remember that the interpretation of results from any study, regardless of the research methodology employed, is an inferential process. The statement "unequivocal results or conclusions" can rarely be made in the scientific literature of chronic pain and clinical outcomes research.

FUNDING ISSUES RELATED TO CHRONIC PAIN RESEARCH

Of course, any discussion of ethical issues in chronic pain research must address the issue of potential conflicts of interest as to who funds such research. In studies with human subjects, much funding has been traditionally provided by the pharmaceutical industry, which has the most to gain, financially, from the development and sale of pain-reduction medications. For example, as an indication of the amount of monies involved in this endeavor, more than 312 million prescriptions for analgesics (137 million for opioids) are written each year (Merck Pharmaceutical, 2002, personal communication with Mark Williams). At the upper limits of costs for medication [$21,500 (37)], the total cost could be as high as $62.5 billion annually!

Because of the great financial incentives, there has been growing scrutiny of pain medications that may have possibly been prematurely "brought to market" before comprehensive clinical trials testing them for all potential negative long-term side effects. For example, the recent revelation of cardiovascular morbidity (mortality side effects of the new line of COX-2 inhibitors, such as Vioxx) has stimulated a storm of controversy about oversight weaknesses. This, in turn, has amplified earlier concerns and accusations that control of data from clinical trials is often in the hands of the sponsoring pharmaceutical company (which has the most financial gain and potential conflict of interest), and that interim reports and the statistical analyses of results are rarely performed by independent groups (38). Other ethical dilemmas involved in such industry-sponsored clinical trials research have also been voiced (39).

As a result of the above, there is now growing scrutiny of major conflicts of interest among investigators, universities, and any companies that collaborate in clinical trials of pain medications, in which the financial benefits to the companies are so large. In a number of articles, this issue of potential conflict, which appears to be endemic, has been revealed and strongly voiced (40,41). Changes in federal oversight guidelines are certain to follow.

CONCLUSIONS

In this chapter, we have discussed important ethical issues faced by investigators conducting research on chronic pain. Three major areas were discussed: (i) laboratory research with human subjects; (ii) laboratory research with animals; and (iii) translating these laboratory research findings to "real world" applications in the clinical treatment arena. As was reviewed, there are different ethical and philosophical issues in each area. Potential financial conflicts of interest with companies that may be sponsoring this research were also highlighted. Accordingly, it is incumbent upon researchers, and their staffs, to obtain appropriate training in ethical principles and standards, and to recognize how these apply to research contexts in which they are working. Fortunately, there is now an array of sources that provide information about these ethical principles and standards. Some of these are listed below.

Website Sources

1. American Psychological Association http://www.apa.org/
2. American Psychiatric Association http://www.psyc.org/
3. National Institutes of Health http://www.nih.gov/
4. National Science Foundation http://www.nsf.gov/
5. American Pain Society http://www.ampainsoc.org/
6. IASP http://www.iasp-pain. org/

FURTHER READINGS

The National Commission for the Protection of Human Subjects of Biomedical and Behavioral Research (1979). The Belmont Report. Washington, D.C.: Department of Health, Education, and Welfare.

International Ethical Guidelines for Biomedical Research Involving Human Subjects. Geneva: The Council for International Organizations of Medical Sciences (CIOMS, 2002. www.cioms.ch/frame_guidelines_nov_2002.htm. accessed august 23, 2006).

World Medical Association (2004). Declaration of Helsinki. Washington, D.C.: U.S. Government Printing Office.

REFERENCES

1. Gatchel RJ. Comorbidity of chronic mental and physical health disorders: the biopsychosocial perspective. Am Psychol 2004; 59:792–805.
2. Gatchel RJ. Clinical Essentials of Pain Management. Washington, D.C.: American Psychological Association, 2005.
3. An Introduction to Health Psychology. Baum A, Gatchel RJ, Krantz DS, eds. 3rd ed. New York: McGraw-Hill, 1997.
4. Vanderpool HY. Introduction and overview: ethics, historical case studies, and the research enterprise. In: Vanderpool HY, ed. The Ethics of Research Involving Human Subjects: Facing the 21st Century. Frederick, Maryland: University Publishing Group, Inc., 1996.
5. Beecher HK. Ethics and clinical research. N Engl J Med 1966; 274:1354–1360.
6. American Psychological Association. Informed Consent to Research. http://www.apa.org/ethics/code2002.pdf. Accessed March 7, 2006.
7. American Psychological Association. Deception in Research. http://www.apa.org/ethics/code2002.pdf. Accessed March 7, 2006.
8. Allen C. Animal pain. Nous 2004; 38:617–643.
9. Allen C, Bekoff M. Animal play and the evolution of morality: an ethological approach. Topoi 2005; 24:125–135.

10. Zimmerman MA. Ethical guidelines for experimental pain in conscious animals. Pain Headache 1983; 16:109–110.
11. American Psychological Association. Humane Care and Use of Animals in Research. Accessed March 8, 2006. http://www.apa.org/science/anguide.html.
12. American Psychiatric Association. Webpage. http://www.psych.org/index-cfm. Accessed March 8, 2006.
13. National Institutes of Health. Revised Guide for the Care and Use of Laboratory Animals. Accessed March 8, 2006.
14. National Science Foundation. Vertebrate Animals. From http://www.nsf.gov/funding/preparing/faq_v.jsp?org=EHR.
15. National Commission for the Protection of Human Subjects of Biomedical and Behavioral Research. The Belmont Report. http://www.hhs.gov/ohrp/humansubiects/guidance/belmont.htm. Accessed March 8, 2006.
16. American Pain Society. Webpage. http://www.ampainsoc.org/. Accessed March 8, 2006.
17. Walters ET. Comparative and evolutionary aspects of nociceptor function. In: Belmonte C, Cervero F, eds. Neurobiology of Nociceptors. New York: Oxford University Press, 1996:92–114.
18. Grau JW, Salinas JA, Illich PA, Meagher MW. Associative learning and memory for an antinociveptive response in the spinalized rat. Behav Neurosci 1990; l04:489–494.
19. Grau JW. Learning and memory without a brain. In: Bekoff M, Allen C, Burghardt GM, eds. The Cognitive Animal Cambridge. Maryland: MIT Press, 2002:77–88.
20. Bradshaw RH. Consciousness in non-human animals. J Consciousness Stud 1998; 5: 108–114.
21. DeGrazia D. Taking animals seriously: mental life and moral status. New York: Cambridge University Press, 1996.
22. Francione G. Animals and us: our hypocrisy. New Sci 2005; 2502:51.
23. Nelkin N. Pains and pain sensations. J Philos I996; LXXXIH:129–147.
24. LaBuda CJ, Fuchs PN. Attenuation of negative affect produced by unilateral spinal nerve injury in the rat following anterior cingulate cortex activation. Neuroscience 2005; 136:311–322.
25. LaBuda CJ, Fuchs PN. A behavioral test paradigm to measure the aversive quality of inflammatory and neuropathic pain in rats. Exp Neurol 2000; 163:490–494.
26. LaBuda CJ, Fuchs PN. Morphine and gabapentin decrease mechanical hyperalgesia and escape/avoidance behavior in a rat model of neuropathic pain. Neurosci Lett 2000; 290:137–140.
27. LaGraize SC, LaBuda CJ, Rutledge MA, Jackson RL, Fuchs PN. Differential effect of anterior cingulated cortex lesion on mechanical hyperalgesia and escape/avoidance behavior in an animal model of neuropathic pain. Exp Neurol 2004; 188:139–148.
28. LaGraize SC, Borzan J, Peng Y, Fuchs PN. Selective regulation of pain affect following activation of the opioid anterior cingulated cortex system. Neurosci Lett 2006; 197(1): 22–30.
29. Gatchel RJ, McGeary D. Cochrane Collaboration-based reviews of health-care interventions:are they unequivocal and valid scientifically, Dr simply nihilistic? Spine J 2002; 2:315–319.
30. O'Leary KD, Borkovec TD. Conceptual, methodological, and ethical problems of placebo groups in psychotherapy research. Am Psychol 1978; 56:821–830.
31. Freedman B. Equipoise and the ethics of clinical research. N Eng J Med 1987; 317(3): 141–145.
32. Levine RJ. The need to revise the declaration of Helsinki. N Eng J Med 1999; 341(7): 531–534.
33. World Medical Association. World Medical Association Declaration of Helsinki: ethical principles for medical research involving human subjects. Paper presented at: 52nd WMA General Assembly; October, 2000; Edinburgh, Scotland.
34. Gatchel RJ, Maddrey AM. Experimental design issues in clinical research of musculoskeletal pain disabilities. Crit Rev Phys Rehab Med 2000; 12:91–101.

35. Concato J, Shah N, Horwitz RI. Randomized, controlled trials, observational studies, and the hierarchy of research designs. N Engl J Med 2000; 342(25):1887–1892.
36. Heinsman DT, Shadish WR. Assignment methods in experimentation: when do nonrandomized experiments approximate answers from randomized experiments? Psychol Methods 1996; 1:154–169.
37. Straus BN. Chronic pain of spinal origin: the costs of intervention. Spine 2002; 27(22):2614–2619.
38. Cleophas GC. Clinical trials in jeopardy. Int J Clin Pharmacol Ther 2003; 41:51–55.
39. Daicos GK. Ethical dilemmas encountered during clinical drug trials. Hum Health Care 2001; 1:E9.
40. Brennan TA, Rothman DJ, Blank L, et al. Health industry practices that create conflicts of interest: a policy proposal for academic medical centers. JAMA 2006; 295:429–437.
41. Puttagunta PS, Caulfield TA, Griener G. Conflict of interest in clinical research: direct payment to the investigators for funding human subjects and health information. Health Law Rev 2002; 10:30–32.

Index